RED
ROGUE

Also by Bruce E. Bechtol, Jr.

The Quest for a Unified Korea:
Strategies for the Cultural and Inter-Agency Process (editor)

RED

THE PERSISTENT CHALLENGE OF NORTH KOREA

ROGUE

BRUCE E. BECHTOL, JR.

POTOMAC BOOKS, INC.

WASHINGTON, D.C.

Library of Congress Cataloging-in-Publication Data
Bechtol, Bruce E., 1959–
    Red rogue : the persistent challenge of North Korea / Bruce E. Bechtol, Jr.
        p. cm.
    Includes bibliographical references and index.
    ISBN 978-1-59797-111-9 (alk. paper)
    1. Korea (North)—Foreign relations. 2. Korea (North)—Economic policy. 3. Korea (North)—Military policy. 4. Nuclear arms control—Korea (North) 5. Korea (North)—Foreign relations—Korea (South) 6. Korea (South)—Foreign relations—Korea (North) 7. Korea (North)—Foreign relations—United States. 8. United States—Foreign relations—Korea (North) I. Title. II. Title: Persistent challenge of North Korea.
    DS935.65.B44 2008
    355'.03305193—dc22
    2007015835

Printed in the United States of America on acid-free paper that meets the American National Standards Institute Z39-48 Standard.

Potomac Books, Inc.
22841 Quicksilver Drive
Dulles, Virginia 20166

First Edition

10 9 8 7 6 5 4 3 2 1

| CONTENTS

| ILLUSTRATIONS

| PREFACE

SINCE THE END OF WORLD WAR II, the Korean Peninsula has been an area that the United States would in many ways like to take off of its "top priorities" list for foreign policy issues. As leaders in Washington prepared to face off with the Soviet Union in a growing Cold War, the threat from North Korea was hardly the first issue the United States expected to confront before the summer of 1950. The Korean Conflict, of course, changed the paradigm perception that the Cold War existed mainly in Europe and not Asia. Since the end of the Korean Conflict, various other issues have taken priority in U.S. foreign policy over the Korean Peninsula. Whether it was the Vietnam War in the 1960s, the arms race with the Soviet Union in the 1970s and 1980s, the Gulf War and the Bosnian Conflict in the 1990s, or the Global War on Terror in the new millennium, the Korean Peninsula, or perhaps to be more specific, the challenges to security and stability in Northeast Asia from a belligerent North Korea, have never been at the top of the priorities list in U.S. foreign policy.

This book addresses why the challenges faced from a rogue regime in North Korea will continue to be among the most important challenges faced by decision makers in Washington, D.C.—despite challenges that are ongoing in Iraq, Afghanistan, and the Global War on Terror. Indeed, in response to the way nearly every nation-state in North Korea's region has adjusted their priorities in the post-9/11 era, leaders in Pyongyang have also been forced to make foreign policy changes, military changes, as well as increasingly emphasize its illicit economic activities and proliferation. As North Korea has skillfully adapted to a changing geopolitical environment, so too must the governments most affected by Pyongyang's rogue behavior—the United States and the Republic of Korea (South Korea). Other nations (particularly China) have and will continue to play a role in dealing with North Korea, but it will be the behavior of these two governments that will in reality have the greatest impact on answering the threat faced from North Korea.

A great number of my colleagues have been extremely helpful in the research and writing of this work. Dr. Doug Streusand has been a wise and patient advisor in reading parts of my manuscript and making suggestions that have made it more accessible to a wider reading audience. Dr. Mark Moyar has been extremely helpful in advising me about the practical mechanics associated with writing a scholarly manuscript and approaches to ensuring it is a credible, scholarly work. Dr. Doug McKenna has been an advisor and mentor who has helped significantly with my approach to conducting research and working with scholars and policy analysts. Of course, as the writing of this manuscript came to a close, Ms. Carol-Anne Parker was invaluable in helping me through the numerous software glitches that an author goes through when attempting to ready a manuscript for publication. All of these patient and highly professional individuals work with me at the Marine Corps Command and Staff College, and they are among the many reasons why being a faculty member at this institution is such a personal and professional pleasure.

I would like to acknowledge a number of Korean Studies specialists and practitioners who have been invaluable in my pursuit of research for this work. Col. David Maxwell is a soldier-scholar well known to anyone who conducts research regarding the North Korean threat. His opinions and analyses have provided me not only with important perspectives but also with insights that have proven to be important to several sections of this book. Also important to my research has been the advice, mentorship, and analyses provided by Park Syungje, a member of the Military Analyst Association of the Republic of Korea. His views on the North Korean and South Korean military were extremely helpful in my research. Finally, the specialist to whom I owe the most is Mr. Robert Collins, a senior staff officer in Combined Forces Command and an individual who has mentored dozens of action officers and foreign area officers for many years. His insights and perspectives regarding the inner workings of the North Korean government, its motivations, and its intent were invaluable to my research for this book. There are many other specialists who have provided important insights and perspectives for my research. Although I cannot acknowledge all of them here, I would like to thank Dr. Richard Bush of the Brookings Institution; Mr. L. Gordon Flake, executive director of the Mansfield Foundation; Dr. Hugo Kim, president of the East-West Research Institute; Dr. Nicholas Eberstadt of the American Enterprise Institute; and Dr. Lee Choong-mook of the Institute of Korean Studies.

I am truly indebted to the Marine Corps University for both supporting and encouraging myself and other faculty members in our research and writing. I am particularly indebted to the president of the Marine Corps University, Maj. Gen. Donald Gardner, USMC (Ret.), whose collaboration, encouragement, and advice have motivated me to reach for higher achievements long before I became a member of his faculty, and whose leadership has made the Marine Corps University one of the icons of professional military education. His efforts will be felt and appreciated long after he has moved on to a much more relaxing life in retirement.

I would like to briefly comment on the transliteration of the Korean language that occurs throughout my book. The written form of the Korean language (Hangul) has never been transliterated in a truly straightforward manner. The form that was used until recently (the McCune-Reischauer system) has typically been the one used by both Western and Korean publications. The South Korean government changed to its own system in 2002, but many publications— even some in South Korea—still tend to use the old system. Thus, any sources that were written before 2002 are under the old system, and some, but not all, publications now use a completely different system for transliteration of the Korean language. Because the McCune-Reischauer system is the one in which I have been trained, this is the one that I use throughout the book whenever possible. When quoting sources that use the new system I quote them exactly as written. Because of this, it may appear that I use different spellings for some of the names in this book. In the interest of consistency, I believe that the methodology described above is the most practical for the reader. In addition, I also used the Korean practice of placing family names first, not last, when quoting Korean individuals unless they have specifically requested otherwise or the sources from which their quotations or information are otherwise articulated. The reader will notice that sometimes I refer to South Korea as the Republic of Korea, the official name of the country. Most scholars and writers accept both terms when referring to this nation—in fact, what Americans would usually refer to as "South Korea" is often referred to as simply "Korea" by the people who live there. While I usually refer to the Democratic People's Republic of

Korea as "North Korea," some sources refer to it as the DPRK, and thus when using these sources I too will refer to it in that manner.

Responsibility for the writing and research of this book is solely my own. The views I express here do not necessarily reflect the policy or position of the Marine Corps Command and Staff College, the Marine Corps University, or the United States Government.

References to Internet sites were accurate at the time of writing. Neither the author nor Potomac Books, Inc., is responsible for websites that may have expired or changed since this book was prepared.

1 | INTRODUCTION

NORTH KOREA AS A TROUBLESOME, threatening regional actor in Northeast Asia is not a new phenomenon. During the Cold War, Pyongyang stood as a bulwark against capitalist ideals in the region and a loyal ally of the Soviet Union.[1] Following the fall of the USSR, North Korea continued without support from the former superpower, first under Kim Il-sung and later following his death, under his son, Kim Chong-il. What has changed since the Kim Il-sung era and the first seven years of the era dominated by his son is the context within which the North Korean government must operate. Following the events of 9/11, many of the paradigms that dominated U.S. foreign policy and the foreign policy of its closest allies in the region experienced significant change. This change has had a profound effect on North Korea's military, economy, and foreign policy.

How has North Korea adapted to the foreign policy challenges of the post-9/11 era? Since 1991, the North Korean regime has survived three major transitions: the fall of the Soviet Union, replacement of Kim Il-sung by his son Kim Chong-il, and changes in the international and regional environment since 9/11. The North Korean regime has used its military forces, illicit economic international activities, and adroit foreign policy maneuvers not only to remain in power but to manipulate the regional agenda. The regime has transformed its methods of dealing with the United States, South Korea, Japan, and China to conform to new realities.

There are important reasons why the context in which foreign policy has been formulated regarding North Korea has gone through such profound paradigm changes in the United States and Washington's two key allies in Northeast Asia—South Korea and Japan (particularly South Korea). Since 1953, the most important deterrent against North Korean aggression no doubt has been the successful ROK–U.S. Alliance.[2] Whereas the Alliance remains intact—at least for now—it is going through a state of flux. The governments in Washington and Seoul have been polarized on the ideological political spectrum (left versus right), but particularly since 2001, they have been on different sides of the fence when dealing with the belligerent state behavior of Pyongyang.[3] This has also led to a polarized political electorate in South Korea and to an extremely difficult (at best) civil-military relationship there that continues to evolve.

Framework of Analysis

This book analyzes the primary issues relating to the security of the Korean Peninsula in the new millennium and intends to provide an in-depth perspective on several key issues relating to North Korea and the policy of both the United States and South Korea (among others) in dealing with these issues. One framework, the Instruments of National Power (IOPs), has been used often by the U.S. Department of Defense as a model for conducting analysis and planning for actions based on an adversary's strengths and vulnerabilities.[4] These IOPs are analyzed in the U.S. Department of Defense document, *Operational Net Assessment*, "a continuously updated operational support tool that provides a JTF (Joint Task Force) commander visibility of effects-to-task linkages based on a 'system-of-systems' analysis of a potential adversary's war-making capabilities."[5] These IOPs are widely considered to be the Diplomatic, Informational, Military, and Economic (DIME) Instruments of National Power.[6] The premise for this framework of analysis is that the stronger the IOPs of the United States and its allies (and the weaker those of its adversary), the more likely the scenario will succeed for manipulating an adversary into state behavior that will be in the national interest of Washington and its allies.[7]

At first glance, one could conclude that North Korea is at a major disadvantage in using the DIME instruments at its disposal when compared to the United States and South Korea. Pyongyang is widely thought to be isolated diplomatically, struggling to maintain its oversized military, naive about how to manipulate information to outsiders, and possessing an economy that has been a "basket case" since the early 1990s. Thus, what are the keys to North Korean strength?

The controversy and brinkmanship that have been inherent in developing and operating Pyongyang's nuclear program have been keys to understanding how the government faces the challenges of operating in the international environment. It is also crucial to understand the proliferation and brinkmanship associated with North Korea's missile programs, as well as to understand how Pyongyang has adjusted to economic realities in revising the doctrine and capabilities of its conventional military forces—and managed to use these forces for provocations. North Korea's strengths and vulnerabilities must include an analysis of North Korea's illicit economic activities and how these activities are used to finance Kim Chong-il's military (including nuclear weapons and missile programs) and lavish lifestyle. Finally, it is important to understand the overarching challenges and motivations for the Kim Chong-il government in the post-9/11 era—and how they have changed.

The Kim Chong-il regime continues to present a wide array of challenges and issues for Northeast Asia and other regions (particularly the Middle East) in the world because of its nuclear and missile programs, weapons proliferation, and illicit activities such as the manufacturing and distribution of illegal drugs, counterfeit currency, and cigarettes. How has the ROK–U.S. Alliance met these challenges amid differing methodologies and ideologies for dealing with the North Korean threat? Indeed, in the midst of an evolving, vibrant democratic society, how has the government in Seoul dealt with its changing civil-military relationship? Furthermore, how has this affected its readiness to engage in a military conflict with the North or work with its most important ally, the United States? These issues are addressed in the following chapters.

Research Strategies and Sources

Recent scholarship relating to the security of the Korean Peninsula has tended to focus on one or two of several significant approaches. While all of these approaches are valuable, to date and for the most part, these issues have generally not been considered together in the context of the post-9/11 era. Thus far these approaches have included:[8]

- Analyzing North Korea's nuclear program
- Examining South Korean internal politics
- Analyzing North Korean internal and foreign policy
- Studying the changing South Korea–United States relationship and/or the North Korea–United States relationship

All of the issues are significant both historically and in the context of contemporary issues that are relevant to foreign affairs in East Asia. Nevertheless, there are other important issues tied in with the studies previously discussed, that are relevant to an analysis of security on the Korean Peninsula in the post-9/11 era. Thus, it is helpful to tie the relevance of North Korea's nuclear program in with its missile programs. Perhaps as importantly, it is relevant to connect these two issues (Pyongyang's nuclear and missile programs) with how they relate to the evolving doctrine, readiness, and capabilities of North Korea's conventional military forces—and how all of these forces are used for brinkmanship and provocations. Using the DIME methodology described earlier, it is also necessary to know how North Korea has financed all of these programs in the face of discontinued subsidies from the Soviet Union that occurred throughout the Cold War. To do this, an analysis is conducted of North Korea's illicit economic activities. Finally, other questions remain. How has Kim Chong-il managed to co-opt and manipulate South Korea? How has he secured badly needed finances from China? How has he managed to control his own people in the face of massive economic hardships? These and other important questions relating to North Korea's challenges and motivations are analyzed when I address how Pyongyang has engaged in preserving its regime.

The issues regarding North Korea are critical because they pose a threat not only to the security and stability of the Korean Peninsula and the region but (because of proliferation) to the balance of power of other volatile regions in the world, such as the Middle East and South Asia.[9] Before understanding such a threat, there must be an in-depth examination of the problems faced by the ROK–U.S. Alliance and the overarching changes to South Korean security faced by a badly deteriorated civil-military relationship in that country. There is very little scholarship available that ties in the relevance of North Korean conventional military forces, how they have evolved in the face of economic realities, and how these forces related to the overall strategy and doctrine of Pyongyang's nuclear and missile forces. In addition, little information exists about North Korea's illicit economic activities and their economic support of North Korea's military forces, diplomatic dealings, and the use of brinkmanship and provocation as a tool in the international community. Finally, the overall strategic picture is completed by tying in the response of the ROK–U.S. Alliance, how it is impacted by the changing civil-military relationship in South Korea, and how the challenges to security on the Korean Peninsula have been affected, particularly during the George W. Bush presidency.

The research conducted in order to write this book comes from a wide variety of sources. These sources include but are not limited to interviews, scholarship, and books by and from experts on both sides of the political spectrum regarding North and South Korean security, papers and presentations from conferences and symposia, analysis of speeches, press releases, press reports, and press conferences; U.S. and South Korean government reports, white papers, and legislative testimony, declassified defector reports, speeches, and statements by policy makers in the United States and East Asia, and a study of papers, reports, and special releases by important think tanks, government agencies, public policy institutes, and universities. To provide further enlightenment on the sources used in this work, a bibliography is included.

Outline of Chapters

The book is organized into two main parts: North Korea in the post-9/11 era: brinkmanship, provocations, illicit activities, and challenges for regime survival; and answering North Korea's troubling state behavior: the changing ROK–U.S. Alliance and splintered South Korean civil-military relationship. Part I addresses not only the threat posed by the North Korean regime in the post-9/11 era, but the motivations and goals behind this threat. Part II addresses how the primary nation-states threatened by North Korea's behavior (South Korea and the United States) have responded to the troubling conduct of the Kim Chong-il regime and the complicated challenges that they have faced in doing so.

Chapter 2 addresses the important aspects relating to both tracks of North Korea's two-track nuclear program—the plutonium program, and the highly enriched uranium (HEU) program. It also addresses the problems and challenges that have been faced by the United States and those in the region in dealing with this program in the post-9/11 era, as well as the threat that the nuclear program has posed in this era. In addition, this chapter makes an analysis of Pyongyang's strategic intentions for its nuclear program and the policy implications that these intentions present to the nation-states who have the most to lose. The six-party talks have been the primary means of negotiation between North Korea, the United States, and regional neighbors since 2003.[10] In September 2005 (at a six-party talks meeting), for example, North Korea agreed to dismantle its nuclear program, but many challenges and unanswered questions emerged soon thereafter. Chapter 3 examines Pyongyang's missile development and how it has evolved in the post-9/11 era. Brinkmanship is now an important aspect of Pyongyang's foreign policy, and missiles are used by the North Korean government as a tool to "raise the stakes" or gain the attention of the international community. Arguably the highest priority when it comes to foreign policy concerns for the United States and Washington's allies in the region and elsewhere is the proven proliferation of missiles by North Korea. This is a concern not only because of the abstract "rogue state" issues that such actions raise, but because of the nations to which North Korea is selling these missiles (largely located in two key volatile regions of the world—the Middle East and South Asia). An analysis of the missile proliferation, and the resulting instability or potential violence caused by this proliferation will be conducted in detail. This chapter also examines the military threat from North Korea's varied missile programs, and show its relevance to the intentions and motivations that Pyongyang has for its missiles—and their key role as a tool of foreign policy.[11]

Chapter 4 focuses on an issue that has garnered little attention since North Korea's two-track nuclear program began to dominate the headlines during the fall of 2002—Pyongyang's conventional military forces. There tend to be two schools of thought regarding Pyongyang's conventional military capabilities, with the first being that North Korea has a military that is badly weakened from severe economic hardship, and is simply trying to "hang on" and defend the paranoid regime in Pyongyang from an attack initiated by the ROK–U.S. Alliance—particularly the United States. The second school of thought opines that North Korea's military—including its doctrine, strategy and capabilities—has changed little since the 1980s, and continues to present an immediate and ominous threat. The North Korean military has in fact greatly evolved in its strategy and capabilities because of economic constraints that the regime has had no control over. Nevertheless, an analysis of how Pyongyang's military has evolved requires an assessment that is significantly more nuanced than either of the two schools of thought discussed above. Thus, in this chapter the changing military capabilities and evolving threats that are posed by North Korean conventional military forces are discussed.[12] In addition, I present the strength and disposition of the ground, air, and naval forces and discuss Pyongyang's motivations for continuing to maintain what I believe my analysis shows is a continued (yet distinctly changed) strong offensive military capability—and a military with forces capable of conducting provocations.

Chapter 5 builds on the evidence discussed in chapter 4, to present the reader with an important case study of how North Korea has used its conventional military forces to conduct provocations and "raise the stakes" in the Kim Chong-il era. This examination is made by conducting an analysis of a naval incident provoked by North Korea during a sensitive time in 2002. This incident and other provocations by Pyongyang in recent years tend to have two things in common: they are intentionally initiated during moments in history when they will have the likelihood of attracting the most attention on the regional and perhaps even the world stage, and they always appear to be events that are small, easily contained, and quickly "resolved." In other words, these incidents are intentionally planned in order to prevent events from spiraling into full-scale war.[13] While the focus of this chapter is on a violent naval battle that occurred in 2002, I also briefly discuss incidents where ground and air forces have been used to conduct provocations. It is my belief that this is an important ancillary aspect of my analysis, as it will show that Pyongyang clearly intends to use all aspects of its armed forces as tools of foreign policy—for provocations and other activities that will "engage" the ROK–U.S. Alliance.

Chapter 6 offers an analysis of North Korea's illicit economic activities, including the inner workings of these operations and the details of the many money-laundering operations. This is important because these illicit activities, and in fact the entire illicit North Korean economy, are key in helping Pyongyang support its military and operate as a state that maintains isolationist policies and belligerent international behavior.[14] North Korea's illegal drug operations are also examined, to include what kind of drugs are being manufactured and marketed, and where these drugs are going, as well as an analysis of the impact these drugs are having in places like Japan. Evidence revealed to the public during 2005 and 2006 shows that North Korea's counterfeit money operations have had a direct impact on the U.S. dollar. Chapter 6 discusses this and examines the nature of these operations, along with a study of Pyongyang's growing counterfeit cigarette program. The nature of all of these programs and where they have the biggest impact is also discussed, as this is what has caused the greatest concern for U.S. policy makers. In addition, the reasons behind Seoul's reluctance during late 2005 and early 2006 to even acknowledge that these programs existed will be carefully analyzed. Finally, estimates looking at how much North Korea actually generates in profit from these activities are discussed, along with an examination of the challenges and implications that this presents to policy makers in the United States and Asia—and the leverage that Washington and other actors in the region can use against Pyongyang to terminate these activities.

Chapter 7 addresses the key issues and challenges that Pyongyang faces in the post-9/11 era. This chapter evaluates how successfully Pyongyang has met these challenges thus far, and why these issues are so important for Kim Chong-il's regime survival. Obvious key challenges include maintaining military readiness, controlling the regime succession process, maintaining nuclear and missile programs in the face of international pressure, maintaining the loyalty of North Korea's second and third-tier leadership, and continuing the isolation and thus the control, of the North Korean populace. But there are other challenges less obvious to casual observers that have become high priorities for the Kim Chong-il regime in recent years. These include maintaining support from the Chinese while conversely controlling the flow of North Korean refugees into China and the international perceptions that it creates. Other important challenges include keeping the South Korean efforts at reconciliation coming (along with vast amounts of aid), while at the same time maintaining momentum in their continuing efforts to drive a wedge into the ROK–U.S. Alliance (and the alienation of the ROK public from the United States in the process). Of course, the regime in Pyongyang (particularly beginning in late 2005 and in 2006) has begun to address the difficult challenge of reinstituting the public distribution system, and will continue to face challenges from the international community—especially the United States—in maintaining its high-profit illicit economic activities. Finally, Kim Chong-il faces the difficult diplomatic and economic challenge of attempting to repair the North Korea–Japan relationship.

Chapter 8 analyzes how the two most important allies in the region (the United States and South Korea) have countered the North Korean threat since the new millennium, and the many challenges that this alliance has faced and continues to face in confronting the unpredictable North Korean regime. The ROK–U.S. Alliance has been in a state of flux almost since the beginning of the Roh Moo-hyun administration in early 2003.[15] To date, many challenges have created debate and controversy on both sides of the Pacific. Issues such as the future role of United States Forces Korea (USFK) on the Korean Peninsula, the cost of maintaining troops and equipment on the Peninsula (and who will pay for it), the transformation of USFK as a military force, the move south of both U.S. Army units close to the DMZ, and three headquarters (UN Command,

Combined Forces Command, and USFK) in Seoul have challenged the alliance. In addition, defense reform in the South Korean military, proposed changes to wartime operational command, and the role of U.S. forces strategic flexibility as applied to the Korean Peninsula, have all been concerns that are addressed in this chapter.

Chapter 9 analyzes how President Roh's policies relating to the South Korean military have created challenges for the ROK–U.S. Alliance and civil-military relations in South Korea. These policy changes became apparent and controversial in the first three years of the Roh administration. Thus, the focus of the analysis presented in this chapter is on the events that occurred during 2003–2005. To understand the challenges and problems inherent in the civil-military relationship in South Korea since 2003, one must first address the unique and rather unprecedented leadership style of Roh Moo-hyun and the historical reasons behind the policy moves he has made. It is also important to understand the strengths and weaknesses that Roh brought to his presidency. Roh's decision making process during his tenure as the leader of South Korea has been significantly different than any of those who have previously served in the Blue House (the executive offices and main residence for the president).[16] An analysis of this unique decision making process and how it has altered the way policy is made (particularly foreign policy and its impact on the current civil-military relationship and the ROK–U.S. Alliance) is made in this chapter. Other important factors in the current civil-military relationship include the vision of the National Security Council and its de facto leader until 2006, Lee Jong-seok, the future of military reform, and the signs of Roh's vision to severely alter the status of the current civil-military relationship.

This book concludes with an assessment of the overall impact that the evolving North Korean strategy has had on the stability and security of the Korean Peninsula and Northeast Asia. This judgment takes into account all of the instruments of national power that North Korea has used in an attempt to continue to advance its interests in the changed global and regional environment that has existed since the beginning of the post-9/11 era. The assessment also ties in all the factors discussed throughout the book in addressing and discussing how successful the Kim Chong-il regime has been in using all of the elements at its disposal to conduct its foreign policy. No consideration of North Korean issues would be complete without also addressing how successful the international community, and in particular, the ROK–U.S. Alliance, has been in dealing with the challenges faced from the Kim Chong-il regime. Indeed, this is perhaps as important as the issues discussed in the first portion of the book, and an assessment of issues and possible policy solutions regarding the ROK–U.S. Alliance will be included. This book addresses the North Korean threat—the entire North Korean threat—with a complete and detailed analysis. It offers a detailed discussion of both the military and political issues that directly relate to answering the challenges of the threat faced from a government in North Korea that remains focused on survival and brinkmanship.

PART I

NORTH KOREA IN THE POST-9/11 ERA:

BRINKMANSHIP, PROVOCATIONS, ILLICIT ACTIVITIES, AND CHALLENGES FOR REGIME SURVIVAL

2 | NORTH KOREA'S NUCLEAR PROGRAM: CONTROVERSY AND BRINKMANSHIP

THE HIGHLY TENSE DIPLOMATIC RELATIONSHIP between the United States and North Korea since 2001 has been filled with rhetoric on both sides and has continued to include nuclear brinkmanship from the government in Pyongyang. Whereas many have argued varying reasons and some have placed the blame for the extremely strained relationship on the Bush administration in Washington—depending on whether this relationship is being analyzed from a left-of-center or right-of-center perspective—no doubt the primary point of contention between these two governments is the North Koreans' nuclear weapons program. As a response to the tensions, the United States worked out a new foreign policy tool with North Korea widely known as the "six-party talks." Since 2003, the six-party talks have been the primary means of negotiation between the United States, North Korea, and its regional neighbors. One result of the talks during September 2005 was that North Korea agreed to dismantle its nuclear program. Since that date, the United States, North Korea, and its regional neighbors have begun the many delicate and often confusing steps to ensure that the issues dealing with North Korea's nuclear program are resolved in a transparent manner satisfactory to all involved.

North Korea's Plutonium Program

North Korea's plutonium-based nuclear weaponization program is widely thought to have been in full gear by the late 1980s and capable of producing nuclear weapons by the early 1990s.[1] This program was relatively easy to track (at the time, and now), because a plutonium-based program is produced in a relatively large facility and difficult to hide, thus easily photographed from the air. This facility in North Korea was located at Yongbyon.[2]

Once it became obvious to the United States and the world that North Koreans may have been developing nuclear weapons at Yongbyon, Pyongyang signed an International Atomic Energy Agency (IAEA) safeguards agreement on January 30, 1992. Following six rounds of inspections by the IAEA that ended in February 1993, analyses indicated that North Korean technicians reprocessed plutonium on three occasions in 1989, 1990, and 1991. When the IAEA requested access to two suspect nuclear waste sites, Pyongyang declared them to be "military sites," and "off limits."[3] This began the first "North Korean Nuclear Crisis" that was eventually resolved in the "Agreed Framework" of 1994.[4] Although the Agreed Framework was hailed at the time as being the solution to a problem that was causing angst both in the United States and throughout the region, there were two critical flaws pointed out by Scott Snyder, Senior Associate at the Asia Society. "First, although U.S. officials did convince the North Koreans to can and store their spent fuel, they were unable to persuade them to give up their nuclear components entirely, as they did with Kazakhstan and Ukraine." Snyder further comments, "The Clinton administration also erred by allowing North Korea to delay its return to the Non-Proliferation Treaty by more than five years."[5] These two key critical flaws would prove to be most problematic during the Bush presidency.

The nuclear confrontation with North Korea that continued into 2006 and beyond is generally agreed to have begun on October 3, 2002, at the first of formal unilateral talks held after the George W. Bush administration took office. Assistant Secretary of State for East Asian Affairs, James Kelly, told North Korean negotiators, Kim Kye-kwan and Kang Sak-ju, that Americans had overwhelming evidence regarding the existence of North Korea's clandestine, highly enriched uranium weaponization program (the "other track" of North Korea's two-track nuclear program). Kelly wanted the program dismantled. It was during these talks that Kang Sak-ju, the North's chief deputy foreign minister, admitted to the program and demanded a non-aggression treaty from the United States (among other demands that the United States was unlikely to meet).[6] The Bush administration released details from this meeting to the public almost immediately, and soon thereafter, leaders in Pyongyang denied having a highly enriched uranium (HEU) program and denied admitting it to James Kelly.[7]

As a result, on December 27, 2002, North Korea announced that it was expelling the IAEA inspectors present at Yongbyon, thus enabling itself to again reprocess plutonium and produce nuclear weapons. On January 10, 2003, North

Korea announced that it was withdrawing from the Non-Proliferation Treaty (NPT).[8] These two events highlight the earlier critical flaws in the Agreed Framework as articulated by Scott Snyder. By only freezing nuclear production, in the event IAEA inspectors were expelled, North Korea could immediately begin the processing of plutonium for weapons. It appears that this is exactly what was done. Soon thereafter, North Korea withdrew from the NPT—thus effectively showing both weaknesses in the Agreed Framework of 1994.

Given the fact that, to date, North Korea has had more than three years to process the plutonium (uninhibited by inspectors) at Yongbyon, how many weapons have they produced? According to Siegfried S. Hecker of Stanford University's Center for International Security and Cooperation, the reactor at Yongbyon was unloaded during April 2005 to extract its plutonium (among other reasons). The reactor was then reloaded, and operations resumed in mid-June 2005. In a paper he presented during November 2005, Hecker suggested that the North Koreans had extracted enough plutonium to produce up to eight nuclear weapons (although he offered no specific numbers). He stated, "Given demonstrated technical capabilities, we must assume they have produced at least a few, simple, primitive nuclear devices."[9] Hecker's analysis was based on a visit to North Korea where he met with officials from the reclusive state. He also provided more analyses following their nuclear test conducted during October 2006, which is discussed later.

Given that the North Koreans' plutonium program has been relatively easy to monitor and the fact that they have had the time to process the materials necessary to produce weapons, it is logical to assume that they now possess several simple plutonium-based nuclear weapons. There has never been any question that North Korea has had this capability all along. However, since 2002 the overriding question has been about North Korea's HEU program, and some (including, when it has been convenient, the North Koreans) have denied that it even exists.

North Korea's HEU Program

Since the bilateral talks between the United States and North Korea in October 2002, there has been a great deal of debate, both within the U.S. policy and academic communities, and to a lesser extent, among allies, whether North Korea actually has an HEU program. In fact, there is even debate regarding the translation of what the North Korean negotiators said.[10] Some have tried to politicize the nuclear confrontation by defining it as a conservative versus liberal issue. In February 2005, Korean analyst and journalist Selig Harrison of the Woodrow Wilson International Center for Scholars wrote that "the Bush administration presented a worst-case scenario as an incontrovertible truth and distorted its intelligence on North Korea (much as it did in Iraq)."[11] From early 2003 to mid-2005 many in the American academic community, as well as some scholars in South Korea and other parts of Asia, openly agreed with Harrison's assertions—although the evidence now appears to dispute his earlier claims.[12]

Although it is understandable that some may not trust assessments made by the U.S. intelligence community, U.S. government officials (among others) have stated that evidence has existed since the late 1990s showing that North Korea has pursued a secret HEU program. U.S. State Department Deputy Spokesman Adam Ereli clarified the reasons why the United States publicized North Korea's pursuit of an HEU weaponization program, why the information did not come out in 2002, and how that information was not based on what the North Koreans told Ambassador Kelly. Ereli stated in December 2004: "There are claims made in the article that we learned about the uranium enrichment program from the North Koreans [when U.S. envoy James Kelly visited Pyongyang in October 2002]. That's not the case. . . . We were already aware of the program before they ever talked to us and we informed them of our knowledge about it in October 2002. And it was at that time that North Korea acknowledged to senior U.S. officials that it was pursuing such a covert program."[13]

Although Selig Harrison's claims are interesting, they appear to be based entirely on what the North Koreans told him, not on any factual evidence. Thus, it is important here to note that others besides "hardliners" within the Bush administration have stated that strong evidence exists of the HEU program. For example, Robert L. Gallucci, a former official in the Clinton administration, had access to highly classified information during the critical period in the late 1990s. In 2004, Gallucci made the strongly worded statement that there is "no doubt" that North Korea had the technology. During an online forum conducted in 2004, Gallucci remarked: "I think the North would like to keep its enrichment program as insurance against U.S. actions. This is something we cannot allow them to do." Gallucci further clarified his statements in an interview with Voice of America, where he stated: "We all should be aware that A. Q. Khan, the Pakistan father of the enrichment program, and sometimes called the father of the bomb in Pakistan, has admitted to transferring centrifuge technology, selling it to North Korea. I do not know why the North Koreans insist refusing to admit this."[14]

It is my belief that enough unclassified evidence has come out since early 2003 to make a clear assessment regarding the existence of Pyongyang's HEU program. It is also clear that the nuclear confrontation will not be resolved until North Korea not only admits (again, openly) to the existence of its HEU program but allows for transparent, verifiable inspections and, ultimately, dismantlement of this program.

During the mid-1990s when North Korea's HEU program commenced, analysts were unaware of it. According to high-ranking North Korean defector Hwang Jang-yop, the program began because of a need to possess nuclear weapons other than those based on the plutonium-based program. The plutonium program was being monitored too closely at the time by the IAEA to continue with developments (and was frozen). Hwang has stated that in a meeting with a high-ranking North Korean official, he realized North Koreans had embarked on a second nuclear track, saying, "Before the fall of 1996, he said we've solved a big problem. We don't need plutonium this time. Due to an agreement with Pakistan, we will use uranium."[15]

James Kelly's accusation to the North Koreans in October 2002 and their subsequent admission to possessing an HEU program (later denied), was only the tip of the iceberg. This is sometimes confusing to those who do not fully understand that the evidence was already available to the United States, and it was not the North Koreans' confession that brought about the confrontation. The confession was merely a reaction to an accusation by Kelly. Soon thereafter, a large amount of unclassified information became available, and Pakistani scientist A. Q. Khan admitted to selling HEU technology to North Korea. Khan reportedly confessed to supplying centrifuge prototypes and blueprints, which enabled North Korea's own centrifuge enrichment program.[16]

The North Korean HEU program (and the exchange of technology and resources) continued into 2000–2001, and the evidence points to it being part of a "missiles for nukes" deal between the two cash-strapped regimes in Islamabad and Pyongyang. During this period, technology, equipment, and blueprints went from Pakistan to North Korea, as missiles went from North Korea to Pakistan. The barter deal was of great benefit to both Pyongyang and Islamabad, with North Korea supplying Pakistan with missiles that could countertarget key areas in India (the No Dong).[17] Pakistani nuclear scientists and North Korean missile technicians were engaged in exchanges throughout the 1990s that lasted well into 2001, even after an alliance had been formed between Washington and Islamabad to fight the Global War on Terrorism and United States troops were headed for Pakistan.

Ironically, according to sources including defectors and press reports, the "missiles for nukes" North Korea–Pakistan shuttles were carried out on American-made C-130s[18] previously sold to the Pakistanis and flown through Chinese airspace. This is an interesting twist as Beijing has made numerous public statements calling for a "nuclear free Korean Peninsula."[19] On one of the trips, one of the C-130s being used to shuttle the weaponry and technology back and forth reportedly broke down at Sunan airfield near Pyongyang, causing a great deal of angst in North Korea at the time, since no spare parts existed there for the American-made aircraft.[20]

Although Pakistan and North Korea tried to keep the exchange of scientists and technicians as secretive as possible, reports continued to leak out revealing the extent of the program. For example, during the summer of 2004 Jeon Sung-hun of the Korean Institute for National Unification remarked, "Nine Pakistani nuclear scientists have been missing since they left their country six years ago, and we cannot rule out the possibility that some of them are in North Korea."[21]

In December 2003, Col. Muammar Gadafi of Libya agreed to cease his efforts to develop nuclear weapons and to turn over all of the materials, equipment, and designs, as well as the uranium that he had acquired from various sources—including North Korea. This agreement, carried out in January 2004, was advantageous for Gadafi because in exchange America and the West opened diplomatic and economic ties with Libya. Gadafi also made available a great deal of information regarding the proliferation network of A. Q. Khan in Pakistan. American Vice President Richard Cheney addressed this in a speech given in April 2004 at Fudan University in China where he remarked, "The Libyans acquired their technical expertise, weapons design, and so forth from Mr. A. Q. Khan, Pakistan. . . . Mr. Khan also provided similar capabilities to the North Koreans. So we're confident that the North Koreans do, in fact, have a program to enrich uranium to produce nuclear weapons."[22]

More evidence was revealed in April 2005 during congressional testimony by then-Director of the Defense Intelligence Agency, Lowell F. Jacoby, before the Senate Armed Services Committee. In response to a question by Senator

Hillary Clinton regarding whether it was his agency's assessment that "North Korea has the ability to arm a missile with a nuclear device?" Jacoby remarked: "My assessment is that they have the capability to do that, yes." This was the first public statement by a U.S. high-ranking intelligence official that states an assessment of North Korea's ability to arm a missile with a nuclear device.[23]

Most analysts agree that it is extremely difficult to manufacture a plutonium-based weapon small enough to be used as a warhead on a missile, and the North Koreans are unlikely to have the technology to do so. In fact, it would be even more difficult to manufacture a nuclear warhead light enough for one of North Korea's long-range missiles such as the Taepo-Dong 1 or 2.[24] However, technology received from Pakistan during the late 1990s may have made this process possible using an HEU warhead.[25] According to press reports, Pakistan supplied Chinese data (the Chinese gave the Pakistanis their nuclear weaponization capability) to both Libya and North Korea that showed how to make a small nuclear warhead for a missile. The documents reportedly included detailed technical instructions for manufacturing components for the device and fitting it atop a ballistic missile. The documents of the warhead design, discovered in Libya after Tripoli agreed to give up its covert nuclear program, showed detailed designs of what appears to be a 500-kilogram warhead.[26] Thus, if Jacoby's assessment presented to the U.S. Senate Armed Services Committee was correct, the most likely type of warhead would have to come from weaponized, highly enriched uranium.

Evidence shows that North Korea is likely already in possession of several plutonium-based nuclear weapons (further proven by the test conducted in October 2006). There is also a great deal of evidence that points to the nation's development of an HEU program. The difference between the two programs is that there is no clear evidence (yet) of how far North Korea's HEU program is in its development, where the weaponization facilities are located, or what kind of weapon is being developed. Additionally, as mentioned, a plutonium-based program is relatively easy to detect, whereas an HEU program is easier to keep in a covert status—certainly a factor that will continue to cause debate and create challenges for U.S. foreign policy.[27] A bomb is the most probable type of weapon for a plutonium-based program, yet it is possible that an HEU warhead could be used on a missile. This, of course, makes an HEU program even more of a threat than the plutonium program.

Nuclear Challenges in the Post-9/11 Era

The problems with North Korea's nuclear program have been twofold. First, in early 2003, the United States called for a "complete, verifiable, irreversible dismantlement" of a two-track nuclear program (which includes both the pluto-nium based weaponization program originating from the Yongbyon facilities and the HEU program), and North Korea responded by proposing a freeze of its nuclear program.[28] This has led to the dilemma (and policy debate) of "freeze versus dismantlement." The second problem has been that North Korea admit-ted in 2002, then denied as of 2007, the existence of an HEU program and has not agreed to discuss it.[29] This will no doubt be the greatest challenge in the six-party talks (which will be discussed in detail later), if North Korea is to actually dismantle all elements of its two-track nuclear program. Of note, in the first official statement made by the North Korean government in which it acknowl-edged it had nuclear weapons (on February 10, 2005), there was no discussion specifically of an HEU program—only "nukes."[30] To date, this issue will likely be the stickiest in the negotiation process and the most likely to create an im-passe in the process, as Washington has asserted that any discussion with Pyongyang about its nuclear weapons must include both the plutonium and HEU programs.

The diplomatic impasse between Washington and Pyongyang began long before the unilateral talks ended unsatisfactorily for both sides in October 2002. First, because of the hotly contested U.S. presidential election in the fall of 2000, the Clinton administration had suspended sensitive talks that had been ongoing during that time. A scheduled trip by envoy Wendy Sherman was can-celed.[31] Second, the Bush and Clinton administrations had extremely different strategies for dealing with North Korea. And perhaps equally important, be-cause there was a delay (because of the difficulties with the presidential elec-tion) in getting their people in and conducting a thorough examination of what the strategy should be regarding North Korea, there was a period of several months where no discussion at all occurred between Washington and Pyongyang. This probably caused an already paranoid government in North Korea to be-come extremely apprehensive about their dealings with the new administration, especially given that the Bush and Kim Dae-jung administrations had stated differences in the diplomatic strategies they wished to pursue with Pyongyang. This caused obvious problems not only with North Korea but within the ROK–U.S. partnership.[32] Talks originally scheduled for July 2002 were delayed to

October because of a violent sea battle between DPRK and ROK naval forces initiated by North Korea resulting in casualties on both sides and the sinking of a ROK naval vessel.[33]

It is true that the government in North Korea was extremely paranoid about dealing with a Republican administration that had campaigned during the elections of 2000 that the policies of the Clinton administration had been far too soft in dealing with the North Korean WMD issues. According to Lim Dong-won, the head of the National Intelligence Service during the Kim Dae-jung administration (and one of Kim Dae-jung's most trusted advisors), Kim Chong-il had planned to visit Seoul in the spring of 2001, months after holding a landmark summit with the former South Korean president. Lim, who also served as chief presidential security advisor during the Kim Dae-jung administration, remarked that Kim Chong-il told him he "had no choice" in canceling his visit, because of the outcome of the U.S. elections, since his advisors had informed him that George W. Bush would take a hard-line policy that would "threaten the North Korean regime." Lim made this disclosure public in a speech at the Young Korean Academy Forum for Unification in Seoul in June 2004.[34] Thus, the problems with discussing North Korea's nuclear program began before 9/11 and were in large part owing to the fact that Kim Chong-il and his government were significantly more hesitant to deal with the Bush administration than with the Clinton administration or their Democratic Party successors (had Al Gore won the election). This problem was exacerbated in part by the confusion regarding East Asian and specifically Korean policy that permeated the Bush administration in its early months of power.

The "freeze versus dismantle" debate within American and Asian policy circles has been a polarizing political issue from 2003 through 2005, with some arguing for a freeze while those with a clearly different perspective on the region arguing for dismantlement of North Korea's nuclear programs.[35] Throughout this process there have been many suggestions and solutions regarding the direction U.S. policy should go. For example, in a rather interesting take on the "freeze versus dismantle" debate, one analyst articulated a "freeze, then dismantle" strategy to deal with North Korea. In February 2005, Leon V. Segal, director of the Northeast Asia Cooperative Security Project wrote,

Agreeing to normalize relations and provide written security assurances makes sense if North Korea agrees to freeze and eliminate any nuclear

programs it has. That means not only plutonium reprocessing but also uranium enrichment, something it has not yet agreed to do. The details of a
verifiable elimination of enrichment could be worked out in the future.[36]

Although there has been a great deal of argument for a U.S. posture that
would once again allow the North Koreans to freeze their two-track nuclear
program, if they were even to admit publicly to having an HEU program—and
then to allow inspectors in to verify such a freeze, there is precedent for not
engaging in such a policy. Pyongyang had previously formally agreed to freeze
their nuclear program in return for alternative energy sources under the Agreed
Framework of 1994.[37] But since 2002, numerous unclassified sources have shown
that Kim Chong-il in fact has pursued his secret HEU weaponization program at
least as far back as 1997 as an alternative way to maintain a nuclear program—
even as IAEA inspectors were monitoring the plutonium-based facility at
Yongbyon.[38]

To further strengthen the argument that freezing is and always has been
merely a temporary fix, the North Koreans then "unfroze" their plutonium facility at Yongbyon following the talks with James Kelly, expelling the IAEA inspectors who had been monitoring the freeze at the facilities and essentially
rendering the Agreed Framework null and void.[39] Pyongyang, of course, eventually followed up these actions with a nuclear test in October 2006.[40] Freezing
North Korea's nuclear program is a flawed option, however, because precedent
suggests the North Koreans will simply pursue an alternative path to nuclear
weaponization or decide to "unfreeze" their program. Then the United States,
its allies, and the region, are in a position where once again nothing seems to
have been accomplished—and North Korea will still have WMD. Agreeing to a
freeze—even a temporary freeze—is also tenuous because North Korea has
frequently and routinely broken agreements when Kim Chong-il and his ad-
ministrators felt it was advantageous for their policy.[41] Thus, only dismantlement of their programs would provide a guarantee for a nuclear-free Korean
Peninsula. To be sure, given North Korea's closed society, even dismantlement
of these programs would be difficult to confirm.

The Six-Party Talks: Challenges and Disappointments

After many of the events during 2001–2002 occurred, the United States worked
out a new foreign policy tool with North Korea widely known as the six-party

talks. The "six parties" include the United States, the People's Republic of China, the *Russian Federation*, Japan, the Republic of Korea (South Korea), and the Democratic People's Republic of Korea (North Korea). The first of these talks began in April 2003.[42] Between April 2003 and the fall of 2005 there were five such sessions of the six-party talks. Most of the sessions were inconsequential, with rhetoric on both sides yielding little, if any results.

One of the few results to come out of the six-party talks before the fall of 2005 was that China, the host of the talks, was perceived as gaining increased clout in manipulating what would happen during the talks, and was able to work more closely than ever before with South Korea in convincing North Korea to change its course.[43] However, no real change in the North Koreans' behavior occurred until Washington and Pyongyang were able to establish a better working agreement..

Suddenly, on September 19, 2005, a breakthrough seemed to emerge when North Korea agreed to abandon its nuclear weapons and programs in exchange for economic assistance, security pledges from the United States, and more international respectability. The deal reportedly involved the United States eventually building a light-water reactor for North Korea (only for peaceful energy purposes) in exchange for complete dismantlement of Kim Chong-il's nuclear program.[44] South Korean Unification Minister at the time, Chung Dong-young, was a few months away from declaring his candidacy for the ROK presidency and seemed to be seeking publicity when he stated in the South Korean press that it was his active efforts in September, several meetings between key U.S. officials and South Korean officials, and active engagement with Kim Chong-il that eventually led to the breakthrough.[45] Although this agreement did not include a specific time frame and many of the basic details remained hazy, without a doubt the agreement was the most hopeful move forward since the nuclear confrontation began during the fall of 2002.

The basic premise of this agreement certainly raised hopes, and at the very least showed that the six-party talks were moving in the right direction. Nevertheless, the largest challenge continued to be the transparent dismantlement of an HEU program that the North Koreans still had not directly addressed since the talks with Kelly in 2002. On September 19, 2005, when a South Korean government official was asked by a reporter if "enriched uranium will be included in the nuclear programs to be scrapped by North Korea," he replied, "It says all nuclear weapons and existing nuclear programs in the agreement."[46]

Verification of the dismantlement of the HEU and other programs remained in the minds of the U.S. negotiators as a crucial issue. As Chief United States Negotiator Christopher Hill stated on September 20, 2005, immediately following the talks, "Verification is the key element of this agreement."[47] His statement was further reinforced on October 5, 2005, when Assistant Secretary of State for Arms Control Stephen G. Rademaker remarked that in order for North Korea to meet its obligations under the accord signed with the United States at the six-party talks in Beijing in September 2005, it would need to scrap both its plutonium and uranium nuclear programs.[48]

Henry Sokolski, executive director of the Nonproliferation Policy Education Center and former deputy for Nonproliferation Policy in the Office of the Secretary of Defense, discussed what a difficult process for the United States and its allies this would be when he wrote, "There's no good way to locate Kim's nukes using special technology. Inspectors will have to ask the regime to learn more, and Kim is sure to demand that the U.S. make concessions for every answer. In this game, Pyongyang's deck will always be larger than ours."[49] This statement is supported by the congressional testimony given to the House International Relations Committee in February 2005, by the deputy director for Nonproliferation at the Carnegie Endowment for International Peace, Jon Brook Wolfsthal, who stated in part, "I repeat, the U.S. has no conclusive way of knowing if North Korea would be willing to eliminate its nuclear capabilities as part of a diplomatic settlement."[50] Although everyone hoped the six-party talks would resume in November 2005 on a positive note, instead Pyongyang officials demanded that the United States release frozen assets of North Korean firms suspected of weapons proliferation as well as stop accusing Pyongyang of counterfeiting U.S. money. The sanctions were imposed by the United States on eight North Korean companies accused of being fronts for the sale of missiles and WMD. The companies were barred from doing business with American citizens or companies, and any of these companies' assets under U.S. jurisdiction were frozen. Additionally, the United States had formally accused the North Koreans in September 2005 of large-scale counterfeiting of hundred-dollar bills.[51]

These new actions caused extreme angst for the North Koreans, and ultimately Kim Chong-il, in the place where it hurt the most—the pocketbook. Nevertheless, the charges do appear to be legitimate. The evidence now shows that Pyongyang's illegal activities include not only counterfeiting and weapons proliferation but a highly lucrative heroin and methamphetamine drug trade that

Japanese officials estimated in 2003 accounted for 43 percent of the Japanese methamphetamine market.[52] Revenues from illegal drugs are estimated to be as high as $1 billion annually (U.S. dollars).[53] In September 2005, after compiling several years of evidence, the U.S. Department of the Treasury designated Banco Delta Asia in Macao as a "primary money laundering concern," citing illegal activities such as counterfeit currency, counterfeit tobacco products, and international drug trafficking.[54] According to experts' information gathered from the fall of 2005 through the spring of 2006, these illicit activities generated almost as much currency for Pyongyang as legal trade and possibly was being used to help fund North Korea's nuclear and missile programs.[55] Whereas the actions against North Korea by U.S. law enforcement were new, this action did not seem based on a desire to end the new initiatives in the six-party talks.

In November 2005, North Korea once again raised issues that created challenges to resolving its nuclear program in the six-party talks, yet during November and December of that year, the United States appeared willing to bring the North Koreans back to the bargaining table. According to sources in the Japanese press, during the fall of 2005 the United States was even considering a peace treaty that would replace the armistice in place since the end of the Korean War in 1953.[56] This was discussed widely in academic and policy circles during the same period in Washington.[57] Special Envoy Joseph DeTrani remarked in November 2005 that "the U.S. is ready to match North Korea word for word and action for action." He also stated that "nobody was asking North Korea to give up its nuclear programs before the U.S. gives up anything."[58] After the round of six-party talks in November 2005, Assistant South Korean Secretary of Foreign Affairs and Trade Song remarked at a press conference in Seoul: "Stopping the operation of the Youngbyeon reactor, the most visible sign of North Korea's nuclear activities, can be a symbolic gesture, and measures (compensation) that match it, should follow." At the same press gathering, U.S. Assistant Secretary of State Christopher Hill also emphasized "the sooner the better for the halt of the Youngbyeon nuclear reactor."[59]

Many issues remained in the six-party talks as 2006 began. North Korea has repeatedly stated in its state-run press and to Chinese and South Korean envoys its insistence that the United States build a light-water civilian reactor before all of Pyongyang's nuclear programs have been verifiably dismantled. On November 17, 2005, President George W. Bush stated, "We'll consider the light-water reactor at the appropriate time—the appropriate time is after they have verifiably given up their nuclear weapons and/or programs." His statement was supported on the same date by President Roh who remarked in part, "a nuclear-armed North Korea will not be tolerated. . . . We have no disagreement at all that this issue must be resolved."[60]

In May and June of 2006, North Korea made extensive preparations for a test launch of the Taepo-Dong 2—including assembling the missile on the launch pad and fueling the missile prior to conducting a launch that caused repercussions throughout Asia. Some analysts thought the move was made to bring Washington back to the six-party talks on Pyongyang's terms. As the launch appeared imminent, Han Song-ryol, deputy head of the North Korean mission to the United Nations made the public statement, "We are aware of the U.S. concerns about our missile launch. So our position is that we should resolve the issue through negotiations." In fact, prior to the launch Pyongyang may have been attempting to tie the easing of tensions created by its imminent missile launch to talks that would include the U.S. agreeing to ease the pressure on North Korea's illicit programs and their ties to banks and other institutions in Macao and elsewhere in Asia. Kim Tae-woo, a senior research fellow at South Korea's Institute for Defense Analysis mentioned this possibility when he said, "The U.S. is now strangling North Korea economically," further commenting, "Their [North Korea's] immediate objective is to make the U.S. step back."[61] Former Pentagon official Chuck Downs also commented:

> Pyongyang has created an opportunity to break out of the negotiating deadlock that has stymied the regime for years, dissolve the international consensus on how to deal with the regime's illicit smuggling and counterfeiting activities, and change politics in South Korea and the U.S.[62]

Using the threat of a missile launch to break the deadlock in the six-party talks could have been an ancillary reason for setting up the test launch—which may have been carried out simply to test a missile that was now ready for deployment and/or proliferation. Nevertheless, as reflected in Han's statement, it also appears obvious that the North Koreans continued to believe brinkmanship was a useful tool in initiating diplomacy—an ongoing tactic in Pyongyang's foreign policy and one that is unlikely to change as long as the Kim Chong-il regime remains in power. While the statement issued during the six-party talks of September 2005 expressed in principle that North Korea would abandon its nuclear weapons in return for economic incentives and security guarantees, as 2006 began, North Korea's issue of U.S. economic sanctions needed to be resolved satisfactorily for both Washington and Pyongyang—and attempts to use the threat of a long-range missile test launch to bring about a breakthrough in the talks did not change Washington's resolve. Given the large amount of money that North Korea's illicit programs generate, this certainly presents a major policy challenge for both the United States and South Korea.

Washington, Seoul, and a Nuclear North Korea

The differences in policy between South Korea and the United States over how to deal with the North Korean nuclear confrontation have often been pronounced and in fact have created major problems in the alliance since the beginning of the Roh presidency in 2003. For example, on a trip to the United States during the fall of 2004, South Korean President Roh Moo-hyun called for a softer stance on North Korea by the United States, saying that there was some validity to the North's claims that their pursuit of nuclear arms was in self-defense.[63] This certainly goes against the U.S. policy of any administration that would be in power in Washington, Democratic or Republican, and likely would have caused a great deal more concern in the U.S. at the time had the Bush administration not been so overwhelmed with events in Iraq. During the same visit, Roh also remarked that U.S. sanctions against North Korea would be undesirable, stating, "We can think about a sanctions policy toward North Korea, but it will just prolong unrest and a threat. It is not a desirable solution." Roh also remarked that the United States should look at providing North Korea with the "security guarantee" it had requested since the nuclear confrontation began in the fall of 2002.[64] Roh's remarks were in sharp divergence with the policy of the United States during the same period, and were troubling because they were made so publicly on U.S. soil.

The Roh administration (both in the persona of the president himself and several members of his cabinet and advisory team) has commented on numerous occasions that North Korea should no longer be perceived through a "Cold War perspective," and some analysts—both in Korea and the United States—have interpreted this to mean that conservatives in both countries are wrong to view Pyongyang in such a light. During a speech given at Georgetown University in November 2005, Dr. Cho Kisuk, who was then the senior secretary to

President Roh for Public Relations remarked (referring to the older, more conservative generation of South Koreans),

> I call it one-dimensional vs. multi-dimensional thinking: it is the difference in the way of thinking between young people and the elderly. Older people see North Korea through a Cold War perspective. In other words, they understand international relations as a dichotomy: North Korea threatens our system whereas the United States safeguards us. Therefore, friendly attitudes toward North Korea are automatically construed as hostility toward the United States.[65]

These remarks reflect an attitude in the Roh administration that the North Korean nuclear threat should not be viewed from a Cold War context and that to do so would make one outmoded—and overly conservative. It is also a rather startling and blunt commentary on how negatively politicians within Roh's administration have felt toward those in the older generation in Korea—an opinion no doubt exacerbated by the fact that the older generation overwhelmingly showed no support of the foreign policy of the Roh administration.

Some have suggested that North Korea cease to be viewed through a Cold War prism because it no longer displays the same behavior as, for example, the USSR did during the Cold War. Yet, the paradigms that existed when the United States and her allies engaged in a face-off with the Soviet bloc seem suspiciously similar to North Korea's current behavior:

- The Soviet Union maintained a nuclear arsenal that threatened the United States and her allies. She also maintained missile platforms to deploy nuclear weapons.
- The Soviet Union maintained a large, forward deployed array of conventional forces that threatened the United States and her allies in Europe.
- The Soviet bloc refused to join the global capitalist economy, instead surviving through trade that existed only among communist nations under a socialist economic system.[66]

No matter what one's political philosophy is, it cannot be denied that all three of these Cold War paradigms exist in North Korea. Pyongyang continues to maintain a nuclear arsenal and the missiles to carry these nuclear weapons.[67]

North Korea also maintains the fifth largest conventional force in the world—forward deployed along the DMZ with long-range artillery, missiles, and special operations forces that can threaten Seoul and other key areas of South Korea with little or no warning.[68] Finally, North Korea has shown little real effort to join the world economy, instead relying on foreign aid, illicit activities, and small economic endeavors for survival.[69] Thus, North Korea has maintained a Cold War in miniature on the Korean Peninsula, despite the fact that the region and the rest of the globe has moved on.[70] Based on these examples of the different policy approaches taken by Washington and Seoul, these two allies have become polarized in dealing with North Korea, from both ideological and methodological perspectives. Both governments have spent a great deal of time and effort to resolve their differences and to find common ground in their foreign policies toward North Korea, as their views have differed on even the most basic level (containment versus engagement). These differences, sometimes very intense and emotional on the ROK side, have been exacerbated since the inauguration of President Roh in 2003 and affect the way the two allies have dealt diplomatically with North Korea regarding the nuclear issue. Because of the wedge driven into the way the alliance has conducted nuclear policy, and the resulting confusion that this often causes, Pyongyang has been in a perfect position to delay, obstruct, and perhaps even halt efforts to bring about a nuclear-free Peninsula.

Crossing the Line: North Korea's Nuclear Test

On October 9, 2006, North Korea announced to the world that it had successfully conducted an underground nuclear test. Analysis by experts from several countries in the region and the United States revealed a small, at least partially successful test of a plutonium nuclear device.[71]

According to Siegfried Hecker who visited North Korea following the test and provided a detailed report of his visit, Chinese nuclear specialists that he discussed the issue with said, "The DPRK aimed for 4 kilotons and got 1 kiloton. That is not bad for the first test. We call it successful, but not perfect." The North Koreans reportedly notified both the Chinese and Russian embassies prior to the underground test and had estimated that the yield of the explosion would be approximately four kilotons. The U.S. Office of Nuclear Intelligence also reportedly confirmed the Chinese estimates that the yield of the underground nuclear test was one kiloton or less. Hecker estimated that before the test, the

North Koreans had separated between forty and fifty kilograms of plutonium, enough for six to eight bombs. He also estimated that they used approximately six kilograms for their first test.[72] Thus, the test appeared to be at least a partial success. Partial fission is not uncommon for nuclear weapons. Reportedly, the U.S. nuclear weapon dropped on Nagasaki in 1945 was successful but only 20 percent of the plutonium used for the warhead fissioned.[73]

The reaction of the international community following the test was predictable with China and Russia—along with the United States, South Korea, Japan and Australia— reacting negatively to the action that still left many questions regarding Pyongyang's nuclear program. Later in October 2006, Kim Chong-il reportedly "expressed regret" for the nuclear detonation, saying that no further tests were in the immediate future.[74] Kim Chong-il reportedly told the Chinese that he was willing to once again return his country to the six-party talks, but the issue of the campaign Washington has conducted against North Korea's illicit programs needed to be addressed.[75] Thus, while North Korea has now crossed a line all had hoped to avoid, everyone in the region (and Washington) were put almost at exactly the same place they had been previously—the six-party talks— having to deal with both the plutonium and HEU programs, and with the United States and North Korea at odds over Pyongyang's illicit programs. The biggest difference since October 9 is that North Korea is no longer a declared nuclear power but a proven one.

Resumption of the Six-Party Talks

If the North Koreans chose to conduct a nuclear test in the fall of 2006 to kick-start the six-party talks, it appears to have worked. In a move that seems to have given the North Koreans much of what they wanted while leaving terms acceptable to the United States extremely vague, in February 2007 the six-party talks brought about an agreement for the eventual dismantlement of Pyongyang's nuclear program. The agreement, articulated in a joint statement released by all six parties on February 13, said that North Korea pledged to shut down the Yongbyon nuclear facility and invite back all IAEA inspectors. It also stated that the DPRK would discuss with other parties a list of all its nuclear programs, including plutonium extracted from used fuel rods. Bilateral talks will begin with both the United States and Japan, and Washington will begin the process of taking North Korea off of the state-sponsored terrorism list. In return for

North Korea complying with phase one of the multiphased process, a shipment of 50,000 tons of heavy fuel oil (HFO) was to occur within sixty days of the February 2007 agreement.[76]

Under the plan discussed above, all parties in the six-party talks also agreed to establish working groups to carry out the initial actions and for the implementation of the joint statement:

- denuclearization of the Korean Peninsula
- normalization of DPRK–U.S. relations
- normalization of DPRK–Japan relations
- economy and energy cooperation, and
- a Northeast Asia peace and security mechanism.

Under the provisions of the agreement, important actions will occur in later phases, including a complete declaration of all nuclear programs by the DPRK and disablement of all nuclear facilities. As these actions occur, North Korea will eventually receive the equivalent of one million tons of HFO. The parties also agreed that steps will be taken to negotiate a permanent peace regime on the Korean Peninsula at an appropriate separate forum.[77]

According to White House spokesman Tony Snow, this agreement was on the right track but many issues still needed to be resolved. Snow's remarks on February 13, 2007, included in part, "We're going to discover in due course whether they, in fact, are going to fulfill their part of the agreement. However, we've already said up here, it is a trust-but-verify situation. . . . This is all conditioned on their behavior."[78] On the same day, when asked troubling questions about why the North Koreans were not pushed to agree to stop nuclear tests and the ambiguity of the wording in the agreement, U.S. Secretary of State Condoleezza Rice said in part, "This is the first step, but there's a step in the follow-on phase which is the complete declaration." When asked about the fact that the North Koreans continued in February to deny the existence of an HEU program, Rice added, " [A]s I said, we are in the first quarter, not the fourth, and we are going to pursue the issue of the highly enriched uranium program. We've made that clear." Rice was also asked about the U.S. assessment of how far along North Korea's HEU program was and whether the issue of the frozen illicit North Korean funds would be released in a Macao bank and she stated,

We've been having good discussion with all of the parties involved in that and we'll look to what kind of remediation needs to take place to resolve our concerns. But that's a legal channel. . . . In terms of the HEU program . . . I can't go much farther beyond saying that we have concerns about the highly enriched uranium program.[79]

As details became public, many conservatives expressed concern. Elliot Abrams, one of Bush's national security advisors, reportedly sent off a series of e-mails criticizing the new plan largely because it suggested that North Korea would be taken of the list of nations that sponsor terrorism. Both the *National Review* and the *Wall Street Journal* editorial pages were highly critical of the plan, with the *National Review* charging that it was essentially the same as the one negotiated by the Clinton administration in 1994. John Bolton, United Nations ambassador to the UN from August 2005 to December 2006 charged that the agreement violated principles that were closely held at the beginning of the Bush administration.[80] Ivan Safranchuk, director of the Moscow office of the Center for Defense Information remarked, "The biggest problem in the agreement is that it does not have any measures to force the North to implement the initial steps."[81] Ruediger Frank, a scholar on North Korea issues at the East Asia Institute at the University of Vienna, said, "I don't see how the North Koreans would be willing to give up weapons they've already produced."[82]

Nicholas Eberstadt of the American Enterprise Institute said in a television interview, "A bad deal with six parties is no better than a questionable deal with two parties. And some of the lessons that North Korea has been learning in this prolonged six-party discussion are hardly likely to make them comply." During the same television interview, liberal scholar and former Clinton administration official Robert Gallucci disagreed, saying, "I actually don't think the modality is all that important in one sense." Gallucci went on to say how important he felt it was for us to be engaging the North Koreans when he remarked in part, "But I don't know how you find out if you don't try. . . . We've had years of not doing this. We had a sanctions resolution. A sanctions resolution that produces what?"[83] Indeed, other liberals have also criticized the Bush administration for reaching an agreement after years of taking what they considered to be a hard-line stance. Democrat Joseph Biden, chairman of the Senate Committee on Foreign Relations called the February 2007 agreement "Back to the Future," and criticized it saying, "Back in 2002, President Bush refused to reach an agreement, which was [the] same with the Beijing agreement, which only made North Korea's nuclear program more dangerous."[84]

Reportedly, the Bush administration embraced the deal in February 2007 because of advice from a few in his administration who had been pushing for engagement, although the majority had been pushing for continued pressure on North Korea. The pro-engagement group was said to be led by Condoleezza Rice and her chief negotiator, Christopher Hill.[85] Indeed, Hill's remarks at a forum at the Brookings Institution certainly reflected his hopes for a pro-engagement process:

> It is unlikely that the North Koreans will roll out of bed in the morning and say we are going to make a strategic decision to get out of all of this. More likely, they are going to make decisions to move on a step-by-step basis, and as they move one step, they will look back and say, this is a better place than we were yesterday, and that will encourage them to take still another step. . . . By no means have we achieved the final step."[86]

Procedures to reach the deal were reportedly much different than in the past during the Bush administration. The past precedent was to vet the details through an interagency process that included the Department of Defense, the office of the vice president, aides at the White House, and other agencies who had previously objected to rewarding North Korea before Pyongyang gave up its weapons, but this did not occur. The change in procedure seems to be what caused the unusually vehement attacks from political conservatives on the February agreement.[87]

There are concerns by many that even if North Korea admits to its HEU program, it will not fully disclose the details or allow inspectors to have complete access to all of its facilities (including plutonium weapons and/or storage facilities). Former Defense Secretary William Perry called possible challenges relating to the HEU program a "deal breaker." Chun Young-woo, South Korea's chief negotiator at the talks said that in Berlin prior to the talks in Beijing, North Korean negotiator Kim Kye-Kwan continued to deny the existence of an HEU program. South Korea's intelligence chief Kim Man-bok reportedly told a closed session of the National Assembly that he believed North Korea does have a secret uranium enrichment program. If and when the HEU program and all of the aspects of the plutonium program are disclosed, experts predict it will take two to three years to conduct full verification because inspectors will be faced with the immense task of verifying Pyongyang's past, present, and future nuclear capabilities.[88] The public at large in South Korea remained skeptical of how well the six-party talks will progress as indicated by a poll of a thousand people conducted by the Korea Security Opinion Institute in February 2007. According to the poll, 65 percent of respondents said the South should resume talks with North Korea depending on Pyongyang's moves to dismantle its nuclear weapons and programs.[89]

As the six-party process continues, concern remains about North Korea's trustworthiness in transparently dismantling its weapons and programs. Tomohiko Taniguchi, a spokesman for Japan's Foreign Ministry recently said, "North Korea is notorious for cheating on its agreements, even with the Chinese."[90] North Korea could—and is likely to—bring up such roadblocks as demanding an end (again) to joint and combined military exercises between the United States and ROK troops. And as it appears now, the issue of North Korea's existing nuclear weapons is likely to be dealt with at the very last stage of the nuclear dismantlement program, according to a high ranking government official in South Korea.[91] As pro-engagement advocate Peter Hayes of the Nautilus Institute has said, "Rather both sides wrestled the other side to a standstill and agreed to talk more."[92]

Ultimately, the deal left the actual abandonment of Pyongyang's nuclear program to a potentially troubled future. No firm timetable was set for a final declaration and dismantlement of programs. Precedent has shown that North Korea has sidestepped previous agreements and the DPRK has countless mountainside tunnels in which to hide projects. The HEU program was not explicitly addressed anywhere in the agreement, so negotiations and disclosure will be at best very difficult. As distinguished East Asian journalist Don Kirk has noted, "North Korea stands to receive a huge amount of aid without forfeiting membership in the nuclear club."[93] The commander of U.S. Forces Korea addressed this in congressional testimony when he said,

> While the agreement last month in Beijing is a positive step, and the ongoing six-party talks continue to offer the best route towards resolution of North Korea's nuclear aspirations, North Korea's record of non-compliance with past agreements suggests a difficult road ahead.[94]

The fact that this process could take years gives it the real potential to unravel over many issues, or it could simply be pulled apart because of disagreement and differing agendas among the six players.

Difficulties in Abandoning the Nuclear Program

During the process of dismantlement, it will be extremely difficult to verify that all of Pyongyang's nuclear programs have been completely dismantled—even when exact details of how it will be done and who will verify it have been agreed to. It appears clear that Kim Chong-il is using his nuclear weapons capability at least partially to make up for the decreases in conventional military capability that came about as a result of economic realities forced on his regime in the 1990s. This makes it difficult to force the North Koreans to truly dismantle their program—no matter what public statements come out of Pyongyang.[95] North Korea can always repeat an underground nuclear test. Preparations to conduct tests have been seen as possible coercion tools in the past as preparations for the test conducted in October were detected (probably because the North Koreans wanted them to be) during August 2006 and reported widely in the international press as the rhetoric went back and forth and several nations urged Pyongyang to back down.[96] Jungmin Kang of Stanford University and Peter Hayes of the Nautilus Institute have predicted that North Korea is likely to conduct another nuclear test.[97] The program also gives the regime in Pyongyang the leverage to engage in bravado using both its nuclear and non-nuclear forces, as has happened on numerous occasions.

If one examines how the international community was able to get two other countries to give up their nuclear weapons, the challenge becomes even more pronounced. When South Africa gave up its nuclear weapons in 1993, the Cold War had ended, and the threat of Soviet and Cuban forces on its border had been lifted. In addition, a new more liberal government had emerged and prompted popular sentiment for the dismantlement. In Libya, the end of international isolation created by the complete dismantlement of its nuclear program eased economic and strategic burdens that had existed since the 1980s. For Pyongyang, nuclear weapons provide Kim Chong-il with a convenient way to preserve his government, as well as compensating for conventional military weaknesses. The nuclear program also serves as leverage for obtaining humanitarian assistance and economic investment from other governments such as Seoul, Tokyo, and Beijing. This would explain North Korea's demands in the fall of 2005 that the United States build a light-water reactor before dismantlement could begin, a demand with the potential to create further delay as the six-party talks progress.[98] Unlike Libya or South Africa, it is actually in the current regime's interest in Pyongyang to maintain its international isolation. Such a condition allows Kim Chong-il to maintain more control over his own people and keep his government in power.[99] Thus, persuading North Korea that completely, verifiably abandoning its nuclear program will be a difficult task until its usefulness as a tool of foreign policy and brinkmanship ceases to exist.

3 | NORTH KOREA'S MISSILES: PROLIFERATION, DEPLOYMENT, TESTING, AND TOOLS OF FOREIGN POLICY

NORTH KOREA'S MISSILE PROGRAM has long been a matter of discussion and concern for the United States and Washington's allies in East Asia even before the events that led to the first nuclear crisis of 1994. The motivations behind North Korea's missile program are no mystery. According to the Nuclear Threat Initiative (a nonprofit research organization in Washington, D.C.), Kim Il-sung made the political decision to seek an indigenous ballistic missile capability sometime around 1965.[1]

If one is to truly understand the challenges for United States policy from North Korea's missiles in the post-9/11 era, it will be necessary first to examine Pyongyang's missile development and how it has brought us where we are today.

During the late 1960s, the North Korean government entered into agreements with both the Soviet Union and China for its fledgling missile program. From the Soviets, it acquired several dozen FROG-5 and FROG-7 (Free Rocket Over Ground) systems. These systems cannot legitimately be considered missiles, because they are not ballistic, and they cannot be easily targeted as a missile can. Nevertheless, it was (and is) an improvement, purely in terms of range, on North Korea's conventional artillery systems. During the same period, North Korea was actively developing a ballistic missile program built around the Chinese DF-61 missile system, a missile that was projected to have a 1,000-kilometer range. This program was eventually terminated (perhaps because of political second thoughts by Beijing), leaving North Korea with no missile program by the mid- to late 1970s. North Korea was in luck though, as Egypt had just begun to completely sever military ties with the Soviet Union in 1979 and was looking for hard currency. Thus, sometime between 1979 and 1981, North Korea acquired its first ballistic missile, the SCUD B (some analysts assess North Korea received the first SCUDS from Egypt as early as 1976).[2] In addition, the North

Koreans received assistance from the Chinese during the development years of the DF-61 that reportedly may have allowed them to reverse engineer the SCUD they received from Egypt and begin indigenous production for their own ballistic missile program.[3]

North Korea successfully tested its own version of the SCUD B ballistic missile during 1984.[4] During this same time period, Pyongyang entered into an agreement with Tehran to receive North Korean missiles in exchange for financial assistance. Many of these missiles were used by Tehran as weapons against the Iraqis during the Iran–Iraq "War of the Cities."[5] Also during this same time, North Korea was upgrading the range of its SCUD missiles and successfully produced and tested its version of the SCUD C during 1986 and then again in 1990—reportedly also selling several versions of this latest missile to the Iranians.[6]

North Korea reportedly began development of the No-Dong missile around 1988. Obviously, this meant that as development, production, and testing of the SCUD missile programs (B and C) were ongoing, a separate program to develop the No-Dong was in place. The No-Dong was derived from SCUD technology (once again showing the great prowess of North Korean technicians at reverse engineering) and was developed largely as an extension of the SCUD, though the No-Dong is a two-stage, liquid-fueled missile with an original range of 1,300 kilometers and the SCUDs are a one-stage weapon.[7] (Fig. 1). The No-Dong reportedly uses a three-gyroscope inertial navigation system that is not precise, whereas the SCUDs are also inaccurate, though this obviously would not be a high priority if it is simply targeting cities or military bases. The No-Dong was successfully tested in May 1993 over the Sea of Japan (when it over-flew Japan). Both Pakistani and Iranian representatives were present at the test firing, and Tehran reportedly also played a role in helping to finance the development of the No-Dong.[8]

Much like the No-Dong project, the Taepo-Dong project was developed while other programs were ongoing. The three-stage Taepo-Dong 1 was likely conceived and developed in the late 1980s but gained the attention of the world when it was test fired in August 1998. An Iranian delegation was believed present at the time. Stages one and two were successful, but the third stage failed. The Taepo-Dong 2 has a significantly longer projected range than the Taepo-Dong 1, although this is as yet unproven in testing.[9]

During May and June 2006, North Korea prepared to launch a Taepo-Dong 2 from a site located in the northeast part of the country. The first indications

FIGURE 1:
North Korean Short- and Medium-Range Missile Capabilities

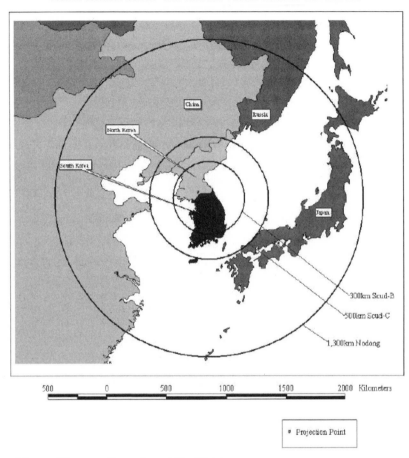

Library of Congress, Geography and Map Division
October 1999

that the missile would be launched were on May 4 when fuselage sections of the system were detected as they were being transported from a missile factory southwest of Pyongyang to another location closer to the launch site.[10] According to numerous press sources, the missile was in the final stages of preparations for a test-launch in June 2006. The missile components were moved in trailers that corresponded to the length of the Taepo-Dong 2 to the site near the North Korean coast. Japanese press sources also reported that radio communications intercepted near the missile test site indicated preparations for a launch.[11]

FIGURE 2:

POTENTIAL OF NORTH KOREAN LONG-RANGE MISSILE CAPABILITIES

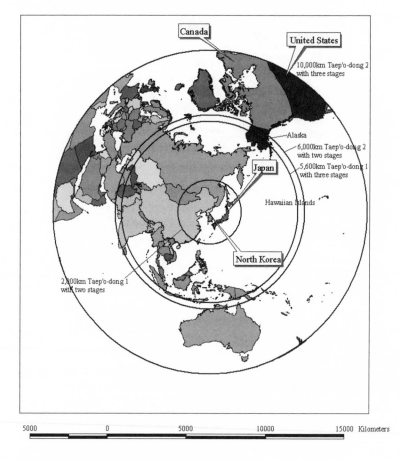

Library of Congress, Geography and Map Division
October 1999

By June 17, 2006, press reports confirmed that the North Koreans had loaded
booster rockets onto a launch pad and moved about ten fuel tanks to the launch
site.[12] An advanced version of the Taepo-Dong 2 has a range of close to 10,000
miles, and as indicated in Figure 2, could potentially hit the western United
States.[13] Reportedly, North Korea has actually had the capability to test-launch
the missile since 2005, two years ahead of the schedule that military analysts

had previously predicted. U.S. Assistant Secretary of State and Department Spokesman Sean McCormack commented during this time that "a missile launch would throw into question North Korea's desire to engage with the international community." The U.S. was considering asking the international community to impose sanctions if the launch occurred.[14]

While the South Korean Roh Moo-hyun administration apparently was in the throes of convincing Kim Chong-il not to launch the Taepo-Dong 2 in June 2006, U.S. capability must have given Pyongyang food for thought. During a test conducted in May 2006, the U.S. Navy for the first time successfully shot down a long-range missile in its final seconds of flight.[15] According to a paper published in 2006 that contained analysis conducted by Japanese specialist Hiromichi Umebayashi, the U.S. Navy has engaged in ballistic missile defense patrols (using Aegis Class ships, among the most sophisticated in the U.S. Navy) near the Japanese island of Okushiri off the southwest coast of Hokkaido. According to the paper, the operations are only in the "experimental stage."[16] The U.S. ground-based missile defense system had reportedly deployed ten or more interceptors and their associated radars in Asia, Alaska, and California by June 2006—though the system was still said to be in "test-mode." A key part of the system includes Aegis-class warships deployed to the waters off the coast of Japan (in the vicinity of North Korea) during this same time.[17]

According to public statements by Pentagon officials, the missile defense system that the United States has now employed, while having a chance to shoot down the Taepo-Dong 2 in mid-flight, was still in the development and testing phase in the summer of 2006. According to Pentagon spokesman Eric Ruff, "Our system is still developing. . . . It's a limited missile-defense system right now."[18] The United States claimed a limited capability to shoot down long-range missiles such as the Taepo-Dong 2, but Washington officials also warned that North Korea would be compromising its best interests to fire the missile. President George W. Bush would have authorized using the missile-defense system and would have done so if the Taepo-Dong 2 had the possibility, once in flight, of posing a direct threat to the United States or its allies.[19] Reportedly, some officials had doubts as to whether the prototype North Korean missile would even fly straight because the capabilities of its guidance systems appear to be unknown.[20] Allies in the region, particularly Japan, were also deeply concerned. In response to Prime Minister Junichiro Koizumi's concerns, the U.S. military deployed advanced Patriot missiles (known as the PAC-3 system) to

Japan in June 2006. As this occurred President Bush called for North Koreans to declare "what they have on top [i.e., a warhead or a satellite] of that vehicle and what are their intentions."[21]

While some on the left in the U.S. had called for strikes on the actual missile site in North Korea to prevent a launch, it appears that cooler heads prevailed in Washington. Ashton B. Carter, former assistant secretary of defense under President Clinton, and William J. Perry, Clinton's secretary of defense, concluded in a June 2006 newspaper editorial: "If North Korea persists in its launch preparations, the United States should immediately make clear its intention to strike and destroy the North Korean Taepo-Dong missile before it can be launched."[22] Former Vice President Walter Mondale supported this statement when he said, "The United States should tell North Korea to dismantle the missile—and if it doesn't we are going to take it out."[23] While such calls for action were interesting (and if carried out could actually have started a new Korean War), reports coming out of the Pentagon focused on the role of missile defense if North Korea's missile launch posed a threat to the United States or its allies.

Clearly Washington's ballistic missile defense has advanced far beyond the stage it was when the Taepo-Dong 1 was launched in 1998. One of the highest priorities of the Missile Defense Agency remains defense from attack from North Korea—and to help Japan in the same manner. Air Force Lt. Gen. Henry A. Obering III testified before the House Armed Services Committee in March 2006 that "North Korea and Iran have not relented in their pursuit of longer-range missiles. . . . Our current and near-term missile defense fielding activities are a direct response to these dangers."[24] Surely North Korea was aware of world opinion and would expect ramifications anytime their missile forces attempted to test-launch long-range ballistic missiles that would fly over Japan and possibly target U.S. bases or U.S. territory. Alas, despite numerous warnings from the United States, other nations in the region, and even their Beijing ally, on July 4, 2006, the North Koreans did in fact test-launch a Taepo-Dong 2 missile. But Pyongyang also shocked the world by launching a total of seven missiles on July 4—and July 5: a Taepo-Dong 2 missile, four SCUD missiles, and two No-Dong missiles. The Taepo-Dong 2 flew for about 40 seconds before the second stage failed to separate and the missile fell harmlessly into the Sea of Japan about 640 kilometers from its original launch site.[25] Reportedly, according to U.S. intelligence, the booster on the Taepo-Dong 2 failed to detach, which caused the crash into the sea.[26]

The test-launches created a firestorm of reaction in the region, not only because they were an obvious act of geopolitical brinkmanship, but also because they violated international law when the North Koreans failed to provide any prior notification of the launches in order to avoid possible accidents with civil aircraft or maritime vessels.[27] About ten minutes before the first missile was launched, a South Korean Asiana Airlines passenger plane crossed the missile's future trajectory above the Sea of Japan (also known as the East Sea).[28] In addition, a missile that fell into the sea several dozen kilometers from the Russian city of Nakhodka reportedly caused quite a stir with the citizens there, who had to be reassured by the mayor that the missiles were launched in "test-mode" and had only dummy warheads.[29]

The test-launches revealed some unexpected results. With the possible exception of the Taepo-Dong 2 airframe, none of the missiles were launched in a trajectory that would take them over Japan—where the United States had missile defense systems online that may have targeted them.[30] This may have been because Pyongyang actually feared the repercussions of negative publicity regarding the capability of their missiles if they were shot down over Japan. The two No-Dongs had the capability to over-fly Japan, and in fact the North Koreans did exactly that when they first tested the No-Dong in 1993.[31]

Kim Chong-il chose to launch seven missiles, and a variety of missiles—a surprise to nearly everyone. It is possible that this was done because once the Taepo-Dong 2 was on the launch pad and fueled, technicians in pre-launch realized that the missile was going to encounter problems in flight. Rather than going through the political embarrassment of taking down the missile after the world had watched them prepare to launch it, the North Koreans chose to launch a real "fireworks display" where the failed Taepo-Dong 2 launch would simply be one event among many. Thus, the headlines would read, "North Korea Launches Seven Missiles," instead of "North Korea's Taepo-Dong 2 Launch Fails." Although this theory remains unproven, it is certainly possible—and the Taepo-Dong 2 remained on the launch pad for longer than most experts expected, leading to assessments that it was encountering pre-launch problems.[32] As military analyst Anthony Cordesman of the Center for Strategic and International Studies has noted,

> It tends to bury the fact that a major series of short/medium range tests took place under the impact of the longer-range test, and the success of

the shorter-range missile tests guarded against the possible failure of the larger, long-range missile.[33]

Reportedly, Iranian military engineers were on hand for North Korea's missile test-launches. This is also an interesting component of the events that occurred on July 4–5, 2006. At least ten members of the Iranian Islamic Revolutionary Guard Corps, all senior engineers, were reported present at the launches. According to Japanese and South Korean press sources, these engineers participated in the preparation for the Taepo-Dong launch and were there for participation in possible Iranian procurement of technology associated with the missile.[34] In another interesting development that may be directly related to the presence of Iranians, it appears that at least one of the missiles that the North Koreans tested was a new SCUD variant. Initial reports after the missile firing indicated that electronic signals associated with at least one of the missiles test-fired were different from previously detected data. Based on analysis and press reports it appears likely that the new missile tested was the extended-range SCUD, or "SCUD ER." The new advanced version of the SCUD is more an evolution than a revolution in missile technology and has an estimated range of 850 kilometers.[35] This gives it a longer range than even the SCUD D. North Koreans may wish to market this new variant to the Iranians and possibly others such as the Syrians.

If the North Koreans had the intention of gaining the world's attention with the multiple missile launches of July 4–5, 2006, they accomplished this goal. If it was their intention to gain concessions from Washington and others by conducting the launch, this strategy backfired. Days after the launch, the United Nations Security Council unanimously backed a resolution against the missile launches. The resolution, passed by a vote of 15 to 0 (including both China and Russia—which is extraordinary), demands that North Korea suspend all activities related to its ballistic missile program and resume its moratorium on long-range missile tests. The resolution also requires all member states to "exercise vigilance and prevent financial resources and missile and missile related items, materials, goods and technology being transferred" to North Korea's missile and WMD programs.[36] In response to the UN resolution, North Korea's Foreign Ministry predictably threatened to "bolster their war deterrent."[37]

To make matters worse for the North Koreans, the Chinese (key suppliers of a large portion of North Korea's energy needs) reportedly reduced a significant amount of their oil shipments to the DPRK following the missiles launches.[38] The Chinese had publicly asked the North Koreans not to launch the missiles, and the incident probably embarrassed Beijing. According to Paul Carroll, a program officer at the Ploughshares Fund NGO who was one of the few foreigners in North Korea during the missile launches, DPRK Vice Foreign Minister Kim Kye-kwan made a reference to the DPRK–PRC relationship that was particularly telling about why the Chinese appear to be disturbed about the launches, "With respect to our missile launch, I am awaiting responses from other parties. What I hear is big brothers saying to little brother 'don't do that' but we are not a little boy, we have nuclear weapons."[39] South Korea also temporarily suspended shipments of food and fertilizer following the controversial missile launches, so it appears that Pyongyang may have underestimated the reactions of those who had previously either supported, or been lenient toward their belligerent state behavior.[40]

In recent years, yet another long-range missile has come to the attention of analysts. This missile (sometimes called the Taepo-Dong X) appears to be based on the design of the old Soviet SS-N-6 design, a submarine-launched (SLBM), nuclear capable missile. The liquid propellant powered missile has a range of 2,500 kilometers, but given the proclivity for reverse engineering that the North Koreans have displayed since the very beginning of the ballistic missile program development, it is possible, in fact likely, that Pyongyang has successfully extended the range of this missile system (data from a launch described later reveals that the range has been extended to about 4,000 kilometers). It is believed that the technology for this system that the North Koreans now have, originated with personnel from the Makeyev Design Bureau in Miass, Chelyabinsk, Russia. A group of twenty missile specialists were detained as they were attempting to depart for North Korea in December 1992. It appears that the sale of the technology to North Korea was not sanctioned by the government—but the technicians had reportedly received approval for their travel from the Ministry of Machine Building and the Ministry of Security in Russia. According to press reports and Russian governmental officials, other groups of missile specialists successfully traveled to North Korea.[41]

The Taepo-Dong X reportedly is already in use (and deployed) in North Korea and is likely also being reproduced. It will likely be a land-launched missile, as the North Koreans would have great difficulty using one of their ships to launch such a vehicle. The United States reportedly believes North

Korea is deploying this missile in "road mobile" mode.[42] Given the fact that this system is already proven to operate effectively, it is not likely to be test-fired by the North Koreans. It can however be proliferated.

Whereas the Taepo-Dong X is a missile that legitimately can be considered to pose a significant threat, the North Koreans have not been idle in acquiring and developing missile technology for their SRBM (short-range ballistic missile) inventory. Details of this activity have also come to light in the post-9/11 era. As discussed earlier, North Korea first acquired FROG systems from the Soviet Union many years ago. The Russians themselves replaced the FROG systems in their own inventory with the SS-21 missile system beginning in 1976. The SS-21 is a ballistic, short-range missile with a modified range of 120 kilometers. North Korea reportedly bought several of the SS-21 systems and their launchers, from Syria in 1996. Pyongyang is now apparently manufacturing their own version of the system (identified as the "KN-02"), which would have the range to target U.S. bases south of Seoul. The system is a considerable improvement on the older FROG systems, because it has a guidance system that would put it within a hundred meters of the aiming point.[43] The missile is a considerable threat because it is road mobile and uses solid fuel, which means it can be deployed and fired more rapidly than other systems.[44] North Korea conducted several test firings of this missile system during 2005 and 2006 that appeared to be successful.[45] United States military officials are reportedly impressed and concerned about the capabilities of this latest edition to North Korea's SRBM inventory. In Congressional testimony during 2006, the commanding general of United States Forces Korea, Gen. B. B. Bell, remarked, "They've again tested short-range ballistic missiles that are in fact a quantum leap forward from the kinds of missiles that they've produced in the past."[46]

North Korea's Proliferation of Missiles

Most experts on North Korea and on national security policy agree that there are two primary threats from North Korean missiles: the military threat to U.S. forces and their allies in Northeast Asia (if a missile were to be fired from North Korea) and the threat of proliferation throughout the Middle East and South Asia. Since 9/11, Pyongyang has had deals for weapons programs with Pakistan, Libya, Egypt, Iran, Syria, Vietnam, and Yemen,[47] although since 2003–2004, Libya has cut off its deals with Pyongyang. In 2004, the SCUD C missiles and their launchers that Libya purchased from North Korea were dismantled under the eyes of inspectors, and the Libyans formally agreed to discontinue all trade in military goods and services with North Korea (among others).[48] The Libyan deal was brought about because of pressure on the government in Tripoli, not because of any actions against North Korea. Libya is the only country that to date has completely, verifiably severed its missile deals with North Korea.

In May 2004, after a train collision in North Korea near the Chinese border resulted in a huge explosion that killed hundreds of people or more, press reports disclosed and U.S. officials confirmed about a dozen Syrian technicians among the casualties. They were accompanying a train car full of missile components and other related equipment.[49] North Korea and Syria are reportedly not only engaged in missile deals developing Syria's SCUD D system (a SCUD system that will have an even longer range than the SCUD C), but also programs for chemical and biological weapons.[50] The SCUD missile system is capable of carrying a chemical warhead.[51]

North Korea's missile proliferation to countries such as Syria makes them much more than simply a regional threat. North Korea has reportedly significantly enhanced the SCUD D missile system for Syria, giving it greater range and accuracy. The first evidence of this came in 2005, when a test-fired SCUD D accidentally veered into Turkey. On examination by the CIA and others it was discovered that the missile had components not in the original model. The improved SCUD D has a range of 700 kilometers and a separating warhead. It also has a warhead capable of delivering chemical weapons, including VX gas.[52]

North Korea could complete weaponization of HEU systems that are capable of being mounted on a much smaller warhead than a plutonium-based system, then sell them to terrorists. To be sure, when weapons brokers from North Korea were working deals in places like Libya and Syria, they could have been contacted by terrorist groups in those countries (although Libya abandoned terrorism as a tool of foreign policy in 2004).[53] Evidence exists that Pyongyang has sold some $2 million worth of conventional arms to a well-known terrorist group in the Philippines, the Moro Islamic Front.[54] North Korean advisors also reportedly helped Hezbollah terrorists construct underground facilities during 2003–2004, a capability Pyongyang's experts have been known to export for years to countries such as Iran, Libya, and Syria.[55]

North Korea has had a relationship through its missile program with both Pakistan and Iran, and these two countries purchased longer range missiles during the post-9/11 era from North Korea: the No-Dong.[56] With Pakistan (a cash strapped regime during most of the period when Islamabad was acquiring missiles from North Korea), the payment for the No-Dong missiles (known as the Ghauri in Pakistan) appears to have been in the form of HEU technology, blueprints, and centrifuges, based on a large number of reports that have surfaced since 2002.[57] With Iran, the purchase of missiles appears to be a trade as well, at least partially based on an exchange of Iranian oil for North Korean missile systems (the Iranian version of the No-Dong is known as "Shahab 3").[58] These No-Dong systems are in addition to the SCUD systems that North Korea continues to proliferate widely to these countries and others.

Starting in the late 1990s, North Koreans helped the Iranians develop their own versions of Taepo-Dong and Taepo-Dong variants, known as the Shahab-4, Shahab-5, and perhaps Shahab-6. Given the extended ranges of these missile programs, the threat to the Middle East, and even to Europe, would be considerable.[59] Recent reports convey that the Iranians bought eighteen other long-range missile packages derived from the SS-N-6 system (sometimes known as the Taepo-Dong X). Iranian President Mahmoud Ahmadinejad reportedly wants to extend the range of the missiles to at least 3,500 kilometers.[60] The Iranians tested the Taepo-Dong X (which is apparently the "Shahab-4) on January 17, 2006. It was successfully launched and reached a distance of nearly 3,000 kilometers and was intentionally destroyed in mid-flight, but the trajectory indicated it could have reached a distance of 4,000 kilometers.[61] The performance data recovered from the flight test also reportedly revealed a range capability of 4,000 kilometers for the missile (which now probably clearly identifies the Shahab-4 as the "Taepo-Dong X") which was carrying a dummy warhead when it was detonated. It is believed that North Koreans were present at the launch.[62]

The Iranians continue to develop the Shahab-5 and Shahab-6 series, which apparently is based on North Korean Taepo-Dong 2 technology and explains the presence of Iranians at the North Korean test-launches on July 4–5, 2006. These missile systems remain untested (except for the Taepo-Dong 2 that failed to reach its second stage during the test-launch conducted on July 4, 2006).[63] Figure 3 shows the dangerous ranges of Iranian missiles acquired from North Korea that have been tested by the Iranians and are deployed or soon will be. The Shahab-3 equates directly to the No-Dong missile (also sold to Pakistan), and the Shahab-4 apparently directly equates to the newly acquired Taepo-Dong X (based on the Russian SS-N-6 design).[64]

FIGURE 3:
Ranges of Iran's Missiles

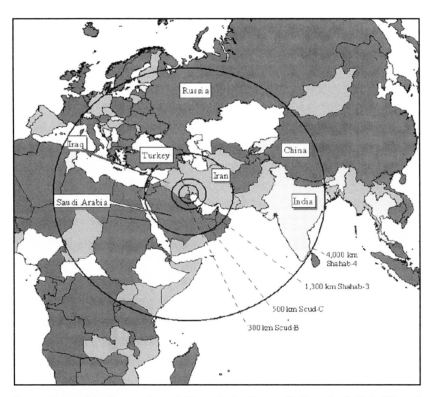

Source: "Recognizing Iran as a Strategic Threat: An Intelligence Challenge for the United States," *Staff Report of the U.S. House of Representatives Permanent Select Committee on Intelligence, Subcommittee on Intelligence Policy*, August 23, 2006, URL: http://intelligence.house.gov/Media/PDFS/IranReport082206v2.pdf#search=%22Recognizing%20Iran%20as%20a%20Strategic%20Threat%3A%20An%20Intelligence%20Challenge%20for%20the%20United%20States%22

As with Libya and Syria, Pakistan and Iran have both been state sponsors of terrorism in the post-9/11 era. Although since becoming officially allied with the United States, Pakistan has been tremedously helpful in fighting the war on terrorism. Nevertheless, its previous proliferation of nuclear technology until 2002 remains troubling.[65] In the case of Iran, the ongoing proliferation of missiles is significantly more troubling.

Iran continues to be a state supporter of terrorism, and though North Korea has signed two documents in the post-9/11 era denouncing terrorists, North

Korean weapons brokers and technicians are likely to have contact with terrorist organizations supported by and currently located in Tehran.[66] In addition, continued weapons sales threaten to destabilize one of the most volatile regions of the world.

It cannot be stressed enough that North Korea will quite literally sell missiles, and/or the technology to develop an independent or semi-independent program (as has been done with Iran and Pakistan) to any nation that is willing to fund such projects, and has already bartered deals with Iran and Pakistan. In the words of one U.S. defense official, "They are becoming The Home Depot for missile sales around the world."[67] Former commanding general of United States Forces Korea, Gen. Thomas A. Schwartz, told the U.S. Senate Armed Services Committee that the North Koreans are the number one proliferators of missiles in the world—and also of conventional weapons.[68]

North Korea uses its missiles as direct tools of brinkmanship and engages in large-scale proliferation of missiles, knowing that eventually, to force Pyongyang to stop these practices will take large amounts of hard currency or foreign aid. President Clinton attempted unsuccessfully to persuade the North Koreans to freeze their missile programs and proliferation in the later stages of his administration in the fall of 2000. Reportedly he was seriously considering offering Kim Chong-il at least several hundred million dollars a year in return for a complete halt to missile sales. It was only at the last minute that he may have been dissuaded from the deal by aides who perhaps felt in was not in the best national security interests of the United States to carry it out.[69]

The Military Threat from Pyongyang's Missile Arsenal

The biggest worry for U.S. policymakers regarding the North Korean threat is the mounting of a nuclear warhead on one or more of its missiles. While North Korean technicians were conducting the testing and evaluation of the No-Dong missile, it is very possible that the North Koreans and Pakistanis were able to stabilize an HEU warhead that could be used on the missile—which during the late 1990s was assessed to have a range of approximately 1,300 kilometers.[70]

Given the possibility that the Pakistanis and North Koreans were able to stabilize such a warhead on the No-Dong/Ghauri, Pyongyang could threaten parts of Japan and U.S. bases on Okinawa with nuclear weapons—and if Pyongyang already has the capability based on technology received from

Islamabad between the late 1990s and 2002, to deploy and fire a No-Dong with a nuclear warhead, it would change the status quo in Northeast Asia. According to press reports from 2005 citing ROK government officials, the No-Dong missile now has a range of 1,500 kilometers, giving it a capability of hitting even more areas in Japan.[71]

Since the nuclear confrontation began in the fall of 2002, Pyongyang has stepped up the deployment of its missiles to newly built sites and conducted experimentation with deploying missiles on easily movable Transporter-Erector-Launchers, widely referred to as TELs. In 2005, engine tests also continued on the Taepo-Dong 2, and were detected and reported on by the South Korean press as recently as May 2005. These tests, of course, led to launch preparations in May and June 2006.[72] Presumably these tests were conducted—at least partially—in order for Washington and Seoul to see them, a methodology that can easily be considered brinkmanship in its own right.

In 2005, the South Korean press also reported that the North Koreans have deployed ten new intermediate-range missiles and five launch pads at Mirim airfield, near Pyongyang. They can be fired from mobile launchers (likely the "TELs" discussed earlier) as opposed to fixed aboveground or underground sites.[73] According to a report by the South Korean Ministry of Defense given to the National Assembly in 2005, North Korea has recently engaged in developing at least eighty tactical sites to conceal field artillery and missiles. What reportedly differs from past efforts is that the sites are not limited to frontline areas but have also been detected in rear areas as well. The Ministry report stated that the precision strike capability demonstrated by the U.S. in Iraq appears to have prompted the effort as Washington's precision weapons will reportedly be deployed to the Peninsula in the case of conflict.[74] South Korean National Intelligence Service Director Kim Seung-kyu revealed in a briefing to the National Assembly in July 2006 that the North Koreans were building new missile bases and silos along their northeast coast. According to the briefing and a report later written by Yun Deok-min of the State-funded Institute of Foreign Affairs and Trade, No-Dong and Taepo-Dong X missile systems are already being deployed to the new bases, which have underground missile bases and silos under construction.[75]

The longer range missiles are important to North Korea's national defense policy, and are also important tools of brinkmanship capable of threatening U.S. bases in Japan as well as other cities and facilities. But North Korea has also developed its SCUD arsenal and the range and deployment of its SCUD missile sites well enough that it can now effectively hit any target in South Korea. Pentagon estimates indicate Pyongyang has more than 500 SCUDs in its arsenal.[76]

In North Korea's conventional forces artillery doctrine, SCUDs (it is likely that the "KN-02" systems also fall into this category) are considered part of the artillery strike force that would assault Seoul and other key areas of both civilian and military importance in the opening barrage of any hostilities that they would initiate with South Korea.[77] Thus, these weapons can (and are) used as a tool of brinkmanship—in essence holding Seoul hostage during any period of increased tensions. Unfortunately, no military base on the Korean Peninsula is truly safe from instant attack by North Korean military forces.

FIGURE 4:
KNOWN NORTH KOREAN MISSILE BASES

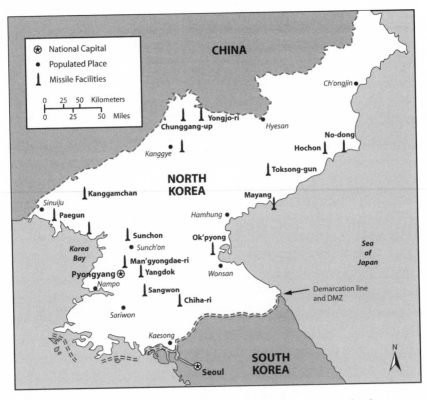

Source: ROK Ministry of National Defense, 2003, URL: http://www.mnd.go.kr

Missiles as a Tool of Policy: Intentions and Motivations

Pyongyang likely has developed its systems in the hope of being able to deter, constrain, and harm the United States and its allies in the region and elsewhere, such as the Middle East.[78] Indeed, it has been suggested that the development of more missiles, longer range missiles, and missiles that could be more widely dispersed and harder to detect (the "TELs" mentioned earlier) is out of a perceived need for security by Pyongyang.[79]

Another legitimate intention that has been seen throughout the development, deployment, and proliferation of North Korean missile systems, is that of economic profit. Pyongyang has sought to gain economic support for its missiles while actively marketing them to anyone who would buy them. Although not the largest source of funds for North Korea's cash strapped regime, the sale of missiles has certainly been one of the larger sources of funds in the post-9/11 era.[80]

Finally, a key intention behind North Korea's varied and continuing missile programs is likely to be a desire to initiate brinkmanship as a tool of foreign policy. Indeed, the testing and deployment of large numbers of ballistic and other types of missiles can reasonably be seen as a way of "raising the stakes" when North Korea is seeking concessions from the United States. These types of activities can be used in conjunction with provocations such as DMZ violations, harassment of U.S. reconnaissance flights, and other activities as a way of raising tensions—a tactic that North Korea has used in recent years on several occasions.[81] When preparing for a test-launch of the Taepo-Dong 2 in 2006, Pyongyang attempted to use the event as a tool for concessions from the United States or others at the six-party talks.

Of course, Pyongyang can continue proliferating its missiles with extended ranges and advancing capabilities and selling them to countries that are likely to disrupt stability and security in their own regions—Iran being a key example.[82] This is likely to continue until Pyongyang can be persuaded that it is not in the best interest of a regime that has over and over again proven that bad behavior usually pays off.

ADJUSTING TO ECONOMIC REALITIES: THE EVOLVING DOCTRINE, READINESS, AND CAPABILITIES OF NORTH KOREA'S CONVENTIONAL FORCES

4

A GREAT DEAL OF DEBATE regarding North Korea's nuclear programs has occurred, as well as some debate regarding its missile programs, but there has been almost no debate regarding its conventional military forces. In fact, scores of Korean analysts, many of whom know little about conventional military forces, tend to take one of two very simplistic schools of thought. The first is that North Korea has a military that is badly weakened from severe economic hardship and is simply trying to "hang on" and defend the paranoid regime in Pyongyang from an attack initiated by the ROK–U.S. Alliance—particularly the United States.[1] Another school of thought opines that North Korea's military—and its strategy and capabilities—has changed little since the 1980s (despite economic hardships) when it was still heavily subsidized by the Soviet Union.[2]

Each of these schools of thought is relatively easy to understand and tends to reflect opposite ends of the political spectrum, in fact the North Korean military has greatly evolved in its strategy and capabilities because of economic constraints over which the regime has had no control over. Thus, an analysis of North Korea's military forces brings us to an assessment that is much more nuanced.

One may correctly assume, simply by looking at Figure 5, that North Korea is an armed camp. The sheer size of North Korea's military makes it the fifth largest in the world.[3] The majority (70 percent) of North Korea's ground, air, and naval forces are deployed to locations south of Pyongyang, putting them in an ideal position for striking South Korea.[4] Many units are also, of course, stationed close to Pyongyang or in the actual city limits[5] and may legitimately be considered the "palace guard" for Kim Chong-il.

FIGURE 5:
NORTH KOREAN DISPOSITION OF FORCES

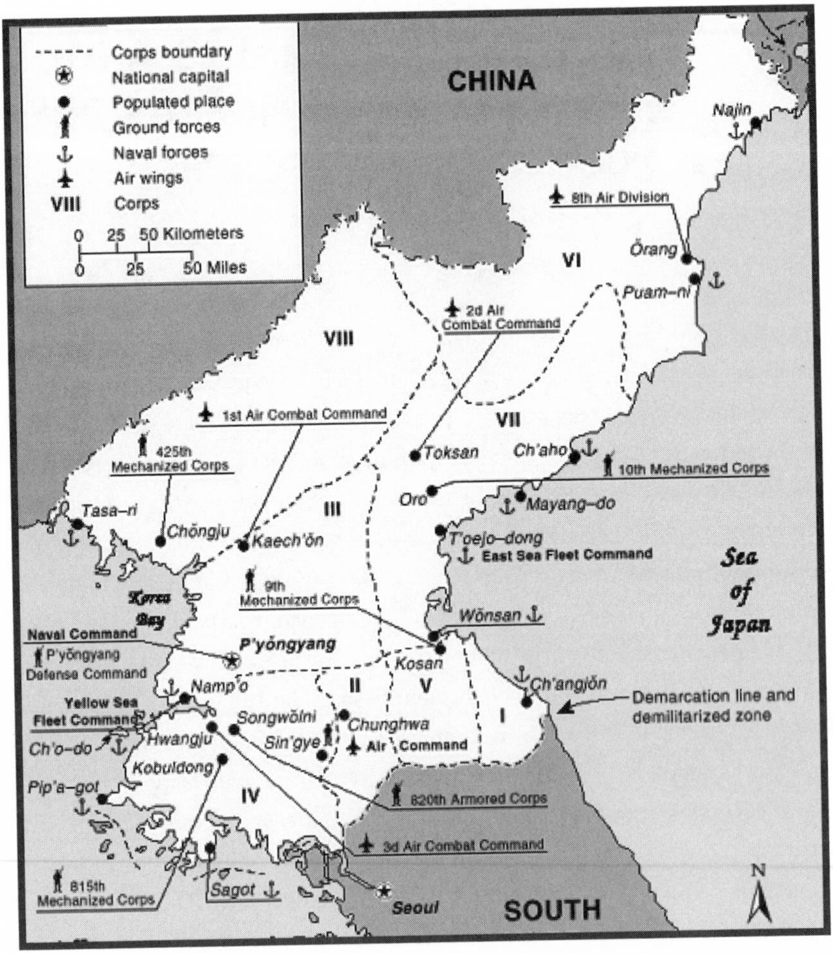

Source: Library of Congress: North Korean Country Study, 2005[6]

Ground Forces

North Korea has an estimated 22.5 million people, and armed forces just below 1.1 million. The Korean People's Army (KPA) makes up the majority at more than 940,000 personnel.[7] KPA equipment includes 3,700 tanks, 3,500 armored personnel carriers, and more than 4,000 self-propelled artillery pieces. The North has a total of nearly 12,000 artillery systems—a staggering number—and is augmented by nearly 800 fighter aircraft[8] (see Fig. 6). Because of the strength and nature of the equipment that the army possesses, its doctrine throughout the 1980s and into the 1990s was built around its armored and mechanized forces in order to conduct a "quick-strike."[9] Order of battle for KPA forces includes twenty corps including four corps in the forward area, four mechanized, one tank and two artillery corps (one of the artillery corps has now been converted to a missile corps), as well as the Light Infantry Training Guidance Bureau (LITGB), which supervises the Special Operations Forces that number up to 100,000. The KPA boasts 176 divisions and brigades that make up the major combat units, including thirty-three infantry divisions/ brigades, and ten security brigades.

The main weaponry of the North Korean ground forces continues to be focused on tanks, armored personnel carriers, and self-propelled artillery. Older model T-54/55/59 tanks comprise the majority of its armor. In the 1990s, Pyongyang domestically produced Chonmaho tanks (North Korea's version of

FIGURE 6:

NORTH KOREAN ARMED FORCES COMMAND AND CONTROL

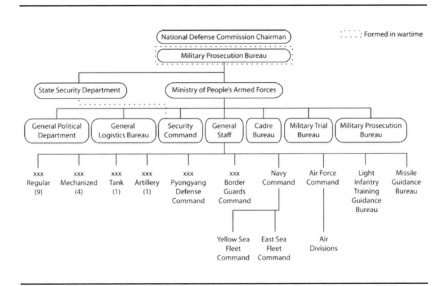

Source: Ken E. Gause, *North Korean Civil-Military Trends: Military-First Politics To A Point,* Strategic Studies Institute Monograph, (Carlisle, PA: U.S. Army War College, September 2006), URL: http://www.strategicstudiesinstitute.army.mil/pdffiles/PUB728.pdf

T-62 tanks) in relatively small numbers. They have been deployed extensively in forward areas and around Pyongyang. The Chonmaho tanks are equipped with snorkels that enable them to cross rivers up to 5.5 meters deep. Additionally, North Korea possesses a large number of multiple rocket launchers (MRLs) ranging from 107mm (with ranges up to about 7,000 meters) to 240mm (with ranges of up to 40,000 meters), which have been moved to the edge of the DMZ.[10] Heavy maneuver forces such as these must be supported by proficient and reliable air forces.

Air Forces

There are six air divisions under direct control of the Air Command, otherwise known as the North Korean Air Force (NKAF). NKAF is organized along old Soviet doctrinal lines with three fighter and bomber divisions, two support aircraft divisions, and one training division. There are approximately 1,700 aircraft, nearly 800 being fighters.

More than half of North Korean aircraft consist of old models such as MiG-15s and 17s and Il-28s. MiG-19s and 21s make up the real fighting punch of the NKAF and are the planes most observed conducting training and exercises. Pyongyang does have more advanced fighters such as MiG-23s and 29s, as well as Su-25s in much smaller numbers in its inventory. All of these newer aircraft were received during the mid- to late 1980s, before the Soviet Union cut off subsidization of the NKPA around 1990.[11] The NKAF also possesses around 300 An-2s (a biplane of a design originally used by the Soviets during World War II) capable of flying slowly at low altitudes. These aircraft are typically used to infiltrate Special Operations Forces in wartime.[12]

Naval Forces

The North Korean navy can legitimately be called a self-defense force and is not truly capable of blue-water operations. However, naval personnel conduct low-level provocations against South Korea and even Japan.[13] The navy is organized into the East Sea and the West Sea Fleets, both of which come under the control of Supreme Navy Command. Combined, the two fleets boast sixteen battle groups. Most North Korean combat vessels are small by western standards, and typical vessels include light destroyers, patrol ships, guided missile boats, torpedo boats, and fire support boats. The biggest threat to United States and ROK naval activity is the approximately forty guided missile boats that are stationed relatively close to the MDL—the naval version of the DMZ. These small, 1950s vintage vessels have the capability of launching missile attacks against much larger vessels and are equipped with two to four 46-kilometer-range Styx antiship missiles. The North Korean navy also has up to fifty Romeo and Shark-class (SANGO) submarines. The Romeos are older, Soviet made vessels, and the SANGOs are indigenously produced. A SANGO submarine was captured on an attempted infiltration mission during 1996.[14]

Two other important threats that the North Koreans have in their naval arsenal—mostly that can be used for harassment and provocation—include indigenously produced landing craft personnel aircushion (LCPA), and 95-kilometer-range ground-to-ship Silkworm missiles on both the east and west coasts. The landing craft could possibly launch Special Forces, whereas the antiship missiles are weapons that the United States and ROK forces would have to take into consideration during any naval engagement near the MDL.[15]

Evolution of the Military Threat[16]

North Korea has faced huge problems since subsidies from a collapsed Soviet Union ceased at the end of the Cold War, namely the impossibility of maintaining the readiness and capabilities of a military (its core being a large, mechanized army) that is poised to attack South Korea, with the goal of achieving unification under the communist regime in Pyongyang.[17] Maintaining a high capability of readiness for a large military that is built around an army dominated by mechanized forces and self-propelled artillery must include providing fuel to conduct field training and exercises on a regular basis. Feeding large military forces is also a major task for any country wishing to maintain its military in a high state of readiness. Fuel and food are commodities that North Korea has been drastically short of since the early 1990s.[18] Anecdotal reporting as late as 2005 suggests that North Korean soldiers in at least some units are still suffering from food shortages.[19]

North Korea's military is limited in what it can do by the unique geography of the Korean Peninsula. Thus, in any invasion scenario, military operations must flow through two key narrow invasion corridors—the Kaesong-Munsan corridor and the Chorwon Valley corridor. The east coast approach, in the case of a North Korean invasion of the South, will only support a small-scale flow of forces[20] (see Fig. 7). These two corridors have always been the key to any invasion into Korea—including those long ago by the Mongols.[21]

Mounting a full-scale invasion through north-south approaches in narrow corridors by mechanized and self-propelled artillery forces must be supported by a modern air force that was capable of combatting U.S. and South Korean aircraft. Otherwise, ground forces will be destroyed as they attempt to navigate roads into the South. The NKAF is lacking in this capability.

Pyongyang's air force was last upgraded in the late 1980s with small-scale acquisitions from the former USSR. Since then North Korea has made feeble

FIGURE 7:
KOREAN INVASION ROUTES

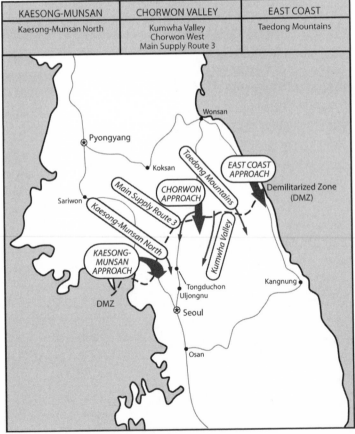

KAESONG-MUNSAN	CHORWON VALLEY	EAST COAST
Kaesong-Munsan North	Kumwha Valley Chorwon West Main Supply Route 3	Taedong Mountains

Source: Republic of Korea Ministry of National Defense, 2001.

attempts to continue the level of capabilities for its air force, such as acquiring forty MiG-21s from Kazakhstan in 1999, but this has simply not been enough to make any real advances in the capabilities of North Korean airpower.[22] Additionally, the air force suffers from the same lack of fuel that troubles the mechanized, armored, and self-propelled artillery forces in Pyongyang's ground forces. As a result, North Korean pilots fly as little as twenty hours a year of flight time in their aircraft—creating the terrible combination of largely antiquated aircraft and poorly trained pilots.[23]

Although many of the aircraft are older models, the North Korean military continues to fly them because they simply do not have anything with which to replace them. A report on commercial satellite pictures released by the Japanese press in 2005 stated that "90 percent of North Korean military aircraft are Korean War vintage . . . newest fighters were those supplied in 1984 and 1988 by the Soviet Union."[24] The report is correct that North Korea's most recent acquisitions of truly modern aircraft came in 1984 and 1988, although the assessment that 90 percent of military aircraft are Korean War vintage is a significant exaggeration.

A report by the North Korean Advisory Group to the U.S. Congress in 1999 noted: "Most recently, South Korean military officials have focused on fuel shortages as a principal cause for the decline in major North Korean military exercises."[25] According to a 2006 paper presented by David Von Hippel, a senior associate at the Nautilus Institute for Security and Sustainable Development, the North Korean military continues to have a huge impact on the country's energy resources, and the lack of these resources has also had an impact on the operations and training of the country's conventional forces—particularly the ground and air forces. At the time Von Hippel presented his paper to the DPRK Energy Expert Study Group Meeting at Stanford University, ground forces activity during 2000 to 2005 was 13 to 20 percent lower than estimated 1990 levels because of shortages of fuel and parts. Von Hippel also revealed that aircraft flight hours per year were at an estimated 50 to 60 percent of estimated 1990 levels by 2000–2005. Additionally, as of 2000, the military accounted for 37 percent of North Korea's oil products demand, and even more strikingly, more than 50 percent of gasoline and diesel use in the country.[26]

If North Korea has undergone a severe degradation of its capability to mount a successful invasion of the South with its conventional military forces, has the threat also severely diminished? The answer is likely to be no. Why? Because during the 1990s, as Pyongyang's capability to mount a successful war of unification on the South diminished, Kim Chong-il's regime concentrated on a new capability—to threaten South Korea (and ultimately the region) with asymmetric forces. Pyongyang has continued to build on, and maintain this capability during the new millennium.

It appears that since the mid-1990s, when Kim Chong-il realized he could no longer maintain previous levels of military readiness and capabilities in armored and mechanized forces (or provide effective air support for them), the regime focused instead on weapons and capabilities that could threaten the security and stability of the government in Seoul but would not be nearly as much of a drain on the dwindling resources of North Korea. This task has been accomplished with an asymmetric force capability developed in the 1990s. This asymmetric capability is maintained with a triad of forces; missiles, long-range artillery, and special operations forces.

Long-range Artillery

Perhaps the most disturbing asymmetric capability that Pyongyang developed and deployed was long-range artillery. During the early 1990s, and continuing late into the decade, North Korea moved a large number of self-propelled, long-range artillery systems to areas just north of the DMZ that target areas in and around Seoul. There are now more than 500 of these systems deployed along the DMZ,[27] with at least 300 aimed at Seoul, potentially causing deaths in the hundreds of thousands.[28] The South Korean Defense Ministry's 2004 version of its Defense White Paper (a defense document that comes out annually and is updated on a detailed basis with each new version), published that North Korea's ability to maintain old equipment had hit a wall, with the number of military tanks and armored vehicles both declining. The conclusion was that a lack of fuel and electricity had made it difficult for Pyongyang to maintain its armament industry and the production of spare parts. The report also noted, however, that North Korea had increased the number of artillery pieces in its arsenal by 1,000 since 2000—a significant improvement.[29] This shows that as one capability to threaten South Korea declined during recent years, the North Korean military was able to replace it with another capability in many ways just as lethal.

Short-range Missiles

The second capability in North Korea's triad of asymmetric capabilities is the missile threat to on-Peninsula forces. North Korea's military planners consider short-range (or SRBM) Scud missiles to be an attack option as part of their artillery doctrine for any attack against South Korea, and its Missile Training Guidance Bureau (also known as "Missile Command" or "Missile Corps") was formed using the staff from a former artillery corps. Thus, the main missile threats to South Korea are the Scud missiles already deployed in North Korea, which are now augmented by the more accurate North Korean version of the SS-21, the KN-02.[30] Estimates vary on how many KN-02 platforms are in Pyongyang's arsenal, but based on recent testing it is likely that several would be deployed in any conflict.[31] Because of their range, as Seoul and other areas of Kyongi Province were coming under artillery attack, the Scud and KN-02 missiles could hit key military and civilian targets that would be out of range of the long-range artillery—such as the U.S. Army Base at Camp Humphries or Osan Air Force Base.

With estimates of at least 500 of these missiles in North Korea's inventory already, some or all of them are likely to have a chemical warhead capability.[32] These missiles could be used concurrently with the long-range artillery already deployed along the DMZ, with little or no warning, and would add significantly to what would already be a casualty count of hundreds of thousands on the first day of a war.

Special Operations Forces

The third capability in North Korea's triad of asymmetric threats is the large and well-trained cadre of special operations forces (SOF) Pyongyang possesses. Estimates vary, but most place the number of personnel up to 100,000—the world's largest. These forces, unlike many in North Korea's military in the re-source-constrained period starting in the early 1990s, seemingly have not been held back by a lack of fuel or food. Special operations forces are able to train year-round, and in fact have not undergone a decline in training seen in many of the other conventional forces that are in Pyongyang's command.

Perhaps as much as anything, it is the very nature of these forces (and Pyongyang's continued cleverness) that allows them to maintain a high level of readiness. For example, special operations forces can practice para-drop training from towers as well as aircraft, so they are not limited by the amount of fuel and/or flight time that their potential aircraft platforms would have. In wartime, these forces have the potential, in large numbers, to attack key command and control nodes, air bases, or any other high-value targets in South Korea. Because of their training and doctrine, they can also conduct "unconventional operations" or even terrorist acts that would severely disrupt morale and alter public opinion in both South Korea and the United States. Their most likely platform for insertion into South Korea is the over 300 AN-2 COLT (WWII Vintage) aircraft in the North Korean inventory. These aircraft are considered relatively easy to fly, and North Korea has made a concerted effort keep its arsenal of AN-2s well maintained.[33] An AN-2 is capable of carrying approximately eight fully combat loaded troops. Multiplying that up with the number of aircraft (100,000 troops, 300 AN-2s), it becomes clear that there are far more SOF troops than there are aircraft to carry them. Thus, it is likely that many of these troops would attempt to infiltrate South Korea through weaker areas of the DMZ.

Two of the areas where such an attempt would be likely are the "Inter-Korean Transportation Corridors" where roads and rail lines are being repaired

FIGURE 8:
INTER-KOREAN TRANSPORTATION CORRIDORS

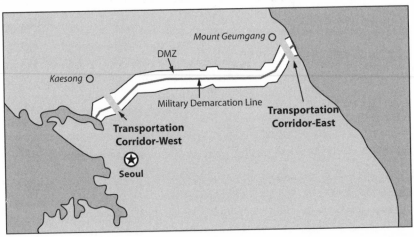

Source: Statement of General Leon J. LaPorte, Commander United Nations Command, Commander, Republic of Korea-United States Combined Forces Command And United States Forces Korea, Before the 108th Congress House Armed Services Committee, URL: http://armedservices.house.gov/openingstatementsandpressreleases/108thcongress/03-03-12laporte.pdf

for future transportation routes, and where barbed wire barriers and mines have been cleared away (see Fig. 8). Not only could troops sneak through these corridors disguised as civilians, but they could also come through at night and this is in addition to forces that would likely infiltrate south through many tunnels that to date remain undiscovered.[34]

An examination of the evidence shows a clear change of direction for North Korea's armed forces that began as their conventional capability began to decline during the 1990s. Because of severely constrained resources, Pyongyang has shifted from a priority of building and maintaining a conventional capability that would ultimately overrun and conquer South Korea, to focusing on a capability that threatens all or most of Seoul, and ultimately disrupts or threatens the security of much of the remaining landmass in the South. Ultimately, this accomplishes many of the same initial objectives. If Seoul is severely degraded as a city, and much of the landmass and or population of South Korea is destroyed or damaged, North Korea will have taken a country that currently has the world's tenth largest GDP back to being a third-world nation.[35] Thus, because Pyongyang has the capability of threatening South Korea's very way of life, and ultimately, Seoul's national security, although the threat of violent reunification has been degraded, the threat of violent war and destruction of life as most South Koreans now know it has not. The North Korean Advisory Group Congressional Report states,

> North Korea is less capable of successfully invading and occupying South Korea today than it was five years ago, due to issues of readiness, sustainability, and modernization. It has, however, built an advantage in long-range artillery, short-range ballistic missiles, and special operations forces. This development, along with its chemical and biological weapons capability and forward-deployed forces, gives North Korea the ability to inflict significant casualties on U.S. and South Korean forces and civilians in the earliest stages of any conflict.[36]

It is important to note that the early stages of a conflict in Korea have long been considered the most important as well as when casualties would be the highest. Because of this, Pyongyang's evolved military threat to South Korea remains an ominous factor that must be deterred by the ROK–U.S. Alliance.

Motivations for Maintaining Conventional Forces

As one looks at North Korea's military with a truly pragmatic, analytical view, an examination of the evidence clearly points to a military that has evolved since the end of the Soviet Union, and certainly since the death of Kim Il-sung and the rise of his son, Kim Chong-il. Because the government in North Korea certainly does not intend to openly express motivations and intentions for the maintenance, training, and equipping of its conventional forces, interested outside observers can only base their analysis on actions taken by the North Koreans. On the surface it may appear that the North Korean conventional military forces no longer have the capability or intention to wage war on the South, and many analysts have assessed that as a tool of foreign policy, North Korea's conventional military forces have been and will continue to be used, only in a defensive manner. In fact, many analysts consider U.S. policy interests best served if the United States reassures a militarily weakened North Korea that it has no intention of attacking.[37] The view that the North Korean military is now in a posture dominated by the defense is espoused most frequently by analysts who have little or no experience in examining capabilities and deployment of conventional military forces.[38] The conclusion that nuclear weapons are a "defensive deterrent" because conventional military forces can no longer reasonably threaten the South is, at best, ill-informed.

If the intentions behind the changes in North Korea's conventional military forces are to be judged as purely "defensive" in nature, the only way that this could seriously be considered legitimate would be if the North Koreans believe "the best defense is a good offense." This takes us back to the Cold War paradigms in that the Soviet forces and their allies in Eastern Europe could threaten NATO forces with unacceptable losses. Of course, to start the war could mean overwhelming loss of life and property for both sides—to such an extent that both sides hoped it would never happen. This amounted to a conventional forces "mutually assured destruction."[39] Indeed, the disposition of conventional forces in North Korea over the past two decades has been specifically designed to adjust to economic realities that have forced Pyongyang out of a Peninsula-unifying attack scenario built around armored and mechanized maneuver forces and into a scenario that involves attacks by long-range artillery, short-range missiles and rockets, and special operations forces focused on Seoul, key areas of Kyongi province, and other strategically important areas. Success would render South Korea a third-world nation and destroy stability throughout Northeast Asia.[40] Thus, the mutually assured destruction theory exists on the Korean Peninsula.

But one must look even deeper to truly understand North Korean intentions for its conventional military forces. Evidence shows that Pyongyang can use these forces as tools of foreign policy by conducting provocations. In the post-9/11 era, North Korean air force units, navy units, and army units, have all been used to conduct provocations against ROK or U.S. forces.

5 | CASE STUDY IN CONVENTIONAL FORCES PROVOCATIONS: THE NORTHERN LIMIT LINE INCIDENT OF 2002[1]

ONE TREND HAS BECOME PREVALENT in all provocations conducted with the conventional forces of the North Korean government. Most of the incidents that have occurred in recent years have in common the intentional initiation during moments in history when they will have the likelihood of garnering the most attention on the regional and perhaps even the world stage, and the appearance of being small, easily contained, and quickly "resolved." In other words, these incidents have been intentionally planned to prevent events from spiraling into full-scale war.

In June 2002 things seemed to be on the upswing on the Korean Peninsula. The Republic of Korea was in the midst of hosting the World Cup soccer championships, the relationship between the United States and North Korea seemed to be warming up—as a scheduled visit to Pyongyang by James Kelly was to occur soon—North-South talks seemed to be making progress on important issues such as a Trans-Korea railway, and South Korean tourists continued to visit the Kum Gang complex near the North-South border.

As has happened numerous times in the inter-Korea relationship since the armistice was declared in 1953, the seemingly docile summer of 2002 was interrupted by what now appears to be a deliberate provocation.[2]

Two North Korean ships crossed the Northern Limit Line (NLL) that separates the two Koreas off the west coast of the Peninsula, with one of the ships actively engaging South Korean patrol boats as it fired directly into the engine room of one of the small patrol craft (or PKM). There were casualties on both sides, with the most badly damaged South Korean boat sinking as it was being towed back into port, and one of the North Korean craft, also badly damaged was photographed smoking heavily (apparently on fire), as it too limped back to port, eventually with the aid of another North Korean vessel. Shortly after the incident occurred, President Kim Dae-jung held an emergency meeting of the National Security Council to discuss Seoul's response to the attack and determine how and why it occurred.[3] Once again, a violent event, initiated by the North Koreans, had increased tensions on the Korean Peninsula.[4]

On June 29, 2002, at 9:54 A.M., a North Korean patrol ship crossed the Northern Limit Line (NLL) that separates North and South Korea off the west coast of the Peninsula at a location about seven nautical miles from Yeonpyong-do (island).[5] Two South Korean patrol craft (PKMs) were sent out to meet the ship. At 10:01 A.M., another North Korean patrol ship also crossed the NLL at a distance about seven miles west of the incursion by the first craft.[6] The two North Korean ships were later identified as the 155-ton "608," and the 215-ton "684."[7] The South Korean ships sent to patrol the area just south of the NLL were now split into two groups, with two patrol craft rushing to meet the first North Korean ship that had crossed the line, and two other craft rushing to meet the ship that had crossed a few minutes later.

FIGURE 9:
BURNING NORTH KOREAN SHIP

Photo courtesy of the Republic of Korea Ministry of National Defense 2002.

At 10:25 A.M., as the second North Korean ship to cross the NLL was approached by the South Korean vessels, the ROK crews were in the midst of broadcasting warnings to "go back to the northern side of the NLL."[8] The North Korean ship closed to 1,000 yards, and the ROK crews then began to use a signal light and sirens to warn the vessel back.[9] The North Korean ship closed to 500 yards and suddenly turned at 30 degrees and aimed its 85-millimeter gun at PKM 357's bridge and steering room. Navy Staff Sergeant Hwang Chan-kyu, described it,

> I could see the number 608 on the North Korean Ship, and thought the distance was pretty close. . . . All of a sudden, I saw a bright light from the enemy ship, and a moment later, our ship was ablaze.[10]

The North Korean ship focused its fire on the bridge and the engine room, using its 85-millimeter gun, 35-millimeter auxiliary gun, and hand-carried rockets. The South Korean patrol boats, including the one being fired upon, unleashed retaliatory fire at the North Korean ship, using 30-millimeter and 40-millimeter guns, and were joined by other ROK ships that had been patrolling nearby. At 10:43 A.M., a loud bang rang out, as huge flames bellowed out of the North Korean ship, which had started the short battle. Soon thereafter, at 10:50 A.M., the North Korean ship, and its sister ship, which had also violated the NLL, headed north back across the NLL into North Korean waters. At 10:56 A.M., the ROK commander on the site ordered that the firing cease and not to pursue the North Korean ships. Rescue operations for the badly damaged South Korean vessel began immediately. As a result of the battle, four South Korean sailors were killed, one was missing (the body was later recovered), and twenty-seven were wounded—all aboard the ship that was originally attacked. The South Korean ship that was attacked at the beginning of the battle subsequently sank at approximately 11:59 A.M as it was being towed back to port.

Immediately after the battle, the South Korean navy estimated that North Korean casualties amounted to about thirty sailors. The North Korean ship that started the attack was later seen being towed back to port.[11] According to the commander of the patrol craft that accompanied the badly damaged PKM 357, Major Kim Chan reported, "In about four minutes, we used all 1,500 rounds of ammunition, with more than 40% hitting the target. Fire poured from the Northern patrol boat, and it was firing with less intensity."[12] Several facts discovered about the events surrounding the battle are worth noting.

FIGURE 10:

SITE OF THE CLASH

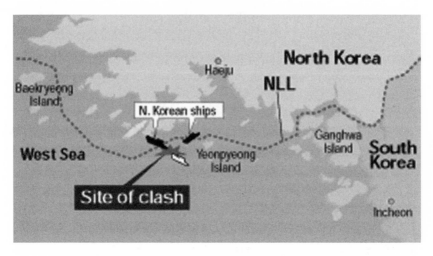

Map Courtesy of the Republic of Korea Ministry of National Defense 2002.

■ The North Korean ships crossed the NLL on their own instead of the normal pattern of crossing along with numerous fishing vessels. All North Korean fishing vessels were distinguishably north of the NLL.[13]

■ The North Korean navy had actually conducted a possible "practice run" the day before. On June 28, two North Korean craft had also crossed the NLL nearly simultaneously at different spots along the disputed line, in what appeared to be a tactic to divide the South's fleet of patrol boats patrolling the area, and leave the lightly armed South Korean PKMs vulnerable to attack. At the time, it appeared to South Koreans to be simply coincidental navigational error.

■ North Korean naval craft had crossed the NLL five times in the previous two weeks before the actual battle occurred, but this had also appeared to be a routine trend, often seen during crabbing season.[14]

Within an hour after it began, according to South Korean military spokesman Whang Yi-dong, South Korean navy corvettes rushed to join the clash and a North Korean ship equipped with STYX missiles activated its targeting radar while moored at one of the North's harbors close to the NLL. Whang stated that "normally, the radar is turned off." Even more ominously, land-based Silkworm antiship cruise missile batteries at nearby Dongsan-got were activated at 11:24 A.M., approximately thirty minutes after the battle was over.[15] The most obvious reason for these actions is that the North made these moves with its military forces in case South Korean naval craft attempted to pursue the North Korean ships into North Korean waters.[16] The STYX missiles have a range of approximately 25 nautical miles and are carried on North Korean guided missile patrol boats. The Silkworm missiles have an even longer range.[17] Both systems were potentially capable of sinking South Korean ships, had they chosen to pursue the DPRK craft back across the NLL.

In the hours and days following the short battle, South and North Korea blamed one another for starting it and for lying about how the events occurred. In South Korea, the Ministry of National Defense and Joint Chiefs of Staff stated that the maritime clash with North Korean vessels was an intentional provocation by the North's warships and that the North started the incident by first shooting at a South Korean patrol boat.[18] North Koreans responded with numerous verbal attacks following the incident. For example, on July 7, the command of the North Korean Navy made an official statement regarding the incident. The statement, carried by KCNA, North Korea's state-sponsored propaganda network, said,

> "The navy of the South Korean Army illegally infiltrated two combat warships into the territorial waters of our side off Kuwol Hill in Kangryong county, South Hwanghae Province, at around 10:30 A.M. today. The provocation in the wake of the armed clash on June 29 is a deliberate move to render the situation in the waters more strained. We warn that the infiltration of the combat warships is a dangerous act which may spark a new armed clash.[19]

The evidence uncovered immediately following the attack was crucial in determining if it was intentional, unintentional, who was lying in statements made following the battle (by the governments of North and South Korea), and if the attack was perhaps the work of a "rogue captain."

One element is the conflict over the NLL, which has gone on for many years. Seoul argues that Pyongyang has tacitly accepted the boundary unilaterally drawn by United Nations Command in 1953, because North Koreans published a map in the 1959 KCNA Annual purportedly recognizing the NLL. Additionally, officials met in 1984 there for food aid and used the NLL-based flight information boundary declared by the International Aviation Authority in 1997. The North counters that in 1953, the UN did not inform North Korea of the boundary, further claiming that some of its waters have been designated unfairly to South Korea.[20] Thus, the disputes over the waters around the NLL are not new—but the naval battles have been an activity that has only occurred there in recent years.

Intentional or Unintentional?

To determine if the attack was a sudden, reactive response from the North Korean ship or a well-planned, violent operation, it is important to note that the two ships crossed the NLL in almost the exact same manner (one ship crossing the line alone, while another ship crossed alone nearly at the same time) on the day previous to the battle. The ships did this during a time when North Korean navy ships frequently were "accidentally" crossing the NLL with fishing boats— although on June 28 the fishing boats remained north of the line, as they did on June 29. According to South Korean Marine Major General Bae Sang-gi who headed the ROK JCS investigation team in 2002,

> "By crossing the border through separate routes, the North Korean forces appear to have intended to split our naval formation for a more effective, concentrated assault on one boat . . . . [T]his year, North Korean warships put their major guns in a shooting position when crossing the border, while previously their gun points were aimed toward the air.[21]

In the hours and days following the attack, according to a South Korean government source, North Korean warships did not mobilize in response to the gun battle. Normally, ships would be expected to rush to the scene, as the South Korean ships did. In addition, the North Korean navy had reportedly been "blocking" communications monitoring by South Korean and U.S. forces by operating under radio silence.[22] Operating under radio silence in an emergency situation would be highly unlikely unless ship movement had been planned in advance. As the second North Korean ship to cross the NLL closed with the closest South Korean patrol boat, it suddenly turned 30 degrees.[23] This is a difficult naval maneuver and one that could not be accomplished without planning, training, and practice. The maneuver appears to have been carried out in order to put the North Korean ship in a position where it was facing "side to side" with the South Korean patrol boat. This would put it in optimal position to aim and fire its 85-millimeter gun at the South Korean craft. In addition, the first shots fired by the attacking ship were aimed directly at the wheelhouse and engine room—the most important, easily destroyed area of the ship, and the portion of the ship most likely to catch on fire and bring maximum casualties to the crew.[24] Again, turning suddenly and making an extreme maneuver, closing with another craft for optimum firepower advantage, and then aiming at and destroying the most important areas of an enemy patrol boat, are all actions that could only be carried out effectively if meticulously planned and trained for.

Because the second North Korean ship headed directly for the two small South Korean patrol craft when it crossed the NLL instead of turning around once it encountered South Korean patrol boats, the action also points to the conclusion that this was a planned operation. As Masao Okonogi, a North Korean expert at Keio University in Tokyo has said, "The circumstantial evidence suggests it's intentional. . . . There are many cross-border incidents, but usually they turn around after being warned."[25] Additionally, the North Koreans activated the radar for weapons systems that could hit South Korean ships without deploying any more vessels of their own, which indicates that a reaction had been planned out in advance.[26] With no civilian fishing boats in the area and no large-scale deployments of naval craft out of port, had the South Koreans taken the option of chasing the ships north of the NLL, the North Koreans could have easily sunk several of their craft.

Finally, Pyongyang refused to accept Seoul's proposal for general officer level talks at Panmunjom to consult on investigations into the incident or to look into future measures for preventing further escalation. Instead, Pyongyang claimed that its actions were taken in self-defense and reiterated its rejection of the NLL's validity.[27] Normally Pyongyang would be expected to be friendly to a meeting at the general officer level where high-ranking North Koreans could rail at South Korean and American generals, demanding aid or other forms of payback in exchange for the easing of tensions. This is another move that indicates possible prior planning. If the North Koreans actually wanted tensions on the Peninsula increased, which would be likely if the incident had been created to gain attention, not agreeing to talks would help ensure that this would happen.

Origins of the Attack

Another point of contention involved what official level the order for the attack came from and where the planning occurred. Following the incident, Scott Snyder of the Asia Foundation postulated that, "Either the incident reflects intentional escalation of tension or it provides further evidence of system breakdown in North Korea."[28] Professor Yoo Ho-yeol of Korea University assessed that the occurrence of the battle may have been evidence of infighting in the North: "I think North Korea intended to shoot this time. The question is who decided." He further speculated that hard-liners in the North's military had staged the confrontation, hoping to derail upcoming U.S.–North Korea talks, fearing their power could be undermined if concessions were made to the United States.[29]

Whereas the assessment that the NLL incident was staged by hard-liners within the North's military is certainly possible, an examination of the North Korean government and its interaction with the military bodes the likelihood to be slim. As the South Korean Ministry of National Defense Report stated following the initial investigation of the attack, "considering the nature of the North Korean political regime, and the circumstantial evidence at the time of the engagement, such claims solicit little credibility."[30] Indeed, command and control within the North Korean military is extremely rigid and tightly controlled. Independent thinking is non-existent, and officers who violate the rigid rules are not the only ones punished. They can also expect to see their families and even close associates punished for deeds that are considered in violation of rules set forth by Kim Chong-il, who directly controls all military functions. As American Deputy Director of Central Intelligence John McLaughlin had said in regard to the Kim regime, Kim Chong-il has "shown his hard side through his purges of the elite, his light regard for suffering of ordinary Koreans, and . . . swift destruction of popular discontent." McLaughlin further pointed out, "the key is that power resides with Kim Chong-il and the cluster of relatives and allies who run the military, the security forces, and the rest of the state and party apparatus.[31]

A good example of the absolute loyalty demanded can be seen if one examines a meeting held in February 2000 by high-ranking political officers in the Korean People's Army, and also that was attended by the top military leaders of the country—including the leadership of the naval command who were in charge of the warships that attacked across the NLL in 2002. A key part of the officer's mission was stated as ensuring that the ideological education of servicemen in their units was conducted in such a way to ensure unconditional loyalty to the "Top Army Commander," Kim Chong-il.[32]

Examples of other incidents that led to tension on the Korean Peninsula demonstrate that absolute loyalty in the armed forces and a fervent rigidity in completing assigned missions appeared to be the order of the day. In 1996 when a North Korean submarine was stranded in South Korea, eleven members of the crew committed suicide, and the rest fought to the last man except for the one man who was captured. On March 1, 2003, two MiG-29s and two MiG-23s suddenly approached an American reconnaissance aircraft flying 150 miles from the coast of North Korea. The North Korean aircraft approached within sixteen meters of the American plane and signaled the pilot to follow them. The pilot refused.[33] The fighters intercepted the U.S. unarmed RC-135S "Cobra Ball" aircraft by shadowing it for more than twenty-two minutes. They also closed to within fifty feet of the U.S. aircraft at one point, and at least one of the fighters may have engaged his fire-support radar and "locked on" to the American aircraft.[34] These incidents show obvious advance planning, and the later incident required intense training for pilots who almost never are observed flying over water or leaving North Korean airspace. While these military operations are probably planned at command levels, they are unlikely to be ordered or carried out without the expressed permission of Kim Chong-il.

Intentional provocations also occurred on land. For example, on July 17, 2003. At 6:10 A.M., North Korean troops initiated a machine-gun battle with their South Korean counterparts across the DMZ line. The North Koreans fired four 14.6-millimeter rounds at ROK army troops with three of the four rounds striking the ROK guard post. The South Korean troops responded with their own machine-gun fire and warning announcements on a loudspeaker.[35] On July 31, 2006, North Korean troops fired two shots at a South Korean observation post along the DMZ. The South Korean soldiers responded with small arms fire, and the South Korean military demanded an apology the next day (which they did not receive). Both of these incidents appeared to be carefully planned in advance, and the later incident was widely assessed by military officials to be directly related to South Korea's negative response to the ballistic missile test-launches conducted by Pyongyang weeks before.[36]

Considering the NLL incident, as we examine the types of intricate maneuvers, the denial and deception carried out in the days leading to the naval attack, and the reaction of the North Korean government immediately following the attack, it becomes obvious that this type of operation had to have been planned at a much higher level than a mere boat captain. Even in the U.S. Navy, coordinating civilian fishing craft, missile batteries, and other ships in nearby ports would have to be extensively planned and trained for at a much higher level than the commanding officer of a single ship. Thus, circumstantial evidence points to the assessment that the planning occurred at least as high as the operational naval command level. Given the apparent coordination with shore batteries, it may have been planned for as high as the Supreme Naval Command level; —in fact, this would be the most likely scenario. According to Park Syung-je, a board member of the Military Analyst Association of the Republic of Korea, the North Korean navy ships would have coordinated with army coastal artillery to ensure they were not hit by friendly fire on their return trip from the battle. In the North Korean military structure, the army and the navy are only allowed to communicate with each other during military operations or exercises, and with the expressed permission of Kim Chong-il.[37] Given the fact that Kim Chong-il insists on a rigid command and control structure, it is also very likely that he ordered the attack, or at the very least, approved it in advance. If this was the case, what were the motivations behind initiating such an attack?

Motivations for the Attack

Given that the North Korean command structure within both the party and the military is extremely rigid and deliberate, the South Korean Ministry of National Defense has assessed four possible reasons why this event was planned and carried out on June 29, 2002.[38]

∎ The attack may have been revenge for the 1999 defeat of the North Korean navy when one of its ships was sunk just south of the NLL during crabbing season. At least thirty North Korean seamen are believed to have been killed in the battle, in addition to the loss of the ship.[39]

∎ The attack was timed to dampen the festive mood in South Korea as Seoul hosted the 2002 World Cup games. This was a widely held view in South Korea immediately following the attack.[40]

∎ The provocation was staged as a gambit for future North-South and North-U.S. relations to gain North Korean leverage in negotiations that were about to occur with the U.S. Such a move might be possible if the aim was to distract from the importance of other issues.[41]

■ The event was staged because Kim Chong-il and his closest advisors wanted to bring the world's attention to the "illegality" of the NLL, an issue the North Koreans had raised on several occasions since the late 1990s. Following the attack, North Korea issued several statements claiming the NLL as a boundary should be reconsidered, including one that stated in part that the NLL was, "a brigandish line unilaterally drawn by the U.S. and the South Korean Military."[42]

Regarding the first possibility—that this was planned and carried out as an act of revenge—some within the South Korean academic community point to the assessment that this attack was "intentionally orchestrated as a part of restoration of the namesake from the June 15, 1999, Yonpyong battle." Others have also made similar remarks, citing the incident as an act of revenge by the North.[43] In fact, since the June 1999 encounter, North Korea asserted on several occasions that, "more bloodshed would be inevitable unless the South Korean intrusion into our territorial waters is checked."[44] This assessment has some merit, particularly considering that between the 1999 naval battle and the 2002 incident, North Korea had reportedly strengthened warship training and target practice with live shells.[45] This is particularly relevant because South Korean warships are more modern, and South Korean seamen routinely receive better training than their counterparts to the North.[46] Thus, to carry out a successful operation of "revenge," North Koreans would need to spend several years planning and training—a particularly daunting process when including the coordination necessary between naval units, shore batteries, and command elements.

There is no direct evidence pointing to the possibility of an attack intended to draw attention away from the 2002 World Cup games. Although North Korea refused to participate, television in the North did broadcast portions of the games, including South Korea's victory over Italy in the second round and over Spain in the quarterfinals.[47] If the reason for the attack on the South was purely to disrupt the World Games, it is likely that the propaganda in the North would have been more negative toward Seoul as a host in the days leading up to the event. It is possible however, that the planning for the provocation had begun and the timeline for the battle drawn up, without considering the events in the South that were gaining worldwide attention. Given the considerable role that denial and deception played in the provocation, it would have been impossible to stage the event at any time other than during crab season—which coincided with Seoul's hosting of the World Cup. Thus, if this was the reason for staging the provocation (as was the popular perception in South Korea), events surrounding June 29 are inconclusive in singling it out.

The third possible reason for the attack is intriguing because if true, it shows a complete misunderstanding of U.S. foreign policy. During the time period leading up to the provocation, talks had been stalled between the Bush administration and the government of Kim Chong-il. North Korean propaganda had been calling for U.S. troop withdrawal, and the government in Pyongyang was reportedly also extremely upset with being characterized as a member of the "Axis of Evil."[48] If the North Koreans meant to draw attention away from such issues as large dispositions of troops on the DMZ or the proliferation of weapons of mass destruction, then they failed to take into account that these are issues the United States considers important to both regional and international security. In fact, as a matter of policy, the Bush administration chose 2001 and 2002 (during the time period leading up to the NLL incident) to take a much more hard-line approach to North Korea than the Clinton White House had.[49] So, if the North Koreans believed that conducting a provocation in the NLL would put them in a position of strength as scheduled bilateral talks with the United States approached, they were actually making a move that created more tension, and made U.S. officials wary of diplomatic dealings with Pyongyang. While it is possible that the incident was staged to deal with the United States from a position of strength, it appears unlikely that even the diplomatically isolated regime in Pyongyang would make such a miscalculation.

The fourth possible reason for staging the provocation is that Pyongyang wished to draw attention to what they considered the "illegal" NLL border area. This is a possibility that rates some discussion. The area is of economic importance to both North and South Korea, and the line as drawn certainly puts North Korean fishing boats at a disadvantage.[50] Further, this possibility makes some sense if viewed in context with the fact that the World Cup games were being held at the same time the incident occurred. If the North wanted to draw attention to what it considers an "illegal" line, what better time to do it, than when world attention was already focused on the Korean Peninsula because of the World Cup? Indeed, this could also match up with the "revenge" reasoning. If North Korea's intention was to achieve revenge over South Korea for the 1999 incident, and gain from the major "loss of face" suffered at the time, what better way to do it than during a time period when much of the world's attention was focused on the Korean Peninsula because of a major sporting event?

Whatever the reason for staging the provocation on June 29, 2002, based on the increased naval training and the obvious meticulous planning, it was an event that was formulated and carried out based on at least months, and probably years, of deliberate, thoughtful, and highly coordinated planning. Given the fact that naval and shore battery training increased dramatically following North Korea's defeat in 1999, the assessment that the incident of 2002 was carried out as an act of revenge appears to carry the most merit. This may not have been the only reason, though. While revenge may have been a primary motivator (particularly given the unique and emotional attitudes of the North Korean government), drawing attention to the perceived illegality of the NLL may have been an ancillary reason for carrying out the attack. In addition, planning the attack for a time period when the world was watching the Korean Peninsula may have been a secondary motivator, especially if the intention was to bring attention to the "plight" of the North Korean fishing fleet. As of the writing of this chapter, no one knows for sure why Pyongyang launched the attack. What is clear is that any advantage the North may have been trying to achieve, whether in foreign policy, military security, or economics, failed to materialize. The only definitive results of the clash were increased tensions—both with South Korea, and the United States.

Implications of the NLL Incident of 2002

One of the first and most important things to occur following the NLL incident was a change in the procedure for the South Korean navy operating along the disputed line. The "rules of engagement" can only be changed by the United Nations Commander (also the Commander of United States Forces Korea), thus, the South Korean navy designated the changes as "standard operating procedure." The new procedure implemented in July 2002 made it more difficult for North Korean ships to conduct a deceptive attack, as the South's ships were authorized to fire "warning shots" in advance, and command and control procedures were streamlined.[51] Since the new procedure was initiated, Northern warships have been turned back several times by warning shots from the South.[52] This obviously reflects South Korea's lack of trust based on North Korea's numerous incursions across the line in recent years, and the absence of transparency regarding the disposition of its naval and civilian fleet on the west coast. It is also a practical force protection measure that has proven to work fairly well in the years since the incident occurred.

In another move reflecting tensions caused by the event, the South Koreans temporarily suspended humanitarian aid shipments of rice previously scheduled to be given to North Korea. The announcement that the rice shipments (which were from "surplus" agriculture supplies) were suspended stated that it was directly attributed to the results of the fatal naval battle. The surplus rice supplies were separate from the aid provided to the North Koreans through the UN World Food Program.[53] While the move was only temporary, it reflected a negativism felt both by the South Korean government, and the population as a whole because of the incident. Aid shipments of rice later resumed, with the first shipment following the incident going to North Korea on September 19 of that year.[54]

In the short term, the incident did not bode well for the South Korean government of Kim Dae-jung and his Sunshine Policy. Immediately following the incident, there was a well-publicized outcry from the families of the sailors killed in the battle, and the political opposition as well as major newspapers in the South, expressed anger over the event, demanding to know why the South Korean navy had not sunk the North Korean ship that started the battle.[55] Ultimately, while Kim's Sunshine Policy was probably tarnished by the incident, during a visit to Japan soon after it occurred, Kim reaffirmed that it would continue, while at the same time acknowledging that South Korea and the United States would boost military surveillance of North Korea.[56]

The incident also did not bode well for North Korea's relationship with the United States. Prior to the incident, after a long absence, talks were finally scheduled to begin with the United States and its formal emissary. On July 2, several days after the incident, State Department Spokesman Richard Boucher announced that the confrontation between the naval vessels of the North and South had created an "unacceptable atmosphere" for the talks, further stating that "We remain committed to the policy of having serious discussions with the North Koreans, but we'll just have to look as things evolve at any questions of rescheduling."[57]

Perhaps because the incident did not garner positive publicity for the North Koreans "plight" over the NLL or provide them with a position of strength in dealing with the Americans (based on the fact that the scheduled security talks were postponed because of the incident), the government of North Korea eventually did issue a formal "statement of regret" over the battle.[58] The North also proposed reopening the North-South ministerial talks, and the two Koreas agreed to have working-level talks at Mt. Kumgang August 2–4. In South Korea, the response was interpreted by many as necessary for the North in order to continue receiving aid from the South that had been stepped up because of Kim Dae-jung's Sunshine Policy. Professor Yoon Young-kwak of Seoul National University interpreted the mere one-month delay of the statement to mean that the "expression of regret," which did not blame the United States or South Korea for the incident (as previous statements had), indicated the North had withdrawn from its previous "hard line." Former Unification Minister Song Young-dae interpreted the expression of regret as

- North Korea's urgent need for food aid and the necessity to resume dialogue,
- North Korea's hope that the next regime in South Korea would continue the Sunshine Policy (thus a hope to influence what were then the upcoming elections in South Korea), and
- North Korea's need to express some sort of indirect appeasing gesture to the United States.[59]

Despite diplomatic moves and statements made following the incident, tension increased dramatically as the bilateral talks between Pyongyang and Washington finally resumed on October 3, 2002. It was at the October 2002 talks that the United States confronted North Korea on the issue of a secret highly enriched uranium (HEU) weaponization program. According to Assistant Secretary of State James Kelly, North Korea's spokesman at the talks, Kang Sak-ju, confirmed U.S. allegations that his country had such a program.[60] The disclosure stunned U.S. and world officials; led to the banishment of IAEA monitors from the Yongbyon plutonium reactor facility; and has led North Korea, the United States, and regional actors, toward the high tension and stalled nuclear and security negotiations that continues today. As of this writing, six-party talks involving North and South Korea, China, Japan, Russia, and the United States have not yet definitively solved the nuclear confrontation issue that was exacerbated during the October 3–5, 2002, talks.[61]

If Kim Chong-il's intention was to create the incident as an act of revenge for the defeat of 1999, he was at least partially successful in achieving his goal. However, any intentions to deal with the United States and South Korea from a "position of strength" backfired—as the event solidified assessments by those who held more hard-line positions that the government of North Korea could not be trusted.

The NLL remains a disputed area, and one that could be a potential flashpoint for naval forces on both sides. Recent high-level military talks have not changed this fact. Though the two Koreas have recently discussed issues and implemented procedures that will lower the chances of bloody conflict along the disputed line, Pyongyang still insists that a new boundary must be established [62] (see Fig. 11). In March 2006, the government in Seoul stated that they would review a proposal made by the North Koreans during talks between high-ranking military officials. Pyongyang requested that the NLL be redrawn based on the Inter-Korean Basic Agreement signed in 1992. The agreement, in Clause 10, chapter 3, states that "There will be continuous consultation about the maritime non-aggression line between South and North Korea. The maritime non-aggression area is defined as the one each side controls until the maritime non-aggression line is established." According to a South Korean official, the review will be undertaken without the prejudice that it will be definitely redrawn—and the official acknowledged that any changes to the NLL would likely meet with strong public resistance in South Korea.[63] South Korean Unification Minister Lee Jong-seok stated in March 2006 that on the issue of the demarcation line, "the aim will be joint supervision."[64]

The confusion, controversy, and debate over the NLL has yet to subside. As a result, the danger of incidents occurring during the peak crabbing season remains a distinct possibility for the foreseeable future. Thus, the short, deadly battle of June 29, 2002, will likely be recorded in history as one more unfortunate provocation by North Korea, among the many that have occurred since 1953.

Clearly, ROK naval forces are superior in technology and crew training to the North. Nevertheless, by using clever planning, deception, and well-thought-out tactics, the North Korean navy was able to sink a ROK naval vessel successfully and regain "status" in the eyes of the Korean Peninsula. And since this was done during a time (the World Cup) when the world's attention was likely to

FIGURE 11:
WEST SEA NORTHERN LIMIT LINE VERSUS THE MARITIME BORDER CLAIMED BY NORTH KOREA

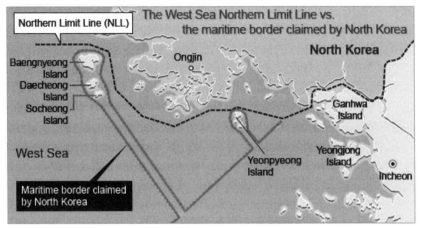

Source: Republic of Korea, Ministry of National Defense 2006.

focus on the event, the North Korean government has shown it intends to con-tinue this practice. On November 11, 2005, on the eve of the APEC Summit hosting national leaders from all over Asia as well as the United States, two North Korean aircraft, probably MiG-21s, crossed into South Korean airspace over the waters of the NLL.[65] The aircraft were in South Korean airspace for about two minutes before they were turned back by ROK fighters. This incident was widely assessed to be a move intended to announce to the world that North Korea continues in its refusal to recognize the NLL—by showing all in atten-dance at the APEC Summit that North Korean conventional forces could vio-late the disputed border at any time.[66]

These provocations demonstrate that North Korea uses its conventional military forces as a tool of foreign policy. Future analysis and assessments on North Korean foreign policy and on the North Korean military should include this key factor. With all of the attention that North Korea's nuclear and missile programs receive it is often easy to forget that Pyongyang does not hesitate to use other elements to flex its military instrument of power. If policy makers were to forget this, the results could be disastrous—as they were on that fateful day in 2002.

6 | FINANCING A ROGUE REGIME: NORTH KOREA'S ILLICIT ECONOMIC ACTIVITIES

OBSERVERS CANNOT TRULY UNDERSTAND how North Korea operates as a state that stubbornly refuses to change its isolationist policies and join the global environment, either politically or economically, until an analysis of Pyongyang's illicit economy is made.

North Korea's illicit activities are varied, diverse, and according to reports from defectors, have been ongoing since at least the mid-1970s when production of illegal drugs began in the mountainous regions of the northeast.[1] In fact, these activities, until recently relatively unknown outside of academic and specialist circles, long ago prompted some who study North Korean issues to dub the government in Pyongyang as "The Family Kim." These undertakings include the manufacture and sale of illegal drugs, counterfeit money production and sales, counterfeit cigarettes production and sales, smuggling (such as the transport of Japanese cars minus strict emission controls across the border into China, and the transport and sale of rare animals), and funds laundering through banks in East Asia and elsewhere.[2]

In 2003, according to congressional testimony by State Department official William Bach, all of these illicit activities were conducted entirely by North Korean government officials, organized first by Kim Chong-il under his father's guidance (while the elder Kim was alive) and continuing—even flourishing in greater numbers—following the rise of Kim Chong-il to the leadership of his autocratic communist state.[3] This activity is specifically operated by an extremely important section of the North Korean government in Pyongyang, with tentacles throughout Asia and the modern crime world.

Such activities have been sponsored, organized, and conducted by the North Korean government for more than thirty years, thus any debate regarding their existence is sheer folly. Not only do they exist, but they have become an important part of financing the Kim Chong-il regime and its other less than honorable programs (the nuclear program, for example) and poses a potential threat to the stability of societies and economic markets in both the region and in the United States.[4]

Illicit Operations and Money Laundering

Unlike some governments with corrupt officials who have at times conspired with drug lords or other mobsters (such as the case in Colombia), Pyongyang is the only government on earth where at the highest levels (Kim Il-sung, Kim Chong-il) a policy decision was made to use the assets of the government to conduct illegal activities commonly associated with organized crime.[5]

During 1974, Kim Il-sung's regime decided that it was short of hard currency and needed to find a way (other than the huge Soviet subsidies it was receiving at the time) to raise more funds.[6] As a result, Kim Il-sung established the Central Committee Bureau 39, otherwise known as "Bureau Number 39." This office was established for the explicit purpose of running illegal activities to generate currency for the North Korean government. It was housed in the heart of Pyongyang and was created originally to generate a "slush fund" under the exclusive guidance of Kim Il-sung's son, Kim Chong-il.[7] Thus, this program has been under the supervision and guidance of the "Dear Leader" since the beginning and long before Kim Il-sung gradually handed over other elements of the government to his son before his death in 1994.[8] Consequently, it is unlikely that Kim Chong-il will dismantle the programs that come under this office, as he has held a personal attachment to their operations since its birth.

The headquarters for Bureau Number 39 is in a rectangular concrete building within a heavily guarded compound, not far from Kim Chong-il's official office building. It also sits in close proximity to the Koryo Hotel where many foreign visitors to Pyongyang stay. This highly secretive organization is responsible for almost all of North Korea's overseas moneymaking operations—but is particularly focused on the illegal activities. Diverse companies, all run by the North Korean government, include but are not limited to Daesung Chongguk (which also has offices in Austria) and Zokwang Trading Company (headquartered in Macao). All are "front companies." Located throughout Asia and other areas of the world, they answer directly to officials at Bureau Number 39. Of course, Bureau Number 39 answers directly to Kim Chong-il.[9]

Macao is one of the key operating centers for the companies that answer to Bureau Number 39 and is often seen as the central overseas point. The former Portuguese colony rose in importance for Pyongyang's illicit activities when the former Soviet Union and its Warsaw Pact communist satellites collapsed. New governments in these nations were more likely to identify front companies from North Korea that were engaged in rather blatant criminal activities. In Macao, however, dozens of North Korean "merchants" holding diplomatic passports have operated the nerve center for many of North Korea's operations in East Asia and other areas of the world for several years, but especially since the end of the Cold War. Until recently Macao has been a city with extremely lax banking laws, making it an ideal place for North Koreans to launder money that has been earned from illegal activities. The diplomatic status of the North Koreans, combined with Macao's lenient banking regulations, has made it relatively easy to launder counterfeit money, or money earned from drug operations (among others) through banks on the tiny, former colonial enclave. Pyongyang has also reportedly used Macao's banks to deposit or exchange currency used in missile deals (when money was used instead of some kind of barter agreement, as was often the case with Libya until 2004).[10]

With a slush fund reportedly worth billions of dollars, Kim Chong-il has used banks in Macao and banks in Switzerland in the past, to hide funds that can be used for whatever purpose is designated "for the good of the people." During 2003, reports in the *Wall Street Journal* quoted intelligence officials in East Asia who estimated the slush fund generated by Bureau Number 39 in the vicinity of $5 billion.[11] Because of recent pressure from the U.S. government and publicity regarding North Korea's holdings, a number of the secret bank accounts have reportedly been moved to banks in Luxembourg.[12] Additionally, in August 2006 reports surfaced that Pyongyang had moved some of its monetary accounts to a bank in Singapore.[13] Evidence of other accounts are likely to surface as the intrigue continues. In February 2006, Macao's banking regulators froze $25 million (USD) worth of North Korean accounts in the Banco Delta Asia, the most notable of the Macao connections that the U.S. government had targeted. In April 2006 press reports affirmed that Zokwang Trading Company, a long-time front company for illicit activities, closed its headquarters on the fifth floor of an office building near Banco Delta Asia. Reportedly, most of its personnel relocated to Zhuhai, just across the border in China proper.[14] Evidence thus shows that the illicit activities run by front companies under the auspices of Bureau Number 39 have become the centerpiece for moneymaking operations used for an illegal slush fund; sponsor other actions the North Korean government would otherwise be too short of hard currency to carry out; are directed through a line of control from Kim Chong-il, to the front companies, to the activities that they carry out, and back to Kim Chong-il; are government operations that have been ongoing since the mid-1970s; show how North Korean officials are good at conducting these activities using banks willing to launder their money; and demonstrates the skill that North Korea has at keeping these programs covert.

Illegal Drug Operations

North Korea's illegal drug trade began in the mid-1970s as land was set aside and farming began for processing opium poppies into heroin.[15] Despite the shortage of farmland in North Korea owing to droughts and well-documented famine, farming of land for the specific purpose of raising opium poppies to manufacture heroin continued to occur well into the post-9/11 era. A U.S. State Department report (2001) stated,

> estimates of the area under cultivation range from 4,200 hectares (10,378 acres) to 7,000 hectares (17,300 acres), and estimates of opium production range from 30 metric tons (MT) to 44 MT annually. Based on those estimates, the expected yield would be approximately 3 to 4.5 MT of heroin, if all opium was exclusively used to produce heroin.[16]

The most well-known incident of North Korean drug trafficking is the capture of the Pong-Su merchant ship in Australia. Heroin seized from the freighter in April and May 2003 was reported by the Australian Federal Police to have an estimated street value of $221 million.[17] This incident brings into question the figures often quoted by U.S. government officials regarding the annual profits that North Korea makes from its illegal drug trade. The $221 million was the total from a single ship in a country North Korea had not previously been known to target as a drug market—and heroin has not been assessed as the major money-maker for Bureau Number 39 and the Kim Chong-il regime.

Although North Korean heroin manufacture and marketing greatly concerns countries in the Pacific Rim, yet a bigger concern is methamphetamines. Most experts agree that North Korea is probably making a great deal more money and focusing more on methamphetamines than on heroin. The difficulties encountered in growing opium poppies during the famines and floods of the mid-1990s accounts for the changed emphasis to manufactured drugs such as methamphetamines. The opium crop was likely greatly reduced, especially after the heavy rains and floods of 1995 and 1996.[18] Beginning in 1995, North Korea increased its imports of ephedrine, a drug used in the manufacturing process of methamphetamines.[19] Methamphetamines are also easier to manufacture and require less overhead than the heroin industry.

In 2003, South Korea's National Intelligence Service issued a report that stated not only had North Korea shifted its focus to the production of methamphetamines but that the North Korean government was operating an illicit narcotics factory inside of a legitimate pharmaceutical facility called "Nanam."[20]

To make a profit, North Koreans smuggle these two key drugs (heroin and methamphetamines) into markets in Asia using government personnel (not just individuals who work for North Korea's government-owned front companies). A variety of sources indicate that this is done (and has been done over a period of many years) on a large-scale basis by Pyongyang's diplomats.[21] The Pong-Su incident, furthermore, points to large-scale use of government-owned, North Korean merchant ships for its drug smuggling efforts.[22] Perhaps the most disturbing element is how North Korean military personnel are being used to smuggle drugs. Infiltration craft (manned by North Korean Special Operations Forces) have been observed in Japanese waters since the late 1990s, and the main reason for their activity appears to be "drug drops."[23] North Korean uniformed personnel have reportedly been involved in the transfer of illegal drugs both off the coasts of Japan and Taiwan.[24]

In keeping with its nickname "The Family Kim," North Korea's illicit activities network run by Bureau Number 39 is confirmed to have close ties with powerful crime syndicates throughout Asia for marketing primarily heroin and methamphetamines. Among these is the Yakuza, the most powerful organized crime group in Japan.[25] North Koreans are also reportedly involved in distribution and other activities related to drugs with organized crime syndicates in China and Taiwan.[26] Given the monetary success of North Korea's illegal drug programs (especially since methamphetamines have been brought in to augment the heroin); the North Korean government logically would tie other illegal programs into its crime network. This is exactly what has happened. In fact, in the post-9/11 era, evidence shows another illegal operation that has been ongoing for many years and has also increased in apparent scope and focus—counterfeiting.

Counterfeit Currency Operations

An activity that constitutes a direct threat to the interests of the United States, but that until the fall of 2005 received little attention, is the large and widely distributed counterfeit currency network run by North Korean operatives. In September 2005, the United States government formally took action against banks in Macao that were laundering North Korean counterfeit U.S. $100 bills.[27] The U.S. Secret Service has been cited as declaring that the counterfeit $100 bills currently in circulation are the most sophisticated in the world.[28]

North Korea's counterfeiting efforts became widely known only recently, but have been ongoing for more than a quarter century, The operation appears to be extremely sophisticated and run by skilled experts. Equipment from Japan, paper from Hong Kong, and ink from France was brought in to manufacture the fake bills. Millions of dollars worth of these counterfeit $100 bills were being distributed by 1989. As with the drug operations, North Korea is the only government in the world known to be running a counterfeit money operation as a matter of state policy. Like their drug network, the North Korean counterfeit network involves an extensive and widely diverse set of operatives including North Korean diplomats, Chinese gangsters, organized crime syndicates in Asia and elsewhere (possibly Russia), banks (especially in Macao), and members of the Irish Republican Army. According to one of the many defectors, a former chemist who is now living in South Korea, "the main motive was to make money, but the secondary motive was inspired by anti-Americanism."[29] Defectors, as well as travelers to China from North Korea, disclosed during 2005 that a factory in the city of Pyongseong prints the counterfeit $100 bills. Reportedly, the bills are often exchanged with Chinese merchants at 50 percent of their "value" and then mixed in with real bills.[30]

According to U.S. lawmakers, more than $45 million dollars worth of North Korean "supernotes" (the nickname given these fake $100 bills because they are of such extraordinary quality) have been seized since 1989. Of interest the North Korean counterfeiting network has been linked for many years to the Irish Republican Army, directly through the head of the Communist Workers Party of Ireland, Sean Garland. Reportedly, nineteen variations of the bill have been produced, each version better than its predecessor. According to defectors, North Korean intelligence services have used the supernotes to finance activities overseas and for foreign purchases made on behalf of Kim Chong-il.

The wide distribution network for the counterfeit bills is staggering. The counterfeits were first discovered in Manila in 1989 and months later were unearthed in Belgrade. The bills have also surfaced in such far away places as Ethiopia, Peru, Germany, and of course, Macao.[31] When they surfaced in Las Vegas during 2005, that development may have raised the concern of U.S. Secret Service officials, as the rise of counterfeiting compromises other economic areas located in the United States. According to Yonhap News Agency, the semi-official information arm of the South Korean government, the number of bogus U.S. bills detected in their country has increased since 2005—again mostly in $100 bills, and again, likely from North Korea.[32]

Like the illegal drug distribution network, it appears that government officials have been involved in distributing counterfeit currency. Diplomats have an ideal cover for traveling from country to country and can easily pass through customs. North Korean merchant ships have been used to transport counterfeit notes out of the country, with such imaginative methods as listing their cargo as "toys," and falsifying the point of origin for the cargo as being China instead of North Korea (since North Korean cargo is now often subject to higher scrutiny based on its past record of illegalities).[33]

The United States is the biggest loser if large-scale distribution of these notes cause world markets to lose faith in the U.S. dollar. What makes this threat even more a matter of concern is that apparently these operations increased in scope and focus as Kim Chong-il consolidated his power in the late 1990s and the regime in Pyongyang has felt more pressure from outside nations in the post-9/11 era.[34] However, some affected nations fear that resolving this issue will somehow override what most analysts and policy makers consider to be the more important issue of North Korea's nuclear weapons.[35]

To exacerbate the problem, the wide-ranging nature of the operation makes calculating its reach difficult. Considering the large number of countries where the bills have been discovered thus far, the magnitude could be huge. Pyongyang has made the issue even more difficult for the United States by tying the issue directly to the six-party talks.[36] This is, in reality, a means at Kim Chong-il's disposal to simply stall instead of resolving a number of issues that deal with threatening state behavior by the regime in Pyongyang.

Pyongyang's dealings with organized crime involving counterfeit currency became apparent in the late fall of 2005. The U.S. State Department and the U.S. Department of the Treasury contacted international agencies and the governments of nations where the organized crime was most pronounced, often presenting compelling evidence regarding the existence of this activity. In early 2006, officials from the Treasury Department visited Hong Kong and Macao and followed up with an even more important visit to Seoul.[37] During this same time, U.S. officials visited Japan, sharing the same information regarding North Korea's counterfeit currency operations and agreeing to work closely with To-kyo officials to improve methods of countering its success.[38] Reportedly, several of Japan's largest banks then voluntarily ceased all transactions with Banco Delta Asia (the Macao-based bank that Washington identified as North Korea's pri-mary money-laundering source).[39] The Japanese government also reportedly decided to intensify measures combating money laundering and drug trafficking at sea—a move undoubtedly aimed at North Korea.[40]

According to press reports that surfaced in early 2006, China conducted a three-month investigation into North Korea's use of banks in Macao to launder counterfeit profits; the investigation confirmed suspicions raised by the U.S. government. According to South Korean diplomats, the Chinese also expressed their concerns during a visit to Beijing by North Korean Kim Kye-kwan (a highly placed diplomat holding the title of Vice Foreign Minister).[41] In Febru-ary 2006, the Chinese reportedly discovered that bank accounts linked to trade in North Korean counterfeit U.S. bank notes had surfaced for the first time in Hong Kong.[42] It remains to be seen how far the Chinese government will go to crack down on its own organized crime networks. In March 2006, the People's Bank of China issued a directive to financial institutions to "increase vigilance" against fake $100 bills. Chinese experts in South Korea at the time remarked that the move was made with North Korea in mind.[43]

During July and August 2006, Washington and Beijing agreed to cooperate more closely to fight organized crime of the kind in which the government in Pyongyang engaged. The agreement came shortly after the Bank of China froze North Korean accounts in its Macao branch.[44] U.S. officials publicly praised the move.[45] Since Banco Delta in Macao cut off its dealings with the North Koreans, the Chinese have become concerned about the allegations of crime and corruption in their own country—particularly as the 2008 Olympics approach and the Chinese have reason to value positive world opinion. Kim Chong-il visited China in early 2006, and the issue most likely was raised with President Hu Jintao, though no reports making this assessment came out of the official press releases of either communist nation.[46]

Counterfeit Cigarettes

North Korea's counterfeit cigarette operations may be less well known than either its illegal drug or counterfeit currency operations, but the manufacture and distribution of illegal cigarettes (packaged to imitate legitimate brands) may be one of the most profitable of North Korea's illicit activities and may be Pyongyang's largest containerized shipping export. Cargoes leaving major ports in North Korea are bound for major ports in China and elsewhere in Asia, and eventually are shipped to locations throughout the world. Several legitimate tobacco corporations in the United States, Japan, and South Korea have identified factories in North Korea producing forged brand-cigarettes and work with government officials from several countries in the region to stop the distribution of the contraband.

As an example of why this practice is so profitable, a standard 40-foot container of counterfeit cigarettes may cost North Korea as little as $70,000 to produce but has a street value of as much as $4 million (USD). As long ago as 1995, the Associated Press reported that authorities in Taiwan seized twenty containers full of counterfeit cigarette wrappers on a ship bound for North Korea that at the time would have rendered a street value of up to $1 billion in cigarettes. It appears that the counterfeit cigarette manufacturing and distribution operations have picked up in recent years, along with other illicit activity, because of the economic straights that the government in Pyongyang has been experiencing.[47]

According to several defectors from North Korea, counterfeit cigarette factories are located relatively close to Pyongyang yet geographically isolated enough so that foreigners do not easily have access. One of these factories reportedly produces nothing but counterfeit Marlboro cigarettes (a very popular brand throughout East Asia). The individuals who work in the counterfeit cigarette factories reportedly belong to a "special workforce team," which entitles them to extra rations—an important factor in a country where food and electricity continues to be in extremely short supply. At least one of the factories, located in a neighborhood in western Pyongyang, also produces counterfeit "Seven" brand cigarettes, a well-known and popular cigarette sold legally in South Korea. The defectors who have reported about this activity have also stated that the distribution of counterfeit cigarettes involves networks in other countries that ensure the cigarettes are sold throughout Asia. Although these networks' methods and participants are not clear, they are likely similar or the same networks that are involved in the distribution of illegal drugs.[48]

American cigarette manufacturers became aware of the illicit trade in their company brand names coming out of North Korea several years ago and mounted a corporate investigation that yielded rather startling results. Corporate investigators were able to trace North Korean counterfeit cigarettes back to where they were manufactured, and then located them in American markets. From 2002 through September 2005, counterfeit Marlboro cigarettes were identified in 1,300 incidents in the United States. Recently filed federal indictments allege that for several years criminal gangs arranged for one 40-foot container of DPRK-sourced counterfeit cigarettes per month to enter the United States for illicit sale. Reliable reports from other investigators working abroad showed that North Korean counterfeit Marlboro cigarettes (and other brands) were also being sold on a large scale in other countries such as Japan, the Philippines, and Singapore. During the course of their undercover operations, the investigators dealt with Chinese criminal intermediaries. Thus, the evidence points to North Korean involvement with Chinese organized crime networks—as well as others.[49]

Sources in the Japanese and South Korean press cite intelligence data from satellites and Japanese maritime police officials and report that North Korea has at times transferred counterfeit cigarettes onto ships registered in Cambodia, Mongolia, and Taiwan, and has carried cigarettes with forged American, Japanese, and British tobacco brands. Increased production of fake cigarettes by North Korea on a mass scale is said to make up for decreased profits from drug trafficking owing to a crackdown by foreign governments. Pyongyang may be earning more money from counterfeit cigarettes than from its other illicit activities.[50]

The illegal industry—there is hardly another term that can be used for these activities except "industry"—has made such large profits for the elite in Pyongyang for so many years that it is unlikely North Korea will be agreeable to halting these illicit actions in a truly verifiable manner. While the activities encompass many franchises, the most important appear to be those discussed already in this chapter—illegal drugs, counterfeit currency, and counterfeit cigarettes. During 2005 and 2006, investigations involving fourteen different U.S. agencies revealed that these activities are operated by agents and organizations (particularly Bureau Number 39) that come directly under the Korean Workers Party and thus Kim Chong-il.[51]

Profitibility of the "Family Kim" Industries

According to the 2005 *CIA World Factbook*, figures from 2004 indicate that North Korea exported approximately $1.275 billion worth of goods legally, placing them just behind such countries as Georgia, Bermuda, and Senegal.[52] Analysts from the Congressional Research Service report that North Korea runs an annual merchandise trade deficit of $1 billion. Foreign aid has been a significant factor in propping up the regime in Pyongyang, especially since 1996, but the amount of foreign aid simply does not make up for the rather large trade deficit.[53]

North Korea must somehow be making money from other sources in order to survive and to keep Kim and the party elite active in the elaborate lifestyle for which they are so well known.[54] Thus, their illegal activities seem to fill a void that otherwise would be hard to explain. While an anecdotal figure on how much profits are being generated can certainly be drawn from much of the evidence presented thus far, several sources have made an analysis based on evidence acquired over a period of several years. According to U.S. Department of Defense officials, North Korea's illegal drug trade generates between $500 million and $1 billion a year.[55] In 2003, Japanese sources placed North Korea as the world's third largest opium exporter and sixth largest heroin exporter, neither of which accounts for the prime source of illegal drug income for Pyongyang—methamphetamines.[56]

Because statistics are only now becoming available on North Korea's profits from such important products as counterfeit currency and cigarettes, it remains unclear exactly how much profit is being generated from these activities every year. Monetary figures discussed earlier such as the $45 million in counterfeit bills confiscated to date as well as the several incidents of large shipments of discovered counterfeit cigarettes probably account for only a fraction of the total. One cigarette manufacturing company has estimated that the U.S. federal government and state governments lose about $736,000 (weighted average) in revenue for each 40-foot shipping container of illicit cigarettes entering the United States.[57] Clearly, these products are likely to be generating profits as high as in the hundreds of millions. Former Senior Advisor for East Asian Affairs in the Department of State, and now adjunct scholar at the Institute of Defense Analysis, David Asher believes that the criminal sector in North Korea may account for as much as 35 to 40 percent of DPRK exports, and a much higher percentage of its total cash earnings.[58] Given the increasing amount of evidence that illegal economic activities comprise such a large part of North Korea's cash earnings, it is no wonder that Pyongyang had such a strong reaction to Washington's actions against these operations. During 2005 and 2006, the actions taken by Washington had a direct impact on North Korea's consent to attend the six-party talks. Perhaps as important, they caused friction in the South Korea–U.S. dealings with the communist state.

Seoul's 2005-2006 Politics and Pyongyang

As discussed earlier in the nuclear chapter, much of the publicity regarding North Korea's illicit economic activities came to light following actions taken against banks in Macao by U.S. policy makers. The most important result of this was that North Korean officials used the actions taken by the U.S. against its illegal operations to once again delay participation in the six-party talks— despite the fact that both Washington and Seoul openly stated that the illicit economic activities should be addressed in a separate forum. During the fall of 2005, attempts by U.S. officials to meet with North Korean officials (including Vice Foreign Minister Kim Kye-kwan) failed over semantic language that was released to the press prior to the planned meeting. Kim and his entourage cancelled a trip to New York that may have made inroads toward resolving the issue.[59]

When asked about talks with North Korea to resolve illicit activities such as counterfeiting and drug smuggling during the same period, Condoleezza Rice bluntly stated, "They don't need to have a bilateral on how to stop counterfeiting other people's money."[60] The South Korean government (despite numerous unclassified reports to the contrary that have been released by the National Intelligence Service) was reticent in acknowledging specifics discussed by the U.S. government. While visiting the United States during December 2005 on a goodwill tour, then-Minister of Unification Chung Dong-young did not mention any of North Korea's illicit activities and how they were affecting peace and prosperity on the Peninsula in his speech given at the National Press Club in Washington. When asked by members of the Korean press if the matter was of concern to the government in Seoul, Chung simply stated that "it should be a separate issue from the six-party talks."[61]

Chung Dong-young's speech and subsequent press conference was one of the first indicators of the difficulties that were to arise between the perspectives of Washington and Seoul regarding North Korea's illicit economic programs. Soon after Chung's speech, Washington's ambassador to South Korea, Alexander

Vershbow said in an interview with a Korean television network that, "In charging North Korea, I have taken into account material, circumstantial and eyewitness evidence, and the evidence I got this time is very reliable." This statement, widely published in the Korean press, followed up an earlier statement the ambassador made, calling North Korea a "criminal regime."[62] Further evidence that South Korea would be hesitant to join the U.S. in a hard-line stance came to light later in December 2005 when Foreign Minister Ban Ki-moon stated, "If it is certain that the North did forge foreign currencies, it has clearly been engaging in illegal activities and must stop immediately."[63] Thus, the question was raised that these were "alleged" activities rather than that the evidence was overwhelming—the approach taken by the United States.

As the South Korean government was making rather ambiguous and noncommittal statements during late 2005, other experts in the country were more forthcoming. Seo Tae-suk of the Korea Exchange Bank discussed the remarkable skill used in making North Korean forged bills when he said, "The materials are so similar that the sense of touch cannot distinguish them, and in that regard the fakes are 90 percent identical to the official currency." Seo also commented that many of the bills seem to be coming out of Yanbian in China, an area heavily populated by ethnic Koreans, and further stated that such complex forgeries would require a powerful and systematic organization behind them. His remarks were supported by other South Korean currency experts in the country.[64]

In early 2006, Seoul had not yet taken a definitive stand regarding the illicit economic activities in the North or their impact on the roles of the United States and North Korea at the six-party talks. Ban Ki-moon stated in an interview that "the gap between the two sides has widened due to the issue. South Korea is deeply concerned about the issue."[65] Ban's statement was clearly meant to distance the government in Seoul from what President Roh Moo-hyun considered a hard-line stance by Washington. Ban also again reinforced the South Korean stance that the discussion (or action taken) regarding the North's activities should be a separate issue from the six-party talks. In an interview with CNN, he was quoted as saying, "We hope that this kind of counterfeiting or illicit activities by North Korea will not stand in the way of the six-party talks."[66] Indeed, Washington preferred separating the illicit activities issue from the six-party talks but not at the expense of cracking down on these illegal and damaging efforts.

The divide between Seoul and Washington over North Korea's illicit activities continued into early 2006. On January 23, 2006, a U.S. team gave a team of South Korean officials extensive briefings on the evidence regarding North Korea's programs.[67] The meetings apparently were not as successful as had been hoped by U.S. officials, as South Korea took the official position that more evidence was needed before taking any action. One South Korean official reportedly suggested that Seoul's continued call for more evidence (in the face of overwhelming evidence already presented) was simply a front, remarking, "I think they had seen enough even before the briefing, but time is needed to figure out how to address the issue while proceeding with the nuclear talks."[68] A South Korean Foreign Ministry official was also quoted as saying that reports of attempts to resolve the issue in Seoul by simply looking the other way "have it completely the wrong way."[69]

The meeting between officials from Seoul and Washington publicized an issue that has had serious national security ramifications for the region as well as for the United States for many years—and has become a much larger issue in the face of events in the post-9/11 era. Washington had apparently urged officials from South Korea to join in American efforts to force North Korea to halt its illicit programs, but Ban Ki-moon stated to reporters soon after the meeting that Seoul needed to take no further steps. A South Korean Foreign Ministry official was quoted as saying, "The nation's financial regulations provide appropriate legal means to conduct investigations and take necessary steps when illegal money laundering or suspected transactions by those connected with terrorist activities occur." When later asked by reporters several times if Seoul accepted Washington's assertion regarding Pyongyang's sponsorship of counterfeiting and other illegal operations, Ban Ki-moon continued to avoid a direct answer, only stating that Seoul was "deeply concerned."[70]

In response to a rather explosive press release by U.S. officials in Seoul that stated American officials had urged South Korea to match U.S. actions, one Foreign Ministry spokesman stated to the press that, "There has been no urging of our government to adopt concrete measures." Another South Korean official noted, "Since North Korea's engagement in illegal activities is not an issue that started recently, we do not think discussion of the issue needs to be extended."[71] These rather confusing statements hint that although Seoul was well aware of Pyongyang's illicit activities (and had been for a long time), the president and his advisors did not believe these activities needed to be addressed, especially in light of the nuclear issues that were at the time considered more pressing for South Korean foreign policy.

As the Lunar New Year approached the "Land of the Morning Calm," President Roh Moo-hyun told the press that,

> The Korean government does not agree with some opinions in the U.S. that apparently want to take issue with and pressure the North Korean regime, sometimes hoping for its collapse. . . . If the U.S. government attempts to resolve the problem that way, there will be friction and disagreements between Seoul and Washington.[72]

When asked by the press if he specifically believed the North Koreans were involved in counterfeiting, Roh responded by saying more time was needed and that it would be "inappropriate for a Korean President to comment now."[73] During a brief to the South Korean National Assembly, the head of the National Intelligence Service stated that his agency knew of counterfeiting by North Korea in the 1990s and was monitoring it, but he used vague terms regarding whether or not he knew the activity was ongoing and implied that the evidence was vague. The briefing statements appeared to be at least partly based on the Roh administration's continued desire to avoid ruffling Kim Chong-il's feathers while sensitive six-party talks were hanging in the balance.[74] When asked about Roh's comments and other issues relating to the Korean Peninsula at a State Department press briefing in Washington, spokesman Sean McCormack remarked,

> We've made it very clear our views with regard to illicit activity, and the United States is going to take steps to protect itself. . . . And we would expect any state would act in a similar manner.[75]

The views of these two long-time allies have been quite different because of the priorities in their perspectives. Washington saw the issue as one of national security and economic order, and Seoul saw it as an issue that may negatively impact the six-party talks and perhaps inter-Korea relations.[76]

Whereas the policy of the Roh administration side-stepped the counterfeiting issue, this was not the case with the opposition GNP party. In February 2006 in a session of the National Assembly, conservative lawmaker Kim Moon-soo produced a counterfeit $100 note dated 2003 that he had acquired in Dandong, China, from a North Korean who worked for one of Bureau Number 39's front companies known as Shinheung Trading. Kim Moon-soo also pointed out the fact that in September 2005 alone, 1,900 fake bills traced to North Korea had been discovered in South Korea. He demanded an explanation from Prime Minister Lee Hae-chan, and accused President Roh and his administration of playing politics with the issue. He cited the testimony of the National Intelligence Service Chief, who hinted that Pyongyang had not been involved in counterfeiting (that they could prove) since 1998. In a transparent attempt to fan the issue away from the North Korean government, Lee stated, "It is unclear whether it was the North Korean government or some individuals doing it," further commenting, "we are working hard to stop the counterfeiting issue from stirring up undesirable debate." This statement, which avoided taking a stand on the counterfeiting issue, was made to appear rather weak when conservative lawmaker Kim Jae-won pointed out that the evidence showed the illegal notes have been distributed by Kwangmyongsong Trading, which manages the private assets of Kim Chong-il.[77] Roh administration officials eventually acknowledged that U.S. allegations regarding the counterfeiting were reliable but said that "it was too early to confirm them."[78]

The rift that occurred between Seoul and Washington regarding North Korea's illicit programs of 2005–2006 is important from the overall context of foreign policy toward North Korea. Roh Moo-hyun's administration largely viewed South Korea's highest priority as improving economic and political engagement with North Korea. South Korean scholar Paik Hak-soon, head of DPRK studies at the Sejong Institute near Seoul articulated the polarization in the policies of Washington and Seoul during the Roh-Bush era:

> Much of the problem comes from the fact there is a clear mismatch of the top priorities of South Korea and the United States. . . . South Korea's priorities under President Roh Moo-hyun have been regional peace, regional prosperity, engagement and eventual long-term unification with the DPRK, while the Bush administration has been interested in fighting both terrorism and military threats.[79]

The polarization in foreign policy perspectives between the Bush and Roh administrations will thus be noted long after both have been replaced by different leaders.

The differing reactions to North Korea's illicit programs can be viewed as only a symptom of the larger problem of how to handle the reclusive government of Kim Chong-il. Because Roh's engagement strategy was the government's highest priority during most of his administration, his policies mostly ignored international security issues such as proliferation and international crime. The reasons for this are simple. Roh's government intentionally and repeatedly avoided any actions that would offend Kim Chong-il's government in Pyongyang or slow down rapidly escalating economic and political engagement. The North Koreans seemed to understand Roh's policies and take advantage of them at every opportunity. Tying their illegal activities to the six-party talks is a perfect example of this.

Countering Illicit Operations

North Korea's illicit activities presented a challenge to the international security environment in East Asia and other parts of the world long before the United States chose to take action. North Korea—particularly North Korea under Kim Chong-il—has always done exactly what the government there thought it could get away with. The perfect example was discussed earlier in this book when the issue of North Korea's two-track nuclear program was addressed. In early 2006, U.S. Envoy to the six-party talks Christopher Hill met with North Korea's top negotiator Kim Kye-kwan, who had stated that North Korea was prepared to follow international rules on money laundering and was also willing to "cooperate internationally." After the meeting, Hill followed up with a statement to the press where he said, "We're not looking for words. We're more interested in actions. We'd like to see this activity cease."[80]

The Bush administration has consistently held a hard-line position regarding its North Korean policy. However, some in South Korea have alleged that U.S. government officials publicizing evidence of North Korea's illicit industries timed the release of the information to disrupt the six-party talks and was further proof that President Bush wanted to bring down the Kim Chong-il regime. But is this really the case? According to David L. Asher, the Bush administration ordered its inquiry into North Korea's illicit programs soon after taking power during 2001, and 150 federal officials took nearly four years to assemble the evidence, much of which remains unavailable to the public. Asher stated that the administration waited until September 2005 in order to give the FBI and other agencies time to finish undercover operations that were focused on members of China's "Triad" organized crime syndicates. The operations ended in August 2005, and the results were quite interesting. Some $4 million worth of supernotes, narcotics, and counterfeit brand cigarettes were uncovered. The operations, known as "Royal Charm" and "Smoking Dragon," ended with the arrest of fifty-nine people, many of whom were lured to the United States where agents conned them into attending a staged wedding. Some of the suspects even offered to sell undercover agents shoulder-fired anti-aircraft missiles. Asher noted that the timing of the disclosure of North Korea's vast illegal operations took as long as it did because, "[U.S. officials] didn't want this to end up being like Iraqi WMDs."[81]

During his first press conference of the year in January 2006, President Bush said,

> We are going to uphold the law and protect the currency of the American people. . . . We think it's very important for the North Koreans to come back to the table [regarding the six-party talks]. We are more than willing to, and want the six-party talks to continue forward.[82]

Bush's remarks indicate that Washington does not wish to tie the issue of North Korea's illicit economic activities to the nuclear issues being discussed in the six-party talks. Bush also made it clear that the actions taken against North Korea's illicit activities were not "sanctions." He stated, "When somebody's counterfeiting our money, we want to stop them from doing that. So we are aggressively saying to North Korea—don't counterfeit our money." The president further commented, "Now, that's different than economic sanctions."[83] Nevertheless, according to press reports quoting Raphael Perl of the Congressional Research Service, an executive order was being drafted in early 2006 that would stop any financial institutions involved in transactions with North Korea from conducting business in the United States.[84] When and if this is initiated, such an order would place even stronger pressure on North Korea—and cause more controversy in the ROK–U.S. alliance.

The Executive Branch is not the only faction of the U.S. government that has acted. On March 27, 2006, the U.S. Senate Judiciary Committee unanimously passed a revised immigration bill in which foreigners with information on weapons of mass destruction (WMD) or counterfeit money will be regarded as political asylum seekers and provided with an "S-type" political asylum visa. Michael Horowitz, a senior researcher at the Hudson Institute, commented at the time that this was likely done with defectors from Iran and North Korea in mind.[85]

No matter what actions the United States takes against North Korea's illicit crime operations, Washington has finally found an effective instrument for economically pressuring North Korea. In fact, senior Bush administration officials have confirmed to members of the press that the actions taken against North Korea's illicit activities have proven far more effective than anyone had dreamed. Many banks around the world have limited their dealings with North Korea, and the pitch of the rhetoric coming out of Pyongyang during late 2005 and early 2006 was unusual even for that government.[86] U.S. Deputy Assistant Treasury Secretary Daniel Glaser noted that Washington's financial restrictions on North Korea were producing "encouraging" results by early 2006. At a conference in Cairo, Egypt, Glaser remarked,

> Our designation of BDA [Banco Delta Asia] has produced encouraging results. Jurisdictions in the region have begun conducting investigations and taking necessary steps to identify and cut off illicit North Korean business. Responsible financial institutions are also taking a closer look at their own operations, terminating or declining to take on such business.[87]

Nam Sung-wook, a North Korean expert at Korea University, conveyed that by July 2006, Washington's measures against Pyongyang's illegal activities had led to an estimated 40 percent decline in North Korean leader Kim Chong-il's income.[88] Although this figure cannot be confirmed, it certainly appears that Washington's efforts during 2005 and 2006 were effective—and were making the North Korean government uncomfortable.

Because North Korea's legal economy is so small and in many ways so ineffective, the only realistic way to influence Pyongyang is to target its illicit economic activities. The evidence supporting this view emerged during a meeting on March 9, 2006, between U.S. officials Kathleen Stephens from the State Department, Treasury official Daniel Glaser, and Li Gun, head of the North American desk at Pyongyang's Foreign Ministry in New York. The Americans conducted a briefing of their knowledge of the North's counterfeiting activities. Li Gun demanded that "sanctions" imposed on Macao banks be lifted before North Korea would return to nuclear negotiations.[89] A spokesman for the United States responded that, "The counterfeiting issue and the six-party talks are unrelated, so we can continue deliberations, but we cannot return to discussions under this kind of pressure."[90]

South Korea's government during the Roh administration clearly has had significantly different views regarding how to target these activities, although their existence cannot be argued. Seoul remains hesitant to support Washington in its efforts to halt or stall North Korea's illegal activities, whereas other nations in the region, namely Japan and China, are likely to join in the effort to target these activities. In January 2006, Chinese authorities arrested (and then released the next day) a vice ministerial level North Korean official, possibly on charges relating to the events described above.[91] The official, Kang Sang-choon, is deputy chief of the Workers' Party "Organization and Guidance" department and is reportedly also in charge of managing Kim Chong-il's private funds.[92]

As a result of separate negotiations between the North Koreans and Washington and a concluded Justice Department investigation in 2007, the funds held in Banco Delta Asia have been released. Nevertheless, law enforcement efforts are likely to continue. As Brad Babson, a retired World Bank official has said,

> It may be that they have spooked enough banks around the world that no one is going to be very interested in opening up new bank accounts even if they have resolved the Banco Delta Asia problem or at least partially resolved it.[93]

One way or the other, in the future North Korea will have much more difficulty prosecuting its illegal activities. Only time will tell how effectively these clever and highly experienced operatives are thwarted in their efforts.

7

PRESERVING THE REGIME: OVERARCHING CHALLENGES AND MOTIVATIONS FOR THE KIM CHONG-IL GOVERNMENT IN THE POST-9/11 ERA

MANY REPORTS DESCRIBING THE KIM CHONG-IL regime have called it similar to that of his father, yet the evidence suggests that in fact his foreign policy has become far more sophisticated. Kim Il-sung's foreign policy dealt almost exclusively with nations within the communist world. He claimed that his nation was part of the "non-aligned movement," while in actuality Kim Il-sung walked a delicate line between the USSR and China—receiving most of his financial support from the former until the end of the Cold War.[1] His son's tactics have changed, largely because of the extensive changes that have occurred in the international system since the end of the Cold War, during which his father's geopolitical skills proved to be so successful. Since Kim Chong-il began to truly consolidate his power following the death of his father in 1994, his position has become one of extremely cautious engagement with the outside world, closer relations with China, and continued belligerence toward the United States. His actions have also attempted to drive a wedge in the ROK–U.S. Alliance while engaging the South, and at the same time conducting the brinkmanship and provocations discussed earlier that have been intended to gain concessions from both South Korea and the United States. Truly, things have changed since the son assumed the mantle of leadership from his father.[2]

The North Korean government has engaged the international community specifically for regime survival. In doing so, it has become more sophisticated in the way that it conducts foreign policy—both in the tactics used and in the persona of the individuals used to employ these tactics. The seemingly unreasonable mix of brinkmanship, provocations, and efforts to reach out to the outside world has often led to confusion and questionable decision making from policy makers who deal with North Korea, resulting in concessions to Pyongyang or stalled attempts to put pressure on the regime.[3] Ultimately, Kim Chong-il's tactics, which have proved to be far more engaging than those used under Kim Il-sung, have enabled North Korea to gain some benefit for the regime and at the same time stave off pressure by the outside world (particularly the United States).

In the post-9/11 era, North Korea has kept the United States at bay with delaying tactics during the six-party talks, which has allowed North Korea continued development of what Pyongyang considers important elements of its national security—nuclear programs, development and deployment of long-range missiles, and illicit activities. These programs serve to strengthen the regime and maintain Kim Chong-il's power. Throughout this period, Kim Chong-il has opened relations with the South. Because the South Korean government has responded to this policy with far more enthusiasm than most would have anticipated during the 1990s, this in turn has created problems within the ROK–U.S. Alliance—a situation that Pyongyang has successfully turned to its advantage.[4]

This chapter addresses the key issues and challenges that Pyongyang faces in the post-9/11 era. These key challenges include maintaining military readiness, maintaining support from the Chinese, keeping the South Korean's efforts at reconciliation coming (along with the vast amounts of aid), controlling the regime succession process, maintaining nuclear and missile programs in the face of international pressure, maintaining the loyalty of North Korea's second and third tier leadership, continuing the isolation (and thus the control) of the North Korean populace, reinstituting the public distribution system, controlling the flow of North Korean refugees into China and the international perceptions that it creates, maintaining their high-profit illicit economic activities, maintaining momentum in their continuing efforts to drive a wedge into the ROK–U.S. Alliance (and the alienation of the ROK public from the United States in the process), and repairing the North Korea–Japan relationship.

Can Kim Maintain His Military With Drastically Limited Resources?

Despite an inability to maintain the readiness and capabilities of its significant armored and mechanized forces and the air support it requires, North Korea has maintained the threat of attack on the South. The asymmetric capability that North Korea has now developed has come with a high price though. North Korea simply cannot maintain the high readiness and capabilities levels of the 1980s with its armored and mechanized forces. Thus, since the mid-1990s, more focus has been placed on its asymmetric forces. In fact, because Pyongyang continues to focus on the ability to maintain threatening conventional forces on the Korean Peninsula, the result has been extreme pressure on the food and fuel supplies for the rest of the country—and even on many conventional forces within the North Korean military that do not receive as much attention as the SRBM units, long-range artillery, and Special Operations Forces.[5] Large amounts of foreign aid for many years has not bolstered the North Korean economy to the point of supporting the basic needs of fuel and food for the populace. A government survey conducted by Seoul in 2003 revealed that South Koreans actually threw away more food than North Koreans ate that year.[6] As the North continues in its aims of maintaining military readiness (apparently at almost any cost), concerns about malnutrition and related health issues in the military will be a concern for the leadership in Pyongyang. Anecdotal reports suggest that in at least some of the military forces, soldiers have been sent home on leave to "recover" from malnutrition.[7] Currently, this has not apparently led to any serious disciplinary actions within the military or any large-scale troop revolts, although in 1995 when famine conditions were at their peak, there was reportedly a corps level revolt within the army in the northeast where conditions were at their worst.[8]

The funding concerns and food and fuel concerns obviously also have an impact on any force modernization dreams that Kim's generals may have for the military. The military has made a concerted effort to maintain an asymmetric capability. But this capability remains centered around special forces that would be lifted by World War II vintage platforms, SRBMs based for the most part on 1950s technology, and indigenously produced long-range artillery of questionable quality (though all it would take to cause thousands of casualties in Seoul is one successful salvo—and the North Koreans are well aware of this). These forces and systems certainly are a clever way of posing a serious threat to security and stability on the Korean Peninsula, yet it is unlikely that North Korea can generate the kind of funds necessary to expand beyond current ca-pability. Maintaining this current capability, and finding ways to get around any actions taken to counter it by the transforming and modernizing ROK–U.S. Alliance, will continue to be a major security concern for the government in Pyongyang. Estimates postulate that Pyongyang spends 25 to 30 percent of its feeble economy maintaining its military forces. As long as this remains the status quo, foreign aid will remain a huge and necessary aspect of North Korea's basic survival needs, and any real economic reforms will be impossible.[9]

Can Kim Maintain Support From China?

If North Korea is able to continue receiving support from China at the levels so badly needed, the government in Pyongyang will need to continue to successfully address several challenges:

■ justify its nuclear program in a way that does not lead to heavy pressure from Beijing to make concessions

■ ensure that the issue of North Korean refugees crossing into China does not cause a backlash in the relationship between Pyongyang and Beijing

■ control China's investment in North Korea to help the economy while avoiding domination and control from Beijing.

During Kim Chong-il's highly publicized visit to China in January 2006, Kim met with Chinese leader Hu Jintao, and they both committed their nations to a peaceful resolution of the nuclear standoff being resolved through the six-party talks. According to KCNA, North Korea's state-run propaganda arm, Kim called for a joint effort with the Chinese to "overcome the difficulties in the six-way talks and to find a way to move forward." The visit came at a time of impasse in the talks and seemed to be overtly aimed at assuring that China was on Kim's side—and at ensuring that the Chinese government would not put too much pressure on North Korea regarding its programs. Kim's visit underscores that fact that while China has far less control over North Korea than many analysts believe, it remains North Korea's last real ally of any kind, and it is in Kim's best interest to maintain a relationship regarding his nuclear program that is acceptable to both nations.[10] North Korea's nuclear test during October 2006 caused problems in their relationship with China, reportedly creating tensions along the border and causing angst among high-level officials in Beijing—although China was influential in urging Pyongyang to return to six-party talks following the test.[11]

The North Korean refugee problem relating to China is also an extremely sensitive issue. Refugees that cross over into China are reportedly badly mistreated by Chinese citizens, sometimes turned back over to the North Korean authorities, and if they remain in China, often end up turning to such occupations as prostitution and illegal manual labor. The refugees also live in constant fear of being discovered and sent back.[12] This in itself presents obvious cause for friction between China and North Korea and even more of a perception problem for China in the eyes of the outside world. The 2008 Olympics is widely regarded as a coming out party for Beijing and its growing economy and world position. The publicity surrounding these refugees—some of whom have been successful in reaching foreign embassies and eventually reaching South Korea—has been largely negative toward Beijing.[13] China does not want human rights issues to dominate the headlines before or during the Olympics. It is unknown if this has been a major item of discussion between Kim and Hu, but good relations with its northern neighbor is certainly a high priority for the North Korean government.

The refugee flow across the border also reveals several problems that are strategically and internally important for North Korea:

- The internal conditions drive individuals to such desperation they will risk their lives and their families to live in squalor conditions in China.[14]
- Internal movement controls have broken down, which now has enabled more access to border areas.[15]
- Poor discipline among North Korean border security units has caused border guards to go on crime sprees, taking bribes from those crossing into China, and engaging in activity that raises the ire of China, enough that it may have prompted Bejing to send 150,000 extra troops to the northeastern frontier of North Korea in a possible attempt to control the situation during 2003.[16]

The third issue involving China and North Korea is a challenge for the Kim Chong-il regime. It concerns Beijing's badly needed economic investment into the isolated communist state. There is also much that can be learned regarding this issue from an analysis of the January 2006 visit that Kim made to China. During the visit, Kim reportedly struck a bargain with the Chinese government where he obtained guarantees of loans and investment. But the bargain came at a heavy price, as Kim promised the Chinese rights to many of his country's most important mineral riches.[17] The South Korean National Intelligence Service has relayed to the National Assembly that North Korea is becoming increasingly dependent on China for economic support and development to the point that it could actually weaken inter-Korean cooperation. According to the briefing, North

Korean and Chinese officials frequently inspect one another's military and economic facilities. China's investment in North Korea increased from $50 million in 2004 to $88 million in 2005.[18] Chinese statistics show that in 2004, foreign direct investment flow into North Korea was $14.1 million—more than a tenfold increase from the previous year. Some South Korean estimates regarding Chinese investment during 2005 postulate another increase of four times that of 2004.[19] According to press reports, China now makes up 50 percent of North Korea's total trade as of 2005, up from 27 percent in 2001, and China reportedly supplies 80 percent of North Korea's oil. In 2005, grain imports to North Korea from China are estimated to have increased by 300 percent from the previous year.[20] Clearly, North Korea has become more dependent than ever before in its history on economic support from China.

The increasing dependence on China for survival means that Beijing may actually be able to gain more control over North Korea's policy. This has not happened yet—despite what many analysts may opine—although China's policies of a continued division of the Korean Peninsula go against the long-term vision of nearly every other country in the region. This also points to another major difference in the foreign policy agenda's of Kim Chong-il and his father. While Kim Il-sung walked a delicate line between the Soviet Union and China while maintaining complete autonomy from both nations, his son now walks the line of attempting to gain important, large-scale economic concessions from China and South Korea.

Can Kim Maintain South Korean Efforts at Reconciliation and Economic Support?

The geopolitical situation in Asia has changed significantly since the end of the Cold War. Since the demise of the Soviet Union, North Korea has grown closer to China, but China is not subsidizing North Korea at even close to the levels the Soviet Union did. Thus, since the mid-1990s, Pyongyang has turned to foreign aid (other than China) in order to ensure regime survival—particularly for food, but also for economic projects. Beginning when Kim Dae-jung took power in South Korea in 1998, and particularly since 2003 when Roh Moo-hyun assumed the reigns of the South Korean presidency, North Korea has turned to that government for aid.[21]

Maintaining the South's efforts at reconciliation includes three key aspects:

- ensuring continued willingness by the South Koreans to provide aid with minimum distribution monitoring[22]
- influencing South Korea to maintain its policy of not criticizing the North Korean regime,[23] and
- focusing on South Korean businesses to subsidize economic projects in Kim's communist state.[24]

South Korea's willingness to provide the North with food and other related types of aid without asking for verification of where the aid is going has largely been based on the policy of the Roh Moo-hyun government. In fact, this "no strings attached" policy has been largely responsible for the North Korean government's 2006 decision to expel NGOs and United Nations aid organizations that had been providing food for the country since the mid-1990s.[25] North Korea continues to be arguably the most isolated country on earth, and prior to the planned withdrawal of aid workers during early 2006, there were only 300 non-Korean residents—five teachers, about 180 diplomats, and the rest working for NGOs or the UN.[26] The problem for Pyongyang has always been that foreign agencies and organizations have insisted on monitoring where the food went—thus limiting Kim Chong-il's ability to first ensure that his military received the badly needed foodstuffs. It appears that the food aid provided by South Korea (with no monitoring of where it went) had increased so much by the fall of 2005 that Pyongyang felt it could expel other foreign aid organizations and still feed its people. By relying on South Korea to replace the aid previously provided by agencies such as the UN World Food Programme (WFP) and World Vision, the North was able to regain its absolute control over where the food went and clamp down on any farmers who had previously been able to operate private plots. The sheer volume of the food aid formerly provided by the WFP shows how much South Korea has picked up the slack. According to its own figures, the WFP feeds about 2.9 million North Koreans a year through its programs.[27] Soon after foreign aid workers left, North Korea requested 150,000 tons of fertilizer from the South, which Seoul indicated it would provide as soon as possible.[28]

The South Korean government of Roh Moo-hyun apparently believes that ignoring human rights violations is the tradeoff required to provide food aid for North Korea in the hopes that it will reach those other than just the military and the government elite. This is an extremely naive policy that has already been proven wrong. Past precedent shows that even under stringent monitoring conditions, the government in North Korea has always sought to first feed the military and party elite.[29] There is no reason to believe that this will change as long as the Kim regime or one like it remains in power. Heo Man-ho, a professor at Kyungpook University, commented during a conference held on March 10, 2006, at the National Human Rights Commission of Korea in Seoul that, "Unconditional food and development assistance from the South Korean government does not necessarily improve North Koreans lives." Heo pointed out the problems that unmonitored aid can create when he stated, "A continuous monitoring by NGOs is badly needed."[30] Maintaining this aid from South Korea will likely be more of a challenge should a more conservative government come to power, but it will undoubtedly remain a high priority for the North Koreans. To lose this aid would mean having to once again reach out to the international community as was done during the mid-1990s.

The second key concern regarding reconciliation and economic support from South Korea that North Korea has is ensuring the South Korean government does not criticize the Kim regime. Ensuring this happens means that South Korea can actually help relieve pressure put on the North by the international community for radical or unlawful state behavior. This policy of not criticizing North Korea, even when state behavior is illegal or a humanitarian concern is exemplified in an event that occurred in November 2005: When a journalist on a visit to North Korea referred to the abduction of citizens by the North, Pyongyang prevented several journalists from covering a reunion of separated families that was ongoing near Mt. KumGang (near the North-South border). The North Koreans reportedly seized the notes of a YTN reporter who had conducted an interview with a fisherman who was allegedly abducted, and confined a television reporter to his hotel room.[31] A representative of the Unification Ministry suggested that "it would be better for South Korean journalists to apologize."[32] In March 2006, a similar incident arose on yet another visit to North Korea by journalists accompanying a reunion of separated families. During the incident, members of the South Korean press were again harassed by the North Korean government. Much like the events of 2005, the response from the South Korean government was notably weak.[33]

The two examples articulated above are relatively minor. Of greater concern has been the reluctance of the South Korean government (during the Roh administration) to comment on human rights violations in the North. During

December of 2005, Unification Minister Chung Dong-young rejected a request for a meeting by visiting Special Envoy for North Korean Human Rights Jay Lefkowitz.[34] A spokesman for the Ministry stated it was "inappropriate" to discuss the issue at this time, perhaps referring to the perceived effect it might have at a sensitive time period of the six-party talks.[35] The Roh government has repeatedly gone out of its way to avoid commenting on human rights issues in North Korea. Perhaps even more disturbing was the South Korean government's decision during November 2005 to abstain from voting at the UN General Assembly on an EU-sponsored resolution condemning North Korean human rights violations.[36] These actions are important, and they serve to help North Korea's foreign policy agenda. By working to ensure that South Korea continues to avoid criticizing its numerous examples of inappropriate and illegal state behavior, Pyongyang is able to sidestep much of the pressure from the international community that would otherwise exist. Clearly, doing everything it can to ensure that Seoul continues to follow this policy will be a high priority for North Korea as events continue to unfold.

The third and final aspect of North Korea's challenge in keeping South Korea down the road of "efforts at reconciliation," is that of ensuring that South Korean business remains willing to subsidize Kim Chong-il's economic projects. Many South Korean business interests have been happy to donate hundreds of millions of dollars into North Korean economic projects that to date have shown no profit. The apparent motivation for this is reconciliation and dialogue with the North. One of the most important examples of these projects that have yielded profits for the North Korean government and nothing for the South is the Mt. KumGang tourism project. Hyundai Corporation funded the entire project and gave the North Korean government $12 million a month in order to keep it going.[37] By mid-2002, the South Korean tourism agency had also kicked in $60 million to keep the project going.[38]

The Mt. KumGang project has provided an opportunity for hundreds of thousands of South Korean tourists to visit the isolated area in North Korea (North Korea keeps the tourists away from all areas except the immediate vicinity of the resort), but less than one third the anticipated number have participated.[39] Hyundai agreed to pay Pyongyang $942 million over six years of the project, and published reports reveal that as of 2003, the corporation had paid over $600 million.[40] As of 2006, the project has accomplished nothing economically except to drain hundreds of millions of dollars in losses from Hyundai.

During January 2006, North Korean officials requested that for future tourism projects they wanted to do business with "anyone but Hyundai," reportedly seeking a partnership with Lotte Corporation for a possible project near Kaesong. Much of the trouble appears to be related to the firing of the previous point man for KumGang, who had funneled the millions to North Korea, by the new leader of Hyundai. North Korea had demanded he be reinstated, and this request was denied.[41]

Easily the most important business venture in the eyes of the Roh Moo-hyun administration is the Kaesong Industrial Park just north of the DMZ. This project, entirely funded by South Korean interests, had fifteen South Korean businesses operating in the Kaesong Industrial Park, employing 5,400 North Korean workers as of late 2005.[42] According to the U.S. State Department, as of April 2005,

> The South Korean Government approved a total of 57 "Economic Cooperation Projects" to North Korea, worth around $5.6 billion. Plans for the complex's first phase envisage participation of 250 R.O.K. companies by 2007 and another 100 technology incentive companies by 2008.[43]

South Korean officials reportedly have made plans to expand the project within a special economic zone to be completed by 2012 that will house 2,000 companies and employ 700,000 North Koreans.[44] Despite the fact that the Roh administration had urged Washington to include products manufactured at Kaesong as being "made in Korea" in the new Free Trade Agreement talks of 2006, the United States refused.[45] South Korea has assumed all of the financial risk for the Kaesong project, having reportedly invested $2 billion by early 2006. Monthly salaries of $57.50 for each North Korean worker are paid directly to the government in Pyongyang, which then gives each worker about $8 per month (according to some U.S. officials, if the real value of North Korean won to dollars is accounted for, the workers are actually paid around $2 USD a month). South Korean efforts to pay the workers directly have been refused. South Koreans, many of whom live for weeks at a time in the complex, have their own cafeteria and their own medical clinic, as well as their own modular housing—all off limits to the North Koreans.[46]

The projects discussed above are just two of the most important projects where South Korean business is "working with" North Koreans. These and other smaller projects that exist in North Korea, are important to Pyongyang for two reasons. First of all, these projects provide badly needed currency that helps to keep the regime in Pyongyang afloat. Secondly, these projects come without a price. Almost without exception, North-South Korean business projects are funded entirely with South Korean money. Thus, in reality, they do not in any way entail "joint ventures." North Korea receives needed capital without having to make any investment, and there are no requirements to fulfill. North Korea largely sets the rules regarding how these projects will be allowed to operate.

Because the Roh administration has a policy that clearly avoids criticizing the Kim regime, South Korea has followed a policy that formulates a vision of economic reconciliation leading to possible confederation. Thus, it appears that generating profits is not the primary reason for pushing South Korean businesses into "joint ventures" in the North. As former Unification Minister and current President of Kyungnam University Jae Kyu Park stated in February 2006, "The North's heavy dependence on the South gives the latter leverage in negotiations, both bilateral and multilateral. Seoul's leverage may be second only to that of Beijing."[47] This statement is important because it shows that if the government in Seoul had the will, pressure could be put on Pyongyang to cease many of the rogue state behavior patterns that have become so well known to analysts and policy makers during the post-9/11 era.

How has the progress in "business relations" paid off as far as getting the North to engage in confidence building measures and easing tensions? Not as well as the South Korean government would hope. Talks to form a joint fisheries measure near the Northern Limit Line in the Yellow Sea (West Sea) were still bogged down as of early 2006 because military talks to resolve the issue were non-existent. Detailed plans to implement flood control measures along the Imjin River had fallen behind schedule during the same time period because of the North's concern that military installations would be "exposed." And two cross-border railroads that connect the two nations (and that had been repaired and constructed largely with South Korean funds) were still not in use by early 2006 because the two militaries could not agree on military safeguard measures to be used. The North has consistently canceled talks between generals from both sides because of routine U.S.–South Korea exercises.[48]

When General Officer level talks were finally held again in March 2006 after a two-year hiatus, things went so bad that the senior member of the North Korean delegation, Lieutenant General Kim Yong-chol summed up the situation by saying, "the meeting did not go well." During the meeting, no agreements were concluded on any of the issues discussed earlier, and in fact, the two sides could not even agree on a joint statement. When the North Korean delegation attempted to meet the press from Seoul by themselves, the South Korean delegation blocked the meeting.[49] After the talks, the Roh government stated that it would "review" the NLL border (as previously discussed). Any change to the border agreed to by Seoul will likely meet stiff public resistance by many in the South.[50] Former South Korean President Kim Dae-jung, who in the past has been an ardent supporter of Roh's policies, summed up the success of Seoul's engagement and integration efforts when he remarked, "It may seem that the inter-Korean relationship has improved greatly after the 2000 Summit, but it has not resulted in any critical change in the bi-lateral relationship." Kim made his remarks at a seminar conducted at Yeungnam University in March 2006.[51]

Unfortunately, the Roh government appears to be unwilling to use any of the leverage at its disposal. Because of this, it will remain an important part of Pyongyang's policy to ensure that South Korean business continues to subsidize economic projects in the North, and provide currency and economic support needed for the North Korean government to conduct business as usual, delay engaging in any substantive confidence building measures, and continue its priority of maintaining a military that can pose a threatening posture to the stability of the Korean Peninsula.

Can North Korea Maintain Momentum in Alienating the South Korean Public from the ROK–U.S. Alliance?

Since the division of the Korean Peninsula in 1945 and the founding of the DPRK, one of the highest priorities for the government in Pyongyang has been to conduct intelligence and clandestine activities in the South.[52] In fact, despite a "warming" in relations between the two Koreas, recent evidence shows that these activities are ongoing. According to a briefing given to the South Korean National Assembly by the National Intelligence Service, North Korea sent as many as 670 secret dispatches to the South in 2001–2005. During this same time, thirteen North Korean spies were arrested in the South.[53]

While the continued clandestine and intelligence collection activities merit consideration, in the post-9/11 era, the North Korean government has focused on what for them would be considered far more sophisticated efforts targeting the South Korean populace. These efforts have been aimed at alienating the populace in the South from conservative politicians, and especially from having a positive stance toward the ROK–U.S. Alliance. Pyongyang has focused on splitting the long-standing alliance between South Korea and the United States, on efforts to target U.S. interests not shared by the government and populace of South Korea, and on efforts to put out information and propaganda campaigns to support left-leaning, "progressive" South Korean politics and policies.

If one examines events that have occurred, especially since 2002, it becomes clear that Pyongyang has made distinct, well-planned efforts to target issues with the potential to intimidate the South and split the ROK–U.S. Alliance. While assailing the South Korean and U.S. military exercises has always been a focus of North Korean propaganda, it appears to have been stepped up since early 2002. Pyongyang has also seized on any move made by the U.S. military on the Korean Peninsula, and put it into a context where it was threatening the North and drawing the South into a "dangerous situation." For example, when a planned withdrawal of U.S. troops from Observation Post Ouellette along the DMZ was announced during 2004, the state-run North Korean press stated, "The U.S. decision . . . indicates that the U.S. preparations for a pre-emptive attack upon the DPRK are underway at a final phase."[54] During the same time period, Pyongyang had in fact earlier temporarily cancelled scheduled talks with Seoul because of a routine exercise conducted yearly by combined ROK–U.S. troops. In a hotline to Seoul citing the exercise, it was announced, "The talks cannot be held as South Korea is launching RSOI/FE exercises with the United States."[55]

As North Korea has taken these actions to vilify the American presence on the Peninsula, they have maintained a continuing effort at letting Seoul know that Pyongyang "feels their pain." For example, in December 2005, Kwon Ho-ung, the lead delegate at inter-Korea cabinet level talks stated, "When the two Koreas live in harmony and put their power together, the fate of Korea will advance smoothly."[56] Just one month later, Pyongyang reacted to a new "Strategic Flexibility" agreement regarding the disposition of U.S. troops in Korea and Asia as a whole, on KCNA (North Korea's most often used propaganda tool) with the statement, "The U.S. purpose for strategic flexibility is to enhance the role of its forces in south Korea and use the south Korean army as its bullet-shields."[57] Thus, the nuance for North Korea during the new millennium has been a concerted effort at putting any moves made by the ROK–U.S. Alliance into a negative light, while playing up their newly found "friendly" relationship with South Korea as the one which will truly lead to peace on the Korean Peninsula.

The second way that the North has used its propaganda campaign to alienate the South Korean public from the ROK–U.S. Alliance is to target U.S. interests not shared by the ROK. In fact, they have been so successful at this, that they have been able to put some issues in a light that gives South Koreans the perception that certain foreign policy moves are being made because of unilateral U.S. interests—even when this is not the case. A good example of this occurred during 2003, when the U.S. government, in a bilateral agreement with South Korea, agreed to withdraw troops from the DMZ and move them farther south to a base at Camp Humphries (about 40 kilometers south of Seoul), Pyongyang announced that this was being done in order for Washington to conduct a unilateral "pre-emptive strike" against North Korea. The reaction by many in the South Korean public at the time was one of negativity and a feeling of "abandonment" toward the United States, when in fact, the move was made originally because of a mutual agreement between the two allies and had nothing to do with any "pre-emptive strike" scenario. Nevertheless, the negative reaction by the public in the South, stirred on by propaganda in the North, caused public relations problems for the U.S. government regarding the movement of its troops.[58] What makes this so interesting is that this was not strictly done out of "U.S. interests," but it was played up that way by the North Korean propaganda, and perceived in the same light by many in the South Korean public.

While the relationship between Seoul and Washington is well documented as deteriorating soon after the Bush administration took office in early 2001, what is not as well known is how North Korea has actively targeted the South Korean electorate, striving to increase the effectiveness of informational vehicles designed to influence the younger generation to support left-leaning "progressive" South Korean politics and policies. This is a skill that Pyongyang appears to have gained proficiency in as time has progressed.

Efforts by the North to influence South Korean politics and policies truly picked up steam during 2004. During March of that year, as South Korean President Roh Moo-hyun was going through the process of being impeached by what was then a National Assembly with a majority from the opposition Grand National Party (GNP), the North Korean state-run press discounted the act for its "illegality and impudence," going on to say that, "The U.S. is chiefly to blame for the incident," and concluding, "The U.S. egged the South Korean political quacks, obsessed by the greed for power, on to stage such an incident in a bid to install ultra-right pro-U.S. regime there."[59] Many in South Korea (particularly conservatives) were reportedly quite offended by this attempted intrusion into Seoul's internal affairs. The reaction from the ROK mainstream press (the three newspapers with the widest distribution were known to have had a very rocky relationship with the Roh administration at the time) was fairly straightforward, including one editorial which read in part, "We do not understand why the North is interfering in the South's domestic affairs. This is a clear violation of the basic principles agreed upon by the two Koreas."[60]

During the spring of 2004, North Korea's attempts to influence the hotly contested National Assembly elections became obvious. During this time period, Pyongyang's print and broadcast outlets urged voters to put the left into power with numerous statements and broadcasts. In one such de facto endorsement of Roh Moo-hyun during April of that year, the DPRK urged South Koreans to vote against "conservative forces" in the elections.[61] During the same week, Pyongyang's press again made statements supporting the left, this time referring to the United States, stating in part, "pro-U.S. conservative forces in South Korea" were plotting to scuttle the National Assembly elections.[62]

Pyongyang's attempted intervention in the elections was analyzed by many as a rather unprecedented effort to build on the division in ROK society that some have seen as being between older conservatives and younger, more liberal voters (widely publicized in ROK and American press outlets), who are more sympathetic to North Korea (the younger voters are also widely viewed as being more "anti-American," another advantage to North Korea). In South Korea, the left-leaning Uri party was at the time fighting a reputation (brought on by some rather unfortunate statements made by its leaders) that it only wanted to appeal to younger and liberal voters.[63] Whether the polarized political climate in South Korea during the National Assembly elections of 2004 was overplayed in the world press or not, the government in Pyongyang clearly felt that it would be at a distinct advantage with a left-leaning government in power in South Korea. Indeed, what makes the propaganda so interesting is that such moves were not made during elections that occurred in South Korea during the 1990s. An analysis of the reasoning behind the moves in their propaganda machinery renders an assessment that Pyongyang's government obviously feels its national interests are best served with a left of center, pro-North Korea government in the Blue House—and that this is a relatively new phenomenon that began to occur only during the later stages of the Kim Dae-jung administration.

The informational barrage in support of left-leaning politics in South Korea did not end in 2004. For example, during October 2005, the North Korean weekly *Tongil Sinbo* criticized the conservative GNP opposition party's reaction to the highly publicized statement by prominent (and very left-leaning) professor Kang Cheong-ku of Seoul's Dongguk University, who had made the highly controversial (and dismissive of the role that the U.S. played during 1950–53) public statement that the Korean War should be regarded as a "war of unification." Of course, many (particularly older, more conservative voters) in the South reacted strongly to the statement, with GNP spokesman Chun Yu-ok remarking, "North Korea should give up its aspiration to communize the Korean Peninsula." The North Korean periodical remarked, "Vigorous political, economic, and military exchanges and cooperation efforts are under way between North and South Korea. The post-June 15 era has long hurled the anti-unification National Security Law into the grave."[64] The remark referred to a law in South Korea that has prohibited strong "pro-North Korea" public statements—when these statements are inaccurate (the National Security Law also prohibits various other activities that are considered "pro-North Korean").[65]

How successful have these attempts to influence the thinking of the South Korean public been? To find the answer, an examination of data compiled by the daily newspaper *Joongang Ilbo* reveals information that is extremely interesting. According to polls conducted by the newspaper and the Survey Research Center at Sungkyunkwan University during 2003 and 2004, South Koreans are now more willing to think about the North as a "partner in cooperation and less as a nation depending on foreign aid for its survival." During 2003, 21 percent of respondents said their most vivid impression of North Korea was that it was a foreign aid recipient. The figure dropped to 20 percent in 2004 and 16 percent in 2005. In the 2003 survey, 36 percent called North Korea a partner in cooperation. The figure rose to 39 percent in 2004, and 43 percent in 2005. According to Park Byeong-jin, a researcher at Sungkyunkwan University, "South Koreans have changed their views in how to treat North Korea based on their sense of relations between the two Koreas." Clearly North Korea has made inroads into the South Korean mindset through its propaganda efforts, but despite these efforts, according to the poll referenced above, when asked to select the country they had the most favorable impression of, the United States ranked first and North Korea second in all three annual surveys.[66]

As North Korea faces challenges to its survival, the government there clearly has placed splitting the ROK–U.S. Alliance and promoting left-leaning politics and policies in South Korea as high priorities on its agenda. An examination of the evidence discussed above shows that Pyongyang has been at least partially successful in meeting these goals. Because of all that can be gained from this policy and the potential disastrous effects that could occur with its complete failure, it is likely that we will continue to see its effects as long as the Kim Chong-il regime exists in North Korea. The regime, and who will run it after Kim Chong-il, has become an issue relatively recently, as Kim Chong-il enters his 60s.

Keeping It in the Family: Can Kim Control the Regime Succession Progress?

Maintaining power, and perhaps in Kim Chong-il's mind, maintaining power in the hands of his family members after his death, is a continuing challenge for the regime in Pyongyang. As Kim ages this has become a priority.

Unusual issues relating to the stability of the Kim Chong-il regime first started to surface during the fall of 2004. These events may show some disturbing trends in the ongoing stability of the Kim regime in North Korea.[67] In early November 2004, unusual reports began to filter out of North Korea that portraits of Kim Chong-il had been removed from honored spots.[68] During the same time, the press in Japan and South Korea reported that North Korea's official media had at least temporarily dropped the glorifying title of "Dear Leader" when referring to Kim Chong-il.[69] Also during the fall of 2004, reports began to surface from China that several generals and high-ranking government officials were defecting, while others had already defected. As many as 130 generals reportedly defected, as well as an unknown number of government officials. According to Zhao Huji, one of China's leading North Korean experts and a researcher at the Communist Party School, " [U]nlike most defectors crossing into China, the high-level defectors and their families did not lack basic necessities. Rather, they were disconcerted with Kim Chong-il's rule."[70]

A North Korean Foreign Ministry official denied the press reports that Kim Chong-il's pictures had been removed from public offices and schools, citing the reports as "groundless fabrication."[71] A North Korean Foreign Ministry spokesman also denied the reports that hundreds of the country's generals had defected to China, stating, "Never mind the generals, not even a single button of their uniforms has crossed the border."[72] Not long after these events were reported, the "top brass" of the North Korean military pledged their support to Kim Chong-il publicly at an event in Pyongyang.[73] Although these reports cropped up rather suddenly and to date have not been confirmed, the confusion surrounding North Korea in the fall of 2004 appears to have possibly been related to purges that Kim was in the process of carrying out. Chang Sung-taek, Kim's brother-in-law, one of his most trusted confidants, and a highly placed official within the North Korean government, was reportedly purged sometime during 2004—perhaps because of succession issues in the government over which he and the "Dear Leader" disagreed.[74] That same year Kim also reportedly purged several of his relatives and up to eighty other officials and their families (reportedly for trying to "seize power," but perhaps over succession issues, as with Chang). In an even more intriguing turn of events, Chang's wife (Kim's sister), Kim Kyong-hee, was reportedly injured in an auto accident during 2004—in an event that is assumed to have been a possible attempt on her life.[75] Kim Kyong-hee may have been in deep depression, and is reported to have undergone medical treatment for alcohol in France, possibly during the same period.[76] Finally, Kim's eldest son, Kim Chong-nam (whose nickname is the "fat bear") reportedly narrowly avoided an assassination attempt while on a trip to Austria. There has also been speculation that this was because of infighting within the inner circle over succession and power issues involving who will wield the reigns of power once Kim Chong-il is gone.[77]

In 2005, rumors began to circulate that Kim had picked his second son, Kim Chong-chol as his successor. Kim Chong-chol has reportedly been put in charge of a department within the Korean Workers Party that will groom him for the leadership of North Korea.[78] Other signs that he may be the elder Kim's successor include that fact that he dined with his father and visiting Chinese leader Hu Jintao during October 2005, and reports that his portrait is being hung at the Central Committee building in Pyongyang. There have been no pictures released to the west of Kim Chong-chol since he was a teenager attending school in Switzerland, and it appears that he holds many of the reclusive habits of his father.[79] Despite signs that Kim's second son may be the heir apparent, there are confusing rumors that may indicate this is a false alarm. According to Lee Kyo-duk, of the Korean Institute for National Unification, the 26-year-old may have a "fatal disease" that results in his suffering from excessive female hormones. Kim Chong-il's former Japanese chef, wrote in his memoirs that the elder Kim considered his second son "too girly" to transfer his power to.[80] Nevertheless, anecdotal indications continue to suggest that Kim's second son is the heir apparent. According to South Korean reports, some North Korean officials were seen wearing lapel pins bearing the image of Kim's second son during the spring of 2006—another possible indicator that he is the "heir apparent."[81]

Eldest son Kim Chong-nam would ordinarily be considered the heir apparent in a Confucianist society, but he is widely known for his drunken binges in Pyongyang hotels and for spending wads of cash on shopping trips to China—as well as trying to sneak into Japan on a fake passport to visit Tokyo Disneyland.[82] Little is known regarding the status of Kim Chong-un, the youngest of the three sons—though according to a Japanese press report during 2006, badges of Kim Chong-il's third son were seen circulating among senior Workers Party of Korea cadres, military officers, and vice ministerial class officials of the government.[83] The situation surrounding the "Family Kim" thus remains confusing, as are the questions regarding who is most powerful in Kim's circle.

Kim's three sons do not have the same mother, as he is noted for being associated with a number of mistresses. Kim Chong-nam is the son of Kim Chong-il's now deceased former mistress, Sung Hae-rim. Kim Chong-chol and Kim Chong-un are the sons of another former mistress, Ko Young-hee, who is now also reportedly dead and was widely known to have been suffering from cancer.[84] As if the picture of who is in the familial circle surrounding Kim is not muddy enough already, he recently was reportedly "married" to his newest longtime "companion," Kim Ok. She has been noted at his side numerous times since Ko Young-hee was reported to have died from cancer during 2004, including his visits to military bases and meetings that he has held with foreign dignitaries. Despite his now widely reported companionship and possible marriage to his latest girlfriend, he is also reported to have other mistresses on the side.[85] This web of intrigue, competition among relatives for his favor, and hazy power circles, presents a confusing, uncertain picture of who Kim favors the most—and who is most influential in his decision-making.

In January 2006, Brent Choi, a North Korea specialist with the *Joongang Ilbo*, wrote that, "Most of the reports on North Korea's successor are 99% wrong. Kim Chong-il's sons might not even make it to the list of candidates. In order to become a successor the prospective leader will have to prove himself in enhancing both economy and ideology."[86] This conjecture was further supported later in 2006 when the German press quoted a University of Vienna professor as saying a junta could replace Kim instead of one of his sons, and that Kim does not necessarily need to stay alive to remain ruler.[87] While both of the examples discussed above are purely educated guesses by experts on North Korean internal politics, they do highlight the mystery surrounding Kim Chong-il's succession plan. The confusing picture surrounding Kim's power circle became all the more mysterious during January 2006, when Chang Sung-taek was "un-purged."[88] While there is a great deal of debate surrounding why this occurred, it may have something to do with succession issues—particularly if Chang has anything to do with helping Kim to pick who his successor will be. Though Chang is apparently back in favor with Kim Chong-il, his personal problems continue, as his daughter, who he had with Kim's sister (Kim Kyong-hee), apparently committed suicide in Paris during July 2006.[89] In any case, any discussion of the "succession issue" is taboo in North Korea, as is any discussion of Kim's sons, their names, ages, and whereabouts.[90]

The prospect of a leader succeeding Kim Chong-il who is not one of his sons obviously rates some discussion. While this is certainly an interesting prospect to consider, there are many factors that come into play here. First of all, if one is to follow historical examples of how succession has occurred in North Korea (the only example we have is obviously the Kim succession), a grooming process would have to begin several years before the new leader would actually emerge. The Kim succession in 1994 is important as a case study because most analysts considered it a *fait accompli* that Kim Chong-il would succeed his father in 1994. There is no such evidence—at least not yet—that any such individual exists today that everyone would consider the heir apparent. More to the point, Kim has not "anointed" any of his military officers or one of his other relatives as the person who might succeed him yet.

Based on the evidence discussed above, it appears that should there be no clear successor to Kim Chong-il when he dies, several scenarios are possible. The first is that there is a violent struggle for power among those in the current power circle in North Korea. Each side would seek to gain the support of the military, as this would appear to be the power base most important to maintaining power in the country. In this case, it would be anyone's guess as to who would emerge as the leader of the country. Another scenario would be that the military itself would seize power. In this case, there is again, no clear indication as to what individual or group of individuals would seek to gain dominance in the government. The absolute power that Kim currently wields, and the

Byzantine web of reporting, counter-reporting, and resultant fear makes it extremely difficult for "factions" to form within the military—at least that are apparent to those analyzing contemporary North Korean issues.

Still another scenario would be that members of the military would seize power following Kim's death and then sue for peace and unification with the South. This scenario is not as far fetched as it may seem. It is a rather well known "secret" that many of the generals in North Korea are rather corrupt, and there are even rumors that many of them are actually on the payroll of the NIS or other agencies. This may be a scenario where the ball will truly be in Seoul's court. Should the South Korean government choose to aggressively pursue unification and dialogue during what would likely be a confusing and important time frame, it may be a chance to actually bring an end to the tyranny that has existed in the North since the end of WWII. Finally, a scenario that has real potential for occurring is that no leadership figure would emerge, the army becomes factionalized, and the country falls into civil war. Again, this may be an opportunity for the government in Seoul, as this would be a significant opportunity (depending on the circumstances) for the ROK to step in and take control of the North—perhaps with minimal use of force.

There is no clear evidence that any potential future leader has emerged yet who is able to take over for Kim should he die. Furthermore, based on the length of time it took Kim Il-sung to prepare the way for Kim Chong-il, we should expect that it would take considerable time to adequately prepare the way for the next successor. Thus, the potential for widespread anarchy in North Korea is very real. This leads to the assessment that Kim is likely extremely concerned about the current situation and a smooth succession process. There is no reason to believe that Kim does not want the legacy of himself and his father to continue. In fact, the evidence suggests that he places this as an important priority.[91]

The rather confusing evidence points to three key challenges and issues for the Kim Chong-il regime regarding succession. Kim Chong-il must

■ prevent political turbulence within the regime caused by division of loyalty between him and his successor—whoever that successor turns out to be, and whenever he is formally announced (if ever)
■ ensure that the propaganda and political mythology process adequately indoctrinates the North Korean populace, and

■ ensure that competition between Kim family members does not affect regime security (it may have been this competition that was at least partially
responsible for Chang's two-year purge).

To prevent turbulence within the regime caused by a division between Kim
Chong-il and his successor, Kim will have to continue to engage in purges as
these divisions occur or as he perceives that they are beginning to occur. Kim
has shown that he will not hesitate to engage in such purges, as he has already
conducted them on several occasions during the mid-1990s and in 2004. This is
probably the only way that he can ensure traditional Confucian loyalties that
tend to rise up in Korean society do not dominate his power circle. The indoctri-
nation and political mythology process has not yet begun. The process must
begin soon in order to ensure a fluid and smooth transition to power following
Kim's death. Of course, the competition between Kim family members, if left
unchecked, can and will threaten the regime security of the DPRK—particularly if members of the military become involved. This may have happened
already, though the evidence is sketchy at best. Nevertheless, Kim is likely to
take whatever measures he deems necessary to ensure that a lid is kept on any
open competition for power among his family members and their allies.

Although anecdotal evidence suggests Kim may already be planning to
choose and more importantly "anoint" his successor, many issues remain up in
the air. Despite his best efforts, no clear base of support or loyalty for Kim's
successor exists. Should the succession process lead to violence, it may cause an
implosion within North Korea, or worse, escalating violence across its borders.

Should Kim's death occur before a clear successor has been anointed and is
clearly set in the minds of the army, the party, and the people, the clear possibility exists that a vicious fight for power will ensue. This is because of the current
situation that exists today, where everybody is compelled to compete with everybody else for power with few natural allies. Thus, if Kim's death occurs with
no clear and credible successor in the wings, what could easily ensue would be
a no-holds barred grab for power between the military, the party, and the security agencies. If so, there is no way to predict the potentiality for implosion or
explosion—or both.

Internationally, many countries will feel the effects of North Korea's change
in leadership:

■ China (and its current autocratic leadership in the Politburo), considers continuation of the North Korean state vital for national security interests. China's current leadership likely feels that they cannot afford an unstable or collapsed North Korea on its border, which might lead to early reunification and remove the current strategic and operational depth from the Americans that currently exists.[92]

■ Russia has no interest in seeing North Korea collapse,[93] because it would remove the last vestiges of influence that Moscow has in Northeast Asia and make its presence in the region almost irrelevant.

■ South Korea cannot afford a collapsed North Korea and the prospect of rebuilding; it has the potential to be devastating economically.[94] Indeed, in an alternative scenario where semi-anarchy or complete anarchy were to occur, Seoul would be very concerned with an exploding or imploding North Korea whose instability would be likely to seep across the border.

■ Japan would be faced with two very unsavory implications, an exploding North Korea, or eventually, a unified Korea that has the potential to be a major economic and military challenge years down the road after recovery from the debilitating effects.

■ For the United States, the biggest concern is control of North Korea's weapons of mass destruction. There are no benign scenarios in an imploding country with a million-man army, and nuclear weapons and missiles, whose control is unknown.

Can Kim Continue the Isolation and Control of the North Korean Populace?

Because of the absolute autocratic nature of the Kim Chong-il government, it remains essential to Pyongyang that the isolation from the outside world and thus the total control of the North Korean populace continues. To carry this isolation and control out, North Korea must suppress social discontent before it becomes dissidence, quarantine the populace from Western ideas, information, and personnel, maintain the North Korean fear of war with America, and resist international efforts at forcing improvements in the human rights situation.

North Korea has been able to suppress social discontent throughout its history. Those who have disagreed openly with the government have usually "disappeared," but open disagreement simply has not existed during the Kim Chong-il regime and was out of the Kim Il-sung regime by the time the elder

Kim had consolidated his power in the late 1950s. Citizens are not allowed to join alumni associations, form clubs, or engage in other activities commonly associated with East Asian society. The way Pyongyang manages to maintain absolute control is through the institution of collective responsibility. The entire North Korean populace is divided into so-called peoples groups or "inminban." This system began in the 1950s and has continued successfully under Kim Chong-il. A typical group consists of twenty to fifty families who live in the same neighborhood, small rural area, or apartment block. These groups are used to indoctrinate the people in Kim's socialist ideas and to control every movement of every member of the groups. Leaders of the groups may inspect any dwelling at any time of day or night, and anyone who sleeps away from their home must first explain why to the leader of the group and receive written authorization. Movement anywhere within the country is tightly controlled, as is money and food, which renders the entire populace completely vulnerable in every aspect of their daily lives.[95]

North Koreans have also been kept completely isolated to every extent possible from those few foreigners who have been allowed to visit their country as changes became necessary during the mid- to late 1990s. This causes problems for numerous aspects of society in maintaining even the basics for the people. For example, a North Korean medical doctor admitted to a traveling reporter during 2004 that, "We are blocked in our dealings with other countries. We want to trade with western and advanced countries. But we have a problem with the system and with sanctions. Experts cannot visit us and we cannot visit them." The populace in general is banned from viewing outside television and from access to the Internet. The Kim regime has managed to keep the fear of war with the United States alive and maintain the populace in a "semi-state of war" status for many years. When the same reporter discussed above had a conversation with a North Korean military officer in 2004, the man remarked,

> America's Bush strengthened his aggressive policy against us. He declared our state as part of the axis of terror. He intends to attack us with nuclear weapons. We do not hide the fact that we have our own nuclear deterrents. There is no war in the Korean Peninsula. There is still an armistice because we have this power.[96]

Kim continues to stress this "semi-state of war" mentality by constantly visiting military units publicly. During 2005, Kim appeared in public 131 times; more than half of these appearances were related to military affairs, while less than 15 percent were related to North Korea's economy. Kim was also frequently accompanied by military generals during these public appearances.[97]

Isolation helps Kim's government resist international efforts at forcing improvements in the North Korean human rights situation. If foreigners do not have access to the numerous restricted areas in North Korea, how can they evaluate the situation and demand improvements? North Korea continues to stall any efforts on sharing important data, allowing access to those who need aid, and any other concerns that would allow the international community to address the numerous human rights concerns that exist there. In fact, North Korea has been accused of actually falsifying reports to the international community.[98]

Can Kim Maintain the Loyalty of the Second- and Third-Tier Leadership?

It appears, despite the events of 2004 and 2005, that Kim maintains the loyalty of those in his inner circle. One of the continuing challenges that the regime in Pyongyang will face is maintaining loyalty in its second- and third-tier leadership. The government will need to control corruption among top party, government, and military officials, adequately reward the regimes leaders and their families, and maintain competence and competition between the regime's numerous police and counterintelligence agencies.

Since President Clinton lifted some sanctions against North Korea during the 1990s, Americans can legally conduct business there, although few companies have taken advantage of this "opportunity." Those who have bring back reports of bribe-seeking officials, a rigid bureaucracy, and a government that has lingering suspicion of Western intentions.[99] This corruption among officials in the middle tiers of North Korea's elite—in essence the ones who run the country—is likely a concern that Kim will have to deal with even more in the future as the country opens up for business on an increasing scale.

Along with keeping the corruption under wraps to a reasonable degree, officials and their families must be kept happy enough that they do not undermine national security. This has continued throughout the Kim Chong-il regime and has created a truly "haves and have nots" society. Indeed, in a Korean Confucian society where family is more important than even other Confucian societies, families have been linked to the well being of their benefactors to such an extent that it often surprises outside observers. Defectors who have been interviewed in South Korea and the United States have declared that their biggest worry was the welfare of their families back in North Korea, who no doubt underwent great hardship because of their defection. The Kim Chong-il regime has used this as a double-edged sword, rewarding family units of those who prove absolutely loyal, and sending those who are not loyal (and their families) to prison camps—or worse.[100] The combination of rewards and punishments has kept these officials in line for the most part.

Perhaps the most important way that Pyongyang has managed to ensure loyalty standards among the country's second- and third-tier leadership is by maintaining competence, redundancy, and competition in the regime's police and counterintelligence agencies. Whereas there are several counterintelligence and police agencies, the two principal domestic intelligence agencies are the Ministry of Peoples Security (MPS) and the State Security Department (SSD). The MPS has more than 144,000 members and operates throughout the country. Members often wear uniforms and report even the slightest misdeed that is perceived to be "anti-Kim,"—even if committed by high officials. MPS operatives are in nearly every workplace and often in housing areas as well. The SSD has many of the same duties and also has thousands of members. The SSD also conducts electronic surveillance of North Koreans (including high party members). See Figure 12.

The SSD and MPS are both headed by high-level military officers and hold equal status with the Ministry of People's Armed Forces (MPAF), answering directly to Kim Chong-il. The MPAF has several counterintelligence agencies that spy on its own officers and soldiers,[101] and all of these agencies spy on each other; everyone is watching over everyone else. In North Korea, any gathering of three to five persons will have at least one of them watching the others.[102] Quite literally, the only person not under surveillance in North Korea is Kim Chong-il himself. There are also numerous other internal spying agencies run out of Pyongyang on a smaller scale—many of whom watch each other as much as the populace.[103]

Kim's position as the strong leader of North Korea appears to be thus far unchallenged. However, the varying aspects of North Korean politics and interaction at the levels below his inner circle remain largely obscure in a society that is more closed to outsiders than any other on earth. The loyalty and political power of those in the second and third tiers of the military, technical, and

FIGURE 12:
NORTH KOREAN PARTY-MILITARY STATE

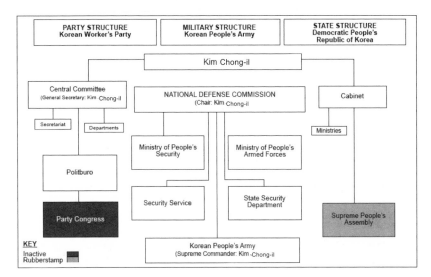

Source: Andrew Scobell, *Kim Chong-Il and North Korea: The Leader and the System,* Strategic Studies Institute Monograph, (Carlisle, PA: U.S. Army War College, March 2006), URL: http://www.strategicstudiesinstitute.army.mil/pdffiles/PUB644.pdf

management elites, as well as their interaction with the members of the Korean Workers Party, is in many ways an enigma to analysts of the regime in Pyongyang.[104]

Can Pyongyang Successfully Reinstitute the Public Distribution System?

Kim Chong-il has placed taking care of his military and elite as a much higher priority than the welfare of the bulk of the populace, which has been obvious since the food crisis reached its peak in the mid-1990s. Nevertheless, the government must adequately take care of its people or it becomes failed state. Many analysts believe that North Korea currently is a failing state—one that many thought would collapse during the 1990s.[105] The food distribution system that had been implemented and "perfected" between the late 1950s and the mid-1960s completely broke down by 1996, escalated by floods and famine. People in the countryside found themselves on their own, and people in the cities received less than half of their normal food rations. The results of this collapse were that markets sprang up all over North Korea, and the international community (largely through the UN's WFP and through international NGOs) began picking up the slack for the badly weakened food distribution system of the North Korean government. Pyongyang initiated economic reforms during 2002 that have done little to kick-start the economy.[106]

From the end of 2005 and into early 2006, North Korea was telling the UN and international NGOs that it was time they go. The government believed it could reinstitute its public distribution system and return North Korea to its earlier methods. However, as recently as January 2005, Amnesty International discussed the distribution system reproachfully, saying,

> The government continued to fail in its duty to uphold and protect the right to food, exacerbating the effects of the long-standing food crisis. Chronic malnutrition among children and urban populations, especially in the Northern provinces, was widespread.[107]

Pyongyang relented slightly in February 2006 and accepted limited food aid from the WFP aimed at small children and pregnant women only, but the move allowed only a fraction of the previous food aid from international contributors into North Korea.[108] After a shutdown of the UN's WFP activities for more than four months, North Korea signed an agreement in May 2006 that allowed the WFP to operate a staff of ten members with a budget of $102 million in order to feed about 1.9 million of the neediest North Koreans over a two-year period. The program was significantly smaller than the previous one—which fed up to six million people under a yearlong $200 million budget, with a forty-eight member staff. Tony Banbury, WFP's Asia Director, reportedly stated that his agency would supply food aid only in areas where distribution could be monitored to ensure the food reached its intended beneficiaries.[109] It is obvious that the food crisis has not ended in North Korea. Since Kim has made it a priority to reinstitute the public distribution system the question is, how will this be accomplished?

The greatest challenge that Pyongyang faces in this regard is to find adequate resources to support the system, particularly fuel and functional transportation assets in remote areas. In late 2004, ReliefWeb stated: "Resources constraints have also led to a significant reduction in the food allocated to FFW activities." The detailed report released by the consortium of NGOs stated that lack of fuel resources and transportation/industrial infrastructure was a continuing concern.[110] It is highly unlikely that North Korea was able to adequately fix these problems between the time of the ReliefWeb report and the time that the NGOs and WFP assets were asked to leave the country (then later allowed to stay but in much smaller numbers).

The important question then becomes, with these rather dismal conditions in effect, how will the public distribution system survive?

It appears the primary means that Pyongyang has used to replace the large void left by departing NGOs and UN relief workers has been through the largesse of China and South Korea.[111] Although China has gradually increased the amounts of its food aid given to North Korea since 2002, the larger amount North Korea receives has been from the South. Kim has allowed these two key benefactors to support his food system—as the government there remains incapable of doing so. China and South Korea are permitted to provide food aid instead of many in the international community because they do not insist on monitoring the distribution.[112] Pyongyang can once again use food as a tool of control over the populace.

This internal policy change was addressed in December 2005 by Stephan Haggard of the University of California, San Diego, and Marcus Noland of the Institute of International Economics, who wrote, "There is evidence that the revived public distribution system is again being used as a tool of control, with favored state employees provided with enhanced access to food in preference to the vulnerable populations targeted by the WFP."[113] Kim has made a policy move that will enhance his control over the populace. The move relies heavily on China's and South Korea's willingness to overlook humanitarian and policy positions of the Kim Chong-il regime. Only time will tell if this move is successful, but it will certainly remain a high priority for Pyongyang as the government there seeks to maintain the status-quo.

Can Kim Maintain His Nuclear Programs in the Face of International Pressure?

Whereas there are many arguments regarding whether or not the North Koreans actually want to keep their plutonium and HEU programs or are maintaining them as a "deterrent" in order to prevent attack by the United States, it is likely that Kim Chong-il's government will do everything it can to keep its nuclear programs intact for as long as possible. Based on past actions North Koreans will manipulate the six-party talks in order to obtain aid while agreeing in principle to dismantle its nuclear programs. The North Koreans effectively gained aid while "freezing" their plutonium program at Yongbyon from 1994 until the breakdown in relations with the United States in the fall of 2002.[114] In September 2005, Pyongyang again agreed, in principle, to dismantle its nuclear program(s). According to published press reports, it did not specify both programs, but this was implied. The agreement in principle stated that North Korea would receive significant energy aid, though it is likely that as the process moves along, Pyongyang will also ask for other types of aid, as this has been their methodology in the past.[115] Based on what was discussed in chapter 2, it appears Pyongyang used the nuclear test conducted in October 2006 as an attempt to coerce Washington to ease up on policing the illicit programs, and to kick-start the six-party talks on terms more favorable to the DPRK. It appears that the test was successful at least partially in accomplishing these goals. The results of the talks in February 2007 left many questions unanswered while providing aid (and opening opportunities for the South to resume large-scale aid) to North Korea.

It is likely that as the six-party process progresses and North Korea agrees to formal and definitive inspection procedures, an attempt will be made to prevent inspection regimes from accessing hidden components of their programs. Because intelligence gaps remain regarding these programs, it is unlikely that Pyongyang will see any advantage to be completely forthcoming. As Condoleezza Rice said during the fall of 2005, "The proof, so to speak, is going to be in the pudding. We are going to now have to have a very clear roadmap for verification, a very clear roadmap for dismantlement, because that is the core issue here." The ease with which the North Koreans can hide these programs is summed up by a statement made by former Special Envoy Wendy Sherman, also made during the fall of 2005, when she stated, "We have no idea where their uranium enrichment program is located. And North Korea is a country filled with mountains and caverns and underground tunnels, and it wouldn't take much to hide such a program."[116] Numerous suggestions have been posed on how to circumvent the significant capability that Pyongyang has for hiding the components of its nuclear programs, but most agree that this will be a difficult process for inspectors.[117]

Finally, and again following precedent determined during the Agreed Framework scenario that began in 1994, it is likely that the North Koreans will end cooperation at the point where vital program elements are threatened but significant aid has been acquired. The North Koreans developed a two-track program during the Clinton administration—although the HEU program has been assessed by most to have not yet been weaponized by October 2002 when the nuclear confrontation occurred—and as their light-water reactors were being developed and foreign aid in the form of energy was coming in, they displayed a sense (at least by North Korean standards) of cooperation. However, this sense of cooperation evaporated when accused by Bush administration officials of having a secret HEU program.[118] It is likely that as negotiations continue, Pyongyang will once again take this tack—at least temporarily and in order to stall—because it will maintain or prolong the existence of their nuclear programs. And Pyongyang sees the existence of their nuclear programs to be to their advantage as long as it can be maintained.

Based on the evidence discussed above, Kim Chong-il's government is likely to consider one of their highest priorities the challenge of maintaining their nuclear program in the face of international pressure to dismantle it. The pressure on Pyongyang since the breakdown of the Agreed Framework during the fall of 2002, has been very gradual, frequently disjointed (between the other members involved in the six-party talks), and in some ways ineffective. Throughout the six-party talks, there have been disagreements between the five participants who are negotiating with North Korea—particularly the United States and China.[119] This situation is to Pyongyang's advantage, and will no doubt be manipulated throughout the process of reaching a solution to North Korea's nuclear question. Thus, it is clear that North Korea will manipulate the six-party talks to obtain aid while agreeing in principle to dismantlement, that they are likely to prevent inspection regimes from accessing hidden components of their programs, and finally (and perhaps most importantly) that, as in the Agreed Framework, they will end cooperation at the point where vital program elements are threatened but significant aid has been acquired.

Can Pyongyang Continue its Illicit Activities and Proliferation?

The challenge for the Kim Chong-il regime as it looks to its survival in the post-9/11 era will be to maintain these activities in the face of mounting pressure from the international community—particularly the United States. As Washington becomes more successful in drawing the international community into programs and initiatives that are used to slow down or stop North Korea's illicit activities and proliferation, the pressure will mount on Kim's regime to find new ways to continue its "less than legal" operations.

One of the key ways that Washington has co-opted allies into its efforts to stop proliferation and illegal activities is through the Proliferation Security Initiative. This is an initiative that involves using mostly maritime forces to interdict illegal shipping activities by nations involved in rogue activities. Current participants include Australia, Canada, France, Germany, Italy, Japan, the Netherlands, Norway, Poland, Portugal, Russia, Singapore, Spain, the UK, and the United States. More than sixty countries have expressed their support for the initiative. While the initiative is widely viewed to be targeted mostly toward North Korea, it was also used to interdict centrifuges headed to Libya (for what was then its developing nuclear weaponization program) during 2003.[120] To date, fourteen exercises have been held in Europe, Asia, and North America, each time led by a different country. Fourteen more exercises were scheduled through the end of 2006.[121] North Korea's government has made it clear that the Proliferation Security Initiative is a threat to its "national security," and with sixty nations now expressing their support for the initiative, it is clear that this makes proliferation a more difficult prospect for Pyongyang.[122]

Since the fall of 2005, U.S. law enforcement agencies have targeted banks that facilitated North Korean money-laundering and counterfeiting activities to try to counter Pyongyang's illegal cash flow. The best known of these banks was Banco Delta Asia, widely known as the "big boy" that North Korea used for many of its illegal financial, criminal, and counterfeiting operations.[123] While it is still too early to determine the overall effects of U.S. actions on North Korea, Pyongyang's crime brokers from Bureau Number 39 will have to develop other money-laundering routes—a real challenge in today's global environment. There are early signs that this is happening already. During February 2006, North Korean diplomatic officials were caught smuggling $1 million (U.S. dollars) and 200 million yen in cash into Mongolia.[124] If the Mongolian example is indicative, North Korea may be willing and ready to adapt to a changing law-enforcement environment.

As a result of international efforts to thwart North Korea, evidence indicates customers are drying up for their missile proliferation programs. As recently as 2001, North Korea was assessed to have earned more than $560 million a year in missile sales, with the largest customers being Pakistan, Libya, and Iran. But since the acceleration of the Global War on Terror, the United States has formed an alliance with Islamabad that has apparently dried up most of the market in Pakistan for North Korean missiles, and Libya agreed in 2004 to stop buying missiles from North Korea, as well as to destroy all of those in its possession. The end of North Korea's missile sales to two of its key customers has dampened profits.[125] Perhaps as important, dwindling profits places more pressure on the government to raise funds through illicit activities such as illegal drug sales and counterfeiting of currency and cigarettes.

The North Korean government must have serious concerns about the future of two of its biggest money generating initiatives—weapons proliferation and illicit criminal activities. Pyongyang must circumvent the Proliferation Security Initiative—perhaps by pressuring Seoul to remain out of the multination project. In addition, North Korea must deal with U.S. law enforcement over its criminal activities, particularly as other nations become concerned and join in these efforts. Finally, finding customers for its weapons of mass destruction—particularly missiles—will remain a challenge that Pyongyang is likely to make one of its higher priorities. North Korea is being pursued and coerced on the world stage where the government is most vulnerable—its pocketbook.

Can Pyongyang Repair DPRK–Japan Relations?

Pyongyang needs to both generate hard currency and maintain the aid pipeline that has steadily increased in volume since 2002 from China and South Korea. One would think that the same would apply to Pyongyang's relationship with Japan, but this is not so. During the 1990s, Japan was extremely generous in providing food aid to the North Koreans, and the government in Pyongyang made little attempt to hide its perspective that the assistance was "owed" because of the well-documented human rights violations of the Japanese colonial past. Unfortunately, Kim Chong-il's open admission that Japanese citizens had been kidnapped by North Korea and subsequently returned fake bones that were supposed to be remains of these citizens created a political frenzy in Japan that led to the shut down of food aid in 2001.[126]

Since relations went sour with Japan following the "abducted citizens" scandal, economic interaction has steadily decreased. In fact, in 2005 trade between North Korea and Japan reached a twenty-eight-year low according to the South Korean trade body Korea Trade-Investment Agency (KOTRA). According to KOTRA, the trade volume between the two nations came to $190 million, the lowest since 1977. The North's exports to Japan amounted to $130 million, and imports from Japan totaled only $60 million. The bilateral trade has declined steadily since 2002. In addition, Japan has boycotted Korean goods.[127] Talks between Japanese and North Korean officials in February 2006 did not ease any of the tensions that have existed between the two nations. Tokyo was reportedly very frustrated with the results of the talks. A senior Japanese Foreign Ministry official was quoted as saying, "The outcome was worse than a stalemate." During the talks, in response to Japanese requests for further action resolving the cases of Japanese citizens who were abducted and used for intelligence training in North Korea, Pyongyang made counter-demands that Japan turn over NGO workers who were helping North Korean defectors.[128] Japan's refusal in February 2007 to contribute to the six-party talks HFO payment to North Korea until this issue was resolved is further proof that the abducted citizen scandal has been important to the people and government of Japan. To say the least, the relationship between North Korea and Japan has cooled because of this issue, causing economic repercussions in Pyongyang.

Conclusions

In today's international environment of globalism, advanced communications, spreading democracy, and blurring lines of corporate and national interests, North Korea stands apart as one of the last bastions of autocratic despotism. To secure the survival of the regime and the continuing existence of its unique autocratic society, daunting challenges must be met with clear planning and ingenuity.

Pyongyang has been successful in meeting many of the challenges, yet the government has been less than successful in meeting others. The North Korean military remains a formidable force in the face of economic hardships, Pyongyang has garnered increased support from both China and South Korea in the post-9/11 era, the regime succession process remains secretive and intact (at least for now), Pyongyang's nuclear program has not yet been dismantled, Kim has been able to maintain the loyalty standards thus far of the second- and third-tier leadership in North Korea, and the general populace remains isolated and highly controlled. Based on polling discussed in this chapter that occurred between 2002 and 2005, North Korea has also been at least partially successful in alienating the South Korean public from positive perceptions regarding the ROK–U.S. Alliance.

There is less potential for North Korea being successful in reinstituting the public distribution system—a challenge dependent on the largesse of China and South Korea. An even bigger challenge will be attempts to mitigate the refugee flow across the Chinese border, a phenomenon that creates problems with the

Pyongyang–Beijing relationship, as well as bad publicity in the world's eyes for both nations. Even more troubling for Pyongyang is its continuing profits from illicit activities and proliferation initiatives. This issue is already showing small signs of cracks. For example, South Korea's Ministry of Unification confirmed that Kim's birthday celebrations in February 2006 were reportedly smaller than those held in 2005 probably because of restrictions the United States had slapped on key banks that were helping North Korea engage in illicit activities. Only forty-seven events were held as compared to fifty-two the previous year.[129] Finally, DPRK–Japan relations have been in a deep freeze because of Pyongyang's bungling of diplomacy, and the challenge to repairing this relationship will be huge.

PART II

ANSWERING NORTH KOREA'S TROUBLING STATE BEHAVIOR:
THE CHANGING ROK–U.S. ALLIANCE AND SPLINTERED SOUTH KOREAN CIVIL-MILITARY RELATIONSHIP

8 | COUNTERING THE NORTH KOREAN THREAT: CHALLENGES FOR THE ROK–U.S. ALLIANCE IN THE POST-9/11 ERA[1]

THE ROK–U.S. ALLIANCE HAS BEEN IN A STATE of flux almost since the beginning of the Roh Moo-hyun administration in early 2003. Many challenges have created debate and controversy on both sides of the Pacific and include the future role of USFK on the Korean Peninsula, the cost of maintaining troops and equipment on the Peninsula (and who will pay it), the transformation of USFK as a military force, the southern move of U.S. Army units close to the DMZ, as well as the three headquarters (UN Command, Combined Forces Command, and USFK) in Seoul, defense reform in the South Korean military, proposed changes to wartime operational command, and the role of strategic flexibility as applied to the Korean Peninsula.

Defending the Republic

The most important task of any national leader is the defense of the nation-state. In doing so, a nation's leader must take into account economy, geography, resources, populace, and enemies. In *all eight* Korean nation-states in the Peninsula's history, geography has been one of the most —if not the most—important factor in securing the security and stability of the nation.[2] Historically Korea has been located between great powers such as China and Japan, Russia and Japan, or as during the Cold War, coveted by both the USSR and the USA. With the threat of a DPRK that continues to use brinkmanship and military might as a tool of foreign policy to the North, China the ever-present larger neighbor to the north of the DPRK, and Japan to the east, geography remains essential to South Korea and for the security and stability of the Peninsula.

Throughout Korea's history, geography has required an alliance structure with a major power in order to protect Korean sovereignty. For more years than not throughout its long history, Korea looked to China in such alliances, but since 1953 it has been the ROK–U.S. Mutual Defense treaty.[3] The purpose of this alliance is *mutual defense*, not only deterrence from attack by North Korea. Deterring an attack from North Korea is the responsibility of the Combined Forces Command (CFC), which includes both a peacetime and a wartime structure of ROK and U.S. forces.[4]

How have the United States and the Republic of Korea (ROK, also frequently referred to as South Korea throughout this book) mutually supported one another in defense of the national interests of each nation-state? The United States has fulfilled its role since 1953 by stationing troops, combat systems, equipment, and logistical support in the ROK. Prior to that, from 1950–1953, U.S. troops conducted defense of the ROK through combat forces under the command of the United Nations.[5] The ROK has supported the mutual defense of the United States by supporting U.S. security actions around the world on numerous occasions, such as peacekeeping operations in places in Cyprus and East Timor, and combat operations in Vietnam. In Vietnam, 313,000 troops rotated through, with 43,000 troops in theater at any given time, and Korea suffered nearly 5,000 deaths and close to the same number of wounded. Currently South Korea supports the United States in Operation Iraqi Freedom and numerous other combat and peacekeeping operations.[6] No other ally has sent more troops to fight or conduct security operations with U.S. troops since World War II except the United Kingdom and Australia. In every way, this alliance has been one that since its inception has truly been mutually supportive—both in reality, and in the perceptions of the citizens of South Korea and the United States.

Security Policies of the Roh Administration

Roh Moo-hyun was certainly not the first president of South Korea to take a "left of center" view of domestic and foreign policy. His predecessor, Kim Dae-jung, also had policies that could legitimately be considered "progressive." However, Roh's policies have been more openly polarized from those of the United States than were Kim's.

Roh's new policies were epitomized by the National Security Strategy released by the Blue House in March 2004. The document emphasized reconciliation with the North and self-reliant national defense. It also declared the North Korean nuclear program to be the greatest threat to the security and stability of the ROK, stating in part, "The North's nuclear development is not only the greatest security threat to our nation but also a hindrance to peace and stability in Northeast Asia."[7] However, there is very little discussion of the North Korean asymmetric threat, commonly agreed among most analysts to consist of

- short-range rockets and missiles capable of carrying chemical warheads (Free Rocket Over Ground systems, and Scud missiles)
- highly trained and well-equipped Special Operations Forces, and
- long-range artillery systems (many of which have been deployed to areas just north of the DMZ since the mid-1990s) within range of Seoul and key areas in Kyonggi province.[8]

The long-range artillery systems are easily the most ominous military threat to Seoul and ultimately the security of the entire ROK.

Based on many public statements made during his campaign for the presidency and since assuming leadership, one of Roh's key foreign policy aims has been to marginalize the ROK–U.S. alliance and (as quickly as possible) to change many of the paradigms that have made it so mutually beneficial for both the United States and Korea for more than fifty years.[9] Indeed, actions taken since 2003 have also pointed to this apparent fact. This should be of concern to the public in South Korea because Korea has always needed an alliance to maintain security, stability, and prosperity. Thus, if Roh's intention was to move away from the ROK–U.S. Alliance, what are the alternatives?

The Republic of Korea as a Balancer: The New "Roh Doctrine?"

In 2005, President Roh unveiled what some have called a "new doctrine." At a graduation ceremony for the Korea Third Military Academy, Roh called for a new role in the geopolitical future of South Korea—that of a "balancer" in Northeast Asia. In his speech to the graduates of the military academy, Roh commented, "Korea will calculate and cooperate if need be, and move forward with its proper authority and responsibility." As has often been the case when Roh has made controversial statements, high-ranking government officials commented on his speech, providing more details. One such official was quoted as saying the order in which Korea plays one leg of the three-way alliance with the

United States and Japan was a product of the Cold War, and that Korea wants to extract itself from a stand-off centered on the Peninsula between a "Southern Alliance" (South Korea, the United States, and Japan) and a "Northern Alliance" (North Korea, China, and Russia). Another official was quoted as saying that as tensions arise between the U.S. and Japan on one hand, and China and North Korea on the other, Seoul will not be cornered into an exclusive alliance with Washington.[10] Predictably, Chinese Ambassador Li Bin later stated that China would give "unreserved" support to Korea if it chose to play the role of a "stabilizer" for peace and prosperity in Northeast Asia, remarking in part, "We can't greet an era of mutual prosperity in this region with such old Cold War thoughts, can we?"[11]

The role that balancer would mean for South Korea shows that Seoul would be locked neither into the U.S.–Japan camp nor the North Korea–Russia–China camp. Most important, it means that South Korea would distance itself from a security alliance that has been the basis of its survival for over five decades, yet South Korea sits in one of the most geopolitically dangerous geographical positions in the world. Currently supported by the world's remaining super power, the United States, South Korea sits just south of the world's number two military power (China) immediately south of a government in North Korea that remains intent on maintaining a 1.2-million-man military (with weapons of mass destruction), and west of the world's second most powerful economic nation, Japan.[12] Russia sits slightly farther away, but it is a major player in the relationship with North Korea and in the six-party talks as well. Both those in the academic and policy community in the United States have expressed concern over Roh's new doctrine. In April 2005, a State Department official (who asked that his name be withheld) urged Korean lawmakers on a visit to the United States to consider the errors of the Chosun dynasty at the end of the nineteenth century when Korea's weakened role because of a lack of major-power alliances made Seoul an easy target for Japanese aggression.[13] A member of the South Korea National Security Council (NSC) responded to criticism of Roh's ambition commenting that South Korea could play a balancing role despite lacking economic, political, and military strength and added that a stabilizing role was the most realistic security strategy for Korea to "survive on the world stage."[14]

Further criticism of the Blue House's balancer vision became public on April 8, 2005, in an address delivered on behalf of the GNP to the National Assembly. Party Chair Park Geun-hye stated,

Being a balancer in Northeast Asia reminds me of Daehanjeguk [the imperial continuation of the Chosun dynasty from 1897 to 1910]. The empire declared its futile neutrality just before the Russo-Japanese War in 1904, 100 years ago. . . . At present, China, Japan, and Russia, as well as North Korea, do not recognize South Korea as a balancer in the region. Under the circumstances, any more isolation outside the framework of the Korea–U.S. alliance would not serve Korea's interests.[15]

During the same time, a group of conservative academics, lawyers, and educators held a press conference to express their opposition to President Roh's view of Korea as a potential balancer, declaring his new doctrine as detrimental to the Korea–U.S. alliance, which they stressed had been the main pillar of Korea's economic development and national security.[16] Perhaps the most surprising critic of the doctrine was Roh's predecessor and supporter during his presidential election campaign, Kim Dae-jung. In early April 2005 in an address to the newly elected Uri party leadership, Kim told Moon Hee-sang and other new ruling-party members that,

Fundamentally, it's best that our diplomatic relations operate within the three frameworks of a strong Korea–U.S. relationship, the tripartite alliance and cooperation between the region's four Great Powers, . . . this is not a choice, but a position we have to accept fatalistically, our destiny.[17]

Kim was apparently articulating to the leadership of Roh's supporting party that geopolitical decisions should not be based on emotional reactions to recent events but rather on pragmatic, practical realities that will safeguard the national security of the state.

Possible Alliance Alternatives

The ROK must have an alliance with a powerful nation-state in order to maintain its stability, security, and prosperity. For much of its history, Korea's main ally was China. China was frequently the benefactor of Seoul in both peace and war up until the nineteenth century when a weakened Beijing was itself plagued by foreign aggression. In fact, in April 2005 the Defense Ministry announced that military exchanges between Korea and China will eventually intensify to a level similar to those between Korea and Japan (which is relatively minor). ROK Minister of Defense Yoon Kwang-ung, who gave the announcement, stated in part,

> There is a need to raise the level of military cooperation between Korea and China to at least that shared between Korea and Japan, and it's worth thinking about plans to help stability on the Korean Peninsula with China's assistance.[18]

Later in April 2005, it was confirmed that the Ministry of National Defense was planning to create a policy desk provisionally dubbed the Department of Northeast Asian Policy. The desk would oversee increased military cooperation with China and Russia. This is the first time in South Korea's existence that a department to head up military exchanges with Russia and China had been created. This recent move would unnerve many high ranking officials and military officers within the Ministry of Defense.[19]

But the twenty-first century does not bode well for choosing China as an ally. The PRC fought on the side of the DPRK in the Korean Conflict and continues to provide economic and military assistance to Pyongyang. In addition, it is well known that Beijing wishes to promote the status quo of two Koreas as long as possible.[20] Indeed, journalist Richard Halloran addressed the issue of Seoul reaching out to Beijing as an ally, and the real motives of the government in Beijing when he stated,

> The fundamental issue is which alliance will prevail in East Asia: the autocratic coalition led by China that seeks to drive the United States from the region or the democratic grouping led by the United States that seeks a stable balance of political and military power in which trade and economic development flourishes.[21]

Seoul must determine (even post-unification), if it truly wants a military alliance with an authoritarian communist regime that in the past supported the unification of the Peninsula under a communist government.

Reasons for not engaging in a long-term or even a short-term alliance with Japan are so numerous that they cannot be covered here sufficiently, but they include cultural, historical, ideological, and economic areas. Strong emotional resentment continues in Koreans against the government of Japan for what happened during the Tok Do Controversy of 2005. That bitter disagreement over small islands shows that close military ties with Japan are simply out of the question.[22] Such an alliance would be highly unlikely to support the long- or short-term goals of the government in Seoul and would be extremely unpopular with the people of Korea. This is exacerbated by the fact that there are long-term territorial disputes with both China and Japan.[23]

Many of the same reasons apply to an alliance with Russia, and Russia is also likely far too weak militarily and economically to be a truly beneficial ally.[24] Thus, alternatives to the current alliance with the U.S. appear to be unlikely, and to the disadvantage of Seoul—which means even for an administration which wishes to change many of the paradigms of the ROK–U.S. Alliance, the best alternative is the restructuring of the alliance as we now know it.

Restructuring the Alliance: Key Concerns

When alliance systems do not work, not just one generation suffers but several generations afterward suffer, too. Key recent examples of this are the occupation of Korea by Japan in the early twentieth century and the Korean Conflict beginning in 1950.[25]

The Roh administration, through its new national security strategy, is attempting major steps to adjust the ROK–U.S. Alliance using the Security Policy Initiative, previously referred to as the Future of the Alliance policy initiative talks. Roh's stated goal is the "rebalancing of the ROK–U.S. relationship."[26] Is this policy an emotional backlash from the traditionally weaker partner in the alliance? It also could be that Roh's political base comes from the "386 Generation," a group of highly placed intellectuals and politicians who are inexperienced politically but who share a common bond—much of which is comprised of an agreement that the relationship with the United States should radically change. As the chief target of the conservatives and the individual who epitomizes the values of the 386 Generation, former NSC Vice Chief Lee Jong-seok (appointed Minister of Unification in 2006) was widely believed to hold extraordinarily powerful influence over national security and military issues, as well as having the ear of the president.[27] Despite the pressure that Roh receives from his bases of political support, the fact remains that Seoul continues to need a strong alliance, just as it always has.

Symptoms of Change: OPLAN/CONPLAN 5029

One of the most confusing and debated issues that has brought operational change to the ROK–U.S. alliance is the controversy during 2005 and 2006 over Operations Plan (OPLAN) 5029, a plan that deals with the military action taken by ROK and U.S. forces in the event that several different contingencies were to occur: the collapse of the North Korean regime, mass exodus of refugees, natural disasters, "civil" war with North Korea, a palace coup, and other events short of a force-on-force conflict.[28] The South Korean National Security Council announced the termination of the OPLAN in April 2005, stating, "We have terminated the U.S.–South Korea Combined Forces Command's efforts to map out a plan, code named 5029, because the plan could be a serious obstacle to exercising Korea's sovereignty."[29]

Several aspects of this recent action are important. An OPLAN is different than a "conceptual" plan—which is what 5029 had been until 2003. Command and control, and flow of troops and equipment is much more rigid in an OPLAN than in a Concept of Operations Plan (CONPLAN). Thus, because the OPLAN version of 5029 had Combined Forces Command under the command of a U.S. general, the NSC of Roh's administration apparently felt that this was "infringing on the sovereignty of South Korea."[30] Furthermore, terminating the plan was a highly unusual move because the decision-making process appears to have been conducted entirely by the ROK National Security Council—not the Defense Ministry. In South Korea, much like in the United States, OPLANs have been considered the exclusive domain of the military with almost no outside involvement from the NSC or other outside bodies.[31] Finally, the disagreement over how to change the plan (because of the involvement of the ROK NSC) reportedly caused tensions in 2005 between Seoul and Washington.[32]

Soon after the controversy erupted, South Korea proposed reverting back to the process of working together on it as a CONPLAN as it had been prior to 2003. The suggestion was made during a visit to the United States by then-ROK NSC Vice Chief, Lee Jong-seok.[33] In June 2005, two months after Seoul announced it wanted the plan shelved, Yoon Kwang-ung and Donald Rumsfeld met in Singapore and agreed to develop and upgrade 5029 as a contingency plan.

According to ROK Defense Ministry spokesman Shin Hyeon-don, the discussions were to be conceptual in nature with the two defense chiefs agreeing not to develop an OPLAN "at the moment." Reportedly, they also agreed to leave out organization of operational units and uses of military force (such as troop numbers),[34] based on agreements reached by the Military Committee.[35] In March 2006, the press announced that under the Security Policy Initiative on Guam, the United States and South Korea had agreed on a draft that would be signed by the defense chiefs of both nations.

Symptoms of change in the ROK government process are evident if one considers several factors:

- change in the decision-making process (National Security Council versus Ministry of National Defense),
- confusion about how the plan would evolve (as evidenced by the resurrection of the old CONPLAN as proposed by Lee Jong-seok after 5029 was at first completely scrapped), and
- tensions that this confusing decision-making process caused with the United States.

There were other controversies regarding the changing of this plan as well, such as its impact on the South Korean Civil–Military relationships. But this is likely to be only a symptom of other upcoming problems the alliance will face on a variety of other issues.

Current Strengths and Weaknesses of the ROK–U.S. Alliance

Both nations share common strategic interests, such as regional stability, preservation of a robust alliance, prevention of war, economic prosperity, non-proliferation, and the fight against the global war on terrorism (since North Korea represents a nexus of nuclear weapons and possible proliferation to terrorist organizations and the rogue states who support them).[36] Currently, the ROK has more than 4,000 personnel in twelve countries and fifteen different locations in support of peacekeeping operations or U.S. efforts.[37] The U.S. currently stations 32,000 troops in the ROK to defend against external aggression.[38]

The two nations also share a unique, combined, war fighting capability. Combined Forces Command (CFC) receives bilateral guidance into a "unity of command" structure. CFC gives common purpose to mission, commander's intent, plans, training, exercises, and integration of capabilities. The structures of the two militaries are complementary. The ROK armed forces bring mass, and the U.S. armed forces bring technology. The ROK forces are groundcentric, and the U.S. brings significant air and naval power.[39] There is also interoperability of systems and personnel, and combined training and exercises, as well as common doctrine: ROK officers train in U.S. schools and employ strategy and tactics from U.S. manuals and operational art; U.S. officers attend ROK Primary Military Education programs.[40] Often less publicized but certainly at least as important, the two nations share a common support for freedom's principles and institutions. The ROK is the United States' seventh largest trading partner, and the United States is the second ranked destination for ROK products.[41]

However, weaknesses in the alliance also have existed in the Roh–Bush era, including differing views regarding the region. Polling data has suggested, for example, that the current majority party in the ROK believes one day China will again gain ascendancy in the region while Japan remains a trade partner but potential enemy.[42] The United States sees Japan as remaining a chief ally. Since 2003 the Roh and Bush administrations have had differing views on North Korea, as President Roh has sought coexistence with Pyongyang through a "gradualism" approach, and the South Korean public has calmed over the North Korean threat following the June 2000 summit. President Bush views the DPRK as a member of the axis of evil and a proliferator of WMD.[43] In addition, during the Roh–Bush era, the Roh government has tended to see North Korea's nuclear program as a threat to the United States, not to the ROK, and the Bush administration consequently has viewed North Korea through the counter-proliferation prism.

Primary Challenges Facing the Security Policy Initiative

The Security Policy Initiative essentially consists of ongoing talks between high-ranking military officials from the two governments that occur several times a year. There are several challenges facing the Security Policy Initiative (SPI):

Strategic flexibility. Because of the changing strategic environment throughout the world, the United States engaged in a global posture review during 2003–2005. The result has been a discussion of turning the forces on the Peninsula into a rapid deployment to respond to a crisis in Asia or elsewhere on short notice.[44]

During a meeting where outgoing USFK Commander Gen. Leon LaPorte said good-bye to the South Korean press, he reiterated the U.S. position that the primary mission (despite the concept of Strategic Flexibility) of American forces on the Korean Peninsula was to defend against North Korean aggression. LaPorte stated that neither he nor his successor had the authority to order Korean troops abroad, and that the term "Strategic Flexibility" only referred to the U.S. deploying its own troops elsewhere.[45] This may have been a response to remarks made to the South Korean press by the apparently ill-informed South Korean Defense Minister, Yoon Kwang-ung. Yoon had remarked during the same week that he opposed any expansion of South Korea's military operations outside the Korean Peninsula because he felt it could cause instability and trigger an arms race in East Asia—apparently he was not referring to operations such as Iraqi Freedom and the numerous peacekeeping deployments that the South Korean military has engaged in over the years. Yoon left no doubt where his position was when he stated, "We should not broaden our forces operations any further outside this Peninsula. Our military forces should focus on promoting peace and stability on the Peninsula and avoid any involvement in regional conflicts."[46]

Despite the planned realignment of forces in Korea, numerous U.S. Defense Department officials have stated that the primary mission of U.S. forces in Korea is to defend and deter against an attack from the North.[47] Roh's administration posits reshaping the alliance and allowing no USFK strategic flexibility at a time when the United States needs all of its forces to accomplish security objectives in a post-9/11 world.[48] In early March 2005, Roh spoke to the 53rd graduating class of the Air Force Academy saying, "Our citizens will not become embroiled in Northeast Asian conflicts without our consent." A high-ranking Blue House official said that Roh's comments were a matter of principle and ways of setting them down formally were being studied in consultation with the U.S. Reportedly, the Blue House at the time wanted to make it mandatory for Washington to get prior consent from Korea when moving USFK forces elsewhere.[49]

The debate is likely to continue between those on the right and those on the left in South Korea regarding strategic flexibility, although in principle an agreement was reached between Washington and Seoul. On January 21, 2006, during what was called the "Strategic Consultation for Allied Partnership," the two sides agreed to the expanded role of the USFK as a "stabilizer in Northeast Asia." South Korean officials confirmed that the language was left at a "broad" level without setting roles or guidelines. The Director-General of South Korea's North American Bureau at the Foreign Ministry, Kim Sook, remarked, "We will be discussing details as situations arise," and added that the agreement should not be a source of concern, considering the agreed principle that South Korea will not get involved in a regional conflict against its will.[50]

The agreement was reached following talks between South Korean Foreign Minister Ban Ki-moon and U.S. Secretary of State Condoleezza Rice. It states that "[Seoul, as an ally], fully understands the rationale for the transformation of the U.S. global strategy, and respects the necessity for strategic flexibility of the USFK." Conversely, "The U.S. respects Korea's position that they will not be involved in regional conflict against the will of the Korean people."[51] Another unidentified South Korean official remarked at the time that, "Our position of not wanting to become entangled in regional conflicts against the will of our people was reflected." Both governments demonstrated their ability to compromise, although the possibility of confrontation will continue between Washington and Seoul should the United States try to use troops from USFK in regional conflicts in Asia.[52]

The reaction to the agreement from the left in South Korea was predictable. Roh's de facto supporting Uri party members in the National Assembly conducted a "legislative review" that called for a watertight mechanism requiring prior consent from Seoul prior to any movements of American troops—or a renegotiation of the Mutual Defense Treaty in the long term.[53] Foreign Minister Ban Ki-moon reacted with some irritation to the negative response from the left, reminding those who were opposed that the agreement with Secretary Rice included a statement by the United States that U.S. troops would not be involved in conflicts elsewhere in the region without Seoul's consent.[54] Noted left-leaning former NSC Vice Chief and newly appointed Minister of Unification Lee Jong-seok responded angrily to the reaction of his fellow left-leaning politicians at a seminar given to top-level South Korean diplomats and remarked sarcastically that it would be better for them to openly argue for a withdrawal of U.S. troops stationed in South Korea.[55] The events surrounding the discussion over Strategic Flexibility have often involved perceptions and politics on the South Korean side that are predictable in a liberal democracy. Such debate is important and healthy, particularly between two such long-standing allies.

Burden sharing. Seoul wants to minimize burden sharing that consists of non-personnel stationing costs. These are typically the kinds of costs associated with bases, infrastructure, non-U.S. base workers, and so on. On March 16, 2005, the two sides announced that an agreement had been reached in principle to reduce Seoul's costs paid over the next two years to help maintain a U.S.

military presence in Korea. Foreign Minister Ban Ki-Moon has repeatedly stated that the ongoing reduction in U.S. troops on the Peninsula must be taken into account when the costs are considered.[56] The effects of the agreement were almost immediate and costly. On April 1, 2005, USFK announced a decision to lay off as many as 1,000 Korean civilian staff because of the reductions in South Korea's cost sharing for the year.[57] Lt. Gen. Charles Campbell said that the U.S. military must reduce spending because the amount that Seoul had agreed to pay was not enough to support workers at U.S. bases. In 2005, Seoul paid 9 percent less than in 2004.[58] South Korean Defense Minister Yoon Kwang-ung later stated that the proportion of the USFK's budget allocation to South Korea for 2005 had been reduced by 8.9 percent.[59] On May 20, 2005, the first Korean workers were laid off when 112 civilians were let go who had worked on Air Force bases in South Korea.[60] Talks between officials during August 2006 revealed great differences in perceptions over how the South Korean government should shoulder its share of costs for U.S. troops stationed on the Peninsula. U.S. officials—including Donald Rumsfeld—were clearly concerned that South Korea should pay for a more equitable amount of the costs, given Seoul's large economy.[61]

In addition, Washington requested that Seoul share the costs for modernizing integrated command and control systems—which often also include communications, computers, and intelligence (C4I)—yet for now it appears Seoul is unwilling to pay these costs.[62] Lieutenant General Campbell, speaking on behalf of USFK, also commented, "We will be required to make tough but necessary decisions in C4I systems, which are currently provided to South Korea's military forces."[63]

If one were to compare the costs of military burden sharing in Korea to what the government in Japan has paid over the years, Seoul's share is significantly smaller.[64] For example, starting in April 2006, Japan planned to allocate $1.86 billion to cover the costs of its bases.[65] Related discussions concerned the cost of the Yongsan (USFK headquarters), relocation to areas farther south near the Camp Humphries U.S. Army base, and land allocation. In this case, Seoul sought to limit relocation payments to less than what the U.S. Department of Defense requested. In February 2006, newly appointed Unification Minister Lee Jong-seok announced that Seoul would have to spend $5.5 billion to relocate U.S. forces to Camp Humphries, a leap of $2.5 billion over the original estimate when Seoul and Washington agreed to move facilities and forces during July 2004.[66] Currently, South Korea has the fourth largest holding of foreign currency reserves ($202 billion) in the world, which were originally acquired to prevent a reoccurrence of the ROK financial crisis of 1997.[67] To date, Seoul has refused to discuss using any of this money to pay for the relocation of the Yongsan Army garrison.

Future command relationships. Roh addressed this issue in his speech at the Air Force Academy graduation, stating that it would be necessary to readjust command relationships over the next ten years.[68] Rumors have circulated in the ROK that the United States will downgrade the rank of the commander of U.S. forces from a four-star to a three-star—despite statements from the U.S. Department of Defense and high-ranking military officials to the contrary. If changes to the rank are made, more than likely they will occur whenever Combined Forces Command is dismantled.[69]

President Roh has called for adjustments to (or complete abolishment of) UN Command and Combined Forces Command. Both of these commands have undergone changes in past years, and it is likely that they will continue to do so as the alliance evolves. In addition, Roh has called for changes to the Status of Forces Agreement (SOFA).[70]

Transformation of USFK. USFK is not the only force to undergo transformation in the U.S. military. In fact, transformation has been ongoing in all of the U.S. military services since late 2001. The problem is that any change to the status quo has been interpreted by the Blue House as a change to the military alliance made without consulting America's ROK allies.[71] A key example of this is the transformation of forces and command and control by 2nd Infantry Division, close to the DMZ.[72] The 2nd Infantry Division's transformation to a rapidly deployable, UEx (or "Unit of Employment") was scheduled to be complete by June 15, 2005.[73] This was done, because of current issues capabilities and troop deployments around the world, but it was interpreted by many South Koreans as initiating strategic flexibility and transformation before it has been addressed properly in the SPI talks. In each of these points, the Roh administration pushed its position very hard. This has caused problems because as the United States seeks to transform its forces to best support the national security needs of the ROK, it appears that Seoul has downplayed the threat that the Blue House appears to be so concerned the United States will not be prepared to defend against. Statements by Roh to this effect have caused concern in the

United States.[74] Statements made by Defense Minister Yoon regarding the North Korean threat have also caused concern.[75] Finally the Ministry of Defense White Paper released to the public in early 2005, which eliminated the term "Main Enemy" (the term "Main Enemy" has routinely been used in past South Korean Ministry of Defense White Papers as the accepted term of reference for North Korea) has caused concern, not only in the United States but in the ROK military as well, where a poll conducted by the *Chosun Ilbo* as the Defense Ministry was considering the move to change the terminology, among 1,447 army officers and soldiers, revealed that 84.8 percent believed the government should in fact retain the terminology.[76] As the change to the White Paper became a reality, an ROK field commander was quoted as saying, "It has become difficult to give our soldiers psychological training, and it will get tougher in the future."[77] Clearly, the change to the designation of North Korea as the "Main Enemy" has caused repercussions in the ROK military.

The actions of the Roh administration in Seoul regarding the North Korean threat also have had a profound effect on members of the U.S. Congress. For instance, Congressional Representative Henry Hyde, chairman of the House International Relations Committee, commented on the 2005 MND White Paper in a prepared statement on March 10, 2005:

> It deleted the designation of Pyongyang as the Main Enemy, although the White Paper stated that, in the event of armed conflict in Korea, the U.S. would dispatch 690,000 troops, over four times the 150,000 serving in Iraq. . . . If you need our help, please tell us clearly who your enemy is.[78]

Former Congressman Hyde's remarks were widely publicized by the ROK press. ROK Unification Minister (at the time) Chung Dong-young responded to the remarks soon thereafter, and was quoted by Unification Ministry spokesman Kim Hong-jae as saying Northeast Asia was trying to move from hostile confrontation to coexistence, reconciliation, and cooperation, further stating that Hyde's confrontational thinking was not helpful in resolving problems on the Korean Peninsula.[79] While Hyde may have been the first member of Congress to speak so bluntly of a perception that now exists among many on both sides of the aisle in Congress, he highlighted a concern regarding perceptions of the threat in the Blue House that will likely have an important impact on the ROK–U.S. Alliance.

This brings us back once again to the dilemma created by the ROK national security strategy during the Roh administration and the contradictions seen in the actions regarding this policy since its introduction in 2004. The Roh security policy appears to have downplayed much of the threat that the North poses, while at the same time taking actions (as discussed above) that have served, at least thus far, to marginalize the ROK–U.S. Alliance. Of importance is the fact that "Self-Reliant Defense" is being stressed in this policy, but until 2005 the ROK government had been unwilling to spend the money necessary to create a military force capable of self-reliant national defense—one of the key examples of the contradictions that seem to be occurring between stated policy and actual implemented programs.

Examining ROK Defense spending in recent years (see Fig. 13) shows budget allocations do not appear to match the goals stated by Roh in 2003 and articulated in the National Security Strategy in 2004. When comparing ROK defense spending to other countries with similar economies or national security concerns, South Korea spent considerably less than others where the military plays a significant role in foreign policy (see Fig. 14). ROK Defense Minister Yoon stated in 2005 that the South Korean military aims to establish "self-reliant defense capabilities" by 2025, and that the Defense budget will "rise back" up to 2.7 percent by the end of President Roh's term. The defense budget share of GDP for 2005 was only about 2.47 percent, less that the 2003 and 2004 budgets.[80]

FIGURE 13:
ROK DEFENSE BUDGET ALLOCATION TREND

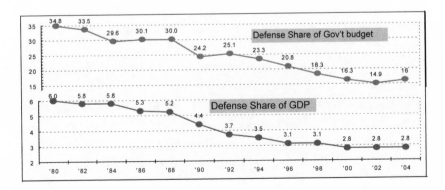

Source: ROK Ministry of National Defense

FIGURE 14:
COMPARISON OF DEFENSE BUDGETS, MAJOR COUNTRIES

DEFENSE SHARE OF GDP (%)	PER CAPITAL DEFENSE BURDEN ($)
Israel 9.7(10th)	**Israel** 1,499(3rd)
Russia 4.8(26th)	**Russia** 333(25th)
China 4.1(31st)	**China** 37(91st)
U.S. 3.3(48th)	**U.S.** 1,138(4th)
Japan 1.0(137th)	**Japan** 290(28th)
Korea 2.8(59th)	**Korea** 266(29th)

DEFENSE SPENDING ON EACH TROOP ($)

Israel 58,929(26th)
Russia 52,862(28th)
China 22,667(53rd)
U.S. 244,219(1st)
Japan 164,583(6th)
Korea 18,986(62nd)

Note: Figures in parenthesis show the world's ranking.
Sources: The Military Balance 2003–2004 and ROK Ministry of National Defense: www.mnd.go.kr

Bruce Bennett of the Rand Institute commented on the contradictions between stated policy and actual military-related implementations in the ROK at a conference held during 2004 in Seoul, remarking that South Korea needs to improve its military equipment, and that the United States does not understand why Korea is shortening its military service period and reducing its troop strength while at the same time telling the United States that American forces in Korea should not leave the country.[81]

A key example of this in the ROK military today is the current C4I structure. The structure remains almost unchanged from a structure that has existed since the 1950s, where quite literally the movement of forces consists of an ROK four-star general picking up the phone and calling an ROK three-star general to tell him where to put a division on the line. Upgrading the ROK C4I structure (and the costs associated with it) has been an important item of discussion between ROK and U.S. defense officials, and to date, the issue remains unresolved.[82]

Sweeping Military Reforms in South Korea

During 2005, the South Korean military announced a massive military reform plan. By 2020 the plan calls for reducing active military personnel from 680,000 to 500,000. The army will take the biggest cut in personnel, reducing divisions from forty-seven to about twenty.[83] Ground and air capability will be increased, and the plan is to cost at least $623 trillion won (Roughly $640 billion at the 2006 monetary exchange rates) by its completion in 2020.[84] The Ministry of Defense will increase capability by procuring $195 billion in new arms. The nation's budget is set to increase by 11 percent annually starting from 2006. Much of the modernization and transformation will occur in the army, as the plan is to expand the operational boundaries of a combat unit from 30 kilometers to 100 kilometers. Next-generation unmanned spy aircraft, armored vehicles, attack helicopters, and self-propelled artillery are scheduled to be deployed. The navy plans to have next-generation submarines, and the air force plans to reduce its number of fighter jets from 500 to 420, but upgrade their capabilities. Next-generation aircraft will include F-15Ks, airborne early warning systems, and airborne tankers.[85] The army's overhaul of its headquarters for greater efficiency began in April 2006.[86] Furthermore, Minister Yoon Kwang-ung announced that the new Defense Ministry would consist of four headquarters with fifteen subordinate departments, with an increase in the number of civilians working for the military from 23,000 to 30,000. Reportedly, military officers in South Korea are worried that without securing the necessary funds to upgrade combat capability (which has to be approved through the National Assembly), the hasty reduction in troop levels could jeopardize the security of South Korea in the face of the North Korean threat.[87]

Two key problems with the new military reforms are finance and transformation. South Korea's biggest obstacle appears to be its budget.[88] Its announced goal of "self-reliant defense" means an "independent capability" that will rely less on support from the United States.[89] However, independent capability probably is not achievable until at least 2015, which is the date that the Roh administration set for achieving a budget of 3 percent of South Korea's GDP.[90] How can the South Korean government actually pay for this? There are currently no bills pending (nor, by South Korean law is this even possible) that will guarantee a stable obtainment of budgets year by year necessary for national defense reforms through a smooth cooperation with governmental agencies and that stipulate specific measures for securing budgets. In other words, there is no guarantee that the budget will not change significantly from year to year or from president to president, between now and 2020.[91]

Another important issue for the South Korean military is transformation—a complicated and difficult issue for Seoul. For example, the South Korean army has been specifically equipped and deployed since 1953 to engage in complementary missions with the U.S. military on the Peninsula. Thus, to truly transform, the ROK military must assume certain important missions, and adapt its capabilities to reach the level currently held by U.S. forces that have conducted these missions. Specifically, the ROK military must transform and upgrade drastically in two very important missions, airpower and C4I (command, control, communications, computers, and intelligence). Otherwise, the large, highly equipped South Korean military will be just like a big powerful football linebacker "without a head"—lots of power, but no ability to direct or support it.

Current C4I changes and initiatives are minor and do not provide an advanced "sensor to shooter" capability. The completion and "test-bed" deployment of South Korea's "advanced digital network" to the Fifth Army Corps during the summer of 2006 is an example. There is no evidence that the system is truly operational, and it is not hooked into national systems—which South Korea does not possess.[92] The launch of "Koreasat 5" (also dubbed "Mugunghwa 5"), South Korea's first combined civil and military communications satellite, falls into the same category—and it will take significant upgrades to provide large-scale C4I capability.[93] Additionally, South Korea is almost completely dependent on the United States for strategic and tactical battlefield information, with currently no plans to significantly upgrade systems or sensors that will give the South Korean military enhanced independent capabilities.[94] Modern C4I is not just about gaining greater communications across the spectrum, but consists of gaining greater sensor to shooter capability and "information dominance." This modern C4I capability (information dominance) is what the United States brings to Combined Forces Command (CFC) and is the key capability that has allowed quick military forces deployment into combat with a flexibility its enemies have been unable to counter in force-on-force conflicts.[95] Current initiatives underway in the ROK military have not addressed this capability completely, and in fact are really just about an advanced spread of C3 (Command and Control Communications)—not information dominance.[96]

Regarding airpower, the South Koreans' purchases of advanced aircraft do not match the capability that U.S. airpower currently gives them. For example, Seoul is only purchasing forty F-15Ks, an aircraft that will give them specific capabilities to take the fight to the North during a force-on-force conflict.[97] Seoul has projected a purchase of twenty more F-15Ks beginning in 2009.[98] The F-15K is a very expensive aircraft, and Seoul's limited purchasing power is only one example of how the ROK air force is lacking (and likely to continue to be lacking) in vital airpower capabilities. Additionally, the South Korean army has seven special-forces brigades for airborne operations (para-dropping and air resupply), plus five independent brigades (two infantry and three counter-infiltration), along with other airborne assets—all of which would need to be airlifted during a conflict. To carry this huge force, the ROK air force transport fleet barely has twenty-five aircraft—ten C-130Hs and fifteen Spanish designed, twin-engine CN-235Ms, an inventory that is sadly lacking in the mission it would be expected to carry out.[99] To date, in planning and in exercises, the South Koreans have relied on the U.S. airlift capability to transport the majority of their airborne troops. To upgrade its own airlift capability will involve a huge investment in aircraft purchases, infrastructure upgrades, maintenance, and training of personnel.

There are other important examples of shortfalls that are important to address if Seoul is serious about building a self-reliant national defense. The ROK Marine Corps is arguably the finest amphibious landing force in East Asia. The training, discipline, and leadership of the ROK Marine Corps is beyond reproach. But a Marine Corps is only as effective as its amphibious lift (specially equipped ships and craft that carry the troops to the fight and provide command and control for these forces as they phase across the beach). Currently, the ROK Navy is completely incapable of providing its Marine Corps the lift necessary to conduct large-scale amphibious operations. This is another example where the capabilities of the United States have been factored in (U.S. Navy ships and the associated command and control) and planned for throughout the history of the alliance. Seoul has built one "LPX" class amphibious assault ship, and construction on three more is expected by 2013—but this and the other smaller craft that the ROK Navy has will still be lacking in the capability to lift all of the landing troops and their associated equipment, and providing the highly important, associated command and control, of the ROK Marine Corps should a large-scale confrontation requiring their services occur.[100]

Yet another striking example of a key gap in South Korea's "independent military capability" becomes obvious if one looks back at North Korea's long-range and short-range missile tests conducted in July 2006. Currently South Korea's military has no indigenous capability for missile defense. The government may purchase some older versions of the Patriot system known as the "PAC-2," but these systems are likely to be ineffective against the more than 500 Scuds that North Korea has pointed at nearly every important node in the South.[101] In fact, the only effective missile defense on the Korean Peninsula remains the PAC-3 Patriot systems manned, maintained, and operated by U.S. Army personnel. USFK deploys a total of sixty-four Patriot (advanced PAC-3 systems) at bases in several locations in South Korea.[102]

One of the most recent examples of shortfalls that occur as missions are handed over from U.S. forces to the forces of South Korea occurred in 2005. As discussed in a previous chapter, North Korea has now moved a large number of long-range artillery systems close enough to the DMZ where they can virtually threaten all of Seoul and many areas of Kyongi Province (the northern-most province in South Korea, and also the area where the largest concentration of South Korean ground forces are located) on a moments notice—with little warning time to U.S. and South Korean forces. Until recently, the ground-based mission of providing counter-fire to this long-range artillery fell to the 2nd U.S. Infantry Division, which operated thirty multiple rocket launcher systems and thirty M109A6 Paladin self-propelled howitzers. In April 2005, as part of the ongoing shift of defense responsibilities on the Korean Peninsula between South Korean and U.S. forces, it was announced that the responsibilities for this mission would shift to the South Korean army, the success of which depends on integration of the South Korean units in the combined ROK–U.S. C4I system on the Peninsula.[103] Unfortunately, one of the key concerns for the U.S. regarding the current state of readiness for South Korean forces on the Peninsula, has been the unwillingness of Seoul to spend the money to upgrade its own C4I infrastructure—or to help with the costs of the current structure.[104] Integration of these newly assigned units into a modern C4I system is vital, because of what the quick reaction time will have to be in grasping the location of North Korean artillery units with radar and destroying them in case the systems have just been fired or are about to be fired.[105] To date, this integration has not occurred and the South Korean army has not provided an indigenous capability that would replace the systems used previously by U.S. forces. The military reforms that the South Korean government has planned for the next several years will be important to the security of the Korean Peninsula. While it is important for the South Korean government to undertake these reforms, to date the government has not addressed many shortfalls that would leave the military vulnerable during a full-scale war. I have only addressed some of the larger issues—but there are most certainly many more. The two overarching challenges of finance and properly initiated transformation are likely to continue to plague Seoul as the military reform continues in coming years.

A Changing Alliance: Wartime Operational Control

The issue that has challenged the alliance since early 2004 is the debate over wartime operational control. The current South Korean constitution states that the president can send his military to war, but he must receive approval from the National Assembly to send troops overseas.[106] If there is a change in wartime operational control (OPCON), the South Korean president will be the sole National Command Authority (NCA) for ROK forces in the case of war with North Korea. Under an agreement signed in 1994, South Korea has peacetime control over all of its armed forces. Only during wartime do *designated ROK forces* chop to the Commander of CFC. As it stands right now, when agreed upon DEFCON conditions have been met, CFC assumes wartime command of all U.S. forces and all South Korean forces who have chopped to CFC.[107] In essence this means that the ROK president, presumably with the advice of the minister of national defense and ROK chairman of Joint Chiefs of Staff, instructs the minister and chairman to chop whatever forces necessary (or previously agreed upon) to CFC. The nature of the crisis would be the key determinant as to when and what ROK units would be chopped to CFC. The same process is generally true for the U.S. side, though technically different, and would presumably involve PACOM. If the crisis is war, combined planning would provide a bilateral understanding as to what ROK and U.S. forces are expected to be apportioned to CFC.

During wartime OPCON the Commander of CFC works for two NCAs: the president of South Korea and the president of the United States, *not* only for the president of the United States. Although the commander of CFC is a U.S. general, there is an ROK–U.S. Military Committee co-chaired by the chairmen of the Joint Chiefs of Staffs, all of which exists under a "dual command system" under the strategic guidance of the presidents and ministers of defense (U.S. Secretary of Defense) of both countries.[108] The commander of CFC carries out decisions based on this strategic guidance passed from the two national authorities through the Military Committee, then uses these decisions to issue operational orders to the combined force. Thus, while designated ROK forces come under the command of CFC during wartime, they do not come under the direct command of the NCA of the United States. They come under a dual-headed NCA.

In December 2005, high-level officials from South Korea and the United States agreed to establish a task force to facilitate discussions on the transfer of wartime command of Seoul's armed forces from the U.S. to South Korea.[109] In January 2006, President Roh called for a change in command relationships between the two militaries so that South Korea could take back wartime OPCON of its forces.[110] He further clarified the actions that he has levied on the ROK Ministry of National Defense in March 2006, during a speech given to the 62nd graduating class of the Korean Military Academy where he stated,

> Through regular meetings with the U.S. and the Security Policy Initiative, we will draw up a road map for regaining operational control in wartime, which includes exact timeframes and precise procedures, and will report on this at the ROK–U.S. Security Consultative Meeting which is scheduled for October [2006].[111]

Action on the task force was formalized in late March 2006, when South Korea and the United States signed an accord to form a joint panel to study a roadmap for South Korea regaining sole operational control of its armed forces during wartime. According to a press release by the South Korean Joint Chiefs of Staff, General Lee Sang-hee, Chief of the South Korean JCS, and Gen. B. B. Bell, commander of USFK, signed a document titled, "Terms of Reference Governing the ROK–U.S. Command Relationships Study and Report." The "Combined Working Group" agreed to discuss ways of presenting detailed measures for the transfer of wartime command and the change in command arrangements.[112]

U.S. Secretary of Defense Donald Rumsfeld reaffirmed Washington's intentions regarding Wartime OPCON in March 2006 when he stated that the United States intends to turn over wartime command of South Korean forces to Seoul, but he did not provide a timetable. He commented that the timing would depend on how quickly South Korea could build the capability to assume the responsibility and further commented that a greater South Korean role would allow further troop reductions on the Peninsula.[113] When asked whether he thought the change in command structure could start this year (2006), Rumsfeld replied: "No, no, I don't at all." Rumsfeld further commented, "The South Korean government has raised the question as to when might it be appropriate to transfer responsibility to the Korean command, and that is something that gets discussed."[114]

In late August 2006, the United States Department of Defense apparently made a decision to conduct a deliberate policy shift regarding Wartime OPCON. Based on the previous statements, Secretary Rumsfeld had been following what appeared to be a policy of turning over Wartime OPCON on a "capabilities-based agenda," in other words, disbanding CFC and forming two separate wartime military commands when the South Korean military had achieved all of the capabilities necessary to independently conduct wartime operations in a war with North Korea. On August 27, 2006, the South Korean Defense Ministry announced that Rumsfeld had sent a formal letter indicating Washington's intention to turn over Wartime OPCON by 2009.[115] This formal announcement indicated a significant policy shift from a "capabilities-based" end of CFC to a "timeline-based" end to CFC. In an even more startling turn of events, Secretary Rumsfeld was quoted in the press as saying that North Korea is not an immediate military threat to South Korea. He remarked in part, "I don't see them, frankly, as an immediate military threat to South Korea."[116] While his remarks may have been taken out of context, they created quite a stir in South Korea, especially because of many earlier conflicting comments on the same issue made by Rumsfeld and because the comments tended to contradict Congressional testimony by USFK commanders (the latest of which was just a month before the Rumsfeld statement).[117] According to a Korean source who was reportedly quoting a U.S. official, in recent bilateral discussions it was obvious that South Korea would not realistically be ready to exercise independent OPCON from CFC by 2012, but since the deadline was politically motivated anyway, there was no reason for Washington to cling to military logic either. Another official reportedly denied that it was this simplistic, but did say that, "Outside of the negotiations, crossing the i's and dotting the t's of what the U.S. said, it does seem to be true that they're getting fed up."[118]

Roh has stated on several occasions that this is a matter of "sovereignty," as his goal is for the South Korean military to become a "self-reliant" force with "independent capability."[119] But does this "call for sovereignty" really make sense? It is important to note that NATO too confers operational control to the NATO commander (a U.S. general), but NATO countries such as the United Kingdom,

Germany, and Italy, have never called for a retrieval of their national sovereignty. During the summer of 2006 Roh stated that Korea was the only country worldwide without wartime operational control. In response to this remark, an anonymous source in Washington deeply involved in CFC operations stated,

> I am not sure whether the remark was intentional or was due to different interpretation or a lack of understanding. . . . Overall, approximately 85% of Korean troops are assigned to the Korea–U.S. combined forces during wartime, but only on the premise that the Korean President and the Joint Chiefs of Staff do not oppose it.[120]

A transfer of Wartime OPCON means that the whole process that has existed since the genesis of the Alliance will cease to exist. To be sure, most conservative lawmakers in the National Assembly, and many in the South Korean public, are opposed to Roh's initiative. As Representative Song Young-sun of the conservative Grand National Party has said during a National Assembly session in 2006, "It is unreasonable to begin full-scale discussions on the issue at a time when South Korea is still dependent on the United States for intelligence and military equipment to deal with North Korea."[121] Indeed, South Korean military officers (though those on active-duty are obviously hesitant to speak publicly) appear to be greatly concerned about the move as well. One reserve officer was recently quoted as saying, "The higher an officer becomes, the more he realizes the power of the U.S. army through CFC training, and understands the importance of the combined forces system of command." Another ROK officer, recently discharged, who had served in CFC stated in part, "The thought that a few high-tech weapons will make a self-reliant national defense is strategically and tactically an illusion."[122]

Conservative lawmakers in South Korea are not the only ones who have questioned this policy move. In June 2006, former Defense Minister and Uri Party lawmaker Cho Seong-tae questioned then Defense Minister Yoon Kwang-ung regarding the readiness of Seoul's military to take over wartime control of its armed forces, asking,

> "Are you confident of retrieving wartime operational control in five to six years? Do we have satellites, early warning systems, and Aegis systems to intercept missiles in mid-flight?"

Yoon responded, "We judge that in about five years we should be able to get ready somehow to achieve that objective."

Cho remarked (in reference to Yoon's statement), "When the President says its possible to regain control within five years, the minister should say it's not a good idea, even at the risk of his ministerial post."[123]

It seems a fait accompli that Wartime OPCON will change. As this occurs, it will likely also eventually mean the end of CFC. In fact this was confirmed to the South Korean National Assembly by Defense Minister Yoon Kwang-ung in August 2006. Yoon's plan involves a roadmap where all concrete plans would be completed by 2011 and CFC would dissolve during 2012—dates that of course conflict with the 2009 timeframe articulated earlier by the U.S. Secretary of Defense.[124] One option, however, would have been to make CFC a Combined Planning Headquarters. At this headquarters, a combined planning staff could write plans and missions for incorporating USFK into the next war. This seems to be practical, but it is unlikely to happen. According to defense experts the most likely option under the new roadmap would be transforming the CFC structure into one based on the Japan–U.S. model. In Japan, U.S. and Japanese troops maintain OPCON of their own troops in peacetime but set up an ad hoc body to deal with joint and combined military operations in case of an emergency (the term "joint" refers to interservice cooperation, while the term "combined" refers to intercountry military cooperation).[125] Government sources in Seoul have said that part of this plan will be to give its military an independent operational center to run an autonomous command that coordinates its troops in a joint or combined operation.[126]

According to press sources in Korea, when the CFC is dissolved, the plan is to shift the U.S. and ROK forces to separate commands. To maintain a "close, cooperative" system, a new center, the "Military Cooperation Center," will be created. This center would essentially become a liaison office and may oversee about ten offices, each staffed equally with Korean and American officers. If the center comes to fruition, it will come under the joint control of two-star generals from Seoul and Washington. The center will address joint military operations during war and peace and will be designed to "be stronger" than the U.S.–Japan model (though it appears strikingly similar) according to South Korean government sources. New operational war plans would need to be constructed to meet the needs of this new command arrangement—and the old ones torn up. The United States has promised to continue to share its military intelligence systems with South Korea even after this separated command and control system is initiated.[127] Gen. B. B. Bell, commander of USFK/CFC/UNC, has been supportive of U.S. forces remaining flexible and providing support to their Korean allies—no matter what the end state of negotiations are. General Bell brought up some questions that must be addressed as the forces on the Peninsula transition:

> First in exercising independent command, what will the ROK government's strategic aims be during a war; and what will the ROK government's desired war end state be? What will be the appropriate U.S. military contributions, given a review of the ROK strategic war aims and end state goals? Next, how will independent command by the ROK of its forces in wartime impact on U.S. consideration for appropriate ground force contributions? Also, how will this new arrangement affect the role of the UN Command, and maintenance of the Armistice agreement? What changes will be required?[128]

While an arrangement similar to the Japanese model is the one many experts think is the most likely to be initiated, another option that could have been considered was to put a South Korean four-star general in charge of CFC with a U.S. three-star deputy. Under this option, the U.S. could keep a four-star in country and that flag-rank officer would remain in command of UN Command (one of the hats of the commander of CFC as of 2007). Of course, this proposal would be as politically volatile in the United States as it would be in South Korea, as it would appear to put U.S. forces under ROK OPCON. Such an option would only work if the ROK four-star general had the same combined staff, resources, and political clout that currently exists within the CFC infrastructure—but again this would be an extremely politically volatile option to initiate. While this option would not work (largely owing to public perception in both countries), a "reinforcement" or expanded role for the UN Command is one that could be significant as new command arrangements fall into place. In fact, in June 2006, the U.S. Senate armed services committee asked the U.S. administration to review possible expansion of the UN forces in Korea. The committee also asked for "discussion of whether and how UN Command members might be persuaded to deploy military forces in peacetime to the ROK to bolster the deterrence mission of the United Nations Command." The role of UN Command, how and when South Korea will participate in it (including the delegation of appropriate armistice authorities and responsibilities), and command arrangements are all likely to be continuing issues.[129]

There are many problems with a parallel arrangement in South Korea largely based on a model of what currently exists in Japan. This would mean many problems relating to command and control of what should be dominate forces in wartime—and could lead to much higher casualties than would be expected if ROK and U.S. forces came under one commander during a contingency. This view is supported by a report from the South Korean National Assembly's National Intelligence Committee (NAIC). According to the NAIC report, which was made public on January 25, 2006:

> The issue of transferring wartime operational control to Korea should not be approached from the hardware view of fostering Korea's own military deterrence against North Korea [further pointing out regarding the C4I]: The Korean army should first improve its capability to collect information, and other deterrence strategies.[130]

According to the Ministry of National Defense White Paper released in 2005, the United States will bring as many as 690,000 forces into the Peninsula (recent reporting suggests that this number will be scaled back somewhat) to help South Korea fight the North in a full-scale war.[131] In such a scenario, huge numbers of military forces would operate in an extremely confined battle space. Does Seoul truly want separate chains of command for so many forces? As Brookings Institution national security analyst Michael O'Hanlon noted, "When all is said and done, the new proposed policy strikes me as a mistake. I would argue against dividing commands sharing a common, constrained, small battlespace."[132] Finally, having an ad hoc group that will determine combined operations on the fly will be much different in Korea than in Japan. Japan does not have an enemy immediately to the North that could attack on a moment's notice. Thus, having an ad hoc body determine operations could result in much higher casualties (military and civilian) than if these operations were determined under one combined command—especially in the early stages of any large-scale war. As Scott Snyder of the Asia Foundation has stated, "Such arrangements are sufficient to support war-fighting capabilities but not to actually fight a war."[133]

In June 2006 an ROK military official disclosed that his government planned to propose an arrangement where, "The nation's armed forces (South Korea) control combined ground troops and the USFK controls or assists maritime and aerial forces."[134] Since the preponderance of ground forces on-Peninsula is composed of ROK units, this seems to be the easiest effort to transfer command and control functions—and in fact is a real possibility after the demise of CFC.[135] South Korean officials stated at a meeting in Singapore during the same period that South Korea hopes to begin a gradual transfer of "wartime operational control" to the ROK military in about 2012. Final decisions regarding bilateral security issues—including transfer of "wartime command" (in actuality an end to the dual-command structure that has existed since 1953) were expected at the annual ROK–U.S. Security Consultative Meeting (SCM) in October 2006—when proposals from the individuals drawing up the "roadmap" from both nations were to be presented.[136]

As events transpired and Defense Minister Yoon held more press conferences, more confusion regarding what the South Korean government was asking for came to light. Yoon's comments suggested that the reports may be incorrect in regard to a division of operational control and an end to CFC as part of the ROK proposal. In addition, Yoon stated that South Korean troop readiness would partly dictate timing (an issue the United States has brought up in the past but one that now appears to have been largely dismissed—perhaps for political, not national security reasons), and Yoon reminded reporters that U.S. forces would counter any threat from North Korea jointly with Korea's military.[137] The defense minister stressed a rather confusing point: that the ROK military will play the leading role on the Korean Peninsula after retaking "wartime operational control" of its forces from the United States and further commented that Seoul and Washington had general agreements on the return of the "wartime command," and would map out a basic master plan later (again referring to the SCM in October 2006).[138]

In June 2006 an ROK military source disclosed that an ROK JCS document called "Joint Military Strategy" announced plans to scrap CFC by 2012. Following the demise of CFC a strengthened role for UN Command under a U.S. commander has reportedly been discussed, or a new formula where each ally commands its own troops.[139] These discussions and the ROK JCS document seem to contradict statements made by Yoon. The transfer of wartime OPCON from CFC to two separate, independent military commands based on a short-term political time frame instead of capabilities of the South Korean military is a move that has also been widely criticized by the majority of retired generals and Defense Ministers in South Korea. In August 2006, sixteen former defense ministers and nine retired generals expressed dismay and fear for Seoul's national security concerns that President Roh and Defense Minister Yoon responded to with open contempt.[140] Perhaps as significantly, on September 4, 2006, as many as 50,000 members of about 200 groups—including the Korean Veterans Association— braved sweltering heat to stage a massive protest in front of Seoul City Hall against Roh's controversial policy.[141]

Hwang Jin-ha, a retired ROK army general and the 2006 chair of the International Relations committee of the GNP and a sitting member of the South Korean National Assembly, articulated the dismantlement of CFC and the change of Wartime OPCON as being dangerous in the following terms:

> First, the security situation on the Korean Peninsula is more fragile than ever. . . . Second, a transfer might encourage North Korea to step up its rogue tactics. . . . Third, the concept of "independent cooperation" is no longer applicable in 21st-century wars. All the militaries of the world are cooperating and delegating commands and responsibilities to each other. This is seen clearly in the North Atlantic Treaty Organization. Operations of the NATO Allied Command are controlled by the commander of the U.S.–European Command.

General Hwang also remarked that the bilateral relationship that exists between the U.S. and Japan has at least unofficially been a partial template for future ROK–U.S. military cooperation, stating in part, "The U.S. and Japan have two separate commands, but this is because Japan's constitution prohibits its Self-Defense forces from being part of any combined war operations."[142]

At the 38th Security Consultative Meeting, the United States and South Korea agreed to an ambiguous date for the dissolution of CFC. Seoul desired a date of 2012 and Washington requested a date of 2009. After the meeting, the two sides agreed that Seoul will have full Wartime OPCON of its troops separately from the United States sometime between October 15, 2009, and March 15, 2012.[143] A joint communiqué issued following the meeting stated:

The ROK and the U.S. are making progress both in pending issues concerning realignment of U.S forces on the Korean Peninsula and in the joint studies on the development of the future ROK–U.S. Alliance. Both sides agreed to continue and to enhance the SPI consultations in 2007 based on the accomplishments of the past two years.[144]

Following Rumsfeld's resignation on February 23, 2007, new U.S. Defense Secretary Robert Gates and Minister Yoon's replacement, Kim Chang-soo, signed a formal agreement to dissolve CFC on April 17, 2012—three years later than Rumsfeld had proposed in 2006.[145] Predictably, this deadline for the end of CFC was criticized by the Korea Retired Generals and Admirals Association.[146]

Conclusions

As CFC changes and the two militaries go into two parallel structures, will there be a combined planning staff, and what model will it be based on? This is a big question that will have to be answered, as CFC in its current structure is designed to support South Korea—not the United States. Any independent structure that evolves for the ROK military will be required to contain all of the same capabilities currently being provided by the United States. In addition, fluid, transparent access to U.S. C4I and national level assets will go away because the two military structures would now no longer be seamless and integrated. This is of particular concern at the highest levels because currently South Korean generals do not have the opportunity to train in equivalent large-scale independent force-on-force operations as their counterparts in the U.S. military, who routinely train at facilities like the U.S. Army's National Training Center at Fort Irwin.[147]

It is very unlikely that the U.S. Congress will allow American troops to come under the permanent wartime command of a military force that is clearly lacking in the basic capabilities, infrastructure, and command and control to lead a large, combined military force. No ROK command structure will lead U.S. forces (at least not in reality). Once CFC is dismantled, a radical change to the structure of USFK will lead to a massive and expensive reorganization. The end of the CFC will also in many ways mean the end of large-scale combined operations and training in what has been called the strongest and most successful alliance in the world.[148] As a movement to two parallel structures and systems occurs, it will likely evolve into a structure similar to the one between Japan and the United States. As this happens, it is possible that as in Japan, the commander of USFK would be downgraded from a four-star to a three-star general. This would also mean that a movement of U.S. military decision making in the alliance would move from Seoul to Pacific Command (PACOM) in Hawaii. In addition, PACOM would be likely to control (much more so than in the current CFC structure) all assets, tasking, and C4I. Certain vital U.S information dominance capabilities would be likely to disappear from the Peninsula. The result in the short term (until the South Korean military can match the U.S. capability—if they are able to do so and if the financial picture allows it) is that South Korea would become more vulnerable to attack from the North.

The policy of self-reliant national defense may be a legitimate goal, but to truly begin the process a self-reliant military must first have its own trained and equipped war fighting command with its own war plans. And of key concern, it is impossible to have a competent, capable war fighting command without a modern C4I system.

Furthermore, because of a reduced conscription pool during 2010–2015, to achieve self-reliant defense, the ROK military must modernize forces that have *Peninsular Operational Flexibility*, not unlike the Strategic Flexibility for which the American military is striving. To achieve this flexibility, the ROK military would need to establish a well-equipped and trained war fighting command; modernize its C4I systems; establish Intelligence, Surveillance, and Reconnaissance (ISR) capabilities at modern levels; and write and exercise its own war plans. These are serious and costly undertakings, but as discussed before, the ROK government has the funds to take on these extremely complicated and expensive tasks in their large holdings of foreign reserves. Even if implementation of all of these recommendations started immediately, the process would be likely to take up to ten years. Hopefully it is clear from the evidence in this chapter that a transition—especially a premature transition—from CFC to two separate independent military commands is a less than optimum way to prepare forces for war. Nevertheless, as long as the two governments and militaries remain flexible, the main goal of defending South Korea from an attack by North Korea will remain intact. This will be very important in coming years as during the transition period South Korea will be vulnerable to belligerent behavior from the North.

CIVIL-MILITARY RELATIONS IN THE ROK: THE IMPACT ON NORTH–SOUTH RELATIONS AND THE ROK–U.S. ALLIANCE[1]

9

CIVIL-MILITARY RELATIONS IN SOUTH KOREA has been a topic of discussion, particularly since the spring of 2003, among many in policy and academic circles, both in the Republic of Korea, and among key allies—particularly the United States. Thus, the focus of the analysis in this chapter is on the events that occurred during 2003–2005 (this is when events occurred that have led to the greatest change in the ROK Civil-Military relationship and the ROK–U.S. Alliance). In order to understand the challenges and problems that have been inherent in the Civil-Military relationship in South Korea since 2003, one must first address the unique and rather unprecedented leadership style of Roh Moo-hyun—and the historical reasons behind the policy moves he has made. It is also important to understand the strengths and weaknesses that he brought to the Presidency. Roh's decision-making process has been radically different than any of those who have previously served in the Blue House.

An analysis of this unique decision-making process and how it has altered the way policy is made (particularly foreign policy and its impact on the current civil-military relationship and the ROK–U.S. Alliance) is made in this chapter. Other important factors in the current Civil-Military relationship include the vision of the National Security Council and its de facto leader until 2006, Lee Jong-seok, the future of military reform, and current signs of Roh's vision to severely alter the status of the current Civil-Military relationship. Finally, Roh's policies relating to the South Korean military have created challenges for the ROK–U.S. Alliance.

The Historical Impact of Civil-Military Relations on the Roh Administration

In past administrations, including the administration of Roh's predecessor Kim Dae-jung, the military has enjoyed a very important role, not only in foreign policy decision making (particularly as it relates to the ROK–U.S. Alliance), but often in domestic policy making and internal politics as well. While the internal political role of the military has been severely downplayed in South Korea since the democratically elected government of Roh Tae-woo came into power in 1988 (and in fact became progressively less important in domestic politics with each new President), many of the memories of the abuses of the military on the ROK populace (most of them made in the name of national security), particularly during the 1980s, remain strong in the minds of those who are now key players in the Roh administration—and are likely in the consciousness of Roh himself.[2]

The key advisors surrounding Roh were very strongly influenced by the events of the 1980s, and in fact speak of these events often today. This in turn has had a strong impact on the Roh policies of dealing with both the ROK military, and Seoul's key ally the United States. Many of these key advisors who helped Roh get elected, and continue to serve in important positions within the ROK government, are known as the "386 Generation" faction. They are now well known in South Korea as individuals who "faced down" South Korea's military rulers at the time, often did hard time in prison for their student and labor activism, and spoke out against the corruption as they saw it, in big business and government in South Korea. The "386 Generation" faction is also noted for being vehement in insisting on a new tone of tolerance for North Korea, and for being at the head of a surge of anti-Americanism in South Korea that reached its zenith with the election of Roh as President in late 2002.[3]

It is important to note the impact of the events of the 1980s on the individuals who have wielded power in the Roh administration (particularly as they impact on civil-military relations and foreign policy), because these events continue to influence the mentality and decision-making process of the ROK government. The icon event of the pre-democratic governments in Seoul is now considered to be the "Kwangju Uprising," an event where ROK Special Forces killed several hundred civilians in Kwangju in putting down a riot, and in the process created a controversy that rages to this day. On May 18, 2005, President Roh spoke of the impact of the Kwangju Uprising on the mindset of his administration saying, "A civil society, which made remarkable progress after the democratic uprising in the 1980s should now improve Korea's level of agreement procedure through creative participation that yields an alternative plan . . . a civil society has now emerged as a principal player in leading national affairs."[4] Such statements suggest Roh feels his is the first administration to seriously address a radically altered role for the military within South Korean society—an argument many would disagree with. In fact, as is often the case following a Roh speech, one of his aides chose to comment to the press, saying,

> The society which Mr. Roh referred to includes civic groups, the press, the opposition parties and local governments. I think Mr. Roh through his remarks suggested that he is now facing difficulties from opponents while he tries to promote diverse policies.[5]

While the Kwangju Uprising was a tragic event in the history of the ROK, tying the event to the foreign policy of the United States is also a tragic mistake. One of the key pillars of the anti-Americanism that is so paramount in the thinking of the leaders of the "386 Generation" faction of the South Korean government is the assertion that the United States knew of the planning for the violent suppression of the riots in Kwangju, and in fact encouraged the South Korean government to take the steps that they did to quell the riots.[6] This will probably remain a subject of great dispute for many years, despite the fact that several key policy makers from that time period have spoken out saying that the United States was completely unaware the South Korean military planned to carry out the violent event—and in fact found out only as it was happening, receiving all of the facts several days later.

There has been a great deal of evidence released to the public that strongly suggests the United States had nothing to do with the suppression of the Kwangju Uprising. Former Ambassador to Korea James Lilley has stated that, "In the case of Kwangju, the Combined Forces Command arrangement made for confusion about American military relations with the ROK, as has been shown in many analyses of events at the time. In 1987, on the other hand, during the democracy demonstrations that brought forth Roh Tae-woo's "June 29th Declaration," there was a steady effort by civilians in the U.S. Government to prevent the use of force."[7] The commander in chief of United States Forces Korea at the time, Gen. John Wickham, specifically stated that neither he nor any of his staff had any idea that ROK forces would be used in the violent suppression of the riots in Kwangju, nor was he informed until it was far too late to do anything about it.[8] Nevertheless, the Kwangju Uprising remains the largest single event in pre-democratized Korea in the minds of most of those in the "386 Genera-tion" faction of Roh's government, and most continue to interpret it as an inci-dent that was encouraged by the United States.

The continuing impact of events that occurred in the 1980s prior to Korean democratization is evident from more recent activities taken by the Roh admin-istration and those in the Uri Party (his de facto supporting political party for most of his presidency). A member of the National Assembly, Lee Kwang-Jae of the Uri party, recently disclosed that he "cut off his finger and wrote a letter of resolve in blood so as not to betray his colleagues in student movements in the 1980s."[9] While this example is rather extreme, it points to the background and anti-military attitude (often complemented by an anti-American attitude) that has existed among many of those in power in the Roh administration and the Uri Party that supported it. Another recent and important event involved the forced resignation of Vice Defense Minister Yoo Hyo-il during 2005. Civic groups in Korea had created an outcry for his unsuitability to remain in office because of his alleged involvement in suppressing the Kwangju Uprising. Despite the fact that the government had argued that at the time his role was minimal, rumors that Yoo had also been involved in an "ideological cleansing" program where students were violently abused eventually forced him to resign.[10]

Finally, the role of the "Truth Committee," a fact-finding committee of citi-zens led by the Rev. Oh Choong-il, in implementing recent reactions to past wrongful events was crucial during 2005. The committee thus far has focused on seven suspicious incidents initiated by the NIS (formerly the KCIA) in which human rights of Korean citizens were severely violated.[11] Many of the incidents occurred during the Park Chung-hee presidency, and it is unclear if the outcry by the left was initiated in order to embarrass his daughter—the leader of the opposition GNP Party during 2005—but to date the investigation is ongoing.[12] Among the most gruesome of the seven incidents was the trial and subsequent execution of seven members of the Peoples Revolutionary Party, based on charges of treason from evidence obtained by then KCIA Director Kim Hyung-wook.[13]

It is clear that the Roh Presidency and those within its power infrastructure has been strongly influenced by the events that occurred in the late 1970s and the 1980s. This was an era when South Korea was transitioning from a third world nation ruled by a military strongman to a strong, vibrant democracy. Be-cause these were the formative years for both President Roh, and many of those who have held key positions within his government, the important events that occurred during those years continue to influence the vision and the policy making of the present administration when it comes to foreign policy making and the future of the civil-military relationship. It is also important to understand the inner workings of the Roh government, and the strengths and weaknesses that he has brought to his presidency.

Strengths and Weaknesses that Roh Moo-hyun Brought to His Presidency

There can be no doubt that the man who came to office in 2003 brought a charismatic and forceful personality to the Blue House. He was well-known as an extremely gregarious individual, a tough infighter in politics, and a savvy politician at the local level—all strengths that he has brought to the presidency. He is also well known for being a man who lifted himself up in society, for example, by passing the bar exam without graduating from college.

Roh brought strengths to his presidency, but he has also brought weaknesses that have affected his administration's ability to govern. He had no significant leadership experience prior to assuming the presidency. He gained his reputation, in fact, through resisting the government, not through working within it. His political experience was mostly limited to labor issues, often defending labor officials against the ROK government. Perhaps even more important in an age where South Korea has become a player on the global scene, Roh's visit to Japan was the extent of his foreign experience prior to assuming the presidency, and he had never visited the United States.[14] This background had a strong influence on Roh's commitments; government reform, populism, raising the average ROK personal income to $20,000 a year (USD)—and perhaps the two most controversial issues of his presidency—less dependency on the United States for national defense, and the decentralization of the ROK government.[15]

Roh Moo-hyun's Decision-Making Process

Unlike past administrations (including that of his predecessor and political ally, Kim Dae-jung), the real power in the Blue House does not lie with Roh's cabinet officers. The result is that the whole decision-making process has become much more ad hoc. The real power in the Blue House lies with the Secretariat,

which screens info and input, and controls output. To date, most cabinet ministers have been unable to counter this power. Secretariat appointments are based
on a history of personal relationships with Roh, thus the result is that in the
decision-making process, personality is emphasized over function (see Fig. 15).

Important aspects of the Secretariat include the fact that, as discussed above,
these individuals are the President's most trusted advisors. Within the Secretariat, most individuals are older, long-term, left-of-center progressives, all
appointed based on long-term relationships, and all intensely loyal to Roh. Arguably the most important advisor to the President since he assumed office when it
comes to National Security decision making, has been former National Security
Council (NSC) vice chief (and later, Unification Minister during most of 2006),
Lee Jong-seok. As NSC vice chief, Lee had direct access past the National Security Advisor (which caused a power struggle between him and earlier NSA Na
Jong-il, who left his post to become the Ambassador to Japan as a result) to
President Roh (as well as his most trusted advisor, Moon Jae-in) and Lee's power
was facilitated by like-minded staffers in the Secretariat. Lee is also widely known
to epitomize the values of the "386 Generation."[16] See Figure 16.

FIGURE 15:
BLUE HOUSE DECISION-MAKING PROCESS

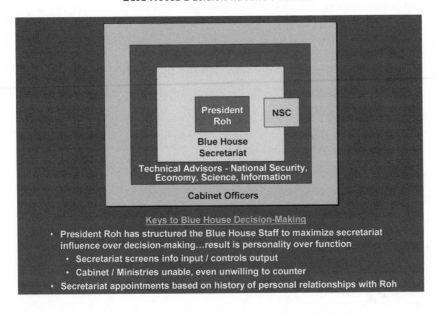

FIGURE 16:
SECRETARIAT (2005)

■ **President** ←	■ NSC Vice Chief
■ Chief of Staff	Lee Jong-seok
Kim U-si	■ Direct access past NSA
■ Policy Planning Chief	■ Facilitated by like-minded
Pak Bong-hum	staffers in Secretariat
■ Policy Planning	
Kwon O-kyu	*President's Closest*
■ Civil Affairs	*Assistants/Advisors*
Moon Jae-in	
■ Civil Society	■ Pre-386 generation, long-
Lee Gang-cheol	term progressives
■ Personnel	■ All with substantiated anti-
Kim Wan-ki	government backgrounds
■ Public Relations	■ Appointed based on long-
Yi Pyong-wan	term relationships, loyalty
	first

Regarding the subject of National Security, the cabinet members who deal with these key issues first have to deal with the Secretariat in order to get to the President. The Ministers of Foreign Affairs and Trade, Unification, National Defense, and the National Intelligence Service, all provide inputs that go from their cabinet ministries to the Blue House Staff, not Minister to President (unlike the role previously played by Lee Jong-seok—who had direct access to the President and the Secretariat and ran the agenda and tone of NSC meetings). Their appointments tend to be based on professional competence, with the probable exception of Ko Yong-goo, who was the NIS Director until resigning under a cloud of controversy (for allegedly mishandling several scandals) in June of 2005.[17] Ko is a former human rights lawyer like Roh, an acknowledged left-leaning protégé of the President, and a former activist who sought the freedom of those who ran afoul of the NIS many years ago—including the now famous Kim Nak-joong case—in which he was able to get a gentleman released from prison after being interned for 14 years by the NIS for visiting North Korea as a young man.[18] Ko was replaced in July of 2005 by former Justice Minister Kim Seung-kyu, who (just as his predecessor) had no prior experience in intelligence. Like Ko, Kim vowed to "change the negative image" of the agency.[19]

Kim resigned in October of 2006, and was reportedly at odds with both the Unification Ministry and many in the Blue House at the time—though it was more likely the underground nuclear test conducted by the North Koreans that same month truly forced his resignation.[20] See Figure 17.

The President's actual National Security Advisors, to include the Economic Policy Advisor, Foreign Policy Advisor, National Defense Advisor, and the man who held the title of National Security Advisor through 2005, Kwon Chin-ho, also appear to have been appointed based on competence and political affiliation. But their input is also screened, much like cabinet members, by the Secretariat. The notable exception during the first three years of the Roh administration was Lee Jong-seok, who though only holding the title of NSC vice chief, was involved in several power struggles with cabinet members that can be characterized as a battle of the "386 Generation" versus experience.[21] As discussed earlier, Lee had direct access to the president, and it is widely believed that the NSC, as dominated by Lee, has led the government's diplomatic and security issues and often been the "epicenter" of policy confusion. Much of the ado has been because of the fact that the forces within the government led by Lee reportedly value Korea's U.S. foreign policy on an equal standing with the United States over the ROK–U.S. Alliance.[22] See Figure 18.

FIGURE 17:
CABINET (NATIONAL SECURITY 2005)

- **President**
  - Secretariat
  - Advisors

- Minister of Foreign Service Affairs and Trade
  Pan Ki-mun

- Minister of Unification
  Chung Dong-yong

- Minister of National Defense
  Yun Kwan-ung

- Director, National Intelligence Service
  Ko Yong-goo

Appointments based on professional competence, NIS on relationship

- Access and input to President screened/ countered by Secretariat/ NSC
- Ministry inputs go from staff to Blue House staff, not minister to President

FIGURE 18:
ADVISORS (NATIONAL SECURITY 2005)

■ **President** ◄───────────	■ NSC Vice Chief Lee Jong-seok
■ Secretariat	■ Lee versus career diplomats . . . battle of 386 versus experience
■ National Security Advisor Kwon Chin-ho	■ Fighting for influence over Roh on security issues
■ National Defense Advisor Currently filled by Kwon	*President's Security Advisors*
■ Foreign Policy Advisor Jung Woo-sung	■ Pre-386 Generation, long-term progressives
■ Economic Policy Advisor Chung Jong-min	■ All with substantiated anti-government backgrounds
	■ Appointed based on long-term relationships, loyalty first

There are several key issues regarding the decision-making process in South Korea as it has existed during the Roh administration. The appointments made by Roh and the structure of the Blue House Staff have isolated functional expertise. The Secretariat has formulated policy, and the ministries have implemented it. The influence battle overall since the early part of 2003 appeared to be between "386 Generation" individuals and "progressives," versus those with significant domestic and foreign policy experience. This is also unique because media manipulation targets public opinion, and the Internet plays a key role in information input and output that it has never played before.[23] This unique, ad hoc system has embarrassed Roh on several occasions to date. The inexperience of the individuals who have wielded the real power in the administration and the rejection of past systems and styles in previous administrations has been very evident to the public at large. The system as it has been set up and managed during Roh's administration has minimized the value of the military and intelligence agencies.

Efforts to Minimize the Role of the Military: The 2004 Naval Incident

The efforts—often cheered on by the younger generation in South Korea, to minimize and "civilianize" control and effectiveness of the military are exemplified by the spring-summer 2004 incident in which both the ROK Navy and the military ended up extremely embarrassed in the eyes of the South Korean public. Because of efforts at reconciliation and the changing (again) of SOP for ROK Navy units operating along the Northern Limit Line (NLL), command and control procedures for Navy units came under heavy fire in the ROK press. The ROK Navy, which has had to deal with an increase in crossings by North Korean patrol craft, essentially now has its hands tied. The problems became public during May and June 2004 and embarrassed both the ROK military and the Blue House, eventually causing the Director of KDIA, the Minister of National Defense, and other high-ranking officers to resign—causing highly publicized bad blood between the Blue House and the military. Morale in the ROK Navy and the military was severely affected.[24]

The role of Lee Jong-seok in dealing with the military has been much more extensive than one would expect from someone in his position. The primary national security advisor on Roh's transition team in 2003, Lee was formerly an academic, who was mentored by well-known advisor Kim Dae-jung and former NIS Director Lim Dong-won. When the NSC started in 2003, it had twenty-seven action officers, by 2005 it had more than seventy—and in reality from 2003 until early 2006 when he "departed" for the Unification Ministry, they worked for Lee, not the "National Security Advisor." Since 2004, he has used his power and influence to ensure that those with a personal stake in the Roh administration are in key positions within MND. The most notable example of this is retired ROK Navy Admiral Yoon Kwan-ung, who moved into the position of Defense Minister when his predecessor resigned following the 2004 naval incident.

As a retired Navy Admiral (and the former commander of 2nd fleet, which was involved in the incident), Yoon understood during the aftermath of the naval incident, how command and control worked within the ROK Navy, and that the incident was largely unavoidable. Nevertheless, he remained silent throughout the negative coverage in the ROK press following the incident. Yoon, who is a strong, vocal supporter of Roh's policies, also went to the same high school as Lee Jong-seok, and is considered a strong ally. Yoon remained in power for a relatively long time for one who was serving in such a tumultuous government. He eventually resigned his position in October, 2006, two weeks after North Korea conducted its first underground nuclear test.[25]

During 2004, Lee Jong-seok informed high-ranking ROK MND officials that the "Main Enemy" reference (discussed earlier) to North Korea was outdated and needed to be dropped as a matter of policy. This also began to cause morale problems in the military. As articulated in an earlier chapter, as the Defense Ministry was considering the move to change the terminology, a poll taken among 1,447 army officers and soldiers revealed 84.8 percent believed that the government should in fact retain the terminology.[26]

The Vision of the National Security Council

The impact of the NSC on the policy making and foreign policy of the Roh administration is clearly much stronger than it has ever been in past presidential administrations. While Lee Jong-seok never officially held the title of "Director" of the NSC (he held the title of "Deputy Chief" and was also sometimes referred to as "Vice Chief"), he was clearly the driver behind the scenes when it came to both foreign policy and defense issues. In fact despite the fact that Lee (who is a North Korean expert) lacks expertise and experience with allied diplomacy and military issues, the evidence suggests that the heads of both the Defense and Foreign ministries often had less access to the president than he has since Roh came to office, and thus often dealt with him as they would a peer (which in fact was probably the reality).[27] This becomes obvious if one simply observes the fact that Lee took the lead on such important issues as South Korea's now highly publicized nuclear tests conducted years ago, and how this issue would be worked out with the United States and the United Nations.[28] As NSC Vice-Chief, Lee was also a key player in the sensitive and important issue of the ROK–U.S. Alliance and Strategic Flexibility.[29] Finally, Lee was frequently seen in public at fora of the highest levels, where he was often seen as a de facto peer of the ministers and Blue House staff members with whom he was seated.[30]

To understand the vision of the previous de facto leader of the NSC, one only has to turn to his writings during the pre-Roh administration. During the spring of 2000, Lee wrote, "Dismantling the Cold War structure on the peninsula will contribute to assurance of a peace regime on the peninsula, consolidating coexistence of the two Koreas, normalization of the U.S.–North Korea and Japan–North Korea relations, lifting economic sanctions against North Korea, inter-Korean economic cooperation, resolution of the North Korean missile and nuclear issues, and the establishment of a peace treaty through the four party talks."[31] These views, expressed as they were before Lee actually came to power in the government, give great insight into the reasons for the current tensions between the members of the NSC and many in the Defense and Foreign ministries.

Of course, as discussed earlier, one of the noteworthy aspects of the "386 Generation" faction of the current South Korean government is the anti-American bias that seems to be inherent in almost all literature and public statements regarding foreign and defense policy, and ultra-sensitivity to those in Korea considered to be "Pro-American." To be fair, this has in many ways been openly encouraged by the president himself. It is a well-known fact that Roh campaigned on an anti-American platform, calling for changes to nearly every aspect of the ROK–U.S. Alliance during his march to the presidency in 2002.[32] This view toward Americans, and the public statements regarding those in South Korea regarded as being strongly "pro-American" were again emphasized on a visit to Turkey, when Roh was quoted as saying, "I feel troubled when I see that there are Koreans who possess a more pro-American way of thinking than Americans themselves."[33] Lee Jong-seok has also made similar comments regarding the relationship with the United States, such as the remarks he made in 2004 regarding the presence of U.S. forces in South Korea when he stated, "It's not an issue that we can solve by grabbing the trouser legs (of U.S. soldiers to prevent them from leaving South Korea)."[34]

The style and vision of key NSC members, and their leader until early 2006, Lee Jong-seok, has caused considerable debate and controversy, with not only the Defense Ministry, but the Foreign Ministry as well (Ministry of Foreign Affairs and Trade). In fact, during 2004, then-Foreign Minister Yoon Young-kwan was forced to resign because of the problems that many in his North America division were having with members of the NSC. The NSC was seen then (and is seen now) as being Roh's real advisory and decision-making body in most issues—including those involving the United States. The issue also came up at that time that some in the Foreign Ministry were seen as being "too pro-American" in their diplomatic activities. Some had also made rather unpleasant remarks about President Roh, as articulated by Uri Party member and National Assembly member Shin Ki-nam. Being seen as "pro-American" has not appeared to be a position popular with many powerful members of the Roh administration.[35]

There also appear to be issues other than the differences in policy vision concerning North Korea and the United States. These issues appear to be very "Confucian" in nature, and involve age, ranking, and "who went to what school" (academic background). Many who have served in the NSC during Roh's Presidency did not go to tier-one universities, as have most of the power brokers who have served in the Foreign Ministry. Nor have most of the members of the NSC attended elite military academies, such as the Korean Military Academy, as the key players in the Defense Ministry have (many of them being Generals and Admirals or retired Generals and Admirals). This may also have caused some of the friction that has existed since Roh came to power in 2003.[36]

One of the most recent controversies that Lee Jong-seok was involved in was the reported investigation into his handling of negotiations with the United States over the future of United States Forces Korea and the concept of Strategic Flexibility as it relates to the future of the ROK–U.S. Alliance and the geopolitical situation in Northeast Asia—particularly as it relates to any future dealings with China. Reportedly, there were two separate, very quiet, investigations into the matter, led by Unification Minister Chung (at the time) and Roh's closest advisor, Moon Jae-in, along with Cheon Ho-seon, Chief of the national security affairs office. There was reportedly both disagreement and confusion among the negotiators with the United States, and while the Blue House has denied that there was an actual "investigation," it appears clear that the government had an internal disagreement over the exact position to take—and the NSC's role in it.[37]

In all of the reports surfacing about this troubling chain of events, there was no mention of involvement by military officials, who appeared to be out of most of the decision-making picture. The same "investigation" was apparently looking into whether the issue of a military plan code-named "5029" had been mishandled. This complicated, highly sensitive, and important military plan was reportedly shelved temporarily during 2005 by order of the NSC, causing a great deal of concern both in the United States and South Korea (as discussed in the previous chapter). Again, the involvement of the ROK military in this appears to be minimal.[38]

In February 2006, Unification Minister Chung Dong-young left his post to work within the Uri party, and transition his focus on building a campaign for the Presidency of South Korea in 2008. To no one's surprise, he was replaced as Unification Minister by Lee Jong-seok. During the final months of Chung's tenure, he also served as the "head" of the NSC—a title that most analysts consider to have meant very little, as Lee was the de facto leader of the NSC from the very beginning of the Roh administration. It appears obvious that Lee then became the real leader of both the NSC and the Unification Ministry, which handles mainly North Korean issues. In fact, this has been confirmed by Blue House spokesman Kim Man-soo, who stated, "For all intents and purposes, Lee has already been in charge of coordinating and managing foreign and security policies of the participatory government . . . taking this into account, the President will ask him to assume the presidency of the council in addition to the post as Unification Minister."[39] Thus, even though Lee "moved on," in early 2006, his presence continued to dominate the NSC, and his power, now consolidated, was the force behind foreign policy in South Korea.

Many in both South Korea and Washington see Lee as the primary source of changes in the ROK–U.S. Alliance, which according to one western diplomat in Seoul who asked to remain anonymous, "had no flaws until Seoul wanted changes made."[40] Those on the right in the National Assembly apparently concur with this assessment. Conservative lawmaker Kim Moon-soo remarked to the ROK press during 2006, that "Lee Jong-seok, who has played a central role to aggravate South Korea–U.S. relations and caused security fears in the nation, is not suitable for the post."[41] An analysis of events occurring between 2003 and early 2006 makes it clear that Roh has placed his trust and confidence in the NSC when it comes to both foreign policy and military issues. It is also clear that the man who was able to consolidate his power so that he came to control both the NSC and the Unification Ministry has been Lee Jong-seok. Thus, it has been his influence and the influence of those who supported him in the NSC, and later the Unification Ministry, that have set the tone and focus for both the Civil-Military relationship in South Korea, and Seoul's alliance with the United States. Lee was later forced to resign in the shake-up of Roh's cabinet that occurred as a result of the first North Korean nuclear test during October 2006.[42]

The Future of Civil-Military Reform

A controversial measure was introduced by the Defense Ministry to the National Assembly in May 2005. The Ministry asked the National Assembly to introduce a bill to allow soldiers to establish residency according to their assigned unit instead of their home of record. Several members of the Uri Party back the bill in which provinces at the bases where soldiers were stationed would be eligible for higher revenue sharing from the central government. If the measure becomes a bill and is voted on, it also has the potential to skew voting demographics in many areas.[43] While on the surface the bill appears to be reasonable, because most conscripts are younger voters—more likely to lean toward the president's Uri Party or other left-leaning parties—its main purpose seems to be to create a political opportunity for the Uri Party and its initiatives, which are often spawned or have been supported by Roh, and seems to have no other clear advantage.

Other measures submitted to the National Assembly are far more controversial. In April 2005, Defense Minister Yoon announced a reform package to go before the National Assembly that would initiate reform on the French Model. The package would include changing the promotion system to allow civilians to sit on promotion boards, initiate structural changes, personnel cuts, and create "balanced development" between the army, navy, and air force. It would also guarantee the minister's right to suggest personnel for key positions, and create a "special mission" to investigate dark episodes in the military's past—once again reaching back to the mindset of the "386 Generation" faction of righting the wrongs of the pre-democratization days of Korea, and opening up old wounds.[44]

The reform, appears to have been strongly influenced by the input of Roh himself. Roh seems to have been impressed with military reform that he has witnessed in Western European nations. At the meeting, in the new government complex's Grand Conference Room, the president stated,

> The legislation should reflect the case of France and be carried out in the long run based on a national consensus. . . . Another task the military must do is to settle past histories . . . just like how Germany's facing its past faults was made possible by their leaders' resolution and courage to face the national pain that history revealed, I hope our military will be born anew by inquiring into the actual matters of the past.[45]

Altering the Civil-Military Relationship

There are many signs—most of them made for public consumption—that Roh actively intends to alter the Civil-Military relationship in South Korea. During Armed Forces Day in 2004, Roh emphasized that civilian control of the military, which intensified as Yoon became defense minister, would be further intensified, stating in part, "We need strong resolution from the Army itself."[46]

Furthermore, the highly publicized investigation into the "promotion scandal" of 2004 involving high-ranking military officers caused added confusion and distrust between the Blue House and the military.[47] Eventually, perhaps because of moving too fast, the prosecutors investigating the scandal were "relieved" by the Blue House. The South Korean public expressed its growing consternation regarding Roh's handling of the military. Later, in 2005, the Blue House reported that President Roh had decided not to attend the Korean Military Academy commencement ceremonies, and that he would only do so every other year. This was largely reported as being a move designed to "even the status" of the army, as compared to the other services.[48]

In February 2005, the Blue House announced it would eliminate the post of National Secretary for Defense and instead create a "Presidential Advisory Committee on national defense development.[49] Further evidence regarding Roh's vision to severely alter the status-quo in Civil-Military relations in the ROK was shown in the announced shelving of an operational plan identified as "5029" in the South Korean press. This move was considered particularly precedent setting because the NSC—not the Ministry of National Defense—initiated the move and organized what proved to be a confused and poorly managed process that caused difficulties in the ROK–U.S. Alliance.[50] Although it is not clear yet what effects the changes in planning will have on the military, once again, the process has changed, and NSC involvement has overridden the decisions of those in the Ministry of National Defense. It is unclear if the Ministry of National Defense was even involved in this decision. The collateral effect of the "2004 Naval Incident," the "Main Enemy" terminology change, and the "Promotion Scandal" has been a noticeable drop in morale among the ROK military. In fact, the continuous lack of clarity regarding the military from the Blue House has left many high-ranking officers apprehensive about decision making, military readiness, and foreign policy.

Conclusion

The effects of a Blue House policy that, based on past actions and public statements, has been designed to drastically change many of the paradigms associated with Civil-Military relations in South Korea and the ROK–U.S. Alliance, have been negative in the short run. This is not to say that these moves will be unsuccessful in the long run. But Roh's leadership style in carrying out his policies and the manner in which the military has been handled has been viewed negatively by the majority of South Koreans. Polls during late 2004 suggested Roh's administration has bungled most attempts at reform targeting infrastructure and command and control of the military.[51] More recent polls taken in May 2005 showed that the approval rate for President Roh and the Uri party was declining.[52]

The worst effect has been on the ROK military itself. Constant maneuvering among the members of Roh's formal and informal power circles has reduced high-ranking military officers and MND officials to bystanders when it comes to real influence in Defense policy making. The treatment of the military by the Roh administration and its key officials has had a profound effect on readiness—most notably at the top, where decision making and leadership have suffered from a lack of clear guidance from the Blue House, public policies that have been perceived as designed to weaken the prestige and infrastructure of the military, and perceived anti-American bias in the Blue House that has strained the ROK–U.S. military Alliance.

10 CONCLUSION: THE IMPACT OF THE POST-9/11 ERA ON KOREAN SECURITY

CONTEMPORARY PERCEPTIONS OF NORTH KOREA'S posture and intentions have often been polarized, contentious, and unfortunately based more on internal political ideology in South Korea and the United States than on a pragmatic analysis of North Korea's capabilities and strategic intentions. The topics of discussion in this book have analyzed all of the capabilities that North Korea possesses and how they have changed because of a radically different global and regional environment that has existed since the tragic events of 9/11. North Korea's approach to diplomacy, its use of information as a tool of coercion (both internally and externally), its use of military forces as a tool of brinkmanship and provocations, and its approach to maintaining a troubled economy, has experienced significant change and shows the Kim Chong-il government's ability to adapt in the face of geopolitical flux.

The governments in Washington and Seoul have both changed in their approaches to dealing with North Korea as a nation-state since 2001. Indeed, this has been the basis of many of the troubles that have increasingly raised concerns regarding the ROK–U.S. Alliance for the past few years. Challenges facing the alliance include

- differing perceptions of the North Korean threat and how to deal with it
- how the South Korean military will be able to raise its independent capabilities to counter the North Korean threat in coming years
- how the U.S. military will adjust its forces, posture, and capabilities to complement the changes in the South Korean military as it evolves, and
- the volatile Civil-Military relationship that exists within the government in Seoul, which raises concerns for the military planning of potential security issues.

North Korea's Use of Diplomacy in the Post-9/11 Era

Throughout this book there have been references to North Korea's highly unusual use of diplomacy. There should be no doubt from the evidence presented
that unlike what may seem to be true, North Korea is not a nation-state that
simply resorts to bluster and military brinkmanship to achieve its goals. Although in many ways bluster and brinkmanship can be considered a tool of
diplomacy, Kim Chong-il's inner circle has proven quite adroit at maintaining
North Korea's nuclear and missile programs in the face of international pressure.[1] This skill has involved driving a wedge into the ROK–U.S. Alliance,
forming closer ties to China (particularly in the post-9/11 era), and warming
relations with other entities in the Western world such as the European Union.[2]

North Korea has made an important move during the Bush–Roh era by
edging closer to China. While Pyongyang and Beijing have been officially allies since the Korean War, ties between the two communist nations cooled during the Cold War as Kim Il-sung moved closer to the Soviet Union and the
subsidies that Moscow offered for his economy and military. In fact, the "Great
Leader" skillfully walked a line between both the Soviet Union and China during much of his tenure as leader of the DPRK.[3] Now, it appears that because of
unmonitored economic aid that Beijing is willing to provide to North Korea,
Kim Chong-il is encouraging growth in relations with China and has allowed
China unprecedented economic investment and trade interests in his nation.[4]
Whereas this has helped North Korea to maintain stability and perhaps provide
some advantage in the six-party talks, it creates the dilemma in Kim's government of drawing closer to China to assure survival while maintaining independence and not turning into a complete Chinese satellite.[5] This is an ongoing
struggle, and coming years will reveal exactly how much influence the Chinese
are able to wield over the North Korean government and its foreign policy.

North Korea has been equally as successful in dealing with South Korea.
The "warming of relations" between North and South Korea began under Kim
Dae-jung's "Sunshine Policy," but as described in detail earlier, it intensified
under Roh Moo-hyun's policy of "Peace and Prosperity" beginning in 2003.
This was a diplomatic coup for Pyongyang because essentially, Kim Chong-il's
government delivered no concessions to Seoul in exchange for numerous eco-
nomic and diplomatic gains delivered by the Roh government. The Kaesong
Industrial Complex, the KumGang Mountain tourist project, large-scale

unmonitored economic aid, and other significant initiatives have yielded no changes in North Korean state behavior. In fact, as articulated throughout this book, Pyongyang continues development of its missile and nuclear programs—as well as the proliferation of many of these programs—maintains its hostile attitude toward such important issues as an inter-Korea railroad and easing tensions along the maritime Northern Limit Line (NLL), and refuses to make any efforts to address human rights concerns that have been an issue for the United States, Japan, and other nations in the region.[6] North Korea continues to test Seoul's will to safeguard its security along the DMZ and NLL with numerous, yet easily controlled border violations.[7] This has not caused the South Korean government to slow any of its initiatives aimed at easing tensions on the Peninsula. Thus, Pyongyang's diplomatic dealings with Seoul can be considered a resounding success for Kim Chong-il's foreign policy.

North Korea's use of diplomacy with the United States has not been nearly as successful. Under the Bush administration, Washington has shown little patience for brinkmanship, cracked down on illicit activities, and repeatedly branded the Kim regime as "evil." Some analysts in both the United States and South Korea have opined that North Korea intends to make no real concessions or confidence-building measures regarding its nuclear or missile programs—not to mention its conventional military—until after the Bush administration leaves office in 2008.[8] It is unclear if advances made during the six-party talks in 2007 will change this, but Washington's concerns about Pyongyang's nuclear and missile programs are unlikely to be completely resolved by the time President Bush leaves office.

Kim Chong-il has also been less than triumphant in his dealings with Japan, which can be considered simply insensitive to Japanese culture and politics. Key issues such as the kidnapping of Japanese citizens, and the returning to Japan of "fake remains" of formerly kidnapped citizens has created an atmosphere of Japanese contempt and resentment toward North Korea.[9]

North Korea's Use of Information as a Tool of Coercion

North Korea uses propaganda as well as lack of information as tools of coercion to control its own people. Thus, the informational instrument of national power is vital to the internal stability of the Kim Chong-il regime. But North Korea has also successfully used information as an instrument when dealing with South Korea. This is quite impressive considering that North Korea is a nation where the Internet and other technological advances are tightly controlled and at best only at primitive levels when compared to other countries.

In North Korean media, Kim Chong-il dominates everything on the daily agenda. In addition, Kim's visits to military units push the dominance of the NKPA in everyday life. This is a message that the North Korean people have no choice to accept because there is simply no other source of information other than the state.[10] North Koreans are brainwashed to believe that attack from the United States is imminent, South Korea is nothing more than Washington's puppet, and that any economic hardships they are facing are a result of negative U.S. policies and other capitalistic societies that only wish to see the downfall of the regime. The heavy-handed control of both the press and severe limits on information from the outside world makes the human rights violations that China commits against its press dim in comparison.[11]

Perhaps as important, North Korea's propaganda machine has evolved to focus on the general populace and the government in South Korea. An excellent example of this can be seen if one examines the breakdown in talks that would have resulted in former President Kim Dae-jung visiting the North for informal talks during 2006 on a reconnected rail line that now runs between North and South Korea. The travel via the rail has strong symbolic meaning for South Koreans (particularly those on the left). North Korea postponed test runs citing security concerns and "unstable conditions in the South" as reasons for the delay. The "unstable conditions" referred to at the time were the conservative groundswell in local elections building in South Korea and some anti-North protests that were highly visible in Seoul.[12] The Roh government in South Korea remained highly committed to engagement with the North. For example, the president publicly stated on a trip to Mongolia in 2006, where he met with ethnic Koreans, that Seoul was ready to make more unconditional concessions to North Korea.[13]

Meanwhile, one of Pyongyang's information operations in 2006 was the intense campaign to urge South Koreans to vote against conservative and pro-American candidates during local elections. A propaganda arm, the "Committee of the Peaceful Reunification of the Fatherland," made a statement preceding the elections that "The United States is seeking to install a puppet regime in South Korea to prepare for a war of aggression on the North." A North Korean website also posted a statement urging South Korean voters to "bring a shameful defeat" to the conservative GNP party in the elections.[14] North Korea's propaganda campaign and skillful use of the informational instrument of national power is an obvious move to encourage continuation of the massive, unmonitored aid coming from the Roh administration. The local elections in 2006 were seen as a measuring stick for presidential elections that will bring the next leader to power following Roh's end of term in February 2008. As with other areas of North Korea's foreign policy, Pyongyang has shown skill in adapting to the situation and has targeted South Korean politics and foreign policy. This has become particularly apparent since 2003 and is likely to continue as long as a left of center government exists in Seoul. Thus, North Korea, a country that is less technologically connected than almost any other nation in Asia, has found ways to be successful in manipulating information to maintain internal control within its borders and external influence in the South.

North Korea's Military Instrument of Power: Threat or Nuisance?

North Korea's military arsenal, which is defined here as nuclear, missile, and conventional forces capabilities, continues to be referred to by many observers as more of a nuisance than an actual threat.[15] Yet North Korea has shown that regardless of the circumstances or political leanings of the U.S. president, it will continue to develop and maintain a nuclear program. For instance, during the Clinton administration, the Agreed Framework became the tool used to freeze North Korea's nuclear program. In return, Pyongyang received shipments of heavy fuel oil and the building of light-water reactors, among other economic concessions.[16] As now publicly disclosed by former high-ranking officials within the Clinton administration such as Robert Gallucci, soon after the Agreed Framework was implemented, Pyongyang pursued an alternate, Highly Enriched Uranium (HEU) weaponization program.[17] In the years since the Bush administration has been in power, North Korea has consistently proven that it will stall any advances toward the transparent dismantlement of its nuclear program. Public disclosure that its program exists in early 2005 and the stalling (once again) of the six-party talks during the fall of 2005 because of the legitimate law enforcement crackdown on its illicit activities by the United States points to the fact that North Korea will do everything in its power to delay, stall, and perhaps deny the existence of parts of its nuclear program.[18] North Korea's first underground nuclear test, conducted in October 2006, proves that the regime has no intention of either listening to its allies (China), its neighbors who have attempted engagement as a policy (South Korea), or the United States that has attempted to pressure the DPRK through numerous measures. Thus, while breakthroughs during 2007 in the six-party talks may yet prove to be an effective tool in convincing North Korea to abandon its nuclear programs, the road to actually accomplishing this feat is a long and treacherous one.

Much like its nuclear program, North Korea has not slowed the development and maintenance of its missile programs. Indeed, in the post-9/11 era, Pyongyang has developed, tested, deployed, and proliferated ballistic missiles with a variety of ranges and capabilities. Two key threats from North Korea's missile programs are the actual missiles deployed by North Korea and the proliferation of missiles in unstable regions such as the Middle East. Whereas missiles such as the North Korean version of the SS-21 threaten the security of the ROK and U.S. forces on the Korean Peninsula, it is the longer range missiles that have garnered the attention and concern of U.S. policy makers. Proliferation of long-range missiles to countries such as Iran threatens the existence of Israel and even Europe—particularly if such missiles are equipped with a nuclear warhead.

Of equally grave concern to U.S. policy makers is the deployment of long-range missiles on North Korean soil. While this is certainly done as a policy move that will threaten the region and possibly even the continental United States, it shows that Pyongyang has no hesitation in using its military instrument of national power as a tool to show the United States that its government will not cave in to pressure from Washington on its illicit activities, nuclear development, and human rights. Events during 2006 point to the assessment that Pyongyang may be using its long-range missiles as tools of coercion. During May and June 2006, government officials in Seoul, Washington, and Tokyo confirmed that the North Koreans were preparing to test-launch a Taepo Dong 2. Reportedly, imagery confirmed that large trailers corresponding to the length that would carry a Taepo Dong 2 missile were located at missile platforms near the northeast coast of North Korea. The missile that was test-fired (unsuccessfully) was reportedly a 35-meter (116 foot) Taepo Dong 2 that could have a range of up to 6,000 kilometers (3,750 miles). North Korea is believed to be developing the missile for a range of up to 10,000 kilometers, which would place the continental United States within striking distance.[19]

The Taepo Dong 2 test-launch preparations that eventually led to the now infamous launches of seven missiles on July 4–5, 2006, make an interesting case study of how North Korea uses its instruments of national power. Pyongyang attempted to gain concessions that would ease sanctions against its illicit economic activities in return for standing down. Kim Chong-il's government also used this as a means for projecting its military might to the world—or as an "information operations" tool—the preparations were slow and conducted in daylight in full view of satellites. Finally, this was an obvious way to turn diplomatic negotiations in their favor. Unfortunately, both China and Russia specifically asked North Korea not to test-launch its missile.[20] And of course, the missiles themselves are a way for North Korea to project military power in the region. Were the primary reasons for launching the missiles economic (sales to Iran) or motivated by politics intended to send a message to Washington and the region?[21] It remains unclear, but the fact that Pyongyang openly prepared to launch during a time when there were numerous issues with the United States regarding its nuclear and illicit economic activities points to the assessment that the missile launches were being used as a tool of coercion.

Given the fact that North Korea has tested and deployed both short-range missiles with increased capabilities (Pyongyang's version of the SS-21), and long-range missiles with increased capability that can potentially threaten the United States (the Taepo Dong 2 and Taepo Dong X), this is an issue that is certainly more than a nuisance. It is a threat that must be taken seriously. Even so, the North Korean threat encompasses more than its nuclear and missile capabilities. Its conventional military forces continue to evolve and maintain capabilities that can threaten South Korea's existence as a prosperous, stable nation. The conventional capabilities that North Korea possesses are now focused around asymmetric forces dominated by short-range missiles and rockets, long-range artillery, and Special Operations Forces. Because these forces (particularly the long-range artillery) can target Seoul with little or no warning, this threat should not be considered merely a nuisance. Throughout the Cold War and now in the post-9/11 era, the factor that has kept North Korea and its large, evolving military at bay has been deterrence from a strong, well-equipped, and trained military force maintained within the security umbrella of the ROK–U.S. Alliance. It is this alliance which has maintained security and stability on the Peninsula through rapidly changing times.

North Korea's Economic "Development": An Instrument of National Power?

Most analysts would agree that North Korea's economy has been a "basket case" since at least the mid-1990s. It was this economic downturn, caused by a combination of a lack of subsidies from the Soviet Union and weather that wiped out crops and caused extensive damage that persuaded Kim Chong-il to turn to the outside world for food aid. Since the famine and widespread starvation in North Korea in the mid- to late 1990s, conditions have improved—largely because of massive amounts of food aid from the United Nations and NGOs in the United States, South Korea, and Western Europe. But in late 2005 and early 2006, North Korea significantly reduced access, numbers of personnel, and amounts of monitored food aid being brought into its country by the World Food Program. Based on an analysis of unmonitored economic aid increases that began coming in (picking up intensity in 2005) in late 2004 from both China and South Korea, it does not appear that the North Korean agricultural sector has "recovered" enough to feed its own people. Instead, China has now chosen to augment its fuel aid with massive food aid, and South Korea under the Roh administration has chosen to provide food aid without any concessions or monitoring, as well as other important economic initiatives that funnel cash, fuel, and food into North Korea. An analysis of these "initiatives" and "partnerships" reveals that they are really nothing more than a handout—and thus far the North Korean economy has shown no real signs of recovery.

Does North Korea have an economy that is a threat or a concern to the United States, South Korea, and the region? The answer is yes. As previously described, as much as half of North Korea's real economy comes from illegal drugs, counterfeit money, counterfeit cigarettes, and proliferation of military weaponry—all of which are of grave concern to Washington's foreign policy.[22] Now it appears that because Washington has finally targeted these activities through international law enforcement agencies, the United States may have leverage that may not have been anticipated. These illicit activities have become such a large part of the North Korean economy that the crack down by Washington and its allies on these programs in late 2005 and early 2006 likely caused a major disruption in Kim Chong-il's decisions.[23]

One thing is clear, Pyongyang does not have the capability of surviving economically on its own, nor is it likely to have that capability in the foreseeable future. Whether it is survival on food handouts from the UN and NGOs, or switching to unmonitored handouts from China and South Korea, North Korea has shown an inability to feed its people or run its economy without massive amounts of aid. Although some have suggested that the way for North Korea to finally turn the corner on its economy is to adapt changes based on the Chinese model, this unlikely to happen.[24] To do so would mean opening up North Korea's borders on a large-scale—and this would undermine the very security and stability of a government focused more on regime survival than any other single issue.

Dealing with a Troubling Neighbor: The ROK–U.S. Alliance and the Foreign Policy of Washington and Seoul

Protecting the stability and security of South Korea is a complicated, expensive, and controversial undertaking. This is not to say that it should be abandoned by Washington or taken lightly by Seoul. Nevertheless, some conclusions regarding the ROK–U.S. Alliance deserve discussion because of the ramifications that they pose for the future.

Although there have been many in President Roh's inner circle who have indicated that distancing South Korea's policies from the United States and moving closer to other regional partners (particularly China) is desirable, this is apparently not a policy supported by the majority of South Koreans.[25] In fact, the Korean Institute for Defense Analysis conducted a poll in March 2006. The poll asked 1,002 people over the age of twenty which nation would pose the most serious threat to Korea in a decade, to which more than 38 percent responded China as the country posing the largest threat, followed by Japan at nearly 24 percent, North Korea at 21 percent, and the United States at 15 percent (the United States was likely cited because of fears of a unilateral strike against North Korea).

Of utmost importance, nearly 82 percent cited the United States as Korea's best friend, while China, Japan, and North Korea all drew single digit responses.[26] Local elections held in May 2006 seem to affirm that the majority of South Koreans did not support Blue House policies distanced Seoul from the United States, engaged but did not contain North Korea, and called for radical change in the ROK–U.S. Alliance. The left-leaning Uri party (Roh's de facto supporting party) fell in resounding defeat in both gubernatorial and mayoral elections—a result that left South Korea's president and the party badly shaken and resulted in the resignation of party chair and former Minister of Unification Chung Dong-young.[27]

Roh's policies that began in 2003 created polarization within the South Korean electorate and tension within the ROK–U.S. Alliance. The "progressive" camp in South Korea has staked out an apparently unpopular policy that seeks more independence from the United States, while the conservative camp in South Korea strives to once again grow closer to Washington. The "progressives" in South Korea have maintained publicly that the North Korean nuclear crisis originates from the U.S. military goading the North while conservatives contend that the ROK–U.S. Alliance has prevented North Korea from provoking war for the past five decades.[28] The debate within South Korea and the differences in pursuit of policy between the governments in Seoul and Washington are all about perception of the security threat from North Korea. Is the Cold War really over on the Korean Peninsula? One could easily argue that the Cold War is over only when both sides make serious moves in state behavior that are indicative of real confidence-building measures. To date, North Korea has taken no such action and instead its actions consist of brinkmanship, pro-vocations, belligerent international behavior, and illicit State-sponsored economic activities.

The debate and disagreement over security issues relating to North Korea has also created a strained Civil-Military relationship in South Korea. Debate over methodologies to deal with the North continues. Ultimately, how much of a threat the North poses has led to a rush by Roh's administration to implement the change in Wartime OPCON and caused serious misperceptions in the South Korean public as a whole about the role U.S. forces should play in wartime, as well as about the relationship the ROK government should have with them. Calls to regain sovereignty during wartime may have made popular rhetoric during 2003–2006 by some in the South Korean public (particularly those on the political left), but the practical realities are that South Korea's sovereignty in wartime combat operations (or the use of American forces on its soil) has never been in question. As Brookings Institution Senior Fellow Michael O'Hanlon has said,

> South Korea should know that under such circumstances, Seoul could veto U.S. use of bases on its territory for operations that did not serve South Korean objectives. Many European allies have done so over the years—as in the 1973 Mideast war [when U.S. aircraft were not allowed to land anywhere except Portugal to refuel] and the 1986 bombing of Libya [when France denied the United States aerial overflight rights].[29]

There can be no doubt that the ROK–U.S. Alliance has gone through difficult times since 2003. Despite the difficulties, challenges, and fluxuations of the alliance, Washington and Seoul publicly and privately want the alliance to continue for the foreseeable future. Ultimately, this is because the liberal democracy that exists in South Korea is able to often disagree with Washington under the very umbrella of security that is provided by U.S. troops and equipment. As the two governments continue to work out their differences regarding the North Korean threat and how to deal with it, the presidents on both sides of the Pacific will make difficult decisions regarding North Korea, the restructuring of military forces on the Peninsula, and (for Roh Moo-hyun's government and the government that follows it) a difficult Civil-Military relationship.

Implications for the Future

Based on North Korea's state behavior, the government there has not decided to engage its neighbor to the south, other nations in the region, or the United States, in any meaningful manner that will end tensions on the Korean Peninsula. Indeed, as other governments in the region (as well as the United States) began to put more pressure on North Korea's proliferation of WMD, Pyongyang seems to have stepped up its illicit economic activities. Thus, any analysis of North Korea's behavior in the post-9/11 era must logically conclude that any attempts at engagement by democratic neighbors (particularly South Korea) are not a policy that will result in a realistic give and take.

North Korea has one overriding goal that trumps all others—regime survival. This is a struggle that will challenge Pyongyang over the coming years. Of course, one of the ultimate concerns for Kim Chong-il is the succession process and ensuring that the DPRK regime remains in power following his death or retirement. Unfortunately for Kim, he seemed to be starting this long, elaborate process only recently, probably beginning around 2004–2005. This leads to grave concerns for the ROK–U.S. Alliance about internal instability in North Korea should Kim pass from the scene. In fact, a North Korea with the potential to fall into a state of anarchy has geopolitical implications for every single nation in Northeast Asia.

Ultimately, only deterrence has kept North Korea from threatening the South, attempting to bully other nations in the region with WMD (such as Japan), and using its government to violate international laws. This deterrence is vital for the security of the Korean Peninsula and the region. Only a strong ROK–U.S.

Alliance can maintain security and stability on the Peninsula. Only a pragmatic, international law-enforcement effort can prevent North Korea from large-scale distribution of illegal drugs, counterfeit currency and cigarettes, and the proliferation of missiles and other WMD related weaponry. Only when North Korea takes legitimate steps to reduce its threatening military stance, its proliferation of weapons, and its illicit activities, should real engagement occur between North Korea, its neighbors, and the international community. Until then, a Cold War will continue to exist on the Korean Peninsula, as containment is the only strategy that has proven even partially successful at keeping the Kim regime in its box.

| NOTES

Chapter 1: Introduction

1. For analysis on the role that North Korea played with the Soviet Union during the Cold War, see Edward A. Olsen, *Korea: The Divided Nation* (Westport, CT: Praeger Security International, 2005): 106–121.

2. "Joint Declaration on the ROK-U.S. Alliance and Peace on the Korean Peninsula," White House Press Release, November 17, 2005, URL: http://www.whitehouse.gov/news/releases/2005/11/20051117-6.html.

3. Mike Shuster, "South Korean President to Meet with Bush," National Public Radio, June 10, 2005, URL: http://www.npr.org/templates/story/story.php?storyId=4697528.

4. "United States Joint Forces Command Glossary," United States Joint Forces Command, 2006, URL: http://www.jfcom.mil/about/glossary.htm#ONA.

5. "Doctrinal Implications of Operational Net Assessment," Joint Warfighting Center, Joint Doctrine Series, Pamphlet 4, February 24, 2004, URL: http://www.dtic.mil/doctrine/education/jwfc_pam4.pdf.

6. Joint Pub 1-02, "Dictionary of Military and Associated Terms," United States Department of Defense, April 14, 2006, URL: http://www.dtic.mil/doctrine/jel/doddict/data/i/02684.html.

7. Jeramy Biggie, "Operational Net Assessment," Paper presented at the conference titled, "Decision Aids/Support to Joint Operations Planning," hosted by the Military Operations Research Society, at the Dougherty Conference Center, Offutt AFB, Nebraska, November 19, 2003, URL: http://www.mors.org/meetings/decision_aids/da_pres/biggie.pdf.

8. For works that have conducted an analysis of issues surrounding North Korea's nuclear program, see Victor D. Cha and David C. Kang, *Nuclear North Korea: A Debate for Engagement Strategies* (New York: Columbia University Press, 2003); Young Whan Kihl and Peter Hayes, eds., *Peace and Security in Northeast Asia: The Nuclear Issue and the Korean Peninsula* (Armonk, NY: M. E. Sharpe, 1997); Michael O'Hanlon and Mike Mochizuki, *Crisis on the Korean Peninsula: How to Deal with a Nuclear North Korea* (Washington, DC: Brookings Institution Press, 2003); and James M. Minnich, *The Denuclearization of North Korea: The Agreed Framework and Alternative Options Analyzed* (Milton Keynes, UK: Lightning Source, 2003). For a recent work that conducts an excellent analysis of South Korean internal politics, see Young

Whan Kihl, *Transforming Korean Politics: Democracy, Reform and Culture* (Armonk, NY: M. E. Sharpe, 2005). For recent works that conduct an analysis of North Korean internal and foreign policy, see Roland Bleiker, *Divided Korea: Toward a Culture of Reconciliation* (Minneapolis, MN: University of Minnesota Press, 2005); Chuck Downs, *Over the Line: North Korea's Negotiating Strategy* (Washington, DC: AEI Press, 1999); and Kongdan Oh and Ralph C. Hassig, *North Korea Through the Looking Glass* (Washington, DC: Brookings Institution Press, 2000).

9. For more information regarding North Korea's weapons proliferation in the Middle East and South Asia, see "CNS Special Report on North Korean Ballistic Missile Capabilities," *Center for Nonproliferation Studies, Monterey Institute of International Studies*, March 22, 2006, URL: http://cns.miis.edu/pubs/week/pdf/060321.pdf.

10. John S. Park, "Inside Multilateralism: The Six-Party Talks," *Washington Quarterly*, vol. 28, no. 4 (Autumn 2005): 75–91, URL: http://www.twq.com/05autumn/docs/05autumn_park.pdf.

11. Sohn Jie-Ae and Suzanne Malveaux, "World Regrets North Korea's Quitting Nuke Talks," *CNN.com*, February 10, 2005, URL: http://www.cnn.com/2005/world/asiapcf/02/10/nkorea.talks/index.html.

12. Bruce Bennett, "N. Korea's Threat to S. Korea," *Rand Institution Commentary*, March 7, 2003, URL: http://www.rand.org/commentary/030703UPI.html.

13. Peter Hayes, "North Korea's Negotiating Tactics and Nuclear Strategy," *Nautilus Institute Special Report*, April 18, 2003, URL: http://www.nautilus.org/dprkbriefingbook/nuclearweapons/nuclearnegotiations.html.

14. "North Korean Drug Ship to be Sunk," *CNN.com*, March 22, 2006, URL: http://edition.cnn.com/2006/world/asiapcf/03/22/nkorea.pongsu/index.html.

15. Alexander Vershbow, United States Ambassador to the Republic of Korea, "The Changing U.S.–ROK Alliance," Remarks to the Republic of Korea at the National Assembly Study Group on Parliamentary Democracy, Seoul, Republic of Korea, November 9, 2005, URL: http://seoul.usembassy.gov/nov_9_2005.html.

16. Stephen Costello, "Foreign Policy in the First Two Years of the Roh Moo-hyun Government," Cheong Wa Dae: Office of the President, March 18, 2005, URL: http://english.president.go.kr/cwd/en/archive/archive_view.php?meta_id=for_your_info&m_def=3&ss_def=4&id=1c1ca47daa77a9da4798752.

Chapter 2: North Korea's Nuclear Program: Controversy and Brinkmanship

1. Larry Niksch, "North Korea's Weapons of Mass Destruction," in *North Korea: The Politics of Regime Survival*, eds. Young Whan Kihl and Hong Nack Kim (Armonk, NY: M. E. Sharpe, 2005), 99–101.

2. "Nuclear North Korea," *CBC News in Depth*, February 22, 2005, URL: http://www.cbc.ca/news/background/northkorea/nuclear.html.

3. "North Korea Profile: Nuclear Overview," *The Nuclear Threat Initiative*, September 2005, URL: http://www.nti.org/e_research/profiles/nk/nuclear/.

4. For a detailed chronology of the events surrounding the Agreed Framework

and leading up to the crisis of 2002, see "Kim's Nuclear Gamble: A Chronology," *PBS Frontline*, URL: http://www.pbs.org/wgbh/pages/frontline/shows/kim/etc/cron.html.

5. Scott Snyder, "The Fire Last Time," book review on *Going Critical: The First North Korean Nuclear Crisis*, Joel S. Wit, Daniel B. Poneman, and Robert L. Gallucci, (Washington, DC: Brookings Institution Press); *Foreign Affairs* (July/August 2004), URL: http://www.foreignaffairs.org/20040701fareviewessay83415/scott-snyder/the-fire-last-time.html.

6. Oh Young-hwan and Jeong Yong-soo, "North's Uranium Put U.S. in Policy Quandary," *Joongang Ilbo*, October 11, 2004, URL: http://joongang daily.joins.com/200410/20041011223125680990092309231.html.

7. Peter Hayes, "The Multilateral Mantra and North Korea," *The Nautilus Institute Online*, February 20, 2004, URL: http://www.nautilus.org/dprkbriefingbook/multilateraltalks/phmultilateralmantra.html.

8. Mark Manyin, Emma Chanlett-Avery, and Helene Marchat, "North Korea: A Chronology of Events, October 2002–December 2004," *CRS Report for Congress* (Washington, DC: Library of Congress, Congressional Research Service), January 24, 2005, URL: http://www.fas.org/man/crs/rl32743.pdf.

9. Siegfried S. Hecker, "Technical Summary of DPRK Nuclear Program," paper presented at the 2005 Carnegie International Non-Proliferation Conference, November 8, 2002 (Washington, DC: Carnegie Endowment), URL: http://www.carnegieendowment.org/static/npp/2005conference/presentations/hecker.pdf.

10. "North Korea's Nuclear Challenge," 2002 Carnegie International Non-Proliferation Conference, November 14, 2002, URL: http://www.ceip.org/files/projects/npp/resources/conference2002/northkorea.htm.

11. Selig S. Harrison, "Did North Korea Cheat?" *Foreign Affairs Online* (January/February 2005), URL: http://www.foreignaffairs.org/20050101faessay84109/selig-s-harrison/did-north-korea-cheat.html.

12. "Dispute Imperils North Korea Nuke Talks," *Associated Press*, February 19, 2004, URL: http://www.military.com/newscontent/0,13319,fl_korea_021904,00.html.

13. Heo Yong-beom, "N.K. Uranium Program Known for Years: U.S. State Department," *Chosun Ilbo*, December 12, 2004, URL: http://english.chosun.com/w21data/html/news/200412/200412120019.html.

14. See Stephanie Ho, "North Korea Pursuing Two Paths Toward Nuclear Weapons," *Voice of America*, June 21, 2004, URL: http://www.iwar.org.uk/news-archive/2004/06-21-3.html; Robert L. Gallucci, "North Korean Nuclear Crisis: An Online Question and Answer Session," *Washington Post*, June 23, 2004, URL: http://discuss.washingtonpost.com/wp-srv/zforum/04/world_gallucci062304.htm.

15. "Defector: North Korea Has Uranium Program," *Associated Press*, February 8, 2004, URL: http://www.nuclearpolicy.org/newsarticleprint.cfm?newsid=1276.

16. Mitchell B. Reiss and Robert L. Gallucci, "Red Handed," *Foreign Affairs Online* (March/April 2005), URL: http://www.foreignaffairs.org/20050301faresponse84214/mitchell-b-reiss-robert-gallucci/red-handed.html.

17. David E. Sanger and James Dao, "U.S. Says Pakistan Gave (Nuclear) Technology to North Korea," *New York Times*, October 18, 2002, URL: http://membres.lycos.fr/tthreat/article24.htm.

18. David E. Sanger, "In North Korea and Pakistan, Deep Roots of Nuclear Barter," *New York Times*, November 24, 2002: A02

19. "High Stakes on the High Seas in Korean Blockade," *Sydney Morning Herald*, July 12, 2003, URL: http://www.smh.com.au/articles/2003/0711105778 3354653.html.

20. Greg Bearup, "Pakistan's Nuclear Bazaar: Dr. Khan's Shady Nuclear Family," *South China Morning Post*, February 11, 2004, URL: http://www.worldpress.org/asia/1825.cfm.

21. "Missing Pakistani Nuclear Scientists in North Korea," *Agence France-Presse*, June 20, 2004, URL: http://www.pakistan-facts.com/article.php?story= 20040620201344967.

22. Richard Cheney, Vice President of the United States, "Vice President Speaks at China's Fudan University April 15," Speech given at Fudan University, China, April 15, 2004, URL: http://helsinki.usembassy.gov/servlet/pageserver?page=today2.html.

23. "Open Letter from Senators Clinton and Levin to Secretary Rice," website of the United States Senate, April 28, 2005, URL: http://clinton.senate.gov/ 4.28.05.html.

24. "N. Korea has 4-13 Nukes, But Not Small Enough for Taepodong-2 Missile," *Kyodo News Service*, June 27, 2006, URL: http://www.kyodonews.com/.

25. "North Korea Issues for the 109th Congress," *East Asia Education Project, The Friends Committee on National Legislation,* January 2005, URL: http://www.fcnl.org/pdfs/north_korea_security_in_109.pdf.

26. See Joby Warrick and Peter Slevin, "Libyan Arms Design Traced Back to China: Pakistanis Resold Chinese-Provided Plans," *Washington Post*, February 15, 2005, URL: http://www.washingtonpost.com/ac2/wp-dyn/a42692- 2004feb14?language=printer; "U.S. Intelligence Concludes Iran, N. Korea Have Chinese Nuke Warhead Design," *East-Asia-Intel.com*, August 9, 2006, URL: http://www.east-asia-intel.com/eai/.

27. David Albright, "Finding our Way Anew to a De-Nuclearized Korean Peninsula," *Center for International Policy Working Paper*, November 19, 2002, URL: http://ciponline.org/asia/reports/task_force/Albright.htm.

28. Mark E. Manyin, Emma Chanlett-Avery, and Helene Marchart, "North Korea: A Chronology of Events, October 2002–December 2004," *CRS Report for Congress* (Washington, DC: Library of Congress, Congressional Research Service), January 24, 2005, 24.

29. "Roh Meets Bush Advisor on Nukes, Alliance," *Korea Update, The Embassy of the Republic of Korea*, July 20, 2004, URL: http://www.koreaemb.org/ archive/2004/7_2/foreign/foreign5.asp.

30. See "Text Statement of the Democratic Peoples Republic of Korea," *KCNA*, February 10, 2005, URL: http://news.bbc.co.uk/2/hi/asia-pacific/4252515.stm; "DPRK 'Manufactured' Nuclear Weapons, To 'Suspend' 6-Way Talks for 'Indefinite Period," *Korean Central Broadcasting Station Statement*, full text of February 10, 2005, statement broadcast over North Korean radio and

television, URL: http://www.nautilus.org/napsnet/sr/2005/0513a_kcbs.html.

31. Michael R. Gordon, "How Politics Sank Accord on Missiles with North Korea," *New York Times*, March 6, 2001, URL: http://www.nytimes.com/2001/03/06/world/06MISS.html.

32. "A Visit by South Korea's Leader," *New York Times*, March 6, 2001, URL: http://www.nytimes.com/2001/03/06/opinion/06TUE3.html.

33. George Gedda, "U.S. Withdraws Offer to Hold Security Talks with North Korea Next Week," *Associated Press*, July 2, 2002, URL: http://www.nautilus.org/napsnet/dr/0207/JUL03.html#item2.

34. See "Former NIS Head Says N.K. Leader Had Planned S.K. Visit in 2001," *Digital Chosun Ilbo*, June 9, 2004, URL: http://english.chosun.com/cgi-bin/printnews?id=200406090013; Bruce E. Bechtol Jr., "The Impact of North Korea's WMD Programs on Regional Security and the ROK–U.S. Alliance, *International Journal of Korean Studies*, vol. 8, no. 1 (Fall/Winter 2004): 141.

35. See Robert Marquand and Donald Kirk, "Ranks Breaking Over North Korea," *Christian Science Monitor*, June 22, 2004, URL: http://www.csmonitor.com/2004/0622/p01s04-woap.html; Ralph A. Cossa, "U.S. Mantra: N Korea Nukes Must Go, But How?" *Asia Times*, May 8, 2004, URL: http://www.atimes.com/atimes/koreafe08dg01.html.

36. Leon V. Segal, "North Korea's Tactics," *Boston Globe*, February 12, 2005, URL: http://www.boston.com/news/globe/editorial_opinion/oped/articles/2005/02/12/north_koreas_tactics.

37. Benjamin Friedman, *Fact Sheet: North Korea's Nuclear Weapons Program*, Nuclear Issues: Center for Defense Information, January 23, 2003, URL: http://www.cdi.org/nuclear/nk-fact-sheet-pr.cfm.

38. See Daniel A. Pinkston, "When Did the WMD Deals Between Pyongyang and Islamabad Begin?" *North Korea Special Collection, Monterey Institute of International Studies, Center for Nonproliferation Studies* (Monterey, CA: Monterey Institute of International Studies, January, 2003), URL: http://cns.miis.edu/pubs/week/021028.htm; Victor D. Cha, and David C. Kang, "The Korea Crisis," *Foreign Policy.com* (September 29, 2003), URL: http://www.foreignpolicy.com/story/story.php?storyID13620.

39. "North Korea Expelling IAEA Inspectors," *CNN.com*, December 27, 2002, URL: http://archives.cnn.com/2002/world/asiapcf/east/12/27/nkorea.expulsions/.

40. Brian Lee, "Atomic Test Jars World," *Joongang Ilbo*, October 10, 2006, URL: http://joongangdaily.joins.com/200610/09/20061009223702733 9900090209021.html.

41. "IAEA Director General Cites DPRK Nuclear Brinkmanship," Texts of December 26 and 27 IAEA press releases on developments in North Korea, URL: http://japan.usembassy.gov/e/p/tp-20021230a7.html.

42. Larry Niksch, "North Korea's Nuclear Weapons Program," *CRS Report for Congress* (Washington, DC: Library of Congress, Congressional Research Service), May 6, 2005, URL: http://www.fcnl.org/pdfs/nk_nuclear_may_6.pdf.

43. Edward A. Olsen, "If the United States Had 'No' Policy toward North Korea," *Strategic Insights*, vol. IV, no. 10 (October 2005), URL: http://www.ccc.nps.navy.mil/si/2005/oct/olsenoct05.asp.

44. Brian Lee, "North Agrees to Give Up its Nuclear Works, *Joongang Ilbo*, September 20, 2005, URL: http://joongangdaily.joins.com/200509/19/200509192255503579900090209021.html.

45. "Chung Broke Deadlock in North's Nuclear Crisis," *Joongang Ilbo*, October 4, 2005, URL: http://service.joins.com/asp/print_article_english.asp?aid=2625262&esectcode=e_special&title=chung+broke+deadlock+in+north's+nuclear+crisis.

46. "Seoul Saved Six-Party Talks: Unification Minister," *Chosun Ilbo*, September 19, 2005, URL: http://english.chosun.com/w21data/html/news/200509/200509190024.html.

47. Brian Lee, "Details Could Stir Controversies," *Joongang Ilbo*, September 20, 2005, URL: http://service.joins.com/asp/.

48. "U.S. Aide Says North Must Scrap Uranium," *Joongang Ilbo*, October 5, 2005, URL: http://joongangdaily.joins.com/200510/04/20051004225416 1839900090209021.html.

49. Henry Sokolski, "Hide and Seek with Kim Chong-il," *Nautilus Institute Policy Forum Online 05-80A*, September 29, 2005, URL: http://www.nautilus.org/fora/security/0580Sokolski.html.

50. Jon Wolfsthal, "No Good Choices: The Implications of a Nuclear North Korea," Testimony to the U.S. House of Representatives International Relations Committee, Sub-Committees on Asia and the Pacific and on International Terrorism and Nonproliferation, February 17, 2005, URL: http://wwwc.house.gov/international_relations/109/wol021705.htm.

51. Kwang-tae Kim, "N. Korea Claims U.S. Undermine Nuke Talks," *Associated Press*, November 10, 2005, URL: http://www.adelphia.net/news/read.php?ps=1012&id=12340267.

52. Nick Green, "Dealing Drugs: North Korean Narcotics Trafficking," *Harvard International Review*, vol. 26, no. 1 (Spring 2004), URL: http://hir.harvard.edu/articles/1201.

53. Ah-Young Kim, "Targeting Pyongyang's Drug Trade Addiction," *Asia Times*, June 18, 2003, URL: http://www.atimes.com/atimes/korea/ef19dg04.html.

54. Treasury Designates Banco Delta Asia as Primary Money Laundering Concern under USA PATRIOT Act," U.S, Department of Treasury Press Release, September 15, 2005, URL: http://www.treas.gov/press/releases/js2720.htm.

55. Raphael F. Perl, "Drug Trafficking and North Korea: Issues for U.S. Policy," *CRS Report for Congress*, Congressional Research Service, Washington, DC, December 5, 2003, URL: http://www.fas.org/sgp/crs/row/RL32167.pdf.

56. "U.S. Mulls Team to Discuss Korea Peace Treaty, *Chosun Ilbo*, November 2, 2005, URL: http://english.chosun.com/w21data/html/news/200511/200511020027.html.

57. The author attended a conference at Georgetown University in November 2005, where the subject of a "Peace Treaty" with North Korea was widely discussed by former U.S. and current South Korean policy makers and academics.

58. "U.S. Vows to Match N. Korea Action for Action," *Chosun Ilbo*, November 3, 2005, URL: http://english.chosun.com/w21data/html/news/200511/200511030015.html.

59. Young-Gun Lee, "Outlook Uncertain as Six-Party Talks End," *Donga Ilbo*, November 12, 2005, URL: http://english.donga.com/srv/service.php3? bicode=050000&biid=2005111283758.

60. Peter Baker and Anthony Faille, "U.S., S. Korea Find Unity against North's Nuclear Arms Program," *Washington Post*, November 17, 2005, 20.

61. See Donald Kirk, "N. Korea's Test Threat Causes Uproar," *Christian Science Monitor*, June 22, 2006, URL: http://www.csmonitor.com/2006/0622/p06s02-woap.html; and (2nd LD) "N. Korea Trying to Shift U.S. Policy with Missile Threats: Official," *Yonhap News Agency*, June 23, 2006, URL: http://english.yonhapnews.co.kr/Engservices/4101000000.html.

62. Chuck Downs, "Right Where He Wants Us," *Wall Street Journal*, Commentary, June 21, 2006.

63. Ser Myo-ja, "Roh Calls for Softer Stance against North," *Joongang Ilbo*, November 15, 2004, URL: http://joongangdaily.joins.com/200411/14/200411142157137909900090309031.html.

64. Jung-Hun Kim, "President Roh Says U.S. Sanctions to N. Korea Would Be Undesirable," *Donga Ilbo*, November 14, 2004, URL: http://english.donga.com/srv/service.php3?biid=2004111590368.

65. Cho Kisuk, "Understanding Public Opinion in Korea," keynote speech presented at Georgetown University, Washington, DC, November 4, 2005, at Georgetown's School of Foreign Service and Korea's Sejong Institute co-sponsored conference titled, "New Era: New Alliance," URL: http://www.kois.go.kr/news/news/newsview.asp?serial_no=20051104015&part=111&searchday.

66. *At Cold War's End: U.S. Intelligence on the Soviet Union and Eastern Europe, 1989–1991*, History Staff, Center for the Study of Intelligence, Central Intelligence Agency, URL: http://www.cia.gov/csi/books/19335/art-1.html.

67. "Special Report on the North Korean Nuclear Weapons Statement," *Center for Nonproliferation Studies, Monterey Institute of International Studies*, February 11, 2005, URL: http://cns.miis.edu/pubs/week/050211.htm.

68. Donald Macintyre, "Kim's War Machine," *Time Asia*, February 17, 2003, URL: http://www.time.com/time/asia/covers/ 501030224/army.html.

69. Marcus Noland, "North Korea and the South Korean Economy," paper presented to Roh government transition team, Seoul, Korea, February 24, 2003, URL: http://www.iie.com/publications/papers/paper.cfm?researchid=242.

70. David L. Asher, "The North Korean Criminal State, its Ties to Organized Crime, and the Possibility of WMD Proliferation," Remarks presented to the Counter-Proliferation Strategy Group, Woodrow Wilson Center, Washington, DC, October 21, 2005, URL: http://www.nautilus.org/fora/security0502asher.html.

71. Daniel Pinkston, "North Korea Conducts Nuclear Test," *Center for Nonproliferation Studies, Monterey Institute of International Studies*, October 10, 2006, URL: http://cns.miis.edu/pubs/week/pdf/061010_dprktest.pdf.

72. Siegfried S. Hecker, "Report on North Korean Nuclear Program," *Center for International Security and Cooperation, Stanford University*, November 15, 2006, URL: http://iis-db.stanford.edu/pubs/21266/dprk-report-hecker06.pdf.

73. Kim Min-seok and Park Bang-ju, "Atomic Test Evidence Shows Partial Success," *Joongang Ilbo*, October 17, 2006, URL: http://joongangdaily.joins.com/200610/16/200610162243083379900090309031.html.

74. Burt Herman, "North Korea May Be Backing Off Showdown," *Associated Press*, October 20, 2006, URL: http://www.washingtonpost.com/wp-dyn/content/article/2006/10/20/AR2006102000273.html.

75. "Report: N. Korea Leader Regrets Test," *Associated Press*, October 20, 2006, URL: http://apnews.myway.com/article/20061020/D8KSA5PG3.html.

76. "North Korea—Denuclearization Action Plan: Initial Actions for the Implementation of the Joint Statement," *U.S. Department of State*, February 13, 2007, URL: http://www.state.gov/r/pa/prs/ps/2007/february/80479.htm.

77. For more details regarding the joint statement of February 13, 2007, see "Initial Actions for the Implementation of the Joint Statement: Joint Statement from the Third Session of the Fifth Round of the Six-Party Talks," *Nautilus Institute Special Report*, February 13, 2007, URL: http://www.nautilus.org/fora/security/07013Statement.html.

78. "Press Briefing by Tony Snow," *White House Press Releases*, February 13, 2007, URL: http://www.whitehouse.gov/news/releases/2007/02/20070213-3.html.

79. "Briefing on the Agreement Reached at the Six-Party Talks in Beijing," *U.S. Department of State*, February 13, 2007, URL: http://www.state.gov/secretary/rm/2007/feb/80496.htm.

80. See Glen Kessler, "Conservatives Assail North Korea Accord," *Washington Post*, February 15, 2007, URL: http://www.washingtonpost.com/wp-dyn/content/article/2007/02/14/AR2007021401695.html; Ben Feller, "White House Calms GOP Base on Korea," *Monterey Herald*, February 15, 2007, URL: http://www.montereyherald.com/mld/montereyherald/news/politics/16706095.htm.

81. "N. Korea Could Expel Nuclear Inspectors," *Donga Ilbo*, February 15, 2007, URL: http://english.donga.com/srv/service.php3?bicode=050000&biid=2007021696018.

82. Tim Johnson, "Nuclear Accord Far From Foolproof, Experts Fear," *Miami Herald*, February 18, 2007, URL: http://www.miami.com/mld/miamiherald/news/world/16725042.htm.

83. "North Korea Agrees to Abandon Nuclear Program, *PBS Online News Hour*, February 13, 2007, URL: http://www.pbs.org/newshour/bb/asia/jan-june07/koreadeal_02-13.html.

84. "Hasty Celebration of Six-Party Talks Worries Critics," *Donga Ilbo*, February 15, 2007, URL: http://english.donga.com/srv/service.php3?biid=2007021571868.

85. David Sanger, "Outside Pressures Broke Korean Deadlock," *New York Times*, February 14, 2007, URL: http://select.nytimes.com/gstabstract.html?res=F30F13F63D5A0C778DDDAB0894DF404482.

86. "Transcript: Update on the Six-Party Talks with Christopher R. Hill," *Brookings Institution Center for Northeast Asian Policy Studies*, February 22, 2007, URL: http://www.brook.edu/comm/events/20070228hill.pdf.

87. David Sanger and Thom Shanker, "Rice is Said to Have Speeded North Korea Deal," *International Herald Tribune*, February 15, 2007, URL: http://www.iht.com/articles/2007/02/16/asia/web.0216.php?page=1.

88. See Brian Lee, "Pyongyang Holds Key for Nuclear Inspection Access,"

Joongang Ilbo, February 20, 2007, URL: http://joongangdaily.joins.com/article/view.asp?aid=2872599; "S. Korea Spy Says NKorea Enriching Uranium," *ABC Radio Australia*, February 21, 2007, URL: http://www.radioaustralia.net.au/news/stories/s1852712.htm; Brian Lee, "Ex-U.S. Official: The Key to Deal is North's Disclosure of Uranium," *Joongang Ilbo*, February 21, 2007, URL: http://joongangdaily.joins.com/article/view.asp?aid=2872644; and Brian Lee, "Seoul Side: Uranium is not Forgotten," *Joongang Ilbo*, February 17, 2007, URL: http://joongangdaily.joins.com/article/view.asp?aid=2872552.

89. Jung Sung-ki, "65% Oppose Hasty Talks With North," *Korea Times*, February 16, 2007, URL: http://times.hankooki.com/lpage/nation/200702/kt2007021619164511990.htm.

90. Magnier, "Many Questions Remain on North Korea Accord," *Los Angeles Times*, February 14, 2007, URL: http://www.latimes.com/news/nationworld/world/la-fg-norkor14feb14,1,2586076.story?coll=la-headlines-world.

91. "Bombs Left for Final Stage of Nuke Talks," *Chosun Ilbo*, February 15, 2007, URL: http://english.chosun.com/w21data/html/news/200702200702150020.html.

92. Peter Hayes, "The Beijing Deal is Not the Agreed Framework," *Nautilus Policy Forum Online 07-014A*, February 14, 2007, URL: http://www.nautilus.org/fora/security/07014Hayes.html.

93. Don Kirk, "Flawed Deal Keeps Kim Ahead of the Pack," *South China Morning Post*, February 17, 2007.

94. Gen. B. B. Bell, Commander, United Nations Command, Republic of Korea–United States Combined Forces Command; Commander United States Forces Korea, *Statement for the Record to the Senate Armed Services Committee*, March 7, 2007, URL: http://armedservices.house.gov/pdfs/FCPACOM030707/Bell_Testimony030707.pdf.

95. Kongdan Oh and Ralph C. Hassig, "North Korea's Nuclear Politics," *Current History*, vol. 103 (September 2004): 274–275.

96. "Seoul Steps up Efforts to Detect North's Nukes," *Taipei Times*, August 21, 2006, URL: http://www.taipeitimes.com/News/world/archives/2006/08/21/2003324147.

97. Jungmin Kang and Peter Hayes, "Technical Analysis of the DPRK Nuclear Test," *Nautilus Institute Policy Forum Online 06-89A*, October 20, 2006, URL: http://www.nautilus.org/fora/security/0689hayeskang.html.

98. For an outstanding example of this "nuclear bravado," see "N. Korean General: We'll Nuke You," *CBS News Online*, January 13, 2006, URL: http://www.cbsnews.com/stories/2006/01/12/60minutes/main1203973.shtml.

99. Bennett Ramberg, "Why North Korea Will Not Give up the Bomb," *International Herald Tribune*, January 6, 2006, URL: http://www.iht.com/articles/2006/01/05/opinion/edramberg.php.

Chapter 3: North Korea's Missiles: Proliferation, Deployment, Testing, and Tools of Foreign Policy

1. "North Korea Profile: Missile Overview," *Nuclear Threat Initiative*, 2003, URL: http://www.nti.org/e_research/profiles/nk/missile/index_1667.html.

2. Joseph S. Bermudez, Jr., "A History of Ballistic Missile Development in the DPRK: CNS Occasional Paper #2," *Center for Non-Proliferation Studies*,

Monterey Institute, 1999, URL: http://cns.miis.edu/pubs/opapers/op2/index.htm.

3. Thomas Woodrow, "China Opens Pandora's Nuclear Box," *China Brief*, vol. 2, no. 24, December 10, 2002, URL: http://www.jamestown.org/publications_details.php?volume_id=18&&issue_id=664.

4. "North Korea Missile Milestones," *The Risk Report*, vol. 6, no. 5, September-October 2000, URL: http://www.wisconsinproject.org/countries/nkorea/missile-miles.htm.

5. "Chronology of North Korea's Missile Trade and Developments: 1980–1989," *Center for Non-Proliferation Studies, Monterey Institute*, 2003, URL: http://cns.miis.edu/research/korea/chr8089.htm.

6. Victoria Samson, "North Korea's Missile Flight Tests," *Center for Defense Information*, November 20, 2003, URL: http://www.cdi.org/friendlyversion/printversion.cfm?documentID=1677.

7. For more detailed analysis of the development of the No Dong missile, see David C. Wright and Timur Kadyshev, "An Analysis of the No Dong Missile," *Science and Global Security*, vol. 4 (1994), URL: http://www.princeton.edu/~globsec/publications/pdf/4_2wright.pdf.

8. "North Korea's Nuclear-Capable Missiles," *The Risk Report*, vol. 2, no. 6, November–December 1996, URL: http://www.wisconsinproject.org/countries/nkorea/nukemiss.html.

9. David C. Wright, "Assessment of the North Korean Missile Program," *Union of Concerned Scientists*, February 25, 2003, URL: http://www.ucsusa.org/global_security/missile_defense/assessment-of-the-north-korean-missile-program.html.

10. Joseph Bermudez, "North Korea Set to Launch Taepo Dong 2," *Jane's Defence Weekly*, July 5, 2006, 4–5.

11. "Paper: N. Korea Preparing for Missile Test," *Associated Press*, June 1, 2006, URL: http://www.usatoday.com/news/world/2006-06-01-nkorea-missile_xhtm.

12. See "North Korea Expected to Test Long-Range Missile," *Los Angeles Times*, June 17, 2006, URL: http://www.latimes.com/news/nationworld/world/la-fg-korea17jun17,1,6609140.story?coll=la-headlines-world&ctrack=1&cset=true; Chisaki Watanabe, "N. Korea Denies It's About to Test Missile," *Associated Press*, June 17, 2006, URL: http://www.forbes.com/entrepreneurs/feeds/ap/2006/06/17/ap2822073.html.

13. See "Major Concern if North Korea Launches Long-Range Missile: U.S.," *Agence France-Presse*, May 23, 2006, URL: http://www.defencetalk.com/news/publish/article_006119.php; "Seoul Tries to Dissuade North from Missile Launch," *Chosun Ilbo*, May 19, 2006, URL: http://english.chosun.com/w21data/html/news/200605/200605190011.html.

14. See "N. Korea Has Been Ready for New Missile Test Since 2005: Sources," *Kyodo News*, May 22, 2006, URL: http://asia.news.yahoo.com/060522/kyodo/d8hog7f00.html; and "U.S. to Seek U.N. Sanctions if N. Korea Fires Long-Range Missile," *Kyodo News*, May 26, 2006, URL: http://finance.comcast.net/rich/news_body.html?id=comtex_CTB_en%3A1148694540&auth.

15. "Navy Shoots Down a Long-Range Missile," *CNN.com*, May 25, 2006, URL: http://edition.cnn.com/2006/U.S./05/24/missile.defense.ap/.

16. Hiromichi Umebayashi, "U.S. Navy Set Missile Defense Operations Area in the Sea of Japan 190 Kilometers West of Okushiri: Japan as a Base for the Defense of the U.S. Homeland," *Nautilus Institute Special Report*, June 2, 2006, URL: http://www.nautilus.org/napsnet/sr/2006/0642Umebayashi.pdf.

17. U.S. Missile Defense System Prepared for Anticipated N. Korean Launch," *East-Asia-Intel.com*, June 7, 2006, URL: http://www.east-asia-intel.com/eai/2006/06_07/12.asp.

18. Matt Kelley, "U.S. Still Working Kinks Out of Defense Shield," *USA Today*, June 21, 2006.

19. "U.S. Dismisses Call to Destroy N. Korea Missile," *MSNBC Online*, June 22, 2006, URL: http://www.msnbc.msn.com/id/13481845/.

20. David Sanger, "Don't Shoot, We're Not Ready," *New York Times*, June 25, 2006, URL: http://www.nytimes.com/2006/06/25/weekinreview25sanger.html?_r=1&oref=slogin.

21. Mari Yamaguchi, "U.S. to Put Patriot Interceptors in Japan," *Associated Press*, June 26, 2006, URL: http://seattlepi.nwsource.com/national/1104ap_japan_us_missile_defense.html.

22. Ashton B. Carter and William J. Perry, "If Necessary, Strike and Destroy," *Washington Post*, June 22, 2006.

23. "Mondale Supports Pre-Emptive Strike Against North Korea," *Associated Press*, June 23, 2006, URL: http://www.startribune.com/587/story511193.html.

24. Steven Donald Smith, "North Korea, Iran Pose Missile Threat to U.S., General Says," *American Forces Information Service*, March 10, 2006, URL: http://www.defenselink.mil/news/mar2006/20060310_4447.html.

25. B. C. Koh, "North Korea's Missile Launches and Six-Party Talks," *Institute for Far Eastern Studies Forum* (August 21, 2006), URL: http://ifes.kyungnam.ac.kr/eng/activity/05_ifes_forum_view.asp?ifesforumNO=181&page=1.

26. "Tokyo, Seoul and U.S. Now Agree on Details of Taepo Dong 2 Explosion," *East-Asia-Intel.com*, August 2, 2006, URL: http://www.east-asia-intel.com/eai/.

27. Peter Hayes, "Embrace Tiger, Retreat to Mountain, Test Nuke," *Nautilus Institute Policy Forum Online 06-60A*, July 21, 2006, URL: http://www.nautilus.org/fora/security/0660Hayes.html.

28. "Asiana Plane in Close Shave as North Launches Missile," *Chosun Ilbo*, July 6, 2006, URL: http://english.chosun.com/w21data/html/news/200607/200607060029.html.

29. "North Korea's Missile Puts Neighbouring Russian City on Edge," *ITAR-TASS*, July 5, 2006, URL: http://www.itar-tass.com/eng/.

30. "North Korea's Missile Programme," *BBC News*, July 5, 2006, URL: http://news.bbc.co.uk/1/hi/world/asia-pacific/2564241.stm.

31. Clarence A. Robinson, Jr., "Missile Technology Access Emboldens Rogue Nations," *SIGNAL* (April 1999), URL: http://www.afcea.org/signal/archives/content/April99/missile-april.html.

32. "Transcript: North Korea Launches Seven Missiles; Enron Founder Dies in Apparent Heart Attack," *CNN.com*, aired July 5, 2006, URL: http://transcripts.cnn.com/TRANSCRIPTS/0607/05/lt.01.html.

33. Anthony Cordesman, "Missile Menace: Weighing the Real Threat From North Korea," *San Diego Union Tribune*, July 9, 2006, URL: http://www.signonsandiego.com/uniontrib/20060709/news_lz1e9cordesma.html.

34. See "Iran Military Engineers on Hand for N. Korea Missile Launch," *World Tribune*, July 12, 2006, URL: http://www.worldtribune.com/worldtribune/06/front2453929.001388889.html; and Barbara Demick, "N. Korea-Iran Ties Seem to Be Growing Stronger," *Los Angeles Times*, July 27, 2006, URL: http://www.latimes.com/news/printedition/asection/la-fgmissile27jul27, 1,6737932.story?coll=la-news-a_section&ctrack=1&cset=true.

35. See Kim Min-seok and Brian Lee, "Pyongyang Reportedly Tests New Scud," *Joongang Ilbo*, July 19, 2006, URL: http://joongangdaily.joins.com/200607/18/2006071821383514799000090309031.html; "North Korea Profile: Missile Overview," *Nuclear Threat Initiative*, August 2006, URL: http://www.nti.org/e_research/profiles/nk/index_1667.html; and "North Korea: Missiles and Diplomatic Strategy," *STRATFOR*, July 18, 2006, URL: http://www.stratfor.com.

36. See (3rdLD) "Security Council Unanimously Backs Resolution Against N.K. Missile Launches," *Yonhap News Agency*, July 15, 2006, URL: http://english.yna.co.kr/engnews/20060716/610000000020060716075653e1.html; "U.N. Unanimously Adopts North Korea Sanctions," *Chosun Ilbo*, July 16, 2006, URL: http://english.chosun.com/w21data/html/news/200607/200607160001.html; and "Security Council Condemns North Korea," *CBS News*, July 15, 2006, URL: http://www.cbsnews.com/stories/2006/07/15/world/main1807134.shtml.

37. "N. Korea Threatens to 'Bolster War Deterrent' in Protest to U.N.," *AFX News Limited*, July 16, 2006, URL: http://www.forbes.com/home/feeds/afx/2006/07/16/afx28811546.html.

38. Bert Herman, "China Reduces Oil Shipment to N. Korea," *ABC News*, August 26, 2006, URL: http://abcnews.go.com/international/wirestory?id=2359069.

39. Paul Carroll, "Trip Report by Paul Carroll," *Nautilus Institute Policy Forum Online 06-59A*, July 20, 2006, URL: http://www.nautilus.org/fora/security/0659tripreport.html.

40. "S Korea Suspends North Food Aid," *BBC News*, July 7, 2006, URL: http://news.bbc.co.uk/2/hi/asia-pacific/5156464.stm.

41. Joseph S. Bermudez, Jr., "North Korea Deploys New Missiles," *Jane's Defence Weekly* (August 2, 2004), URL: http://www.janes.com/defence/news/jdw/jdw040802_1_n.shtml.

42. Paul Kerr, "New North Korean Missile Suspected," *Arms Control Today*, September 2004, URL: http://www.armscontrol.org/act/2004_09/nk_missile.asp.

43. James Dunnigan, "North Korea's SS-21 Missiles," *Strategy Page*, May 12, 2005, URL: http://www.strategypage.com/dls/articles/2005512213718.asp.

44. Paul Kerr, "North Korea Increasing Weapons Capabilities," *Arms Control Today*, December 2005, URL: http://www.armscontrol.org/act/2005_12/dec-nkweapons.asp.

45. See "N.K. Fired Russian Missile: Official," *Korea Times*, May 4, 2005, URL: http://times.hankooki.com/lpage/nation/200505kt2005050422050611

990.htm; "U.S. Responds to Latest N. Korean Missile Test," *Chosun Ilbo*, March 10, 2006, URL: http://english.chosun.com/w21data/html/news/200603/200603100010.html; and Jack Kim, "N. Korean Missiles Tested are Quantum Leap: U.S. General," *Reuters*, March 10, 2006, URL: http://www.defensenews.comstory.php?f=1589997&c=asiapac.

46.   For more details on General Bell's Congressional Testimony regarding North Korean missiles, see Gen. B. B. Bell, Commander, United Nations Command, Republic of Korea-United States Combined Forces Command; Commander United States Forces Korea," *Statement for the Record to the Senate Armed Services Committee*, March 7, 2006, URL: http://www.senate.gov/~armed_services/statemnt/2006/march/bell%2003-07-06.pdf.

47.   See Joby Warrick, "North Korea Shops Stealthily for Nuclear Arms Gear," *Washington Post*, August 15, 2003, URL: http://www.washingtonpost.com/ac2/wp-dyn?pagename=article&node=&contentID; and Joby Warrick, "On North Korean Freighter, a Hidden Missile Factory," *Washington Post*, August 14, 2003.

48.   Paula A. DeSutter, "Completion of Verification Work in Libya," *Testimony to the U.S. House of Representatives Subcommittee on International Terrorism, Nonproliferation and Human Rights*, September 22, 2004, URL: http://www.state.gov/t/vci/rls/rm/2004/37220.htm.

49.   "N. Korean Rail Explosion Foiled Missile Shipment to Syria," *World Tribune.com*, May 18, 2004, URL: http://216.26.163.62/2004/ss_syria_05_18.html.

50.   See "Syrians With Secret CBW Material on Train that Exploded?" *IMRA.com*, May 15, 2004, URL: http://www/imra.org.il/story.php3?id=20828; and "Source Notes Syrian Technicians Killed in Yongch'on Train Explosion," *Tokyo Sankei Shimbum*, May 7, 2004.

51.   "The Gulf War: Weapons: SS1 SCUD," *PBS Frontline*, 1991, URL: http://www.pbs.org/wgbh/pages/frontline/gulf/weapons/scud.html.

52.   "Syria Improves Its SCUD D Missile With Help From North Korea," *Geostrategy-Direct*, February 22, 2006, URL: http://www.geostrategy-direct.com/geostrategy%2ddirect/.

53.   "Patterns of Terrorism," Released by the Office of the Coordinator for Counterterrorism, U.S. Department of State, 2003, URL: http://www.state.gov/s/ct/rls/pgtrpt/2003/31644.htm.

54.   "Rebels Bought Arms From North Korea Spy," *United Press International*, March 13, 2003, URL: http://www.upi.com/view.cfm?storyid=20030313-062155-7264r.

55.   See Con Coughlin, "North Korea to Help Iran Build Secret Missile Bunkers," *Daily Telegraph*, December 6, 2005, URL: http://www.telegraph.co.uk/news/main.jhtml?xml=/news/2005/06/12/wnkor12.xml&sSheet=/news/2005/06/12/ixnewstop.html; and "Report: North Korea Supervised Building of Hezbullah Underground Facilities," *East-Asia-Intel.com*, September 13, 2006, URL: http://www.east-asia-intl.com/eai/2006/09_13/12.asp.

56.   "No-Dong," *Missile Threat.com*, A Project of the Claremont Institute, January 8, 2006, URL: http://www.missilethreat.com/missiles/no-dong-2_north_korea.html.

57.   See Charles R. Smith, "Asian Arms Race Result of Appeasement Policy,"
      NewsMax.com, February 8, 2003, URL: http://www.newsmax.com/archives/
      articles/2003/1/7/164846.shtml; Jess Altschul, "Pakistan–North Korea
      Weapons Trade Continued Through 2002," *Jewish Institute for National
      Security Affairs*, September 9, 2003, URL: http://www.jinsa.org/articles/
      articles.html/function/view/categoryid/169/documentid/2202/history/
      3,2360,652,169,2202; Matthew Pennington, "Pakistan: We're Sharing Nuke
      Finds," *CBS News Online*, April 13, 2004, URL: http://www.cbsnews.com/stories/
      2004/04/13/world/main611610.shtml; and Sharon A. Squassoni, "Weapons of
      Mass Destruction: Trade Between North Korea and Pakistan," *CRS Report for
      Congress,* Congressional Research Service, March 11, 2004, URL: http://
      www.fas.org/spp/starwars/crs/RL31900.pdf.

58.   See Choe Sang-hun, "Iran-North Korea Talks May Harden U.S. Stance,"
      International Herald Tribune, November 27, 2005, URL: http://www.iht.com/
      articles/2005/11/27/news/korea.php; "Tehran to Pyongyang: Trade Oil for
      Nuke Help," *WorldNet Daily*, November 27, 2005, URL: http://www.world
      netdaily.com/newsarticle.asp?article_id=47597; and "Iran's Long-Range Missile
      Program: Nato's Next Challenge," *Defense Update News Commentary*,
      January 19, 2005, URL: http://www.defense-update.com/2005/01/irans-long-
      range-missile-program-natos.html.

59.   "Iran's Ballistic Missile and Weapons of Mass Destruction Programs," Hearing
      before the International Security, Proliferation, and Federal Services
      Subcommittee of the Committee on Governmental Affairs, U.S. Senate, 106th
      Congress, Second Session, September 21, 2000, URL: http://www.fas.org/
      irp/congress/2000_hr/hr_092100.html.

60.   See Alon Ben-David, "Iran Acquires Ballistic Missiles from DPRK," *Jane's
      Defence Weekly*, December 29, 2005, URL: http://www.janes.com/security/
      international_security/news/jdw/jdw051229_1_n.shtml; and "Iran Bought 18
      North Korean Missiles," *Taipei Times*, December 17, 2005, URL: http://
      www.taipeitimes.com/news/world/archives/2005/12/17/2003284803.

61.   "Iran Develops Missile With 4,000-KM Range," *Middle East Newsline*, March
      2, 2006, URL: http://www.menewsline.com/stories/2006/march03_02_1.html.

62.   Charles P. Vick, "Has the No-Dong B/Shahab-4 Finally Been Tested in Iran
      for North Korea?" *Global Security.org*, May 2, 2006, URL: http://
      www.globalsecurity.org/wmd/library/report/2006/cpvick-no-dong-
      b_2006.htm.

63.   Charles P. Vick, "The Closely Related Collaborative Iranian, North Korean,
      and Pakistani Strategic Space, Ballistic Missile and Nuclear Weapon
      Programs," *Global Security.org*, May 23, 2006, URL: http://
      www.globalsecurity.org/wmd/world/iran/missile-development.htm.

64.   Uzi Rubin, "The Global Range of Iran's Ballistic Missile Program," *Jerusalem
      Issue Brief, Institute for Contemporary Affairs*, vol. 5, no. 26 (June 20, 2006),
      URL: http://www.jcpa.org/brief/brief005-26.htm.

65.   Touqir Hussain, "U.S.–Pakistan Engagement: The War on Terrorism and
      Beyond," Special Report no. 145, *United States Institute of Peace*, August
      2005, URL: http://www.usip.org/pubs/specialreports/sr145.html.

66.   "Pyongyang Urged to do More," *Asia Times*, November 30, 2001, URL: http://
      www.atimes.com/koreas/ck30dg02.html.

67. Bill Gertz, "The North Korean Missile Threat," *Air Force: Journal of the Air Force Association*, vol. 83, no. 1, January 2000, URL: http://www.afa.org/magazine/jan2000/0100missile.asp.

68. Bertil Linter, "North Korea's Missile Trade Helps Fund its Nuclear Program," *Yale Global Online*, May 5, 2003, URL: http://yaleglobal.yale.edu/display.article?id=1546.

69. Michael E. O'Hanlon, "A Master Plan to Deal with North Korea," Policy Brief no. 114, Brookings Institution, January 2003, URL: http://www.brookings.org/comm/policybriefs/pb114.htm.

70. Randall Parker, "Pakistan Buys North Korean Missiles," *ParaPundit.com*, March 31, 2003, URL: http://www.parapundit.com/archives/001086.html.

71. "N. Korea No Dong Missile Could Reach all of Japan, Nikkei Says," *Bloomberg.com*, June 1, 2004, URL: http://quote.bloomberg.com/apps/news?pid=10000101&sid=aeehgknrjafs&refer=japan.

72. Kim Min-seok, "North Appears Set to Test New Missile Engines," *Joongang Ilbo*, May 5, 2004, URL: http://joongangdaily.joins.com/200405/05/200405052351452109900090309031.html.

73. "North Deploys New 4,000Km Range Missiles," *Chosun Ilbo*, May 5, 2004, URL: http://english.chosun.com/cgi-bin/printnews?id=200405040031.

74. Kim Min-seok, "North is Said to Reinforce Military," *Joongang Ilbo*, July 8, 2004, URL: http://joongangdaily.joins.com/200407/07/200407072259173579900090309031.html.

75. See "N. Korea Building New Missile Bases, Silos Along East Coast: Report," *Yonhap News Agency*, August 3, 2006, URL: http://www.freerepublic.com/focus/f-news/1676857/posts; and "N. Korea Has Eight Medium-Range Missile Pads: NIS," *Chosun Ilbo*, July 12, 2006, URL: http://english.chosun.com/w21data/html/news/200607/200607120018.html.

76. *Report No. 2000/09: Ballistic Missile Proliferation,* Perspectives, Canadian Security Intelligence Services, March 21, 2001, URL: http://www.csis-scrs.gc.ca/en/publications/perspectives/200009.asp.

77. "Flashpoint: North Korea," *PBS Online News Hour*, April 14, 2003, URL: http://www.pbs.org/newshour/bb/asia/jan-june03/nkorea_04-14.html.

78. Robert D Walpole, National Intelligence Officer for Strategic and Nuclear Programs, "The Iranian Ballistic Missile and WMD Threat to the United States Through 2015," Statement for the record to the International Security, Proliferation and Federal Services Subcommittee of the Senate Government Affairs Committee, September 21, 2000, URL: http://www.cia.gov/nic/testimony_wmdthreat.html.

79. For more information regarding North Korea's perceived security needs, and its use of missiles as one of the tools to satisfy those needs, see Andrew Scobell, *North Korea's Strategic Intentions*, Strategic Studies Institute Monograph (Carlisle, PA: U.S. Army War College, July 2005), URL: http://www.nautilus.org/napsnet/sr/2005/0569scobel.pdf.

80. James Dao, "U.S. Shaping North Korea Sanction," *New York Times*, February 27, 2003, URL: http://www.globalpolicy.org/security/sanction/nkorea/2003/0305san.htm.

81. Edward A. Olsen, "U.S.–North Korea: From Brinkmanship to Dialogue," *Strategic Insight*, (Monterey, CA: Center for Contemporary Conflict), April

1, 2003, URL: http://www.ccc.nps.navy.mil/rsepresources/si/apr03/eastasia.asp.

82. Thomas H. Henriksen, "Using Power and Diplomacy To Deal With Rogue States," *Hoover Institution Essays in Public Policy*, February 1999, URL: http://www.hoover.org/publications/epp/default.html.

Chapter 4: Adjusting to Economic Realities: The Evolving Doctrine, Readiness, and Capabilities of North Korea's Conventional Forces

1. For more analysis on this school of thought, see Richard A. Matthew and Ted Gaulin, "Time to Sign the Mine Ban Treaty," *Issues in Science and Technology*, Spring 2003, URL: http://www.issues.org/issues/19.3/matthew.htm; and David Kang, "Transcript: North Korea's Nuclear Program, an Online Question and Answer Session," *Washington Post*, May 4, 2005, URL: http://www.washingtonpost.com/wp-dyn/content/discussion/2005/05/03/DI2005050300593.html.

2. For more detailed analysis on this school of thought, see Homer T. Hodge, "North Korea's Military Strategy," *Parameters*, Spring 2003, URL: http://carlisle-www.army.mil/usawc/Parameters/03spring/hodge.htm.

3. "North Korea: Suspicious Minds," *PBS Frontline* Transcript Online, January 2003, URL: http://www.pbs.org/frontlineworld/stories/northkorea/facts.html.

4. *White Paper: 1998,* Republic of Korea, Ministry of National Defense, chapter 3, 1998, URL: http://www.mnd.go.kr/english/html/02/1998/133.html.

5. "Democratic Peoples Republic of Korea," *Asia Source*, October 2002, URL: http://www.asiasource.org/policy/northakorea.cfm.

6. The map, from 2005, showing North Korean military forces disposition, is the latest map posted by the Library of Congress. The disposition and name for some units may have changed based on data that is unavailable in the unclassified domain at this time. Nevertheless, the general strength and disposition of forces shown on the map gives the reader an excellent general description of type and location of conventional combat units deployed throughout the North Korean land mass. URL: http://lcweb2.loc.gov/frd/cs/korea_north/kp05_03a.pdf.

7. "Korean Peoples Army," *Federation of American Scientists*, June 15, 2000, URL: http://www.fas.org/nuke/guide/dprk/agency/army.htm.

8. Library of Congress, *North Korea: A Country Study*, URL: http://lcweb2.loc.gov/frd/cs/kptoc.html.

9. *White Paper: 1996,* Republic of Korea, Ministry of National Defense, chapter 3, 1996, URL: http://mnd.go.kr/mnd/mnden/sub_menu/w_book/1996/232.html.

10. *White Paper: 1999,* Republic of Korea, Ministry of National Defense, chapter 3, 1999, URL: http://www.mnd.go.kr/cms.jsp?p_id=01902000000000&cmstrans=/jsps/w_book1.jsp&src=/english/html/02/1999/index.html.

11. "Korean Peoples Army Air Force," *Global Security.org*, 2002, URL: http://www.globalsecurity.org/military/world/dprk/airforce.htm.

12. *White Paper: 1999,* Republic of Korea, Ministry of National Defense, chapter 3, 1999.

13. Todd Crowell and Laxmi Nakarmi, "Battle of the West Sea: Behind the Latest Clash Between the Koreas," *Asia Week*, June 25, 1999, URL: http://www.asiaweek.com/asiaweek/99/0625/nat5.html.

14. Adrei Lankov, "Still Waters Run Deep," *Korea Times*, October 4, 2005, URL: http://times.hankooki.com/lpage/opinion/200510/kt2005100416 444754140.htm.

15. *White Paper: 2000,* Republic of Korea, Ministry of National Defense, chapter chapter 3, 2000, URL: http://www.mnd.go.kr/cms.jsp?p_id=01902000 000000&cmstrans=/jsps/w_book1.jsp&src=/english/html/02/2000/index.html.

16. Portions of the analysis in this section were previously published: Dr. Bruce E. Bechtol, Jr., "The Future of U.S. Airpower on the Korean Peninsula," *Air and Space Power Journal*, vol. XIX, no. 3 (Fall 2005): 75-84. Whereas only small sections of the research published in the article may be reflected as close similarities to analysis in this section, any and all similarities or quotations attributed to the article are printed with the expressed written permission of the *Air and Space Power Journal.* The author wishes to express thanks and gratitude to the editor of the *Air and Space Power Journal* during 2005, Lt. Col. Paul D. Berg, Ph.D.

17. Barry Rubin, "North Korea's Threat to the Middle East and the Middle East's Threat to Asia,*" Middle East Review of International Affairs* (Book Studies), URL: http://meria.idc.ac.il/books/brkorea.html#Author.

18. Rebecca MacKinnon, "Food, fuel and medicine shortages plague North Korea," *CNN.com*, December 14, 1999, URL: http://archives.cnn.com/1999/ asianow/east/12/14/nkorea.crisis/.

19. Kurt Achin, "Video Shows N. Korean Soldier Allegedly Suffering from Malnutrition," *Voice of America*, July 28, 2005, URL: http://www.voanews .com/english/archive/2005-07/2005-07-28-voa9.cfm.

20. "Phase One: DPRK Attack," *Global Security.org*, URL: http://www.global security.org/military/ops/oplan-5027-1.htm.

21. Alexandre Mansourov, "Enigma of the Land of Morning Calm: Korean Shrimp or Roaring Tiger?" CNAPS Working Paper, Brookings Institute, September 2000, URL: http://www.brookings.edu/fp/cnaps/papers/2000_mansourov.htm.

22. "N. Korea Boosts Border Defenses," *BBC World News*, London, England, Broadcast, December 4, 2000.

23. Richard Halloran, "How Good are North Korean Forces?" *Korea Herald*, June 28, 2004, URL: http://www2.gol.com/users/coynerhm/how_good_ are_north_korean_forces.htm.

24. "Satellite Photos Show Outdated N. Korean Military Forces," *Kyodo Press*, January 6, 2005, URL: http://asia.news.yahoo.com/050106/kyodo/ d87ed3b00.html.

25. "Report to the Speaker of the U.S. House of Representatives," North Korea Advisory Group, November 1999, URL: http://www.fas.org/nuke/guide/dprk/ nkag-report.htm.

26. David Von Hippel, "Estimated DPRK Military Energy Use: Analytical Approach and Draft Updated Results," paper presented at the "DPRK Energy Expert Study Group Meeting," Stanford University, CA, June 26–27, 2006, URL: http://nautilus.org/dprkenergymeeting/papers/dvh_dprk_military.ppt.

27. Gen. Thomas A. Schwartz, "Statement of Commander in Chief, UNC/CFC and United States Forces Korea," Before the Senate Armed Forces Committee,

March 7, 2000, URL: http://www.shaps.hawaii.edu/security/us/schwartz_2000.html.

28. Donald Macintyre, "Kim's War Machine," *Time Asia*, February 17, 2003, URL: http://www.time.com/time/asia/covers/501030224/army.html.

29. Brian Lee, "Defense Paper: North Boosts Artillery but Cuts Tanks, Armor," *Joongang Ilbo*, February 5, 2005, URL: http://joongangdaily.joins.com/200502/04/200502042241418509900090309031.html.

30. Joseph Bermudez, "Moving Missiles," *Jane's Defence Weekly*, July 27, 2005, URL: http://www.janes.com/defence/land_forces/news/jdwjdw 050727_1_n.shtml.

31. "Annex 8. North Korea and Weapons of Mass Destruction: U.S. Department of Defense Estimate of North Korean Actions and Intentions Involving Nuclear, Biological, and Chemical Weapons," *Analytical Center for Non-Proliferation Problems*, 2005, URL: http://npc.sarov.ru/english/digest/52002/appendix8.html.

32. See: "KN-02 Short Range Ballistic Missile," *Global Security.org*, URL: http://www.globalsecurity.org/wmd/world/dprk/kn-2.htm; and North Korea Primer," National Defense University, November 3, 2005, URL: http://merln.ndu.edu/merln/mipal/reports/northkoreaprimer03nov05.doc.

33. See "United Nations Command/Combined Forces Command Backgrounder No. 13," Public Affairs Office, United States Forces Korea, January 1998, URL: http://www.korea.army.mil/pao/backgrounder/bg13.htm; and "North Korean Military Threat," Republic of Korea Ministry of National Defense *White Paper: 1998*, URL: http://www.mnd.go.kr/english/html/02/1998/133.html.

34. "South Korea's Tunnel Hunters," *BBC News Online*, April 29, 2003, URL: http://news.bbc.co.uk/2/hi/asia-pacific/2982213.stm.

35. "Korea as World's 10th Largest Economy," *Korea.net*, January 31, 2005, URL: http://www.korea.net/news/issues/issuedetailview.asp?board_no=6103.

36. "Report to the Speaker of the U.S. House of Representatives," North Korea Advisory Group, November 1999.

37. Charles Knight, "General Trainor's Korean War Scenario is Only Half the Story," *Project on Defense Alternatives*, June 4, 1997, URL: http://www.comw.org/pda/trainor.htm.

38. For examples of assessments that North Korea is "on the defensive," see Ivan Eland, "Nuking Our Strategy on North Korea," *Chicago Tribune*, February 16, 2005, URL: http://www.independent.org/newsroom/article.asp?id=1465; and Hy-Sang Lee, "Allow Two Nukes for North Korea," *Nautilus Institute Policy Forum Online: PFO 05-22A*, March 10, 2005, URL: http://www.nautilus.org/fora/security/0522A_Lee.html.

39. Graham Allison, Joseph S. Nye, and Albert Carnesale," Defusing The Nuclear Menace," *Washington Post*, September 4, 1988, URL: http://bcsia.ksg.harvard.edu/publication.cfm?ctype=article&item_id=868.

40. William C. Potter and Phillip C. Saunders, "Double Trouble: North Korean Talks are Imperative," Center for Non-Proliferation Studies, Monterey Institute, March 18, 2003, URL: http://cns.miis.edu/research/korea/potsaund.htm.

Chapter 5: Case Study in Conventional Forces Provocations: The Northern Limit Line Incident of 2002

1. The majority of research and writing for this chapter was originally published as: Bruce E. Bechtol Jr., "The Northern Limit Line of 2002: Motivations and Implications," *Pacific Focus*, vol. 19, no. 2 (Fall 2004): 233–264. Reprinted with the expressed written permission of the publisher of *Pacific Focus* and the Center for International Studies, Inha University, Inchon, Republic of Korea.

2. Dick K. Nanto, "North Korea: Chronology of Provocations, 1950–2003," *CRS Reports for Congress* RL300004 (Washington, DC: Library of Congress, Congressional Research Service), March 18, 2003, CRS 17–19.

3. Sohn Jie-Ae, "South, North Korea Clash at Sea," *CNN.com*, June 29, 2002, URL: www.cnn.com/2002/world/asiapcf/east/06/29/korea.warships/index.html.

4. "Koreas Clash in Sea Battle," *BBC News*, June 29, 2002, URL: http://news.bbc.co.uk/1/low/world/asia-pacific/2073694.stm.

5. Jeong Yoomi, "Brink of War in South Korea," *International Action Center*, July 2, 2002, URL: http://www.iacenter.org/korea_yonpyong.htm.

6. "The Naval Clash on the Yellow Sea on 29 June 2002 Between South Korea and North Korea: The Situation and ROK's Position," Ministry of National Defense, Republic of Korea, July 1, 2002, URL: http://www.globalsecurity.org/wmd/library/news/rok/2002/0020704-naval.htm.

7. Yoo Yong-won, "Military Admits Early Error," *NKchosun.com*, July 7, 2002, URL: http://nk.chosun.com/english/news/news.html?ACT=detail&cat=3&res_id=6650.

8. Ministry of Defense, Republic of Korea, July 1, 2002.

9. Yang Geun-man, "Sailors Recount Bloody Ambush," *Digital Chosun Ilbo*, June 30, 2002, URL: http://english.chosun.com/w21data/html/news/200206/200206300039.html.

10. "Koreas Trade Blame in Gunboat Clash," *CBSNews.com*, June 30, 2002, URL: http://www.cbsnews.com/stories/2002/06/29/world/main513817.shtml.

11. Ministry of National Defense, Republic of Korea, July 1, 2002.

12. Yang, "Sailors Recount Bloody Ambush," June 30, 2002.

13. "Koreans Battle Briefly at Sea," *St. Petersburg Times*, June 30, 2002, URL: http://www.sptimes.com/2002/06/30/news_pf/Worldandnation/Koreans_briefly_battl.shtml.

14. "South Korean Probe says North Planned Sea Attack," *NKchosun.com*, July 7, 2002, URL: http://nk.chosun.com/english/news/news.html?ACT=detail&cat=3&res_id=6656.

15. "West Sea Clash," *Yonhap News Agency News*, July 11, 2002, URL: http://www.yonhapnews.co.kr/engservices/.

16. "North Korean Military Ready for Action in the West Sea," *Kimsoft.com*, URL: http://www.kimsoft.com/2002/westsea.2b.htm.

17. "North Korea Country Handbook," United States Department of Defense, May 1997, URL: http://www.dia.mil/public/foia/nkor.pdf.

18. Yu Yong-won, "JCS Says N.K. Opened Fire First," *Digital Chosun Ilbo*, June 29, 2002, URL: http://english.chosun.com/w21data/html/news/200206/200206290009.html.

19. "Command of KPA Navy Makes Public Press Release," *KCNA*, July 7, 2002, URL: http://www.kcna.co.jp/index-e.htm.

20. Mark J. Valencia and Jenny Miller Garmendia, "Yellow Sea Clash: North Korea Has a Point," *Northeast Asia Peace and Security Network Special Report*, December 23, 1999, URL: http://www.nyu.edu/globalbeat/asia/Valencia122399.html.

21. Hwang Jang-jin, "North Korea Premeditatedly Provokes Naval Skirmish in West Sea," *Korea Herald*, July 13, 2002, URL: http://kn.korea herald.co.kr/SITE/data/html_dir/2002/07/13/200207130003.asp.

22. Yoo Yong-wan, "Circumstantial Evidences Show Planned Attack," *Digital Chosun Ilbo*, July 4, 2002, URL: http://english.chosun.com/w21data/html/news/200207/2002070400013.html.

23. Yang, "Sailors Recount Bloody Ambush," June 30, 2002.

24. Yu, "JCS Says N.K. Opened Fire First," June 29, 2002.

25. "Koreans Battle Briefly at Sea," June 30, 2002.

26. "North Korean Military Ready for Action in the West Sea."

27. Ministry of National Defense, Republic of Korea, July 1, 2002.

28. Scott Snyder, "Disciplining North Korea: The Bush Administration & U.S. Policy Toward North Korea," paper presented at the *Korea Political Science Association*, "Inter-Korean Relations: Status and Prospects," July 25, 2002, URL: http://asiafoundation.or.kr/asiafoundation/download/kpsa—disciplining_bush_pol.doc.

29. "Koreans Battle Briefly at Sea," *St. Petersburg Times*, June 30, 2002.

30. Ministry of National Defense, Republic of Korea, July 1, 2002.

31. John E. McLaughlin, "North Korea: Engagement or Confrontation," speech delivered at Texas A&M, April 17, 2001, URL: http://www.cia.gov/cia/public_affairs/speeches/2001/ddci_speech_04172001.html.

32. "Meeting of Army Political Officers Focuses on Loyalty to Kim Chong-il," *No. 75 Yonhap News Agency News Agency*, March 2, 2000, URL: http://www.yonhapnews.co.kr/services/2208620000.html.

33. Han Ho-suk, "North Korea's War Strategy of Massive Retaliation Against U.S. Attacks," *Association for Asian Research*, May 1, 2003, URL: http://www.asianresearch.org/articles/1359.html.

34. T. Rhem, "North Korea Intercepts Air Force Aircraft," U.S. Air Force Press Releases, March 4, 2003, URL: http://www.findarticles.com/p/articles/mi_prfr/is_200303/ai_2878134602.

35. "Korea Demilitarized Zone Incidents," *GlobalSecurity.org*, 2003, URL: http://www.globalsecurity.org/military/ops/dmz.htm.

36. See "DMZ Shots: Premeditated Provocation?" *Donga Ilbo*, August 2, 2006, URL: http://english.donga.com/srv/service.php3?biid=2006080296928&path_dir=20060802; Brian Lee, "North, South Soldiers Exchange DMZ Gunfire," *Joongang Ilbo*, August 2, 2006, URL: http://joongangdaily.joins.com/200608/01/200608012151356039900090309031.html; and "N. Korea Fires Shots Across DMZ," *Chosun Ilbo*, August 1, 2006, URL: http://english.chosun.com/w21data/html/news/200608/200608010016.html.

37. Park Syung-je, board member, Military Analyst Association of the Republic of Korea, Seoul, Republic of Korea, email interview by author, May 29, 2004.

38. Ministry of National Defense, Republic of Korea, July 1, 2002.

39. "Koreas Fight Sea Battle: 5 Killed," *Pakistan Herald*, June 30, 2002, URL: http://www.dawn.com/2002/06/30/int6.htm.

40. "Koreas Trade Blame in Gunboat Clash," *CBSNews.com*, June 30, 2002.

41. Ministry of National Defense, Republic of Korea, July 1, 2002.

42. Paul Eckert, "N. Korea Demands Redrawing of Sea Border with South," *Reuters*, July 9, 2002, URL: http://www.nautilus.org/napsnet/dr/0207/JUL10.html#item2.

43. Quotes from Professor Ko Yoo-hwan of Dong-Kuk University and Professor Ryu Kil-jae of the North Korean graduate study program at Kyung-Nam University, in Jeong Yoomi, "Brink of War in South Korea," *International Action Center*, July 2, 2002 URL: http://www.iacenter.orgkorea_yonpyong.htm.

44. Nanto, "North Korea," CRS-19.

45. Yu Yong-won, "JCS Says N.K. Opened Fire First," *Digital Chosun Ilbo*, June 29, 2002.

46. Michael O'Hanlon, "Sensible Plan for South Korea," *Japan Times*, November 29, 2003, URL: http://www.brook.edu/views/op-ed/ohanlon/20031129.htm.

47. Don Kirk, "Four Killed as North and South Korean Navy Vessels Trade Fire," *New York Times*, June 29, 2002, URL: http://www.usasurvival.org/ck63002a.shtml.

48. "N. Korea Tells U.S. That Road to Resuming Talks Begins with Troop Pullout," *Stars and Stripes*, January 12, 2002, URL: http://www.globalsecurity.org/wmd/library/news/dprk/2002/dprk-020112-article2.htm.

49. Congressman David Price, Keynote speech presented at North Carolina State University, Centennial Campus Engineering Graduate Research Center, "Korean Peninsula: Time of Diplomacy and Development," April 24, 2003, URL: http://www.house.gov/price/issue_north_korea.htm.

50. Kenji Hall and Soo-jeong Lee, "Crab Season Peaks, So Does Korean Clash," *Miami Herald*, June 5, 2003, URL: http://www.miami.com/mld/miamiherald/news/world/6017994.htm?1c.

51. Lee Chul-hee, "Rules of Engagement to Change," *Joongang Ilbo*, June 30, 2003, URL: http://english.joins.com/Article.asp?aid=200206302344 36&sid=200.

52. Kenji Hall and Soo-jeong Lee, "Crab Season Peaks, So Does Korean Clash," *Miami Herald*, June 5, 2003.

53. Cho Mee-young, "South Korea May Halt Rice Aid to North Korea," *Reuters*, July 2, 2002, URL: http://www.nautilus.org/napsnet/dr/0207 JUL03 .html#item3.

54. "First Rice Shipment Goes Sept. 19th," *Joongang Ilbo*, September 2, 2002, URL: http://www.reliefweb.int/w/rwb.nsf/6686f45896f15dbc852567 ae00530132/533f5af45d9ba90f49256c2800089b20?opendocument.

55. "South Koreans Angry at North Over Sea Battle Deaths," *AFP*, URL: http://sg.news.yahoo.com/020701/1/302po.html.

56. Song Jung-a and Teruaki Ueno, "South Korea's Kim Retains Sunshine Policy Despite Clash," *Reuters*, July 1, 2002, URL: http://story.news.yahoo.com/news?tmpl=story&cid=838&ncid=731&e=2&u=/nm/20020701/wl_asia_nm/asia_113120_3.

57. George Gedda, "U.S. Withdraws Offer to Hold Security Talks with North

Korea Next Week," *Associated Press*, July 2, 2002, URL: http://www.nautilus
.org/napsnet/dr/0207/jul03.html#item2.

58. "Northern Limit Line West Sea Naval Engagements," *Global Security.org*,
November 21, 2002, URL: http://www.globalsecurity.org/world/war/nll.htm.

59. Song Young-dae and Yoon Young-kwak, "Interview: North Korea's Regret is
a Countermeasure for Food Shortage Problem," Interview conducted by Cho
Hee-cho, *Chosun Ilbo*, July 28, 2002, URL: http://nk.chosun.com/english/
news/news.html?ACT=detail&res_id=7014.

60. George Gedda, "DPRK Nuclear Weapons Program Acknowledgement,"
Associated Press, October 16, 2002, URL: http://www.nautilus.org/napsnet/
dr/0210/oct16.html#item1.

61. James Kelly, Assistant Secretary of State for East Asian and Pacific Affairs,
"Opening Remarks Before the Senate Foreign Relations Committee," U.S.
Congress, Senate, Washington, DC, March 2, 2004, URL: http://
www.state.gov/p/eap/rls/rm/2004/30093pf.htm.

62. Chae Byung-gun and Brian Lee, "Koreas Extend Military Parley," *Joongang
Ilbo*, June 6, 2004, URL: http://joongangdaily.joins.com/200406/03/
200406032249476179900090309031.html.

63. "Seoul to Review Maritime Border with N. Korea," *Chosun Ilbo*, March 9,
2006, URL: http://english.chosun.com/w21data/html/news/200603/
200603090006.html.

64. "USFK Not Up for Debate in Peace Talks: Minister," *Chosun Ilbo*, March 16,
2006, URL: http://english.chosun.com/w21data/html/news/200603/
200603160028.html.

65. "On APEC's Eve, North Korea Sends Aircraft South," *Joongang Ilbo*,
November 12, 2005, URL: http://joongangdaily.joins.com/200511/11/
200511112241072879900090209021.html.

66. See "N. Korean Fighters Violate S. Korean Airspace," *Chosun Ilbo*, November
11, 2005, URL: http://english.chosun.com/w21data/html/news/200511/
200511110025.html; and "N. Korean Fighter Violate National Airspace," *KBS
Global*, November 11, 2005, URL: http://english.kbs.co.kr/news/
newsview_sub.php?menu=8&key=2005111133.

Chapter 6: Financing a Rogue Regime: North Korea's Illicit Economic Activities

1. For an example of a detailed defector report on North Korea's illicit activities,
see statement of former North Korean high-ranking government official,
"Drugs, Counterfeiting, and Weapons Proliferation: The North Korea
Connection," testimony before the Senate Committee on Governmental
Affairs, May 20, 2003, URL: http://hsgac.senate.govindex.cfm?fuseaction=
hearings.testimony&hearingid=73&witnessid=257.

2. Anthony Spaeth, "Kim's Rackets: To Fund His Lifestyle—and His Nukes—
Kim Jong Il Helms a Vast Criminal Network," *Time Asia* June 2, 2003, URL:
http://www.time.com/time/asia/covers/501030609/story.html.

3. William Bach, Office of African, Asian and European Affairs, Bureau for
International Narcotics and Law Enforcement Affairs, Department of State,
"Hearing on Drugs Counterfeiting and Arms Trade," Senate Sub-Committee

on Financial Management, the Budget, and International Security, May 20, 2003, URL: http://hongkong.usconsulate.gov/ushk/state/2003/052001.htm.

4. See Seung-Ryun Kim, "North Korea's Counterfeiting Mistake," *Donga Ilbo*, December 24, 2005, URL: http://english.donga.com/srvservice.php3? bicode=060000&biid=2005122473898; and Bertil Linter, "North Korea's Missile Trade Helps Fund its Nuclear Program," *Yale Global Online*, May 5, 2003, URL: http://yaleglobal.yale.edu/display.article?id=1546.

5. See Winifred Tate, "Paramilitaries in Colombia," *Brown Journal of World Affairs,* vol. 8, no. 1 (Winter/Spring 2001), URL: http://www.watsoninstitute .org/bjwa/archive/8.1/essays/tate.pdf.

6. For more detailed analysis on the large-scale subsidies that the Soviet Union provided North Korea during the 1970s, see Nicholas Eberstadt, "The Persistence of North Korea," *Policy Review*, no. 127 (October/November 2004), URL: http://www.policyreview.org/oct04/eberstadt.html.

7. Anthony LoBaido, "N. Korea's Slush Fund: Dictator Reportedly Stashed $2 billion in Austrian Bank," *World Net Daily*, March 19, 2000, URL: http:// www.worldnetdaily.com/news/article.asp?ARTICLE_ID=19068.

8. For detailed analysis of Kim Chong-il's gradual rise to power under his father's guidance, see Alexandre Y. Mansourov, "Inside North Korea's Black Box: Reversing the Optics," *Brookings Institution Paper*, June 2004, URL: http:// www.brookings.edu/views/papers/fellows/oh20040601ch4.pdf.

9. Spaeth, "Kim's Rackets: To Fund His Lifestyle—and His Nukes—Kim Jong Il Helms a Vast Criminal Network," *Time Asia,* June 2, 2003, URL: http:// www.time.com/time/asia/covers/501030609/story.html.

10. Mike Chinoy, "Will China End North Korea's Illegal Activities in Macao?" *CNN.com*, December 18, 1999, URL: http://archives.cnn.com/1999/ ASIANOW/east/macau/stories/macau.north.korea/index.html.

11. Jay Solomon and Hae Won Choi, "Money Trail: In North Korea, Secret Cash Hoard Props Up Regime," *Wall Street Journal*, July 14, 2003.

12. "N. Korean Leader Moved Secret Bank Accounts to Luxembourg: Report," *Yonhap News Agency*, December 27, 2005, URL: http://english.yna.co.kr/ engnews/20051227/430100000020051227194320e2.html.

13. "Singapore: N. Korea's New Money Haven," *Donga Ilbo*, August 5, 2006, URL: http://english.donga.com/srv/service.php3?bicode=060000& biid=2006080539518.

14. Barbara Demick, "No More Gambling on N. Korea," *Los Angeles Times*, April 6, 2006, URL: http://www.latimes.com/news/printedition/la-fg-macao6apr06,1,7483991.story.

15. Richard C. Paddock and Barbara Demick, "N. Korea's Growing Drug Trade Seen in Botched Heroin Delivery," *Washington Post*, May 21, 2003, URL: http://opioids.com/korea/.

16. "International Narcotics Control Strategy Report," *United States Department of State*, March 2001, URL: http://www.state.gov/p/inl/rls/nrcrpt/2000/ 891.htm.

17. "Media Release: Extra 75kg of heroin linked to 'Pong Su'," *Australian Federal Police*, May 27, 2003, URL: http://www.afp.gov.au/afp/page/media/2003/ 0527pongsu.htm.

18. Raphael F. Perl, "Drug Trafficking and North Korea: Issues for U.S. Policy," *CRS Report for Congress*, Library of Congress, Congressional Research Service, December 5, 2003, URL: http://www.fas.org/sgp/crs/row/rl32167.pdf.

19. Mike Nartker, "North Korea: Pyongyang Funds WMD Programs by Selling Drugs, Counterfeit Currency," *Global Security Newswire*, May 21, 2003, URL: http://www.nti.org/d_newswire/issues/2003/5/21/2s.html.

20. Charles R. Smith, "North Korean Heroin," *NewsMax.com*, May 7, 2003, URL: http://www.newsmax.com/archives/articles/2003/5/7/30830.shtml.

21. See "Dozens of North Korean Diplomats Caught Smuggling Drugs," *Radio Free Asia*, December 15, 2004, URL: http://www.rfa.org/english/news/social/2004/12/15/nkorea_drugs; Todd Crowell, "North Korea, the 'Sopranos' state," *Asia Times*, January 18, 2004, URL: http://www.atimes.com/atimes/Korea/HA18Dg01.html; and Kim Young Il, "North Korea and Narcotics Trafficking: A View from the Inside," *North Korea Review*, vol. 1, no. 1 (March 1, 2004), URL: http://www.jamestown.org/publications_details.php?volume_id=398&issue_id=2915&article_id=23572.

22. "U.S. Says North Korea Dealing in Illegal Drugs," *Join Together*, March 5, 2004, URL: http://www.jointogether.org/sa/news/summaries/reader/0,1854,569738,00.html.

23. "North Korean Ship Sunk," *Association of Former Intelligence Officers*, December 24, 2001, URL: http://www.afio.com/sections/wins/2001/2001-50.html.

24. Smith, "North Korean Heroin," *NewsMax.com*, May 7, 2003, URL: http://www.newsmax.com/archives/articles/2003/5/7/30830.shtml.

25. Mindy L. Kotler, "Toward an 'Asian' North Korea," *Nautilus Institute Policy Forum Online*, PFO 03-28, April 8, 2003, URL: http://www.nautilus.org/fora/security/0328_kotler.html.

26. For more analysis on North Korea's involvement with illegal drugs in China, see Gavan McCormack, "North Korea and the U.S.: Strategic Decision," *Japan Focus*, December 2005, URL: http://www.japanfocus.org/article.asp?id=498.

27. "Treasury Designates Banco Delta Asia as Primary Money Laundering Concern under USA PATRIOT Act," *United States Department of Treasury Press Release*, September 15, 2005, URL: http://www.treas.gov/press/releases/js2720.htm.

28. Sheena E. Chestnut, "Sopranos State? North Korean Involvement in Criminal Activity and Implications for International Security," *Nautilus Institute Special Report*, January 19, 2006, URL: http://www.nautilus.org/napsnet/sr/2006/0605Chestnut.pdf.

29. Josh Meyer and Barbara Demick, "Counterfeiting Cases Point to North Korea," *Los Angeles Times*, December 12, 2005, URL: http://www.tobacco.org/scripts/jump.php?article_id=212369&url=http://www.latimes.com/news/printedition/la-fg-counterfeit12dec12,1,1659491,full.story.

30. "Defectors: Counterfeit Bills Printed at Press in Pyeongseong, North Korea," *East Asia Intel.com*, December 7, 2005, URL: http://www.east-asia-intel.com/eai/2005/12_07/4.asp.

31. Bill Gertz, "N. Korea Charged in Counterfeiting of U.S. Currency," *Washington Times*, December 2, 2005, URL: http://www.washingtontimes.com/world/20051201-103509-5867r.htm.

32. "N. Korean Supernotes Surfaced In Las Vegas Casinos," *East-Asia-Intel.com*, January 11, 2006, URL: http://www.east-asia-intel.com/eai/2006/01_11/3.asp.

33. David L. Asher, "The North Korean Criminal State, its Ties to Organized Crime, and the Possibility of WMD Proliferation," Remarks presented to the Counter-Proliferation Strategy Group, Woodrow Wilson Center, Washington, DC, October 21, 2005, URL: http://www.nautilus.org/fora/security/0502asher.html.

34. See: Asher, "The North Korean Criminal State, its Ties to Organized Crime, and the Possibility of WMD Proliferation," URL: http://www.nautilus.org/fora/security/0502asher.html; and Chestnut, "Sopranos State? North Korean Involvement in Criminal Activity and Implications for International Security," URL: http://www.nautilus.org/napsnet/sr/2006/0605chestnut.pdf.

35. Burt Herman, "Kim Says He Wants to End Nuclear Standoff," *Associated Press*, January 18, 2006, URL: http://www.adelphia.net/news/read/read.php?ps=1012&id=12506130.

36. Choe Sang-Hun, "N. Korea ties talks to end of U.S. sanctions," *International Herald Tribune*, December 6, 2005, URL: http://www.iht.com/articles/2005/12/06/news/korea.php.

37. Ser Myo-ja, "South Warns North on Counterfeits," *Joongang Ilbo*, January 23, 2006, URL: http://joongangdaily.joins.com/200601/22/200601222235223879900090309031.html.

38. "Japan, U.S. huddle over Pyongyang counterfeiting," *Japan Times*, January 26, 2006, URL: http://www.japantimes.co.jp/cgi-bin/getarticle.pl5?nn20060126a7.htm.

39. "Japanese Banks Match U.S. Sanctions on N. Korea," *Chosun Ilbo*, February 2, 2006, URL: http://english.chosun.com/w21data/html/news/200602/200602020013.html.

40. "Japan to Tighten Check on Remittances to N. Korea," *Chosun Ilbo*, March 13, 2006, URL: http://english.chosun.com/w21data/html/news/200603/200603130029.html.

41. "China Finds N. Korea Guilty of Money Laundering," *Chosun Ilbo*, January 11, 2006, URL: http://english.chosun.com/w21data/html/news/200601/200601110019.html.

42. "N.K. Counterfeit Bill Accounts Surface in Hong Kong," *Chosun Ilbo*, February 27, 2006, URL: http://english.chosun.com/w21data/html/news/200602/200602270018.html.

43. See: "China Cracks Down on Counterfeit Dollars," *Chosun Ilbo*, March 19, 2006, URL: http://english.chosun.com/w21data/html/news/200603/200603190006.html; and Gordon Fairclough, "North Korea Might Be Exporting Fake $100 Bills," *Wall Street Journal*, March 24, 2006, URL: http://www.washingtonpost.com/wp-dyn/content/article/2006/03/23/AR2006032301534.html.

44. See Choi Hyung-kyu and Brian Lee, "U.S., China Agree to Help Attack North Counterfeiting," *Joongang Ilbo*, August 1, 2006, URL: http://joongangdaily.joins.com/200607/31/200607312148443009900090309031.html; Lindsay Beck, "Analysis—China Grapples with North Korea's Illicit Dealings," *Reuters*, August 1, 2006, URL: http://www.hses.comn06080107.htm; and Elizabeth Wishnick, "Nuclear Tension Between China, N Korea," *International*

Relations and Security Network, August 11, 2006, URL: http://www.isn.ethz.ch/news/sw/details.cfm?id=16511.

45. Lee Sang-il and Brian Lee, "U.S. Hails Bank of China's Freeze," *Joongang Ilbo*, July 28, 2006, URL: http://joongangdaily.joins.com/200607/27/200607272127545339900090309031.html.

46. Tim Johnson, "North Korea's Leader Reportedly Visits China After Talks Hit Impasse," *Mercury News*, January 10, 2006, URL: http://www.mercurynews.com/mld/mercurynews/news/world/13593100.htm.

47. Asher, "The North Korean Criminal State, its Ties to Organized Crime, and the Possibility of WMD Proliferation," URL: http://www.nautilus.org/fora/security/0502Asher.html.

48. Park Syung-je, Board Member, Military Analyst Association of the Republic of Korea, Seoul, Republic of Korea, email interview by author, January 22, 2006.

49. Peter A. Prahar, Director, Office of African, Asia and Europe/NIS Programs, Bureau for International Narcotics and Law Enforcement Affairs, Department of State, "Prepared Statement: North Korea: Illicit Activity Funding the Regime," Senate Sub-Committee on Financial Management, Government Information, and International Security, Senate Homeland Security and Government Affairs Committee, April 25, 2006, URL: http://hsgac.senate.gov/_files/042506prahar.pdf.

50. See Yeh Young-june, "Report: North Ships Caught with Fake Cigarettes," *Joongang Ilbo*, May 16, 2006, URL: http://joongangdaily.joins.com/200605/15/200605152229094209900090309031.html; and "Vessels from N.K. Carry Fake Cigarettes," *KBS World Radio*, May 15, 2006, URL: http://world.kbs.co.kr/english/news/news_detail.htm?no=36221.

51. "U.S.: N.K. Gov't Approves Illegal Activities," *KBS Global Online*, January 19, 2006, URL: http://english.kbs.co.kr/news/newsview_sub.php?menu=8&key=2006011933.

52. *CIA World Factbook*, 2005, URL: http://www.cia.gov/cia/publications/factbook/rankorder/2078rank.html.

53. Dick K. Nanto and Emma Chanlett-Avery, "The North Korean Economy: Background and Policy Analysis," *CRS Reports for Congress*, RL32493 (Washington, DC: Library of Congress, Congressional Research Service), February 9, 2005: 7–18.

54. "Answers to Questions from the Senate Select Committee on Intelligence, World Wide Threat Hearing," *Defense Intelligence Agency*, March 21, 2002, URL: http://www.fas.org/irp/congress/2002_hr/020602dia.html.

55. Paddock and Demick, "N. Korea's Growing Drug Trade Seen in Botched Heroin Delivery," 2003, URL: http://opioids.com/korea/.

56. Kim Ah-young, "A Narcotic State: Halt North Korea's Drug Habit," *International Herald Tribune*, June 18, 2003, URL: http://www.iht.com/articles/2003/06/18/edkim_ed3_.php.

57. Prahar, "Prepared Statement: North Korea: Illicit Activity Funding the Regime," URL: http://hsgac.senate.gov/_files/042506prahar.pdf.

58. Asher, "The North Korean Criminal State, its Ties to Organized Crime, and the Possibility of WMD Proliferation," URL: http://www.nautilus.org/fora/security/0502asher.html.

59. Glenn Kessler, "Semantic Dispute Cancels N. Korea, Treasury Meeting," *Washington Post*, December 1, 2005, URL: http://www.washington post.com/wp-dyn/content/article/2005/11/30/ar2005113002168.html.

60. "No Need for Talks on Counterfeiting with N. Korea: Rice," *Chosun Ilbo*, November 30, 2005, URL: http://english.chosun.com/w21data/html/news/200511/200511300021.html.

61. Chung Dong-young, Minister of Unification, Republic of Korea, "Korean Peace Economics," Speech presented at the National Press Club, Washington, DC, December 19, 2005.

62. "U.S. Envoy Has Evidence of N. Korean Counterfeiting," *Chosun Ilbo*, December 22, 2005, URL: http://english.chosun.com/w21data/html/news/200512/200512220025.html.

63. "Seoul Swings Behind U.S. in N. Korea Forgery Charge," *Chosun Ilbo*, December 22, 2005, URL: http://english.chosun.com/w21data/html/news/200512/200512210025.html.

64. "S. Korean Experts Agree Bogus Dollar Trail Leads North," *Chosun Ilbo*, December 22, 2005, URL: http://english.chosun.com/w21data/html/news/200512/200512220033.html.

65. "Interview: Ban Credited With Improved Seoul-Washington Ties," *Yonhap News Agency,* January 24, 2006, URL: http://english.yna.co.kr/engnews/20060102/5001000000 20060102090531e5.html.

66. Ser Myo-ja, "South Warns North on Counterfeits," *Joongang Ilbo*, January 23, 2006, URL: http://joongangdaily.joins.com/200601/22/200601 22223522387990009030903l.html.

67. "U.S. To Give Counterfeiting Report," *Donga Ilbo*, January 23, 2006, URL: http://english.donga.com/srv/service.php3?bicode=050000&biid=2006012334298.

68. Brian Lee, "In Fake Cash Talks, Mum's the Word," *Joongang Ilbo*, January 24, 2006, URL: http://joongangdaily.joins.com/200601/23/200601 23222638397990009030903l.html.

69. "U.S. Investigators Smash Hopes of N. Korea Compromise," *Chosun Ilbo*, January 23, 2006, URL: http://english.chosun.com/w21data/html/news/200601/200601230015.html.

70. Brian Lee, "Ban Ducks on Bogus Cash, North," *Joongang Ilbo*, January 25, 2006, URL: http://joongangdaily.joins.com/200601/24/20060124221952 5139900090209021.html.

71. "Seoul Raps U.S. Mission Over N.K. Sanctions Bombshell," *Chosun Ilbo*, January 25, 2006, URL: http://english.chosun.com/w21data/html/news/200601/200601250015.html.

72. "Roh Defiant in Korea-U.S. Tension," *Chosun Ilbo*, January 25, 2006, URL: http://english.chosun.com/w21data/html/news/200601/20060125 0021.html.

73. Brian Lee, "U.S., Seoul, Differ Publicly on Action Call," *Joongang Ilbo*, January 26, 2006, URL: http://joongangdaily.joins.com/200601/25/2006012522243393399000909030903l.html.

74. Brian Lee, "Intelligence Chief Walks Tightrope on Bogus Cash," *Joongang Ilbo*, February 3, 2006, URL: http://joongangdaily.joins.com/200602/02/2006020222234096179900090309031.html.

75. "Washington Glosses Over N. Korean Spat With Seoul," *Chosun Ilbo*, January 26, 2006, URL: http://english.chosun.com/w21data/html/news/200601/200601260015.html.

76. Jong-Koo Yoon, "U.S., Korea, Split on Counterfeiting Issue," *Donga Ilbo*, January 28, 2006, URL: http://english.donga.com/srv/service.php3?biid=2006012808048.

77. Ser Myo-ja, "Opposition Hits Seoul Over Fake Cash Inaction," *Joongang Ilbo*, February 24, 2006, URL: http://joongangdaily.joins.com/200602/23/200602232221584679900090309031.html.

78. "Seoul Given Proof of Recent N. Korean Forgeries: U.S.," *Chosun Ilbo*, February 23, 2006, URL: http://english.chosun.com/w21data/html/news/200602/200602230007.html.

79. "Crackdown On North Korea Strains U.S.-South Ties," *Reuters*, January 28, 2006, URL: http://www.nautilus.org/napsnet/dr/index.html#item3.

80. Brian Lee, "U.S. Aide Skeptical of North's Overture," *Joongang Ilbo*, January 27, 2006, URL: http://service.joins.com/aspprint_article_english.asp?aid=2677759&esectcode=e_politics&title=us+aide+skeptical+of+north's+overture.

81. Martin Fackler, "North Korean Counterfeiting Complicates Nuclear Crisis," *New York Times*, January 29, 2006, URL: http://www.nytimes.com/2006/01/29/international/asia/29korea.html?_r=1&pagewanted=print.

82. Brian Lee, "Bush Tells North to Stop Printing $100 Bills," *Joongang Ilbo*, January 26, 2006, URL: http://joongangdaily.joins.com/200601/27/200601272054063309900090209021.html.

83. "Bush Says No to Compromise on N.K. Financial Sanctions," *Chosun Ilbo*, January 27, 2006, URL: http://english.chosun.com/w21data/html/news/200601/200601270017.html.

84. "U.S. In Sweeping Plan to Strangle N. Korea's Cash Flow," *Chosun Ilbo*, January 27, 2006, URL: http://english.chosun.com/w21data/html/news/200601/200601270027.html.

85. Seung-Ryun Kim, "U.S. Bill Grants WMD Informants Asylum," *Donga Ilbo*, March 30, 2006, URL: http://english.donga.com/srvservice.php3?biid=2006033068298.

86. Joel Brinkley, "U.S. Squeezes North Korea's Money Flow," *New York Times*, March 10, 2006, URL: http://select.nytimes.com/gst/abstract.html?res=f70c1ffe38550c738dddaa0894de404482.

87. Daniel Glaser, Deputy Assistant Secretary of Treasury, "The Importance of AML/CFT Controls in Financial Institutions," Prepared remarks presented to the International AML/CFT Inaugural Conference of the U.S./MENA Private Sector Dialogue, Cairo, Egypt, March 22, 2006, URL: http://www.treas.gov/press/releases/js4132.htm.

88. Brent Choi, "Experts Say Money Squeeze on North is Working," *Joongang Ilbo*, July 21, 2006, URL: http://joongangdaily.joins.com/200607/20/200607202241523609900090309031.html.

89. Brian Lee, "After Meeting, Nuclear Talks Are No Nearer," *Joongang Ilbo*, March 9, 2006, URL: http://joongangdaily.joins.com/200603/0820060308214 3315779900090309031.html.

90. "N. Korea–U.S. Meeting Makes Little Progress," *Chosun Ilbo*, March 8, 2006,

URL: http://english.chosun.com/w21data/html/news/200603200603080020.html.

91. "North Korean Official's Arrest in Macao Unrelated to Counterfeiting," *KBS World Online*, January 29, 2006, URL: http://world.kbs.co.kr/english/news/news_today.htm.

92. "Report: Kim Jong-Il's Top Aide Arrested in Macau during Kim's Visit to China," *East-Asia-Intel.com*, February 1, 2006, URL: http://www.east-asia-intel.com/eai/2006/02_01/7.asp.

93. Donald Greenlees, "U.S. Wraps up its Investigation of North Korean Financial Charges," *International Herald Tribune*, February 26, 2007, URL: http://www.iht.com/articles/2007/02/26/news/north.php.

Chapter 7: Preserving the Regime: Overarching Challenges and Motivations for the Kim Chong-Il Government in the Post-9/11 Era

1. Aidan Foster-Carter, "Castro and Kim: Ill-Suited Comrades," *Asia Times*, March 5, 2003, URL: http://www.atimes.com/atimes/korea/ec05dg04.html.

2. For analysis showing how Kim Chong-il's policies differed from those of his father, see Hwang Jang-yop, "Testimonies of North Korean Defectors," Republic of Korea, National Intelligence Service, 1999, URL: http://www.fas.org/irp/world/rok/nis-docs/hwang6.htm.

3. Morton Abramowitz, Michael J. Green, and James T. Laney, "North Korea Task Force Press Conference," *Council on Foreign Relations*, July 27, 1999, URL: http://www.cfr.org/publication/3212/north_korea_task_force_press_conference.html?breadcrumb=default.

4. Jon Herskovitz, "Crackdown on North Korea strains U.S.–South ties," *Reuters*, January 28, 2006, URL: http://news.yahoo.com/s/nm/korea_north_usa_dc.

5. See "Analysis of the North Korean Threat: Backgrounder No. 12," United Nations Command, Combined Forces Command, January 1998, URL: http://www.korea.army.mil/pao/backgrounder/bg12.htm; and "Overcoming Humanitarian Dilemmas in the DPRK: Special Report 90," *United States Institute of Peace*, July 2002, URL: http://www.usip.org/pubs/specialreports/sr90.html.

6. Tom Barnes, "America & North Korea: A New Cold War?" *Victorian Peace Network*, 2004, http://www.vicpeace.org/stories/10/1279.html.

7. Kurt Achin, "Video Shows N. Korean Soldier Allegedly Suffering from Malnutrition," *Voice of America*, July 28, 2005, URL: http://www.voanews.com/english/archive/2005-07/2005-07-28voa9.cfm?cfid=5394580&cftoken=53605521.

8. Danny Gittings, "China Props Up An Evil Regime," *Asian Wall Street Journal*, January 16, 2003, URL: http://www.freerepublic.com/focus/news/823973/posts.

9. Michael O'Hanlon and Mike Mochizuki, "Bridging the Roh–Bush Divide on Korea," *Yale Global Online*, May 14, 2003, URL: http://yaleglobal.yale.edu/display.article?id=1615.

10. Burt Herman, "Kim Says He Wants to End Nuclear Standoff," *ABC News International*, January 18, 2006, URL: http://abcnews.go.com/international/wirestory?id=1517226.

11. "China Urges 'Punitive' Steps, Tightens Border with North Korea," *Radio Free Asia*, October 10, 2006, URL: http://www.rfa.org/english/news/politics/2006/10/10/nkorea_china/.

12. Donald MacIntyre, "Nowhere to Run, Nowhere to Hide," *Time Asia*, June 25, 2001, URL: http://www.time.com/time/asia/news/magazine/0,9754, 131024,00.html.

13. "China: Crackdown on Illegal Immigrants Likely to Target North Korean Refugees," Amnesty International, March 27, 2002, URL: http://web.amnesty.org/library/index/engasa170132002?open&of=eng-prk.

14. Shahid Ilyas, "Security Environment in Northeast Asia," *Regional Studies*, vol. 23, no. 4 (Autumn 2005), URL: http://irs.org.pk/publregional studies.htm#_ftnref4.

15. Lee Keum-soon, "Cross-Border Movement of North Korean Citizens," *East Asian Review*, vol. 16, no. 1 (Spring 2004), URL: http://www.ieas.or.kr/vol16_1/16_1_3.pdf.

16. Cortlan Bennett, "China Moves to Curb Crime By North Korean Soldiers," *San Francisco Chronicle*, September 19, 2003, URL: http://www.cank or.ligi.ubc.ca/issues/136.htm.

17. "Analysts: Desperate Kim Jong-il Secured Second Bailout From China in 3 Months," *East-Asia-Intel.com*, January 25, 2006, URL: http://www.east-asia-intel.com/eai/2006/01_25/8.asp.

18. "N. Korea Getting More Dependent on China, NIS Warns," *Chosun Ilbo*, November 24, 2005, URL: http://english.chosun.com/w21data/html/news/200511/200511240015.html.

19. Wonhyuk Lim, "Kim Jong-il's Southern Tour: Beijing Consensus with a North Korean Twist?" Presentation given in Washington, DC, at the Korea–China Forum titled, "China's Economic Reforms: A Model for the DPRK?" Co-hosted by the Atlantic Council and the Korea Economic Institute, February 13, 2006, URL: http://www.nautilus.org/fora/security/0616lim.pdf.

20. Han Ki-heung, "Opinion: China's Next Province?" *Donga Ilbo*, March 23, 2006, URL: http://english.donga.com/srv/service.php3?biid=2006032360828.

21. Shim Jae Hoon, "Protect Regime Now, Feed People Later," *Yale Global Online*, October 18, 2005, URL: http://yaleglobal.yale.edu/display.article ?id=6385.

22. "Statement of Stephan Haggard and Marcus Noland for Hearings on the North Korean Human Rights Act of 2004: Issues and Implementation," Subcommittee on Africa, Global Human Rights, and International Operations, United States House of Representatives, April 28, 2005, URL: http://www.iie.com/publications/papers/noland0405.pdf.

23. Sekai Nippo, "Korea in Crisis: 2007 Presidential Race Will Be 'Watershed'," *World Peace Herald*, February 4, 2006, URL: http://www.wpherald.com/print.php?storyid=20060203-105835-1064r.

24. Scott Snyder, "Three Months of Unrequited Korean Love," *Asia Times*, April 26, 2005, URL: http://www.atimes.com/atimes/korea/gd26dg01.html.

25. Andrei Lankov, "Aid Strengthens Kim's Regime," *Nautilus Institute, Policy Forum Online 05-96A*, December 1, 2005, URL: http://www.nautilus.org/fora/security/0596lankov.html.

26. Jonathan Watts, "North Korea Turns Away Western Aid," *Guardian Unlimited*, October 2, 2005, URL: http://www.guardian.co.uk/korea/article/0,,1583051, 00.html.

27. Ser Myo-ja, "Aid Agencies Question North's Food Capability," *Joongang Ilbo*, November 19, 2005, URL: http://joongangdaily.joins.com/200511/18/ 2005111822244816099000903090 31.html.

28. "N. Korea asks for aid from South," *CNN.com*, February 9, 2006, URL: http://www.cnn.com/2006/world/asiapcf/02/08/koreas.aid.ap/index.html#.

29. Masood Hyder, "In North Korea: First, Save Lives," *Washington Post*, January 4, 2004, URL: http://www.washingtonpost.com/ac2wpdyn?pagename=article &node=&contentid=a50820-2004jan2&notfound=true.

30. "Generosity Does Not Improve the Human Rights Situation in North Korea," *Donga Ilbo*, March 11, 2006, URL: http://english.donga.com/srv/ service.php3?biid=2006031195708.

31. "North Korea Attempts to Control Our Press With Impunity," *Chosun Ilbo*, November 10, 2005, URL: http://english.chosun.com/w21data/html/news/ 200511/200511100027.html.

32. Jae-Young Kim, "Unification Ministry Remarks Cause Stir," *Donga Ilbo*, November 12, 2005, URL: http://english.donga.com/srv/service.php3? bicode=040000&biid=2005111283738.

33. See Ser Myo-ja, "Reporting Spat Delays Return of Reunion Kin," *Joongang Ilbo*, March 23, 2006, URL: http://joongangdaily.joins.com/200603/22/ 2006032222230346799000903090 31.html; and Seo Dong-shin, "Tensions Rise Over N.K.'s Press Censorship," *Korea Times*, March 21, 2006, URL: http:// times.hankooki.com/lpage/nation/200603 kt2006032117322610510.htm.

34. "Atrocities Unchallenged," *Joongang Ilbo*, December 9, 2005, URL: http:// joongangdaily.joins.com/200512/09/2005120922064600099000901090 11.html.

35. Ser Myo-ja, "U.S. Aid Asks Seoul to Press Rights in North," *Joongang Ilbo*, December 10, 2005, URL: http://joongangdaily.joins.com/200512/09/ 2005120922105263390009020902 1.html.

36. "Uri Party Sees Vote on N.K. Human Rights as Counter-Productive," *Chosun Ilbo*, November 18, 2005, URL: http://english.chosun.com/w21data/html/ news/200511/200511180020.html.

37. "Renegotiation Kumgang Project," *N. K. Chosun*, May 5, 2001, URL: http:// nk.chosun.com/english/news/news.html?ACT=detail&key=2&res_id=4113.

38. "KNTO To Put W5 Billion into Kumgang Tours," *N. K. Chosun*, August 19, 2002, URL: http://nk.chosun.com/english/newsnews.html?ACT=detail&linkv =9&res_id=7227.

39. Sang-Hun Choe, "North Korea Proves Tough Sell as Tour Destination," *Washington Times*, February 20, 2004, URL: http://www.washtimes.com/ world/20040219-094837-7967r.htm.

40. Larry A. Niksch, "U.S.–Korea Relations: Issues for Congress," *CRS Report for Congress* (Washington, DC: Library of Congress, Congressional Research Service), June 16, 2005, URL: http://www.fas.org/sgp/crs/row/IB98045.pdf.

41. See "N.K. Seeks to Exclude Hyundai From New Tour Projects," *Korea Times*, January 20, 2006, URL: http://times.hankooki.com/lpage/nation/200601/ kt2006012020420311990.htm; "North Korea Digs in Heels Over Kaesong Tourism," *Chosun Ilbo*, July 21, 2006, URL: http://english.chosun.com/ w21data/html/news/200607/200607210016.html; and "Miffed North Korea Cuts Mt. Kumgang Visitor Quota," *Chosun Ilbo*, August 29, 2005, URL:

http://english.chosun.com/w21data/html/news/200508/200508290022.html.

42. Chung, Dong-young, Minister of Unification, Republic of Korea, "Korean Peace Economics," Speech presented at the National Press Club, Washington, DC, December 19, 2005.

43. "Background Note: North Korea," *Bureau of East Asian and Pacific Affairs, United States State Department*, November 2005, URL: http://www.state.gov/r/pa/ei/bgn/2792.htm.

44. Norimitsu Onishi, "North Korea's Well-Isolated Capitalism," *International Herald Tribune*, July 18, 2006, URL: http://www.iht.com/articles/2006/07/18/news/pyongyang.php.

45. See "U.S. Rejects Free Trade in Kaesong Products," *Joongang Ilbo*, February 9, 2006, URL: http://joongangdaily.joins.com/200602/08/200602082141182639900090309031.html; and "North Korea Industrial Zone to be Excluded from Korea FTA," *World Trade/Interactive*, February 10, 2006, URL: http://www.strtrade.com/wti/wti.asp?pub=0&story=0&full_articles=yes&date.

46. See Barbara Demick, "A One-Hour Commute to Another World," *Los Angeles Times*, February 28, 2006, URL: http://www.latimes.com/news/nationworld/world/la-fg-commute28feb28,0,2034290.story?coll=la-headlines-world; and "Seoul Dismisses U.S. Claims About Kaesong Complex," *Chosun Ilbo*, March 31, 2006, URL: http://english.chosun.com/w21data/html/news/200603/200603310014.html.

47. Jae Kyu Park, President, Kyungnam University, Former Minister of Unification, Republic of Korea, speech presented at the Woodrow Wilson Center for International Scholars, Washington, DC, January 17, 2006, videotape recording of the presentation can be viewed online at URL: www.wilsoncenter.org/index.cfm?fuseaction=events.event_summary&event_id=161541.

48. Chae Byung-gun, "Military Ties Lag in Efforts By 2 Koreas," *Joongang Ilbo*, November 28, 2005, URL: http://joongangdaily.joins.com/200511/27/200511272247301939900090309031.html.

49. Brian Lee, "Generals End 2-Day Talks: No Progress," *Joongang Ilbo*, March 4, 2006, URL: http://joongangdaily.joins.com/200603/03/200603032131292809900090209021.html.

50. "Seoul to Review Maritime Border with N. Korea," *Chosun Ilbo*, March 9, 2006, URL: http://english.chosun.com/w21data/html/news/200603/200603090006.html.

51. "Time for Kim Jong-il to Visit Seoul: Kim Dae-jung," *Chosun Ilbo*, March 21, 2006, URL: http://english.chosun.com/w21data/html/news/200603/200603210024.html.

52. Aiden Foster-Carter, "Spies R Us: Inter-Korean Infiltration," *Asia Times*, November 18, 2001, URL: http://www.atimes.com/koreas/ck10dg01.html.

53. Song Mun-hong, "North Korea's Continuing Intelligence Campaign," *Donga Ilbo*, November 26, 2005, URL: http://english.donga.com/srv/service.php3?bicode=100000&biid=2005112677728.

54. "N. Korea Accuses U.S. of Preparing Attack," *Las Vegas Sun*, April 25, 2004, URL: http://www.lasvegassun.com/sunbin/stories/w-asia/2004/apr/25/042505126.html.

55. "North Korea Pushes Back Inter-Korean Talks over U.S.-South Korea Exercise," *Asia-AFP*, March 22, 2004, URL: http://news.yahoo.com/news?tmpl=story&u=/afp/20040322/wl_asia_afp/skorea_us_military_1.

56. Ser Myo-ja, "North Stresses Kinship With South at Meeting," *Joongang Ilbo*, December 14, 2005, URL: http://joongangdaily.joins.com/200512/13/200512132150214009900090309031.html.

57. "Repeal of Agreement on "Strategic Flexibility" Urged," *KCNA*, January 25, 2006, URL: http://www.kcna.co.jp/index-e.htm.

58. Kongdan Oh, "Misunderstandings About the Relocation of U.S. Bases in Korea," *Brookings Institution Paper*, June 21, 2003, URL: http://www.brookings.edu/views/op-ed/fellows/oh20030621.htm.

59. "KCNA Slams Parliamentary Coup in S. Korea," *KCNA*, March 17, 2004, URL: http://www.kcna.co.jp/item/2004/200403/news03/18.htm.

60. "Editorial: Butt Out, Pyongyang," *Joongang Ilbo*, March 17, 2004, URL: http://joongangdaily.joins.com/200403/17/20040317214327663990009010901 1.html.

61. Andrew Ward, "N Korea Endorses Roh's Party in South's Poll," *Financial Times*, April 7, 2004, URL: http://www.nautilus.org/archives/napsnet/dr/0404/APR07-04.html#item8.

62. "Pyongyang Warns of Election Plotting," *Joongang Ilbo*, April 9, 2004, URL: http://joongangdaily.joins.com/200404/09/2004040900421071099000093 09031.html.

63. See Pak Du-shik, "Elderly Voters Can Stay Home," *Chosun Ilbo*, April 1, 2004, URL: http://english.chosun.com/w21data/html/news/200404/200404010026.html; and Bruce E. Bechtol Jr., "The Impact of North Korea's WMD Programs on Regional Security and the ROK-U.S. Alliance," *International Journal of Korean Studies*, vol. 8, no. 1 (Fall/Winter 2004): 142-157.

64. "North Korean Press Attacks GNP," *Donga Ilbo*, October 21, 2005, URL: http://english.donga.com.

65. For a detailed description of South Korea's National Security Law, see "South Korea's National Security Law," *World History Archives*, October 1, 1996, URL: http://www.hartford-hwp.com/archives/55a/205.html.

66. Ser Myo-ja, "Warm Feelings Increase for North Korea," *Joongang Ilbo*, December 23, 2005, URL: http://joongangdaily.joins.com/200512/22/200512222218174309900092309231.html.

67. "What Do Strange Signs in North Korea Mean?" *Chosun Ilbo*, November 18, 2004, URL: http://english.chosun.com/w21data/html/news/200411/200411180035.html.

68. James Brooke, "Monitors of North Korean News Note Dip in Reverence for Kim," *New York Times*, November 18, 2004, URL: http://www.nytimes.com/2004/11/18/international/asia/18korea.html?oref=login&pagewanted=print&position.

69. "North Korean Media Drop Kim Jong-il's Dear Leader Title," *Chosun Ilbo*, November 18, 2004, URL: http://english.chosun.com/w21data/html/news/200411/200411180014.html.

70. "North Korean Generals, Officials Defecting, But Kim Jong-il Still Strong," *AFP*, December 9, 2004, URL: http://story.news.yahoo.com/news?tmpl=

story&cid=1530&ncid=2181&e=10&u=/afp/20041209/wl_asia_afp/nkoreachinadefection_041209040849.

71. "N.K. Foreign Ministry Denies Removal of Kim Jong-il Portraits," *Chosun Ilbo*, November 19, 2004, URL: http://english.chosun.com/w21data/html/news/200411/200411190019.html.

72. "North Korea Denies Defection of Generals," *Joongang Ilbo*, December 14, 2004, URL: http://joongangdaily.joins.com/200412/13/2004121322 34036479900090209021.html.

73. "N. Korean Military Leaders Pledge Loyalty to Kim Jong-il," *Yonhap News Agency*, February 8, 2005, URL: http://english.yna.co.kr/Engnews/20050208/320000000020050208161124E0.html.

74. Barbara Demick, "Kim Ousts Relative, a Potential Rival, From N. Korean Government," *Los Angeles Times*, December 9, 2004, URL: http://www.latimes.com/news/nationworld/la-fgpurge9dec09,0,4477486.story?coll=la-headlines-world.

75. Jasper Becker, "Portrait of a Family at War: Kim Jong-il Purges Relatives After Alleged Coup Bid," *The Independent*, December 28, 2004, URL: http://news.independent.co.uk/world/asia/story.jsp?story=596607.

76. "N. Korean Leader's Younger Sister Alive: Source," *Yonhap News Agency*, February 7, 2005, URL: http://english.yna.co.kr/englishnews/20050207/320000000020050207175052E8.html.

77. "N.K. Leader's Son Avoids Assassination Plot in Austria," *Chosun Ilbo*, December 19, 2004, URL: http://english.chosun.com/w21data/html/news/200412/200412190013.html.

78. Yoo Kwang-jong, "Efforts to Hand Over North's Reins," *Joongang Ilbo*, November 24, 2005, URL: http://joongangdaily.joins.com/200511/23/200511232222205639900090309031.html.

79. Lee Young-jong, "North's Second Son Watched as Probable Heir," *Joongang Ilbo*, November 23, 2005, URL: http://joongangdaily.joins.com/200511/22/200511222228384209900090309031.html.

80. See Aidan Foster-Carter, "Cook and Tell: Another Chef Spills the Beans," *Asia Times*, July 2, 2003, URL: http://www.atimes.com/atimes/korea/eg02dg02.html; and Seo Dong-shin, "Speculation Rekindled Over N.K. Power Succession," *Korea Times*, February 17, 2006, URL: http://times.hankooki.com.

81. See Kim Hyung-jin, "N. Korea Appears to be Ready to Anoint one of Kim's Sons as Heir: S. Korean officials," *Yonhap News Agency*, April 5, 2006, URL: http://english.yna.co.kr/engnews/20060405430100000020060405102217e2.html; "Lapel Pins Hint at Kim's Successor," *CNN.com*, April 5, 2006, URL: http://www.cnn.com/2006/world/asiapcf/04/05/nkorea.succession.ap/index.html; and Rian Jensen, "On Pins and Needles over Kim Jong-il's Heir," *Asia Times*, April 28, 2006, URL: http://www.atimes.com/atimes/korea/hd28dg01.html.

82. Matthew Rusling, "Kim's Birthday No Retirement Party," *Asia Times*, February 16, 2006, URL: http://www.atimes.com/atimes/korea/hb16dg01.html.

83. "Badges of Kim Jong Il 3rd Son Said 'Circulating' Among DPRK Officials Since Mid-Feb," *Tokyo Sentaku*, April 1, 2006: 21.

84. "North Korea's Secretive First Family," *BBC News*, February 15, 2006, URL: http://news.bbc.co.uk/2/hi/asia-pacific/3203523.stm.

85. "Kim Jong-il Marries Former Secretary," *Chosun Ilbo*, July 24, 2006, URL: http://english.chosun.com/w21data/html/news/200607/2006072 40003.html; and "N. Korean Leader Kim Has New Wife: Sources," *Seoul Times*, September 17, 2006, URL: http://theseoultimes.com/st/?url=/st/db/read.php?idx=3725.

86. Brent Choi, "Looking for Mr. X: North Korea's Successor," *Nautilus Institute*, Special Report 06-03A, January 10, 2006, URL: http://www.nautilus.org/napsnet/sr/2006/0603choi.html.

87. "Junta Could Succeed N. Korean Leader," *KBS World Radio*, February 18, 2006, URL: http://rki.kbs.co.kr/english/news/news_detail.htm?no=33819.

88. Lee Young-jong and Ser Myo-ja, "Kim Kin's Return Just as Puzzling as His 2-Year Exile," *Joongang Ilbo*, January 31, 2006, URL: http:/service.joins.com/asp/print_article_english.asp?aid=2678791&esectcode=e_nkor&title=kim+kin's+return+just+as+puzzling+as+his+2-year+exile.

89. See Lee Young-jong, "Kim's Niece Kills Herself in Paris," *Joongang Ilbo*, September 19, 2006, URL: http://joongangdaily.joins.com/200609/18/200609182229417739900090309031.html; and "Kim Jong-Il's Niece Dies of Overdose," *Chosun Ilbo*, September 15, 2006, URL: http://english.chosun.com/w21data/html/news/200609/200609150030.html.

90. "Kim Jong-il's Succession Remains Taboo," *Chosun Ilbo*, November 30, 2005, URL: http://english.chosun.com/w21data/html/news/200511200511300020.html.

91. Alexandre Y. Mansourov, "Korean Monarch Kim Jong Il: Technocrat Ruler of the Hermit Kingdom Facing the Challenge of Modernity," *Nautilus Institute: DPRK Briefing Book*, URL: http://www.nautilus.org/DPRKbriefingbook/negotiating/issue.html.

92. David Shambaugh, "China and the Korean Peninsula: Playing for the Long Term," *Washington Quarterly*, vol. 26, no. 2 (Spring 2003), URL: http://www.twq.com/03spring/docs/03spring_shambaugh.pdf.

93. James Clay Moltz, "Russian Policy on the North Korean Nuclear Crisis," *Center for Non-Proliferation Studies*, May 5, 2003, URL: http://cns.miis.edu/research/korea/ruspol.htm.

94. For details on the economic burden that will be put on the government in Seoul in a post-unification scenario, see Marcus Noland, "Some Unpleasant Arithmetic Concerning Unification," *Institute for International Economics, Working Paper 96-13*, October 23, 1996, URL: http://www.iie.com/publications/wp/wp.cfm?researchid=169.

95. For detailed information on the system used to repress the population and maintain political control in North Korea, see Andrei Lankov, "The Repressive System and the Political Control in North Korea," *North Korea: Yesterday and Today*," 1995, originally published in Russian by *Moscow Literatura*, 1995, available in English on the internet at URL: http://www.fortunecity.com/meltingpot/champion/65/control_lankov.htm.

96. "Inside North Korea: A News Hour with Jim Lehrer Transcript," *PBS News Hour Online*, June 29, 2004, URL: http://www.pbs.org/newshour/bb/asia/jan-june04/nkorea_6-29.html.

97. Lee Young-jong, "Generals Still Surround Dear Leader in Public," *Joongang Ilbo*, January 25, 2006, URL: http://joongangdaily.joins.com/200601/24/200601242226090139900090209021.html.

98. "Setting a Humanitarian and Human Rights Agenda for North Korea: Meeting Report," *Brookings Institution*, March 4, 2004, URL: http://www.brookings .edu/dybdocroot/fp/projects/idp/20040304idpnkorea.pdf.

99. Heidi Brown and Susan Kitchens, "Trading With the Enemy," *Forbes Asia* February 27, 2006, URL: http://www.forbes.com/global/2006/0227/ 046A.html.

100. Doug Struck, "Opening a Window on North Korea's Horrors," *Washington Post*, October 4, 2003, URL: http://www.washingtonpost.com/ac2/wp-dyn/ a41966-2003oct3?language=printer.

101. Kongdan Oh and Ralph C. Hassig, *North Korea Through the Looking Glass* (Washington, DC: Brookings Institution Press, 2000), 135–139.

102. "The Secret of the North Korean Regime's Surprising Resilience," *The Daily N.K.*, January 19, 2001, URL: http://www.dailynk.com/english/keys/2000/1/ 09.php.

103. For a detailed listing of all of North Korea's police and counterintelligence agencies, see "Agency profile—North and South Korea," *Twentieth Edition of the N&O Column / Spooks Newsletter*, December 3, 1999, URL: http:// www.cvni.net/radio/nsnl/nsnl020/nsnl20kr.html; and "A Country Study: North Korea," *Library of Congress Country Studies*, 2005, URL: http://rs6.loc.gov/ frd/cs/kptoc.html.

104. For more analysis on the many enigmas associated with conducting analysis on this issue, see Charles Wolf, Jr. and Kamil Akramov, *North Korean Paradoxes: Circumstances, Costs, and Consequences of Korean Unification* (Santa Monica, CA: Rand Defense Research Institute, 2005), URL: http:// www.rand.org/pubs/monographs/2005/rand_mg333.pdf.

105. See Stephen Bosworth, "Tufts Expert Offers Insight On North Korea," *Tufts E-News*, January 30, 2006, URL: http://www.tufts.edu/communications/ stories/013006tuftsexpertoffersinsightonnorthkorea.htm; and "The Failed States Index," *Foreign Policy* (July/August 2005), URL: http://foreignpolicy .com/story/cms.php?story_id=3098.

106. Andrei Lankov, "North Korea's Antique Food Rationing," *Asia Times*, January 15, 2005, URL: http://www.atimes.com/atimes/korea/ga15dg01.html.

107. "North Korea Report: 2005," Amnesty International, 2005, URL: http:// web.amnesty.org/report2005/prk-summary-eng.

108. "Pyongyang Relents Over International Food Aid," *Chosun Ilbo*, February 23, 2006, URL: http://english.chosun.com/w21data/html/news/200602/ 200602230024.html.

109. See Edward Cody, "U.N. to Resume Food Aid to N. Korea," *Washington Post*, May 12, 2006, URL: http://www.washingtonpost.com/wp-dyn/content/ article/2006/05/11/AR2006051100627.html?nav=rss_world/asia; Choe Sang-hun, "North Korea Allows Food Aid to Resume," *International Herald Tribune*, May 12, 2006, URL: http://www.iht.com/articles/2006/05/11/news/ korea.php; and "World Food Program to Resume N. Korea Aid," *MSNBC Online*, May 10, 2006, URL: http://www.msnbc.msn.com/id/12729278/.

110. "DPRK 2004," ReliefWeb, 2004, URL: http://www.reliefweb.int/cap/ workshops/bestpractice/chap/resplan/cap_2004_dprk.doc.

111. "U.S. threat Over N Korean Food Aid," *BBC News Online*, December 30, 2005, URL: http://news.bbc.co.uk/2/hi/asia-pacific/4568182.stm.

112. Mark Manyin, "U.S. Assistance to North Korea: Fact Sheet," *CRS Report for Congress* (Washington, DC: Library of Congress, Congressional Research Service), February 11, 2005, URL: http://www.fas.org/sgp/crs/row/rs21834.pdf.

113. Stephan Haggard and Marcus Noland, "A U-Turn on Reforms Could Starve North Korea," *International Herald Tribune*, December 22, 2005, URL: http://www.iie.com/publications/opeds/oped.cfm?researchid=589.

114. "Q&A With Zain Verjee: Transcript," *CNN.com*, October 21, 2002, URL: http://transcripts.cnn.com/transcripts/0210/21/i_qaa.01.html.

115. For more on North Korea's delaying methods during the six-party talks and their demands for aid, see David Albright and Corey Hinderstein, "Dismantling the DPRK's Nuclear Weapons Program: A Practicable, Verifiable Plan of Action," *United States Institute for Peace: Peaceworks No. 54*, January 2006, URL: http://www.usip.org/pubs/peaceworks/pw54.pdf.

116. "North Korea Halts Nuclear Program: Transcript," *CNN.com*, September 19, 2005, URL: http://transcripts.cnn.com/transcripts/0509/19/i_ins.01.html.

117. Lew Kwang-chul, "Don't Just Trust, Verify—Dismantling North Korea's Nuclear Program," *Arms Control Today* (May 2004), URL: http://www.armscontrol.org/act/2004_05/lew.asp#bio.

118. For details of the breakdown in the Agreed Framework process and North Korean cooperation with the Bush administration, see Jonathan Pollack, "The United States, North Korea, and the End of the Agreed Framework," *Naval War College Review*, vol. 56, no. 3 (Summer 2003), URL: http://www.nwc.navy.mil/press/review/2003/summer/art1-su3.htm.

119. For more information and opinion regarding the disagreement among the nations involved in the six-party talks process with North Korea, see Dana Bash, "Cheney Pushes China on N. Korea," *CNN.com*, April 14, 2004, URL: http://edition.cnn.com/2004/WORLD/asiapcf/04/14/cheney.asia/index.html; and Ray Midkiff, "U.S. Regional Strategy for North Korea," *U.S. Army War College Strategy Research Project*, March 18, 2005, URL: http://www.strategicstudiesinstitute.army.mil/pdffiles/ksil198.pdf.

120. "Proliferation Security Initiative," Australian Government, Department of Foreign Affairs and Trade, URL: http://www.dfat.gov.au/globalissues/psi/.

121. The Honorable Alexander Downer, "Proliferation Security Initiative: Media Release," Minister for Foreign Affairs, Australia, May 30, 2005, URL: http://www.foreignminister.gov.au/releases/2005/fa070_05.html.

122. Patrick Goodenough, "N. Korea: U.S. Naval Drill Spells 'Nuclear War'," *NewsMax.com*, September 16, 2003, URL: http://www.newsmax.com/archives/articles/2003/9/16/110926.shtml.

123. Kang Chan-ho, "U.S., North to Discuss Fake Bills," *Joongang Ilbo*, February 25, 2006, URL: http://joongangdaily.joins.com/200602/242006022421349360990009030903.html.

124. "N.K. Officials Caught Smuggling Currency into Mongolia," *KBS World Radio*, February 23, 2006, URL: http://english.kbs.co.kr/news/newsview_sub.php?menu=8&key=2006022313.

125. Jay Solomon and Gordon Fairclough, "North Korea's Counterfeit Goods Targeted," *Wall Street Journal*, June 1, 2005, URL: http://online.wsj.com/

public/article/sb111756528456047297-xmynzpg5ux6fndvs11xzb8lsv8e_
20060601.html?mod=tff_main_tff_top.

126. Miwa Murphy, "Knowledge, Not Speculation, Key to North Korea, Expert Says," *Japan Times*, February 23, 2006, URL: http://search.japan times.co.jp/cgi-bin/nn20060223f2.html.

127. "North's Japan Trade Slumps Amid Tensions," *Joongang Ilbo*, February 13, 2006, URL: http://joongangdaily.joins.com/200602/12/2006021222203 487399000905T09051.html.

128. "Japan Terms N. Korea Talks Worse than Stalemate," *GeoStrategy-Direct*, February 22, 2006, URL: http://www.geostrategy-direct.com/geostrategy %2ddirect/.

129. "Illicit Cash Flow Crisis Blamed for Curtailed Birthday Blowout for Kim Jong-il," *East-Asia-Intel.com*, February 22, 2006, URL: http://www.east-asia-intel.com/eai/2006/02_22/11.asp.

Chapter 8: Countering the North Korean Threat: Challenges for the ROK–U.S. Alliance in the Post-9-11 Era

1. Portions of the research and writing for this chapter was originally published as: Bruce E. Bechtol Jr., "The ROK–U.S. Alliance During the Bush and Roh Administrations: Differing Perspectives for a Changing Strategic Environment," *International Journal of Korean Studies*, vol. 9, no. 2 (Fall/ Winter 2005), 87–115. Reprinted with the expressed written permission of the publisher of the *International Journal of Korean Studies* and the International Council on Korean Studies, Washington, DC.

2. "Korea in Brief: History," *Tour 2 Korea*, 2004, URL: http://english.tour2 korea.com/01tripplanner/koreainbrief/history.asp?kosm=m1_1&konum=5.

3. Tim Lambert, "A Short History of Korea," *Local Histories.org*, 2004, URL: http://www.localhistories.org/korea.html.

4. "U.S., Asia-Pacific Security Alliances*," U.S. State Department Fact Sheet, 1998,* URL: http://usinfo.state.gov/journals/itps/0198/ijpe/pj18fact.htm.

5. Rhonda L. Cornum, "North Korea and the United States: Learning How to Wage Peace in the Twenty First Century," *U.S. National War College Paper*, 2003, URL: http://www.ndu.edu/library/n4/n035601m.pdf.

6. See "ROK Participation in U.S. Peacekeeping Operations," Ministry of National Defense, Republic of Korea, 2003, URL: http://www.mnd.go.kr/; and "History of ROK Military Operations," Ministry of National Defense, Republic of Korea, 2001, URL: http://www.mnd.go.kr/.

7. Participatory Government's National Security Policy Initiative: Peace, Prosperity, and National Security," Republic of Korea, National Security Council (Seoul: Republic of Korea, 2004), 7–19.

8. Donald Macintyre, "Kim's War Machine," *Time Asia*, February 17, 2003, URL: http://www.time.com/time/asia/covers/501030224/army.html.

9. David Scofield, "South Korea: No More Kowtowing to Uncle Sam," *World Press Review*, vol. 51, no. 4 (April 2004), URL: http://www.worldpress.org/Asia/1849.cfm.

10. "Roh Hints at New East Asian Order," *Chosun Ilbo*, March 22, 2005, URL: http://english.chosun.com/w21data/html/news/200503/200503220024.html.

11. "Chinese Ambassador Backs Roh's NE Asia Doctrine," *Chosun Ilbo*, April

7, 2005, URL: http://english.chosun.com/w21data/html/news/200504/200504070022.html.

12. "Again Roh Fails to Consult the People," *Chosun Ilbo*, March 22, 2005, URL: http://english.chosun.com/w21data/html/news/200503/200503220037.html.

13. Kang Chan-ho, "U.S. Official Cautions Korea Over Seeking Balancer Role," *Joongang Ilbo*, April 16, 2005, URL: http://joongangdaily.joins.com/200504/15/200504152154211209900090030903l.html.

14. Shin Jeong-rok, "NSC Rebuffs New Doctrine's U.S. Critics," *Chosun Ilbo*, April 27, 2005, URL: http://english.chosun.com/w21data/html/news/200504/200504270023.html.

15. Seung-Heon Lee, "GNP Chairman Park Geun-hye's National Assembly Speech," *Donga Ilbo*, April 8, 2005, URL: http://english.donga.com/srv/service.php3bicode=050000&biid=2005040943218.

16. Lee Chul-hee and Jung Myung-jin, "GNP Leader Derides Roh Over Balancer Doctrine," *Joongang Ilbo*, April 9, 2005, URL: http://joongangdaily.joins.com/200504/08/20050408223013350990009030903l.html.

17. "Kim Dae-jung Tells New Uri Leaders to Accept Alliance," *Chosun Ilbo*, April 8, 2005, URL: http://english.chosun.com/w21data/html/news/200504/200504080032.html.

18. "Korea Steps up Military Cooperation with China," *Chosun Ilbo*, April 4, 2005, URL: http://english.chosun.com/w21data/html/news/200504/200504040020.html.

19. Sang-Ho Yun, "Proposed Bureau to Oversee Ties with China and Russia," *Donga Ilbo*, April 6, 2005, URL: http://english.donga.com/srvservice.php3?bicode=050000&biid=2005040704868.

20. Song Moon-hong, "After the Perry Report: The Korean Peninsula Game Enters the Second Round," *East Asian Review*, vol. 11, no. 4 (Winter 1999), URL: http://www.ieas.or.kr/vol11_4/songmoonhong.htm.

21. Richard Halloran, "China-Korea Alliance Appears to Have Edge," *Honolulu Advertiser*, April 24, 2005, URL: http://the.honoluluadvertiser.com/article/2005/Apr/24/op/op05p.html.

22. "Tension Mounts Between Korea and Japan Over History, Islets," *Chosun Ilbo*, March 14, 2005, URL: http://english.chosun.com/w21data/html/news/200503/200503140010.html.

23. Peter Rutland, "Distant Neighbors," *CDI Russia Weekly*, vol. 2, no. 2 (January 21, 2003), URL: http://www.cdi.org/russia/241-9-pr.cfm.

24. Robert Conquest, "You are Strong, You are Weak: Mother Russia," *Hoover Digest*, no. 1 (1998), URL: http://www.hooverdigest.org/981/conquest.html.

25. Henry Em, "Between Colonialism and Nationalism: Power and Subjectivity in Korea, 1931-1950," *Journal of the International Institute*, vol. 9, no. 1 (2003), URL: http://www.umich.edu/~iinet/journal/vol9no1/em.html.

26. Jim Geramone, "U.S. Welcomes Talks With South Korea to Re-Balance Forces," American Forces Information Service, February 19, 2002, URL: http://www.globalsecurity.org/wmd/library/news/rok/2003/rok-030219-afps01.htm.

27. Yeon-Wook Jung, "Revamp the NSC to Restore the South-U.S. Alliance," *Donga Ilbo*, November 4, 2004, URL: http://english.donga.com/srv/service.php3?bicode=050000&biid=2004110580768.

28. Jong-Koo Yoon, "CONPLAN 5029 Not to be Elevated to Status of OPLAN," *Donga Ilbo*, June 6, 2005, URL: http://english.donga.com/srvservice.php3?biid=2005060609528.

29. Kim Min-seok and Ser Myo-ja, "Seoul Halts Joing Plan for North Collapse," *Joongang Ilbo*, April 16, 2005, URL: http://joongangdaily.joins.com/200504/15/200504152203130939900090309031.html.

30. Sang-Ho Yun, "Friction Over Military Plan Between South Korea and the U.S.," *Donga Ilbo*, April 15, 2005, URL: http://english.donga.com/srv/service.php3?biid=2005041659058.

31. "Seoul Shelves Combined Forces N.K. Contingency Plan," *Chosun Ilbo*, April 15, 2005, URL: http://english.chosun.com/w21data/html/news/200504/200504150031.html.

32. "Nukes Won't Change Power Balance In Korea: USFK," *Chosun Ilbo*, June 29, 2005, URL: http://english.chosun.com/w21data/html/news/200506/200506290027.html.

33. Kang Chan-ho, "Seoul Proposes Discussing Collapse Plan with U.S.," *Joongang Ilbo*, May 2, 2005, URL: http://joongangdaily.joins.com/200505/01/200505012215393179900090309031.html.

34. Kim Min-seok, "Plan is Revived to Deal with North Collapse," *Joongang Ilbo*, June 6, 2005, URL: http://joongangdaily.joins.com/200506/05/200506052352176279900090309031.html.

35. "Korea, U.S. Close to Agreeing N.K. Contingency Plan," *Chosun Ilbo*, March 6, 2006, URL: http://english.chosun.com/w21data/html/news/200603/200603060012.html.

36. "The Threat of Weapons of Mass Destruction," *Defence: Australia's National Security*, 2003, URL: http://www.defence.gov.au/ans2003/section5.htm.

37. Ministry of National Defense, Republic of Korea, 2005, URL: http://www.mnd.go.kr/.

38. USFK Web Site at URL: http://www.korea.army.mil/.

39. "Missions of Combined Forces Command," *Combined Forces Command*, 2005, URL: http://www.korea.army.mil/cfc.htm.

40. The author is a professor at the United States Marine Corps Command and Staff College, a regionally accredited, graduate-level, master's degree granting institution, attended every year by a field grade officer of the ROK Marine Corps. U.S. military officers also attend the ROK Army, Navy, and Air Force Command and Staff Colleges, and similar exchange programs routinely occur at several levels within both governments.

41. "Foreign Relations–Diplomacy–Politics," *Korea Update*, vol. 15, no. 4 (March 1, 2004), URL: http://www.koreaemb.org/archive/2004/3_1/pdfkoreaupdate_3_1_2004.pdf.

42. "63 Percent of Uri Lawmakers Value China Over U.S.," *Chosun Ilbo*, May 4, 2004, URL: http://english.chosun.com/cgi-bin/printnews?id=200404280042.

43. Ser Myo-ja, "Roh Calls for Softer Stance Against North," *Joongang Ilbo*, November 15, 2004, URL: http://joongangdaily.joins.com/200411/14/200411142157137909900090309031.html.

44. Adam Ward and James Hacket, "U.S. Troop Withdrawals From South Korea: Beginnings of the End for the Alliance?" *Strategic Comments: The International*

Institute of Strategic Studies, vol. 10, no. 5 (June 2004), URL: www.iiss.org/ stratcom.

45. "Outgoing USFK Chief Reflects on Forces Command," *Chosun Ilbo*, January 26, 2006, URL: http://english.chosun.com/w21data/html/news/200601/ 200601260029.html.

46. Jin Dae-woong, "Yoon Opposes Military's Expanded Role Abroad," *Korea Herald*, January 23, 2006, URL: http://www.koreaherald.co.krlist.asp?kpage= 69&kppage=6&scode=fa&art_id%22.

47. "USFK Top Priority is to Deter North Korean Aggression," *Chosun Ilbo*, March 9, 2005, URL: http://english.chosun.com/w21data/html/news/200503/ 200503090010.html.

48. Ahn Sung-kyoo, "Talks to Decipher Future U.S. Military Role," *Joongang Ilbo*, February 3, 2005, URL: http://joongangdaily.joins.com/200502/02/ 200502022242232879900090309031.html.

49. Shin Jeong-rok, "Roh Says No to Greater USFK Role in Northeast Asia," *Chosun Ilbo*, March 8, 2005, URL: http://english.chosun.com/w21data/html/ news/200503/200503080028.html.

50. Jung Sung-ki, "Seoul Agrees on Strategic Flexibility," *Korea Times*, January 21, 2006, URL: http://times.hankooki.com/lpage/200601/kt20060120 17073010440.htm.

51. "Ban, Rice Compromise on USFK Strategic Flexibility," *Chosun Ilbo*, January 20, 2006, URL: http://english.chosun.com/w21data/html/news/200601/ 200601200010.html.

52. Jong-koo Yoon, "U.S., South Korea Issue Joint Statement," *Donga Ilbo*, January 21, 2006, URL: http://english.donga.com/srv/service.php3? bicode=050000&biid=2006012121958.

53. "National Assembly Says No to USFK Flexibility," *Chosun Ilbo*, February 6, 2006, URL: http://english.chosun.com/w21data/html/news/200602/ 200602060020.html.

54. "Ban Assures Koreans On Use of U.S. Troops," *Joongang Ilbo*, February 8, 2006, URL: http://joongangdaily.joins.com/200602/07/200602072232 399009900090309031.html.

55. Brian Lee, "Minister Berates Critics of U.S. Troops Flexibility," *Joongang Ilbo*, February 17, 2006, URL: http://joongangdaily.joins.com/200602/16/ 2006021621505753799000090309031.html.

56. Brian Lee, "Korea, U.S. Seal Agreement On Defense Costs," *Joongang Ilbo*, March 16, 2005, URL: http://joongangdaily.joins.com/200503/15/ 20050315222342007990009030903 1.html.

57. "Upset at Cost-Sharing Demands, USFK to Cut 1,000 Korean Workers," *Chosun Ilbo*, April 1, 2005, URL: http://english.chosun.com/w21data/html/ news/200504/20050404010029.html.

58. Ser Myo-ja, "USFK Sees Cut of 1,000 Korean Workers," *Joongang Ilbo*, April 2, 2005, URL: http://joongangdaily.joins.com/200504/01/ 20050401211380682399000090309031.html.

59. Sang-ho Yun, "Proportion of the USFK's Budget Allocated to South Korea Declines," *Donga Ilbo*, April 5, 2005, URL: http://english.donga.com/srv/ service.php3?bicode=050000&biid=2005040567918.

60. "USFK Lays Off First 112 Koreans," *Chosun Ilbo*, May 20, 2005, URL: http://english.chosun.com/w21data/html/news/200505/200505200021.html.

61. See Jung Sunk-ki, "U.S. Asks Korea to Pay More USFK Budget," *Korea Times*, August 27, 2006, URL: http://times.hankooki.com/lpage/nation/200608/kt2006082717074011990.htm; and "Korea-U.S. Military Budget Talks End in Failure," *Chosun Ilbo*, August 10, 2006, URL: http://english.chosun.com/w21data/html/news/200608/200608100021.html.

62. Brian Lee, "Meetings Cover Seoul's Share of Military Costs for U.S. Forces," *Joongang Ilbo*, January 19, 2005, URL: http://joongangdaily.joins.com/200501/18/200501182245109209900090309031.html.

63. Sang-ho Yun, "USFK Unhappy With Funding Shortfall," *Donga Ilbo*, April 2, 2005, URL: http://english.donga.com/srv/service.php3?bicode=050000&biid=2005040225518.

64. Robert A. Manning, "The U.S.–Japan Security Alliance in the 21st Century," *Council on Foreign Relations*, 2005, URL: http://www.cfr.org/pub2775/robert_a_manning/the_usjapan_security_alliance_in_the_21st_century.php#.

65. "Japan Commits 1.2B For U.S. Bases," *Agence France-Presse*, January 23, 2006, URL: http://www.defensenews.com/story.php?F=1484602&C=landwar.

66. "Moving U.S. Bases More Expensive Than Planned," *Chosun Ilbo*, February 6, 2006, URL: http://english.chosun.com/w21data/html/news/200602/200602060007.html.

67. For more information regarding the reasons Korea has acquired such large foreign reserves, see "Foreign Exchange Reserves in East Asia: Why the High Demand?" *FRBSF Economic Letter*, April 25, 2003, URL: http://www.frbsf.org/publications/economics/letter/2003/el2003-11.html.

68. Jung-Hun Kim, "Roh Rejects Idea of Deployment of USFK Against Korea's Will," *Donga Ilbo*, March 8, 2005, URL: http://english.donga.com/srv/service.php3?bicode=050000&biid=2005030978598.

69. Heo Yong-beom, "No Reduction in Rank of USFK: Lawless," *Chosun Ilbo*, November 8, 2004, URL: http://english.chosun.com/w21data/html/news/200410/200410080031.html.

70. Shin Jeong-rok, "Government Makes Public Future Security Policy," *Chosun Ilbo*, March 4, 2004, URL: http://english.chosun.com/cgi-bin/printNews?id=200403040015.

71. See "Talks Open on Shape of U.S. Forces In South Korea," *Agence France Presse*, February 4, 2005, URL: http://www.iht.com/bin/print_ipub.php?file=/articles/2005/02/03/news/korea.html; and Ho-Won Choi, "Future of the Security of the Korean Peninsula and USFK," *Donga Ilbo*, November 3, 2004, URL: http://english.donga.com/srv service.php?bicode=050000&biid=2004110467718.

72. Sang–Ho Yun, "U.S. 2nd Infantry Division to Transform Into a Next-Generation Unit This Summer," *Donga Ilbo*, March 6, 2005, URL: http://english.donga.com/srv/service.php?bicode=050000&biid=2005030750118.

73. Kim Min-seok, "U.S. Division Revamp Nearly Complete," *Joongang Ilbo*, May 25, 2005, URL: http://joongangdaily.joins.com/200505/24200505242244093179900090309031.html.

74. Jung-Hun Kim, "President Roh Says U.S. Sanctions to N. Korea Would Be

Undesirable," *Donga Ilbo*, November 14, 2004, URL: http://english.donga
.com/srv/service.php3?biid=2004111590368.

75. "North Attack Called Unlikely," *Joongang Ilbo*, October 18, 2004, URL: http://
joongangdaily.joins.com/200410/18/200410182307543909900
90309031.html.

76. "Soldiers Clamor Against Hardened Definition of N. Korea as Main Enemy,"
Chosun Ilbo, November 14, 2004, URL://english.chosun.com/w21data/html/
news/200411/200411140014.html.

77. Yu Yong-won, "N. Korea No Longer Main Enemy in Defense White Paper,"
Chosun Ilbo, January 12, 2005, URL: http://english.chosun.com/w21data/
html/news/200501/200501280038.html.

78. "Opening Remarks of Chairman Henry Hyde: Full Committee Hearing on
the Korean Peninsula: Six-Party Talks and the Nuclear Issue," U.S. Congress,
House, 109th Session, March 10, 2005, URL: http://wwwc.house.gov/
international_relations/109/hyde031005.htm.

79. "Unification Minister Gives U.S. Hardliner Short Shrift," *Chosun Ilbo*, March
14, 2005, URL: http://english.chosun.com/w21data/html/news/200503/
200503140025.html.

80. Kim Min-seok and Ser Myo-ja, "Ministry Seeks Independence for Military,"
Joongang Ilbo, April 29, 2005, URL: http://joongangdaily.joins.com/200504/
28/200504282219391539900090309031.html.

81. Cho Hyung-rae, "Korea–U.S. Alliance Should be a Mutual Relationship,"
Chosun Ilbo, June 9, 2004, URL: http://english.chosun.com/w21data/html/
news/200406/200406090039.html.

82. "U.S. Requests Koreans Share in C4I Modernization Costs," *Chosun Ilbo*,
November 18, 2004, URL: http://english.chosun.com/w21data/html/news/
200410/200410180019.html.

83. "Military to be streamlined by 2020," *Chosun Ilbo*, September 5, 2005, URL:
http://english.chosun.com/w21data/html/news/200509/2005090
50015.html.

84. Sang-ho Yun, "Defense Ministry: 623 Trillion Won Needed for National
Defense Reforms," *Donga Ilbo*, October 26, 2005, URL: http://english
.donga.com/srv/service.php3?bicode=050000&biid=2005102617208.

85. Ser Myo-ja and Kim Min-seok, "Ministry of Defense Announces Details of
Military Reform Plan," *Joongang Ilbo*, September 14, 2005, URL: http:/joong
angdaily.joins.com/200509/13/200509132306 448309900090309031.html.

86. Kim Min-seok, "Military Advances on Army Headquarters Reform," *Joongang
Ilbo*, December 2, 2005, URL: http://joongangdaily.joins.com/200512/01/
200512012154248679900090309031.html.

87. Brian Lee, "Defense Chief Plans Reforms for Ministry," *Joongang Ilbo*,
December 9, 2005, URL: http://joongangdaily.joins.com/200512/08/
200512082215045139900090309031.html.

88. "Military Reform Faces Serious Obstacles," *Chosun Ilbo*, September 5, 2005,
URL: http://english.chosun.com/w21data/html/news/200509200509
050035.html.

89. Editorial, "The Bill for Self-Reliant Defense from the U.S.," *Donga Ilbo*,
April 18, 2005, URL: http://english.donga.com/srv/service.php3?biid=
2005041995778.

90. "Military Spending to Account for 3 Pct of GDP by 2015," *Yonhap News Agency*, October 27, 2005, URL: http://english.yna.co.kr/Engservices/3000000000.html.

91. For specific details on how the budgeting process works in the government of South Korea, see "General Provisions of the Korean National Assembly," National Assembly of the Republic of Korea, October 29, 1987, URL: http://korea.assembly.go.kr/board/down.jsp?boarditemid=1000000155&dirname=/eng_data/1000000155e1.pdf.

92. See "Army Takes IT to the Front Line," *Chosun Ilbo*, June 26, 2006, URL: http://english.chosun.com/w21data/html/news/200606/200606260026.html; and Jin Dae-woong, "Korean Army Completes C4I Command System," *Korea Herald*, June 27, 2006, URL: http://www.koreaherald.co.kr/SITE/data/html_dir/2006/06/27/200606270039.asp.

93. "Korean Satellite Launch is a Success," *Donga Ilbo*, August 23, 2006, URL: http://english.donga.com/srv/service.php3?biid=2006082373498.

94. South Korea is dependent on the United States to provide both strategic and tactical battlefield and potential battlefield information. For details, see Sang-ho Yun, "Korea Depends on U.S. for Data on North," *Donga Ilbo*, June 22, 2006, URL: http://english.donga.com/srv/service.php3?bicode=050000&biid=2006062283888.

95. For detailed information regarding the "information dominance" capability that United States forces have brought to the Korean Peninsula, see John DiGenio, "Command, Control, Communications, Computers and Intelligence Challenges in the Korean Theater," *Army Communicator* (Fall 2001), URL: http://www.gordon.army.mil/ac/fall/fall%2001/koreac4i.htm.

96. See "Integrated Army Information System Ready Soon," *Chosun Ilbo*, October 16, 2006, URL: http://english.chosun.com/w21data/html/news/200510/200510160019.html; and Brian Lee, "Army Gets Modern C4I," *Joongang Ilbo*, October 16, 2005, URL: http://joongangdaily.joins.com/200510/16/200510162212568939900090309031.html.

97. See Sang-Ho Yun, "F-15K, Welcome to Korea," *Donga Ilbo*, September 29, 2005, URL: http://english.donga.com/srv/service.php3?biid=2005092943028&path_dir=20050929; and "F-15K Aircraft," *Republic of Korea Air Force*, 2005, URL: http://www.airforce.mil.kr/eng/pc/pcbe0100.html.

98. "Seoul to Buy 20 More F-15Ks," *Korea Overseas Information Service*, May 19, 2006, URL: http://www.defense-aerospace.com/cgi-bin/client/modele.pl?prod=69009&session=dae.20820725.1147973885.rgywcoa9duaaauyya8&modele=release.

99. Lt. Gen. So Chin Tae, "Recasting the Viability of a Small Ally's Airpower: South Korea in Focus," *Air and Space Power Journal: Chronicles Online Journal* (October 1, 2002), URL: http://www.airpower.maxwell.af.mil/airchronicles/cc/tae.html.

100. For more information regarding the capabilities of the "LPX" class ship, see "Asia's Largest Landing Ship-LPX, 'Dokdo'," *KBS Global News*, March 14, 2006, URL: http://english.kbs.co.kr/news/zoom/1356843_11781.html; "Navy to Launch Region's Biggest Troop Landing Ship," *Chosun Ilbo*, July 4, 2005, URL: http://english.chosun.com/w21data/html/news/200507200507040024.html; and "LP-X Dokdo (Landing Platform Experimental) Amphibious Ship,"

GlobalSecurity.org, September 22, 2005, URL: http://www.globalsecurity.org/ military/world/rok/lp-x.htm.

101. See Sang-Ho Yun, "Korea's Aging Missile Defense System," *Donga Ilbo*, July 7, 2006, URL: http://english.donga.com/srv/service.php3?bicode= 050000&biid=2006070714838; and Mingi Hyun, "Protecting What Has Become the South Korean Way of Life," *Joongang Ilbo*, August 19, 2006, URL: http://joongangdaily.joins.com.

102. "U.S. to Withdraw Patriot Missiles From Gwangju," *Chosun Ilbo*, August 24, 2006, URL: http://english.chosun.com/w21data/html/news/200608/ 200608240011.html.

103. Kim Min-seok and Brian Lee, "Key Defense Mission to go to Korean Military," *Joongang Ilbo*, April 11, 2005, URL: http://joongangdaily.joins.com/200504/ 10/2005041022534456799000090309031.html.

104. "U.S. Requests Koreans Share in C4I Modernization Costs," *Chosun Ilbo*, October 18, 2004.

105. Sang-ho Yun, "1,000 Guided Missiles to Be Introduced to Counter North Korean Artillery," *Donga Ilbo*, April 11, 2006, URL: http://english.donga.com/ srv/service.php3?biid=2005041158378.

106. "South Korea—Constitution," *International Constitutional Law Project*, November 2004, URL: http://www.oefre.unibe.ch/law/icl/ks00000_.html.

107. For details regarding Wartime and Peacetime OPCON and DEFCON conditions, see "ROK–U.S. Alliance and USFK," Republic of Korea, Ministry of National Defense, June 2003, URL: http://www.mnd.go.kr/english/scm/ documents/rok-us_alliance_and_usfk.pdf.

108. Hong Kwan-hee, "Viewpoint: Slow Down on Transfer of Control," *Joongang Ilbo*, March 8, 2006, URL: http://joongangdaily.joins.com/200603/07/ 200603072227529509900090109012.html.

109. Jin Dae-woong, "Korea–U.S. Agreed to Establish Task Force Team on Wartime Command Transfer," *Korea Herald*, December 8, 2005, URL: http:// www.koreaherald.co.kr/site/data/html_dir/2005/12/0820051208 0008.asp?kpage=1&kppage=0&scode=FA&art_id%22.

110. Jung Sung-ki, "Seoul Seeks Speedy Wartime Command Talks with U.S.," *Korea Times*, January 25, 2006, URL: http://times.hankooki.com/lpage/nation/ 200601/kt2006012517104711950.htm.

111. Yeon-wook Jung, "Roh Still Wants Korean Wartime Command," *Donga Ilbo*, March 4, 2006, URL: http://english.donga.com/srv/service.php3? bicode=050000&biid=2006030490648.

112. Jung Sung-ki, "ROK, U.S. to Form Joint Panel on Command Transfer," *Korea Times*, March 29, 2006, URL: http://times.hankooki.com/lpage/nation/200603/ kt2006032920183711990.htm.

113. "Wartime Control Transfer 'Desirable' But no Time Set: Rumsfeld," *Yonhap News Agency*, March 24, 2006, URL: http://english.yna.co.kr/engnews/ 20060324/9100000000020060324065111e3.html.

114. William C. Mann, "Rumsfeld Says No Agreement On S. Korean Wartime Command For Its Military This Year," *Associated Press*, March 23, 2006, URL: http://www.signonsandiego.com/news/military/20060323-1440-us-skorea-military.html.

115. Kim Min-seok and Kim Soe-jung, "Rumsfeld: U.S. to Give Back War Control

in 2009," *Joongang Ilbo*, August 27, 2006, URL: http://joongang daily.joins.com/200608/27/200608272306415779900090309031.html.

116. Brian Lee, "Rumsfeld: South is Not Now at Risk of Attack by North," *Joongang Ilbo*, August 29, 2006, URL: http://joongangdaily.joins.com/ 200608/28/200608282158090939900090309031.html.

117. "U.S. U-Turn on N. Korean Threat Raises Eyebrows," *Chosun Ilbo*, August 29, 2006, URL: http://english.chosun.com/w21data/html/news/200608/ 200608290023.html.

118. "Korea, U.S. in War of Nerves Over Troop Control," *Chosun Ilbo*, August 7, 2006, URL: http://english.chosun.com/w21data/html/news/200608/ 200608070021.html.

119. "What We Lose From Gaining Operational Control," *Chosun Ilbo*, October 12, 2005, URL: http://english.chosun.com/w21data/html/news/200510/ 200510120029.html.

120. "Insider Gives Command Issue Orders," *Donga Ilbo*, August 18, 2006, URL: http://english.donga.com/srv/service.php3?biid=2006081812988.

121. Reuben Staines, "Lawmakers Debate Wartime Command," *Korea Times*, October 10, 2005, URL: http://times.hankooki.com/lpage/nation/200510/ kt2005101019431711990.htm.

122. "Wartime Command Worrying Say Officers," *Donga Ilbo*, August 10, 2006, URL: http://english.donga.com/srv/service.php3?biid=2006081096348& path_dir=20060810.

123. See Chae Byung-gun and Kim Jung-wook, "Uri Trains Its Guns on Roh Aides at National Assembly," *Joongang Ilbo*, June 26, 2006, URL: http:// joongangdaily.joins.com/200606/25/200606252214277379900009 0309031.html; and "Look Around Before Dismantling the Pillar of Our Security," *Chosun Ilbo*, June 23, 2006, URL: http://english.chosun.com/ w21data/html/news/200606/200606230032.html.

124. "National Assembly Told of End to Combined Forces Command," *Chosun Ilbo*, August 17, 2006, URL: http://english.chosun.com/w21data/html/news/ 200608/200608170031.html.

125. Jung Sung-ki, "Seoul Seeks New Joint Military Structure With U.S.," *Korea Times*, February 28, 2006, URL: http://times.hankooki.com/lpage/200602/ kt2006022817584553460.htm.

126. "Seoul Wants to Scrap Combined Forces Command," *Chosun Ilbo*, February 28, 2006, URL: http://english.chosun.com/w21data/html/news/200602/ 200602280020.html.

127. See Brian Lee, "After Transfer, New Agency Will be Liaison," *Joongang Ilbo*, August 12, 2006, URL: http://joongangdaily.joins.com/200608/11/ 200608112240234679900090309031.html; Sohn, Suk-jo, "S. Korea, U.S. to Set Up Joint Headquarters after Disbanding Combined Command," *Yonhap News Agency*, August 17, 2006, URL: http://english.yna.co.kr/engnews/ 20060817/540000000020060817135931e7.html; "Post-Command Shift Joint HQ Planned," *Donga Ilbo*, August 18, 2006, URL: http://english.donga.com/ srv/service.php3?bicode=050000&biid=2006081812778; Brian Lee, "U.S.– Korea Liaison to Be at War Office," *Joongang Ilbo*, August 18, 2006, URL: http://joongangdaily.joins.com/200608/17200608172228022939 9 00090309031.htm; and Jung Sung-ki, "U.S. to Share Military Intelligence

After Command Transfer," *Korea Times*, August 17, 2006, URL: http://times.hankooki.com/lpage/nation/200608/kt2006081717281911990.htm.

128. Gen. B. B. Bell, "Speech to Korean National Assembly Security Forum," Presented to the National Assembly of the Republic of Korea Security Forum, July 13, 2006, URL: http://www.usfk.mil/usfk/index.html?/org/fkpa/sptr/index.html.

129. See "U.S. Senate Asks for Report on Possible UNC Expansion in Korea," *Yonhap News Agency*, July 4, 2006, URL: http://www.yonhapnews.co.kr/engservices/3000000000.html; and "U.S. Troop Reductions in Korea Will Not Affect Combat Ability: Official," *Yonhap News Agency*, August 7, 2006, URL: http://www.yonhapnews.co.kr/engservices/3000000000.html.

130. "Command Issue Could Hurt Korea–U.S. Ties," *Donga Ilbo*, January 26, 2006, URL: .http://english.donga.com/srv/service.php3?bicode=050000&biid=2006012680278.

131. *White Paper: 2004*, Republic of Korea, Ministry of National Defense, 2004, URL: http://www.mnd.go.kr/etext2/main.jsp?dir=002&subdir=000&name=&popup=n&currentpage=1.

132. Michael O'Hanlon, "A Disunited Allied Force?" *Washington Times*, August 28, 2006: 14.

133. Scott Snyder, "[OVERSEAS VIEW] The Time is Right to Take Over the Defense," *Joongang Ilbo*, April 27, 2006, URL: http:/joongangdaily.joins.com/200604/26/200604262139202839900090109012.html.

134. "Korea, U.S. Mulling Halfway House for Wartime Control," *Chosun Ilbo*, June 2, 2006, URL: http://english.chosun.com/w21data/html/news/200606/200606020035.html.

135. Kim Min-Seok, "Seoul Seeks Leadership of Ground Forces Here," *Joongang Ilbo*, June 3, 2006, URL: http://joongangdaily.joins.com/200606/02/200606022132540339900090309031.html.

136. Park Song-wu, "Seoul to Get Back Wartime Command in 5 to 6 Years," *Korea Times*, June 4, 2006, URL: http://times.hankooki.com/lpage/200606/kt2006060417383810220.htm.

137. Brian Lee, "Yoon Denies 2 Reports of War Control Changes," *Joongang Ilbo*, June 6, 2006, URL: http://joongangdaily.joins.com/200606/05/200606052215557709900090309031.html.

138. "Military to Play Leading Role on Peninsula," *KBS World Radio*, June 5, 2006, URL: http://rki.kbs.co.kr/english/news/news_detail.htm?No=36771.

139. "Pillar of Korea–U.S. Military Alliance for the Scrapheap," *Chosun Ilbo*, June 5, 2006, URL: http://english.chosun.com/w21data/html/news/200606/200606050001.html.

140. See Jung Sung-ki, "Ex-Defense Chiefs Oppose Command Transfer," *Korea Times*, August 6, 2006, URL: http://times.hankooki.com/lpage/200608/kt2006080617551653460.htm; and "Roh Under Fire Over Wartime Command Withdrawal," *Chosun Ilbo*, August 10, 2006, URL: http://english.chosun.com/w21data/html/news/200608/200608100014.html.

141. "Thousands Protest Command Transfer," *Donga Ilbo*, September 4, 2006, URL: http://english.donga.com/srv/service.php3?biid=2006090452318.

142. Jin Ha Hwang, "Just Say No (To Roh)," *Wall Street Journal*, September 14, 2006.

143. See Brian Lee, "Defense Chiefs Defer Decision on War Control," *Joongang Ilbo*, October 23, 2006, URL: http://joongangdaily.joins.com/200610/22/200610222244570309900090209021.html; "Korea, U.S. Compromise on Troop Control Transfer," *Chosun Ilbo*, October 21, 2006, URL: http://english.chosun.com/w21data/html/news/200610/200610210010.html; and Sohn Suk-joo, "S. Korea to Take Over Wartime Control from U.S. Between 2009 and 2012," *Yonhap News Agency*, October 20, 2006, URL: http://english.yonhapnews.co.kr/engnews/20061021/610000000002006 1021124806e6.html.

144. "The 38th Security Consultative Meeting Joint Communiqué," *Defense Link*, October 20, 2006, URL: http://www.defenselink.mil/news/Oct2006/d20061020uskorea.pdf.

145. "Secretary Gates Holds Consultations with ROK Minister of National Defense," *Defense Link*, February 23, 2007, URL: http://www.defenselink.mil/news/Feb2007/d20070223sdrok.pdf.

146. "Former Generals Criticize Seoul–Washington Deal on Wartime Control Transfer," *Yonhap News Agency*, February 26, 2007, URL: http://english.yonhapnews.co.kr/Engnews/2007022661000000002 0070226140348E0.html.

147. For details regarding the training at the U.S. Army's National Training Center, see "The National Training Center and Fort Irwin," URL: http://www.irwin.army.mil/channels.

148. Jim Geramone, "General Says U.S.–Korean Alliance Relevant, Ready," Armed Forces Information Service, February 4, 2006, URL: http://www.defenselink.mil/news/feb2006/20060204_4111.html.

Chapter 9: Civil-Military Relations in the ROK: The Impact on North–South Relations and the ROK–U.S. Alliance

1. The majority of research and writing for this chapter was originally published as Bruce E. Bechtol Jr., "Civil-Military Relations in the Republic of Korea: Background and Implications," *Korea Observer*, vol. 36, no. 4 (Winter 2005): 603–630. Reprinted with the expressed written permission of the publisher of the *Korea Observer* and the Institute of Korean Studies, Seoul, Republic of Korea.

2. Chaibong Hahm, "An Election Without Issues," *Asia Update: The 1997 Korean Elections, The Asia Society.com*, November 1997, URL: http://www.asiasociety.org/publications/update_elections.html.

3. Moon Ihlwan and Mark L. Clifford, "Korea's Young Lions," *Business Week Online* February 24, 2003, URL: http://www.businessweek.com/magazine/content/03_08/b3821011.htm.

4. Jung-Hun Kim and In-Jik Cho, "President Roh: Civil Society Plays Key Role in National Affairs," *Donga Ilbo*, May 18, 2005, URL: http://english.donga.com/srv/service.php3?bicode=050000&biid=2005051905768.

5. Min Seong-jae and Kang Joo-an, "President Lauds Kwangju Uprising Victory," *Joongang Ilbo*, May 19, 2005, URL: http://joongangdaily.joins.com/200505/18/2005051821420509399000090309031.html.

6. Tim Shorrock, "Special Report: The U.S. Role in Korea in 1979 and 1980,"

Kimsoft.com, 1996, URL: http://www.kimsoft.com/korea/kwangju3 .htm#incident.

7. Donald Clark, "The Korean War: Forgotten No More," Conference summary of Korean War Conference conducted June 23–25, 2000 at Georgetown University, sponsored by the Korea Society, URL: http://www.koreasociety .org/main/kwarconferencerpt/kw_confsummary.htm.

8. John A. Wickham Jr., *Korea on the Brink: From the "12/12 Incident" to the Kwangju Uprising, 1979–1980* (Washington, DC: NDU Press, 1999*)*, URL: http://www.ndu.edu/inss/press/ndupress_books_titles.htm.

9. Yong-Gwan Jung, "I Wrote a Letter in Blood Not to Betray My Student Activist Colleagues," *Donga Ilbo*, May 19, 2005, URL: http://english.donga.com/srv/ service.php3?bicode=050000&biid=2005052024408.

10. Brian Lee, "Top Defense Aide is Forced Out," *Joongang Ilbo*, May 5, 2005, URL: http://joongangdaily.joins.com/200505/04/20050504215324277 9900090309031.html.

11. "Truth Committee Picks Seven Suspicious NIS Incidents," *Chosun Ilbo*, February 3, 2005, URL: http://english.chosun.com/w21data/html/news/ 200502/200502030015.html.

12. "NIS History Probe Must Maintain Strict Neutrality," *Chosun Ilbo*, February 3, 2005, URL: http://english.chosun.com/w21data/html/news/200502/ 200502030037.html.

13. "Executions Still Smart 30 Years After," *Chosun Ilbo*, April 8, 2005, URL: http://english.chosun.com/w21data/html/news/200504/200504080025.html.

14. "Young, Liberal and in Command, *Economist.com* (April 16, 2004), URL: http://www.economist.com/agenda/displayStory.cfm?story_id=2606595.

15. "Liberal Wins South Korean Presidential Election," *PBS News Hour Online*, December 19, 2002, URL: http://www.pbs.org/newshour/updates/skorea_12- 19-02.html.

16. "The United States and South Korea; Reinvigorating the Partnership, Joint U.S.–Korea Academic Studies Vol. 14, 2004," Proceedings of symposium conducted by the Stanford Asia Pacific Research Center, the Korea Economic Institute, and the Korea Institute for International Economic Policy, October 22–24, 2003, URL: http://www.keia.com/2-publications/2-3-monograph/ monograph2004/monograph2004.pdf.

17. "NIS Chief Tenders Resignation," *KBS World Radio Online*, June 1, 2005, URL: http://english.kbs.co.kr/news/newsview_sub.php?menu=2&key= 2005060101.

18. John Larkin, "Cleaning House: South Korea's shady spy agency is being overhauled, but will it still be able to catch North Korean spooks?" *Time Asia*, June 16, 2003, URL: http://www.time.com/time/asia/magazine/article/ 0,13673,501030616-457404,00.html.

19. Kim Jung-wook, "New Intelligence Chief Vows to Overcome Past," *Joongang Ilbo*, July 12, 2005, URL: http://joongangdaily.joins.com/200507/11/ 200507112250192909900090409041.html.

20. Chun Su-jin, Lee Jung-min and Kim Jung-wook, "Spy Chief Adds Fuel to the Fire Over His Ouster," *Joongang Ilbo*, October 31, 2006, URL: http:// joongangdaily.joins.com/200610/30/200610302216139239900090 409041.html.

21. Shim Jae-yun, "Foreign Minister Resigns over U.S. Policy Flap," *Korea Times*, January 15, 2004, URL: http://times.hankooki.com/lpage/200401/kt2004011516343110440.htm.

22. Yeon-Wook Jung, "Revamp the NSC to Restore the South–U.S. Alliance," *Donga Ilbo*, November 4, 2004, URL: http://english.donga.com/srv/service.php3?bicode=050000&biid=2004110580768.

23. See "Roh to Hold Internet Conversation with the Nation," *Chosun Ilbo*, March 22, 2006, URL: http://english.chosun.com/w21data/html/news/200603/200603220025.html; and Park So-young, "Study Shows Slippage in Uri Grip on Netizens," *Joongang Ilbo*, May 9, 2005, URL: http://joongangdaily.joins.com/200505/08/2005050822335273399000090309031.html.

24. For more information regarding this incident and the aftermath, see Kim Min-seok and Ser Myo-ja, "Defense Chief Resigns, Naval Dispute Goes On," *Joongang Ilbo*, July 27, 2004, URL: http://joongangdaily.joins.com/200407/27/200407272232190439900090209021.html; Shin Jeong-rok, "Defense Minister Hands in His Resignation," *Chosun Ilbo*, July 27, 2004, URL: http://english.chosun.com/w21data/html/news/200407/2004070044.html; "S. Korean Generals Stripped of Rank While N. Korea Willfully Violates NLL," *Chosun Ilbo*, July 26, 2004, URL: http://english.chosun.com/w21data/html/news/200407/200407260048.html; and Ho-Won Choi, "Another N. Korean Patrol Boat Crosses NLL on Tuesday," *Donga Ilbo*, November 10, 2004, URL: http://english.donga.com/srv/service.php?bicode+050000&biid=2004111146408.

25. Donald Greenlees, "2 Ministers in S. Korea Quit Over Bomb Test," *International Herald Tribune*, October 25, 2006, URL: http://www.iht.com/articles/2006/10/25/news/korea.php.

26. "Soldiers Clamor Against Hardened Definition of N. Korea as Main Enemy," *Chosun Ilbo*, November 14, 2004, URL://english.chosun.com/w21data/html/news/200411/200411140014.html.

27. "What Was Wrong with NSC's Grey Eminence?" *Chosun Ilbo*, May 17, 2005, URL: http://english.chosun.com/w21data/html/news/2005052005051700 36.html.

28. Park Shin-hong, "Seoul Asks U.S. Help Bar U.N. Nuclear Query," *Joongang Ilbo*, March 17, 2005, URL: http://joongangdaily.joins.com/200411/16/2004111622181264799000090309031.html.

29. "KNSC Official in Mystery Investigation," *Chosun Ilbo*, May 17, 2005, URL: http://english.chosun.com/w21data/html/news/200505/200505170034.html.

30. See "Government to Seek Balanced Pragmatic Diplomacy: Minister Ban," *Korea Update*, April 15, 2005, URL: http://www.koreaemb.org/archive/2005/4_1/foreign/foreign11.asp; and "President Roh Says No Change in Dispatch Plan," *Hot Issues in Korea*, June 23, 2004, URL: http://www.ipr.co.kr/eng/ipr4-p3-v.asp?id=ISSUE&index=list&page=8&seq=47%09%09%09%09%09&keyword=&ssubject=0&sname=0&scontent=0.

31. Lee Jong-seok, "Dismantling the Sole Remaining Cold War Structure and the Engagement Policy," *East Asian Review*, vol. 12, no. 1 (Spring 2000), URL: http://www.ieas.or.kr/vol12_1/leejongseok.htm.

32. Sook-Jong Lee, "The Rise of Korean Youth as a Political Force: Implications

for the U.S.–Korea Alliance," *Brookings Institution Papers*, 2005, URL: http://www.brook.edu/fp/cnaps/papers/survey2004/2korea2.pdf.

33. Choi Hoon and Park Shin-hong, "Roh Aide Explores the Meaning of Pro-American," *Joongang Ilbo*, April 21, 2005, URL: http://joongang daily.joins.com/200504/20/200504202243226309900090309031.html.

34. Park Song-wu, "U.S. Pullout Inevitable: NSC Official," *Korea Times*, May 16, 2005, URL: http://times.hankooki.com/lpage/200405/kt200405 3015524510230.htm.

35. Ralph Cossa, "U.S.–ROK: Tough Times Ahead?" *PacNet: Pacific Forum CSIS*, January 27, 2004, URL: www.csis.org/pacfor/pac0454.pdf.

36. For more information on perspectives regarding this issue through the socio-cultural prism, see Brent Choi, "Don't Misunderstand Firing of South Korean Foreign Minister," *Nautilus Institute Policy Forum Online 04-01*, February 5, 2005, URL: http://www.nautilus.org/fora/security/0401_choi.html.

37. Jung-Hun Kim, "What's Going On in the Security Control Tower?" *Donga Ilbo*, May 17, 2005, URL: http://english.donga.com/srv/service.php3? bicode=050000&biid=2005051884218.

38. Min Seoung-jae, "Security Aide Reportedly under a Cloud," *Joongang Ilbo*, May 18, 2005, URL: http://joongangdaily.joins.com/200505/17/20050517 2235423609900090309031.html.

39. "New Unification Minister to Assume NSC Post," *Chosun Ilbo*, January 3, 2006, URL: http://english.chosun.com/w21data/html/news/200601/ 200601030019.html.

40. Brian Lee, "New Policymaker for North Preceded by His Reputation," *Joongang Ilbo*, January 14, 2006, URL: http://joongangdaily.joins.com/ 200601/13/200601132224256439900090309031.html.

41. Annie I. Bang, "Lee Firmly in Roh Inner Circle," *Korea Herald*, February 8, 2006, URL: http://www.koreaherald.co.kr/archives/result_contents. asp?id=200602080034.asp.

42. Don Kirk, "Seoul Dodges the Dragon But Feels the Heat," *Asia Times*, October 28, 2006, URL: http://www.atimes.com/atimes/Korea/HJ28Dg01.html.

43. Jeon Jin-bae, "Army Trying to Make Bases More Palatable," *Joongang Ilbo*, May 19, 2005, URL: http://joongangdaily.joins.com/article/view.asp? aid=2570667

44. "Military Reform on French Model Planned," *Chosun Ilbo*, April 28, 2005, URL: http://english.chosun.com/w21data/html/news/200504/2005042 80021.html.

45. Sang-Ho Yun, "Preparing for Military Personnel Reduction and Structural Reform Legislation," *Donga Ilbo*, April 28, 2005, URL: http:// english.donga.com/srv/service.php3?bicode=050000&biid= 2005042978638.

46. Jung-Hun Kim, "Continuing Civilian Control Over the Army and Military Reform," *Donga Ilbo*, October 1, 2004, URL: http://english.donga.com/srv/ service.php3?biid=2004200281618.

47. "S. Korea Army Chief Offers To Quit," *BBC News*, November 25, 2004, URL: http://news.bbc.co.uk/2/hi/asia-pacific/4041057.stm.

48. Sang-Ho Yun, "President Roh to Attend Military Academy Commencement Every Other Year," *Donga Ilbo*, February 15, 2004, URL: http://

english.donga.com/srv/service.php3?bicode=050000&biid=2005021603208.

49. Choi Hoon, "Experts Head Blue House Military Group," *Joongang Ilbo*, February 11, 2005, URL: http://joongangdaily.joins.com/200502/10/200502102110327679900090309031.html.

50. "Seoul Shelves Combined Forces N.K. Contingency Plan," *Chosun Ilbo*, April 15, 2005, URL: http://english.chosun.com/w21data/html/news/200504/200504150031.html.

51. Ho-Won Choi, "Poll: President Roh is Wrongfully Managing State Affairs," *Donga Ilbo*, November 7, 2004, URL://english.donga.com/srv/service.php3 bicode=050000&biid=2004110809418.

52. Yeon-Wook Jung, "President and Ruling Party Suffer Declining Approval Rate After Elections," *Donga Ilbo*, May 12, 2005, URL: http://english.donga .com/srv/service.php3?bicode=050000&biid=2005051305368.

Chapter 10: Conclusion:
The Impact of the Post-9/11 Era on Korean Security

1. Andrew J. Coe, "North Korea's New Cash Crop," *Washington Quarterly*, vol. 28, no. 3 (Summer 2005), URL: http://www.twq.com/05summer/docs/05summer_coe.pdf.

2. For more information on North Korea's warming of ties with the EU, see "North Korea Comes in from the Cold: EU Establishes Diplomatic Ties, Starts on 'Very Long . . . and Stony Road'," *CNN.com*, May 14, 2001, URL: http://archives.cnn.com/2001/fyi/news/05/14/eu.nkorea/index.html.

3. Sergey Radchenko, "The Soviet Union and the North Korean Seizure of the USS *Pueblo*: Evidence from Russian Archives," Cold War International History Project: Working Paper Number 47, URL: http://www.wilson center.org/topics/pubs/cwihp_wp_47.pdf.

4. Michael Rank, "North Korea Banks on China," *Asia Times*, May 24, 2005, URL: http://www.atimes.com/atimes/korea/gc24dg02.html.

5. For an analysis of the complex China–North Korea relationship, see Denny Roy, "China and the Korean Peninsula: Beijing's Pyongyang Problem and Seoul Hope," *Asia-Pacific Center for Security Studies Paper*, vol. 3, no. 1 (2004), URL: http://www.apcss.org/publications/apsss/chinaandthekorean peninsula.pdf.

6. For an analysis of several key South Korean initiatives and how they have influenced North Korea's state behavior, as well as the priorities the South Korean government has pursued in its "Peace and Prosperity" agenda, see Don Kirk, "Never Mind the Missiles, Stay on the Rails," *Asia Times*, May 26, 2006, URL: http://www.atimes.com/atimes/korea/he26dg01.html.

7. North Korea continues to conduct DMZ and NLL violations that are probably designed to be easily controllable and to test the resolve of the South Korean military; a recent example occurred in May 2006, as North Korean troops conducted a minor DMZ violation when troops briefly crossed the line long enough to gain the attention of South Korean troops before being forced back by warning shots; see "N. Korean Soldiers Briefly Violate Inter-Korean Border," *Yonhap News Agency*, May 26, 2006, URL: http://english .yonhapnews.co.kr/engnews/20060526/430100000020060526170217e7.html.

8. See "N. Korea Hibernating Till Bush Goes," *Chosun Ilbo*, March 24, 2006,

URL: http://english.chosun.com/w21data/html/news/200603/20060
3240023.html; and Ben Johnson and Gordon Cucullu, "On North Korea, Don't
Blame Bush," *FrontPage Magazine*, February 11, 2005, URL: http://www.front
pagemag.com/articles/readarticle.asp?id=17007.

9. See "Japan Protests to North Korea Over Fake Evidence," *China Daily*,
    December 8, 2004, URL: http://www.chinadaily.com.cn/english/doc/2004-
    12/08/content_398468.htm; and "DNA Tests Reveal New Information—
    Husband of Japanese Abductee Yokota is Abducted ROK National," *Foreign
    Press Center Japan*, April 13, 2006, URL: http://www.fpcj.jp/e/mres/
    japanbrief/jb_622.html.

10. Mike Chinoy, "North Korea's Propaganda Machine," *CNN.com*, February
    28, 2003, URL: http://www.cnn.com/2003/world/asiapcf/east/02/28/
    nkorea.propaganda/index.html.

11. Robert Marquand, "N. Korea News: One Source Tells All," *Christian Science
    Monitor*, June 17, 2005, URL: http://www.csmonitor.com/2005/0617/p06s01-
    woap.html.

12. Kirk, *Asia Times*, URL: http://www.atimes.com/atimes/korea/he26dg01.html.

13. "President Roh's Pledge to Make Bigger Concessions to Pyongyang," *KBS
    World Radio*, May 18, 2006, URL: http://world.kbs.co.kr/english/event/
    nkorea_nuclear/now_02_detail.htm?No=87.

14. Jong-Heon Lee, "Analysis: N. Korea Keen on S. Korea Election," *United
    Press International*, May 30, 2006, URL: http://www.upi.com/
    internationalintelligence/view.php?storyid=20060529-044126-3920r.

15. For more analysis on the debate regarding North Korea being a "threat" or a
    "nuisance," see Don Oberdorfer, "The United States and South Korea: Can
    This Alliance Last?" *Nautilus Institute: Policy Forum Online 05-93A*,
    November 17, 2005, URL: http://www.nautilus.org/fora/security/
    0593oberdorfer.html; and Kurt M. Campbell and Celeste Johnson Ward, "New
    Battle Stations?" *Foreign Affairs* (September/October 2003), URL: http://
    www.foreignaffairs.org/20030901faessay82507/kurt-m-campbell-celeste-
    johnson-ward/new-battle-stations.html.

16. Mary Crane, "North Korea: The North Korean Disarmament Talks," *Council
    on Foreign Relations*, July 27, 2005, URL: http://www.cfr.org/publication/
    8079/.

17. "Clinton Administration Knew of Secret North Korean Uranium-Based
    Weapons Program, Experts Say," *NTI Global Security Newswire*, May 28,
    2006, URL: http://www.nti.org/d_newswire/issues/2006_5_26.html#
    e4ed60ef.

18. Paul Kerr, "North Korea, U.S. Talks Inch Forward," *Arms Control Today* (April
    2006), URL: http://www.armscontrol.org/act/2006_04/nkustalksinch.asp.

19. "Major Concern if North Korea Launches Long-Range Missile: U.S.," *Agence
    France-Presse*, May 23, 2006, URL: http://www.defencetalk.com/news/
    publish/article_006119.php; "U.S. to Seek U.N. Sanctions if N. Korea Fires
    Long-Range Missile," *Kyodo News*, May 26, 2006, URL: http://
    finance.comcast.net/richnews_body.html?id=comtex_ctb_en%3
    a1148694540&auth; and "Seoul Tries to Dissuade North from Missile
    Launch," *Chosun Ilbo*, May 19, 2006, URL: http://english.chosun.com/
    w21data/html/news/200605/200605190011.html.

20. See Brian Lee, "China and Russia Ask North Not to Test-Fire Missile," *Joongang Ilbo*, June 24, 2006, URL: http://joongangdaily.joins.com/200606/23/200606232142338479900090309031.html; and Myoung-Gun Lee, "China Could Help Defuse ICBM Crisis," *Donga Ilbo*, June 26, 2006, URL: http://english.donga.com/srv/service.php3?biid=2006062639788.

21. Myoung-Gun Lee, "ICBM Test Delay Keeps World Guessing," *Donga Ilbo*, June 20, 2006, URL: http://english.donga.com/srv/service.php3?biid=2006062045888.

22. See Stuart Levey, "Prepared Remarks by Under Secretary Stuart Levey: Terrorism and Financial Intelligence," Presented to the Netherlands' Terrorist Financing Conference, March 16, 2006, URL: http://www.treasury.gov/press/releases/js4119.htm; and Nicholas Eberstadt, "Pyongyang's Option: 'Ordinary' Stalinism," *Far Eastern Economic Review*, March 21, 2005, URL: http://www.aei.org/publications/filter.all,pubID.22158/pub_detail.asp.

23. "North Korea Arms Push May Be Stymied by Banking Rules (Update 1)," *Bloomberg.com*, March 7, 2006, URL: http://www.bloomberg.com/apps/news?pid=10000101&sid=akgisnckqyua.

24. Park Song-wu, "N.K. Should Open Up Like China: Wolfowitz," *Korea Times*, May 30, 2006, URL: http://times.hankooki.com/lpage/nation/200605/kt2006053017352511990.htm.

25. See Christian Caryl, "Is Three a Crowd? At Odds with Washington Over How to Handle North Korea, South Korea is Drawing Ever Closer to China," *Newsweek International*, June 20, 2006, URL: http://www.msnbc.msn.com/id/8185488/site/newsweek/from/RL.5/; and Ahn Sung-kyu and Min Seong-jae, "Prime Minister Seeks Strategic Independence," *Joongang Ilbo*, March 31, 2005, URL: http://joongangdaily.joins.com/200503/30 2005033 0215414180990009003090 31.html.

26. Kim Min-seok, "Poll Cites China as Korea's Big Security Threat in Next Decade," *Joongang Ilbo*, March 20, 2006, URL: http://www.world securitynetwork.com/showArticle3.cfm?article_id=12713.

27. See "A Tough Choice for President after Election Defeat," *Chosun Ilbo*, May 31, 2006, URL: http://english.chosun.com/w21data/html/news/200605/200605310012.html; "Uri Party Chairman Falls on His Sword," *Chosun Ilbo*, June 1, 2006, URL: http://english.chosun.com/w21data/html/news/200606/200606010020.html; Lee Soo-ho and Chun Su-jin, "Some Fingers Point at Blue House," *Joongang Ilbo*, June 3, 2006, URL: http://joongangdaily.joins.com/200606/02/20060602213527067990009 0309031.html; Chun Su-jin, "Stunned Uri Head Quits," *Joongang Ilbo*, June 2, 2006, URL: http://joongangdaily.joins.com/200606/01/200606012218155 679900090309031.html; and Jung Sung-ki, "Roh's Policy Line Not Attractive to Young Voters," *Korea Times*, June 4, 2006, URL: http://times.hankooki.com/lpage/200606/kt2006060417452768040.htm.

28. Lee Kyo-kwan, "Seoul and Washington Closer to Divorce," *Asia Times*, March 7, 2006, URL: http://www.atimes.com/atimes/korea/hc07dg03.html.

29. Michael O'Hanlon, "Future of U.S.-Seoul Ties," *Washington Times*, December 18, 2005, URL: http://www.washingtontimes.com/commentary/20051218-125507-7793r.htm.

| SELECTED BIBLIOGRAPHY

Abramowitz, Morton, Michael J. Green, and James T. Laney, "North Korea Task Force Press Conference." *Council on Foreign Relations*, July 27, 1999. URL: http://www.cfr.org/publication/3212/north_korea_task_force_press_conference.html?breadcrumb=default

Albright, David. "Finding our Way Anew to a De-Nuclearized Korean Peninsula." *Center for International Policy Working Paper*, November 19, 2002. URL: http://ciponline.org/asia/reports/task_force/Albright.htm

Albright, David, and Corey Hinderstein. "Dismantling the DPRK's Nuclear Weapons Program: A Practicable, Verifiable Plan of Action." *United States Institue for Peace: Peaceworks Number. 54*, January 2006. URL: http://www.usip.org/pubs/peaceworks/pw54.pdf

Altschul, Jess. "Pakistan-North Korea Weapons Trade Continued Through 2002." *Jewish Institute for National Security Affairs*, September 9, 2003. URL: http://www.jinsa.org/articles/articles.html/function/view/categoryid/169/documentid/2202/history/3,2360,652,169,2202

"Annex 8. North Korea and Weapons of Mass Destruction: US Department of Defense Estimate of North Korean Actions and Intentions Involving Nuclear, Biological, and Chemical Weapons." *Center for Non-Proliferation Problems,* 2005. URL: http://npc.sarov.ru/english/digest/52002/appendix8.html

"Answers to Questions from the Senate Senate Select Committee on Intelligence, World Wide Threat Hearing." *Defense Intelligence Agency*, March 21, 2002. URL: http://www.fas.org/irp/congress/2002_hr/020602dia.html

Asher, David L. "The North Korean Criminal State, its Ties to Organized Crime, and the Possibility of WMD Proliferation." Remarks presented to the Counter-Proliferation Strategy Group, Woodrow Wilson Center, Washington DC, October 21, 2005. URL: http://www.nautilus.org/fora/security/0502Asher.html

At Cold War's End: US Intelligence on the Soviet Union and Eastern Europe, 1989–1991. History Staff, Center for the Study of Intelligence, Central Intelligence Agency. URL: http://www.cia.gov/csi/books/19335/art-1.html

Bach, William. Office of African, Asian and European Affairs, Bureau for International Narcotics and Law Enforcement Affairs, Department of State.

"Hearing on Drugs Counterfeiting and Arms Trade." *Senate Sub-Committee on Financial Management, the Budget, and International Security.* May 20, 2003. URL: http://hongkong.usconsulate.gov/ushk/state/2003/052001.htm

"Background Note: North Korea." *Bureau of East Asian and Pacific Affairs, United States State Department,* November 2005. URL: http://www.state.gov/r/pa/ei/bgn/2792.htm

Bechtol, Bruce E. Jr. "The Impact of North Korea's WMD Programs on Regional Security and the ROK–U.S. Alliance." *International Journal of Korean Studies*, vol. 8, no. 1 (Fall/Winter 2004): 141.

———. "The Northern Limit Line of 2002: Motivations and Implications." *Pacific Focus*, vo. 19, no. 2 (Fall 2004): 233–264.

———. "Civil-Military Relations in the Republic of Korea: Background and Implications." *Korea Observer*, vol. 36, no. 4 (Winter 2005): 603–30.

———. "The ROK-US Alliance During the Bush and Roh Administrations: Differing Perspectives for a Changing Strategic Environment." *International Journal of Korean Studies*, vol. 90, no. 2 (Fall/Winter 2005): 87–115.

———. "The Future of US Airpower on the Korean Peninsula." *Air and Space Power Journal*, vol. 19, no. 3 (Fall 2005): 75–84.

Bell, B. B. *Statement for the Record to the Senate Armed Services Committee.* March 7, 2006. URL: http://www.senate.gov/~armed_services/statemnt/2006/March/Bell%2003-07-06.pdf

———. *Statement for the Record to the Senate Armed Services Committee.* March 7, 2007. URL: http://armedservices.house.gov/pdfs/FCPACOM030707/Bell_Testimony030707.pdf

———. "Speech to Korean National Assembly Security Forum." Presented to the National Assembly of the Republic of Korea Security Forum, July 13, 2006. URL: http://www.usfk.mil/usfk/index.html?/org/fkpa/sptr/index.html

Ben-David, Alon. "Iran acquires ballistic missiles from DPRK." *Janes Defence Weekly*, December 29, 2005. URL: http://www.janes.com/security/international_security/news/jdw/jdw051229_1_n.shtml

Bermudez, Joseph S. Jr. "A History of Ballistic Missile Development in the DPRK: CNS Occasional Paper #2." *Center for Non-Proliferation Studies, The Monterey Institute*, 1999. URL: http://cns.miis.edu/pubs/opapers/op2/index.htm

———. "Moving Missiles." *Janes Defence Weekly*, July 27, 2005. URL: http://www.janes.com/defence/land_forces/news/jdw/jdw050727_1_n.shtml

———. "North Korea Deploys New Missiles." *Janes Defence Weekly*, August 2, 2004. URL: http://www.janes.com/defence/news/jdw/jdw040802_1_n.shtml

———. "North Korea Set to Launch Taepo Dong 2." *Janes Defence Weekly*, July 5, 2005, 4-5.

Biggie, Jeramy. "Operational Net Assessment." Paper presented at the conference titled, "Decision Aids/Support to Joint Operations Planning," hosted by the Military Operations Research Society, at the Dougherty Conference Center, Offutt AFB Nebraska, November 19, 2003. URL: http://www.mors.org/meetings/decision_aids/da_pres/Biggie.pdf

Bleiker, Roland. *Divided Korea: Toward a Culture of Reconciliation* (Minneapolis, MN: University of Minnesota Press, 2005).

"Briefing on the Agreement Reached at the Six-Party Talks in Beijing." *U.S. Department of State*, February 13, 2007. URL: http://www.state.gov/secretary/rm/2007/feb/80496.htm

Campbell, Kurt M., and Celeste Johnson Ward. "New Battle Stations?" *Foreign Affairs*, September/October 2003. URL: http://www.foreign affairs.org/20030901faessay82507/kurt-m-campbell-celeste-johnson-ward/new-battle-stations.html

Carpenter, Ted Galen, and Doug Bandow. *The Korean Conundrum: America's Troubled Relationship with North and South Korea* (New York: Palgrave MacMillan, 2004).

Carroll, Paul. "Trip Report by Paul Carroll." *Nautilus Institute Policy Forum Online 06-59A*, July 20, 2006. URL: http://www.nautilus.org/fora/security/0659TripReport.html

Cha, Victor D. and David C. Kang. *Nuclear North Korea: A Debate for Engagement Strategies* (New York: Columbia University Press, 2003).

———. "The Korea Crisis." *Foreign Policy.Com*, September 29, 2003. URL: http://www.foreignpolicy.com/story/story.php?storyID13620

Cheney, Richard. "Vice President Speaks at China's Fudan University April 15." Speech given at Fudan University, China, April 15, 2004. URL: http://helsinki.usembassy.gov/servlet/PageServer?Page=today2.html

Chestnut, Sheena E. "Sopranos State? North Korean Involvement in Criminal Activity and Implications for International Security." *Nautilus Institute Special Report*, January 19, 2006. URL: http://www.nautilus.org/napsnet/sr/2006/0605Chestnut.pdf

"China: Crackdown on Illegal Immigrants Likely to Target North Korean Refugees." *Amnesty International*, March 27, 2002. URL: http://web.amnesty.org/library/Index/ENGASA170132002?open&of=ENG-PRK

Cho, Kisuk. "Understanding Public Opinion in Korea." Keynote speech presented at Georgetown University, Washington, DC, 4 November 2005, at Georgetown University's School of Foreign Service and Korea's Sejong Institute co-sponsored conference entitled, "New Era: New Alliance." URL: http://www.kois.go.kr/news/news/newsView.asp?serial_no=20051104015&part=111&SearchDay=

Choi, Brent. "Looking for Mr. X: North Korea's Successor." *Nautilus Institute*, Special Report 06-03A: January 10, 2006. URL: http://www.nautilus.org/napsnet/sr/2006/0603Choi.html

————. "Don't Misunderstand Firing of South Korean Foreign Minister." *Nautilus Institute Policy Forum Online 04-01*, 5 February 2005. URL: http://www.nautilus.org/fora/security/0401_Choi.html

"Chronology of North Korea's Missile Trade and Developments: 1980–1989." *Center for Non-Proliferation Studies, The Monterey Institute*, 2003. URL: http://cns.miis.edu/research/korea/chr8089.htm

Chung, Dong-young, Minister of Unification, Republic of Korea. "Korean Peace Economics." Speech Presented at the National Press Club, Washington, DC, December 19, 2005.

CIA World Factbook, 2005. URL: http://www.cia.gov/cia/publications/factbook/rankorder/2078rank.html

Clark, Donald. "The Korean War: Forgotten No More." *Conference Summary of Korean War Conference Conducted on 23-25 June, 2000, at Georgetown University, Sponsored by the Korea Society*. URL: http://www.korea society.org/MAIN/KWarConferenceRpt/KW_ConfSummary.htm

"CNS Special Report on North Korean Ballistic Missile Capabilities." *Center for Nonproliferation Studies, Monterey Institute of International Studies*, March 22, 2006. URL: http://cns.miis.edu/pubs/week/pdf/060321.pdf

Conquest, Robert. "You are Strong, You are Weak: Mother Russia." *Hoover Digest*, no. 1 (1998). URL: http://www.hooverdigest.org/981/conquest.html

Costello, Stephen. "Foreign Policy in the First Two Years of the Roh Moo-hyun Government." *Cheong Wa Dae: Office of the President*, March 18, 2005. URL: http://english.president.go.kr/cwd/en/archive/archive_view.php ?meta_id=for_your_info&m_def=3&ss_def=4&id=1c1ca47daa77a9da4798752.

Crane, Mary. "North Korea: The North Korean Disarmament Talks." *Council on Foreign Relations*, July 27, 2005. URL: http://www.cfr.org/publication/8079/

DeSutter, Paula A. "Completion of Verification Work in Libya." *Testimony to the U.S. House of Representatives Subcommittee on International Terrorism, Nonproliferation and Human Rights*. September 22, 2004. URL: http://www.state.gov/t/vci/rls/rm/2004/37220.htm

DiGenio, John. "Command, Control, Communications, Computers and Intelligence Challenges in the Korean Theater." *Army Communicator*, Fall 2001. URL: http://www.gordon.army.mil/AC/Fall/Fall%2001/koreac4i.htm

"Doctrinal Implications of Operational Net Assessment." *Joint Warfighting Center, Joint Doctrine Series, Pamphlet 4*, February 24, 2004. URL: http://www.dtic.mil/doctrine/education/jwfc_pam4.pdf

Downer, Alexander. "Proliferation Security Initiative: Media Release." *Minister for Foreign Affairs, Australia*, May 30, 2005. URL: http://www.foreign minister.gov.au/releases/2005/fa070_05.html

Downs, Chuck. *Over the Line: North Korea's Negotiating Strategy* (Washington, DC: AEI Press, 1999).

"DPRK 'Manufactured' Nuclear Weapons, To 'Suspend' 6-Way Talks for 'Indefinite Period." *Korean Central Broadcasting Station Statement*. Full Text of 10 February 2005 Statement broadcast over North Korean Radio and

Television. URL: http://www.nautilus.org/napsnet/sr/2005/0513A_ KCBS.html

"DPRK 2004." *ReliefWeb*, 2004. URL: http://www.reliefweb.int/cap/workshops/ BestPractice/CHAP/ResPlan/CAP_2004_DPRK.doc

Eberstadt, Nicholas. "The Persistence of North Korea." *Policy Review*, no. 127, (October–November 2004). URL: http://www.policyreview.org/oct04/ eberstadt.html

————. "Pyongyang's Option: 'Ordinary' Stalinism." *Far Eastern Economic Review*, March 21, 2005. URL: http://www.aei.org/publications/ filter.all,pubID.22158/pub_detail.asp

Em, Henry. "Between Colonialism and Nationalism: Power and Subjectivity in Korea, 1931–1950." *Journal of the International Institute*, vol. 9, no. 1 (2003). URL: http://www.umich.edu/~iinet/journal/vol9no1/em.html

"F-15K Aircraft." *Republic of Korea Air Force*, 2005. URL: http://www .airforce.mil.kr/ENG/PC/PCBE0100.html

"The Failed States Index." *Foreign Policy*, July/August 2005. URL: http:// foreignpolicy.com/story/cms.php?story_id=3098

"Foreign Relations—Diplomacy—Politics." *Korea Update*, vol. 15, no. 4 (March 1, 2004). URL: http://www.koreaemb.org/archive/2004/3_1/pdf/ koreaupdate_3_1_2004.pdf

Friedman, Benjamin. "Fact Sheet: North Korea's Nuclear Weapons Program." *Nuclear Issues: Center for Defense Information,* January 23, 2003. URL: http://www.cdi.org/nuclear/nk-fact-sheet-pr.cfm

Gause, Ken E. *North Korean Civil-Military Trends: Military-First Politics to a Point.* Strategic Studies Institute Monograph (Carlisle, PA: U.S. Army War College, September 2006). URL: http://www.strategicstudiesinstitute .army.mil/pdffiles/PUB728.pdf

"General Provisions of the Korean National Assembly." *National Assembly of the Republic of Korea*, October 29, 1987. URL: http://korea.assembly.go.kr/ board/down.jsp?boarditemid=1000000155&dirname=/eng_data/ 1000000155E1.pdf

Gertz, Bill. "The North Korean Missile Threat." *Air Force: Journal of the Air Force Association*, January 2000, vol. 83, no. 1. URL: http://www.afa.org/ magazine/Jan2000/0100missile.asp

Glaser, Daniel. "The Importance of AML/CFT Controls in Financial Institutions." Prepared remarks presented to the International AML/CFT Inaugural Conference of the U.S./MENA Private Sector Dialogue, Cairo, Egypt, March 22, 2006. URL: http://www.treas.gov/press/releases/js4132.htm

"Government to Seek Balanced Pragmatic Diplomacy: Minister Ban." *Korea Update*, April 15, 2005. URL: http://www.koreaemb.org/archive/2005/4_1/ foreign/foreign11.asp

Green, Nick. "Dealing Drugs: North Korean Narcotics Trafficking." *Harvard International Review*, vol. 26, no. 1 (Spring 2004). URL: http://hir.harvard .edu/articles/1201

Hahm, Chaibong. "An Election Without Issues." *Asia Update: The 1997 Korean Elections, The Asia Society.com,* November 1997. URL: http://www.asiasociety.org/publications/update_elections.html

Han, Ho-suk. "North Korea's War Strategy of Massive Retaliation Against U.S. Attacks." *Association for Asian Research,* May 1, 2003. URL: http://www.asianresearch.org/articles/1359.html

Harrison, Selig S. "Did North Korea Cheat?" *Foreign Affairs Online,* January/February 2005. URL: http://www.foreignaffairs.org/20050101faessay84109/selig-s-harrison/did-north-korea-cheat.html

Hayes, Peter. "The Beijing Deal Is Not the Agreed Framework." *Nautilus Policy Forum Online 07-014A,* February 14, 2007. URL: http://www.nautilus.org/fora/security/07014Hayes.html

———. "Embrace Tiger, Retreat to Mountain, Test Nuke." *Nautilus Institute Policy Forum Online 06-60A,* July 21, 2006. URL: http://www.nautilus.org/fora/security/0660Hayes.html

———. "The Multilateral Mantra and North Korea," *The Nautilus Institute Online,* February 20, 2004. URL: http://www.nautilus.org/DPRKBriefingBook/multilateralTalks/PHMultilateralMantra.html

———. "North Korea's Negotiating Tactics and Nuclear Strategy." *Nautilus Institute Special Report,* April 18, 2003. URL: http://www.nautilus.org/DPRKBriefingBook/nuclearweapons/NuclearNegotiations.html

Hecker, Siegfried S. "Report on North Korean Nuclear Program." *Center for International Security and Cooperation, Stanford University,* November 15, 2006. URL: http://iis-db.stanford.edu/pubs/21266/DPRK-report-Hecker06.pdf

———. "Technical Summary of DPRK Nuclear Program." Paper presented at the 2005 Carnegie International Non-Proliferation Conference, November 8, 2005. URL: http://www.carnegieendowment.org/static/npp/2005conference/presentations/hecker.pdf

Henriksen, Thomas H. "Using Power and Diplomacy To Deal With Rogue States." *Hoover Institution Essays in Public Policy,* February 1999. URL: http://www.hoover.org/publications/epp/default.html

"History of ROK Military Operations." *Ministry of National Defense, Republic of Korea,* 2001. URL: http://www.mnd.go.kr/

Hodge, Homer T. "North Korea's Military Strategy." *Parameters,* Spring 2003. URL: http://carlisle-www.army.mil/usawc/Parameters/03spring/hodge.htm

Hussain, Touqir. "U.S.-Pakistan Engagement: The War on Terrorism and Beyond." *Special Report Number 145, United States Institute of Peace,* August 2005. URL: http://www.usip.org/pubs/specialreports/sr145.html

Hwang, Jang-yop. "Testimonies of North Korean Defectors." *Republic of Korea, National Intelligence Service,* 1999. URL: http://www.fas.org/irp/world/rok/nis-docs/hwang6.htm

"IAEA Director General Cites DPRK Nuclear Brinkmanship," *Texts of December 26 and 27 IAEA press releases on developments in North Korea.* URL: http://japan.usembassy.gov/e/p/tp-20021230a7.html

Ilyas, Shahid. "*Security Environment in Northeast Asia.*" *Regional Studies,* vol. 23, no. 4 (Autumn 2005). http://irs.org.pkPublRegionalStudies.htm#_ftnref4

"Initial Actions for the Implementation of the Joint Statement: Joint Statement from the Third Session of the Fifth Round of the Six-Party Talks." *Nautilus Institute Special Report*, February 13, 2007. URL: http://www.nautilus .org/fora/security/07013Statement.html

"International Narcotics Control Strategy Report." *United States Department of State*, March 200. URL: http://www.state.gov/p/inl/rls/nrcrpt/2000/ 891.htm

"Iran's Ballistic Missile and Weapons of Mass Destruction Programs." *Hearing before the International Security, Proliferation, and Federal Services Subcommittee of the Committee on Governmental Affairs*, United States Senate, 106th Congress, Second Session, September 21, 2000. URL: http:// www.fas.org/irp/congress/2000_hr/hr_092100.html

Kang, Jungmin, and Peter Hayes. "Technical Analysis of the DPRK Nuclear Test." *Nautilus Institute Policy Forum Online 06-89A*, October 20, 2006. URL: http://www.nautilus.org/fora/security/0689HayesKang.html

Kelly, James, Assistant Secretary of State for East Asian and Pacific Affairs. "Opening Remarks Before the Senate Foreign Relations Committee." *U.S. Congress, Senate,* Washington, DC, March 2, 2004. URL: http://www.state .gov/p/eap/rls/rm/2004/30093pf.htm

Kerr, Paul. "New North Korean Missile Suspected." *Arms Control Today*, September 2004. URL: http://www.armscontrol.org/act/2004_09/NK_ Missile.asp

———. "North Korea Increasing Weapons Capabilities." *Arms Control Today*, December 2005. URL: http://www.armscontrol.org/act/2005_12/Dec-NKweapons.asp

———. "North Korea, US Talks Inch Forward." *Arms Control Today*, April 2006. URL: http://www.armscontrol.org/act/2006_04/nkustalksinch.asp

Kihl, Young Whan. *Transforming Korean Politics: Democracy, Reform and Culture*, (Armonk, NY: M. E. Sharpe, 2005).

Kihl, Young Whan, and Peter Hayes (eds.). *Peace and Security in Northeast Asia: The Nuclear Issue and the Korean Peninsula* (Armonk, NY: M. E. Sharpe, 1997).

Kim, Young Il. "North Korea and Narcotics Trafficking: A View from the Inside." *North Korea Review*, vol. 1, no. 1 (March 1, 2004). URL: http:// www.jamestown.orgpublications_details.php?volume_id=398&issue_id= 2915&article_id=23572

Knight, Charles "General Trainor's Korean War Scenario is Only Half the Story." *Project on Defense Alternatives,* June 4, 1997. URL: http://www.comw.org/ pda/trainor.htm

"KN-02 Short Range Ballistic Missile." *Global Security.Org*. URL: http:// www.globalsecurity.org/wmd/world/dprk/kn-2.htm

Koh, B. C. "North Korea's Missile Launches and Six-Party Talks." *Institute for*

Far Eastern Studies Forum, August 21, 2006. URL: http://ifes.kyun gnam.ac.kr/eng/activity05_ifes_forum_view.asp?ifesforumNO= 181&page=1

"Korea as World's 10th Largest Economy." *Korea.Net,* January 31, 2005. URL: http://www.korea.net/news/issues/issueDetailView.asp?board_no=6103

"Korean Peoples Army." *Federation of American Scientists*, June 15, 2000. URL: http://www.fas.org/nuke/guide/dprk/agency/army.htm

"Korean Peoples Army Air Force." *Global Security.Org,* 2002. URL: http:// www.globalsecurity.org/military/world/dprk/airforce.htm

Kotler, Mindy L. "Toward an 'Asian' North Korea." *Nautilus Institute Policy Forum Online*, PFO 03-28: 8, 2003. URL: http://www.nautilus.org/fora/ security/0328_Kotler.html

Lankov, Andrei. "The Repressive System and the Political Control in North Korea." *North Korea: Yesterday and Today,* 1995. Originally published in Russian by *Moscow Literatura*, 1995. URL: http://www.fortunecity.com/ meltingpot/champion/65/control_lankov.htm

Lee, Hy-Sang. "Allow Two Nukes for North Korea." *Nautilus Institute Policy Forum Online: PFO 05-22A,* March 10, 2005. URL: http://www.nautilus .org/fora/security/0522A_Lee.html

Lee, Jong-seok. "Dismantling the Sole Remaining Cold War Structure and the Engagement Policy." *East Asian Review*, vol. 12, no. 1 (Spring 2000). URL: http://www.ieas.or.kr/vol12_1/leejongseok.htm

Lee, Keum-soon. *"Cross-Border Movement of North Korean Citizens." East Asian Review*, vol. 16, no. 1 (Spring 2004). URL: http://www.ieas.or.kr/ vol16_1/16_1_3.pdf

Lee, Sook-Jong. "The Rise of Korean Youth as a Political Force: Implications for the U.S.-Korea Alliance." *Brookings Institution Papers*, 2005. URL: http://www.brook.edu/fp/cnaps/papers/survey2004/2korea2.pdf

Levey, Stuart. "Prepared Remarks by Under Secretary Stuart Levey: Terrorism and Financial Intelligence." *Presented to the Netherlands' Terrorist Financing Conference*, March 16, 2006. URL: http://www.treasury.gov/press/ releases/js4119.htm

Lew, Kwang-chul. "Don't Just Trust, Verify—Dismantling North Korea's Nuclear Program." *Arms Control Today,* May 2004. URL: http://www.arms control.org/act/2004_05/Lew.asp#bio

Library of Congress. *North Korea: A Country Study*. URL: http://lcweb2.loc.gov/ frd/cs/kptoc.html

Linter, Bertil. "North Korea's Missile Trade Helps Fund its Nuclear Program." *Yale Global Online*, May 5, 2003. URL: http://yaleglobal.yale.edu/ display.article?id=1546

"LP-X Dokdo (Landing Platform Experimental) Amphibious Ship." *GlobalSecurity.Org*, September 22, 2005. URL: http://www.global security.org/military/world/rok/lp-x.htm

Manning, Robert A. "The U.S.–Japan Security Alliance in the 21st Century."

Council on Foreign Relations, 2005. URL: http://www.cfr.org/pub2775/ robert_a_manning/the_usjapan_security_alliance_in_the_21st_ century.php#

Manyin, Mark. "U.S. Assistance to North Korea: Fact Sheet." *Congressional Research Service Report for Congress,* February 11, 2005. URL: http:// www.fas.org/sgp/crs/row/RS21834.pdf

Manyin, Mark, Emma Chanlett-Avery, and Helene Marchat. "North Korea: A Chronology of Events, October 2002–December 2004," *Congressional Research Service,* Library of Congress, January 24, 2005. URL: http:// www.fas.org/man/crs/RL32743.pdf

Mansourov, Alexandre. "Enigma of the Land of Morning Calm: Korean Shrimp or Roaring Tiger?"*CNAPS Working Paper, The Brookings Institution,* September 2000. URL: http://www.brookings.edu/fp/cnaps/papers/2000_ mansourov.htm

———. "Inside North Korea's Black Box: Reversing the Optics." *Brookings Institution Paper,* June 2004. URL: http://www.brookings.edu/views/papers/ fellows/oh20040601ch4.pdf

———. "Korean Monarch Kim Jong Il: Technocrat Ruler of the Hermit Kingdom Facing the Challenge of Modernity." *Nautilus Institute: DPRK Briefing Book.* URL: http://www.nautilus.org/DPRKbriefingbook/negotiating/ issue.html

Matthew, Richard A. and Ted Gaulin. "Time to Sign the Mine Ban Treaty." *Issues in Science and Technology,* Spring 2003. URL: http://www.issues.org/ issues/19.3/matthew.htm

McCormack, Gavan. "North Korea and the US: Strategic Decision." *Japan Focus,* December 2005. URL: http://www.japanfocus.org/article.asp?id=498

McLaughlin, John E. "North Korea: Engagement or Confrontation." Speech delivered at Texas A&M, April 17, 2001. URL: http://www.cia.gov/cia/ public_affairs/speeches/2001/ddci_speech_04172001.html

Minnich, James M. *The Denuclearization of North Korea: The Agreed Framework and Alternative Options Analyzed* (Milton Keynes, UK: Lightning Source, 2003).

"Missions of Combined Forces Command." *Combined Forces Command,* 2005. URL: http://www.korea.army.mil/cfc.htm

Moltz, James Clay. "Russian Policy on the North Korean Nuclear Crisis." *Center for Non-Proliferation Studies,* May 5, 2003. http://cns.miis.edu/research/ korea/ruspol.htm

Nanto, Dick K. "North Korea: Chronology of Provocations, 1950–2003." *CRS Reports for Congress* RL300004 (Washington, DC: Congressional Research Service, Library of Congress, March 18, 2003).

Nanto, Dick K., and Emma Chanlett-Avery. "The North Korean Economy: Background and Policy Analysis." *CRS Reports for Congress,* RL32493 (Washington, DC: Congressional Research Service, Library of Congress, February 9, 2005).

"The Naval Clash on the Yellow Sea on 29 June 2002 Between South Korea and North Korea: The Situation and ROK's Position." *Ministry of National Defense, Republic of Korea*, July 1, 2002. URL: http://www.global security.org/wmd/library/news/rok/2002/0020704-naval.htm

Niksch, Larry A. "North Korea's Nuclear Weapons Program," *Congressional Research Service, Library of Congress*, May 6, 2005. URL: http://www.fcnl.org/pdfs/NK_Nuclear_May_6.pdf

———. "North Korea's Weapons of Mass Destruction." in *North Korea: The Politics of Regime Survival* (eds). Young Whan Kihl and Hong Nack Kim (Armonk, New York: M.E. Sharpe, 2005).

———."US–Korea Relations: Issues for Congress." *Congressional Research Service, Library of Congress*, June 16, 2005. URL: http://www.fas.org/sgp/crs/row/IB98045.pdf

"No-Dong." *Missile Threat.Com, a Project of the Claremont Institute*, January 8, 2006. URL: http://www.missilethreat.com/missiles/no-dong-2_north_korea.html

Noland, Marcus. "North Korea and the South Korean Economy." Paper presented to Roh government transition team, Seoul Korea, February 24, 2003. URL: http://www.iie.com/publications/papers/paper.cfm?ResearchID=242

———. "Some Unpleasant Arithmetic Concerning Unification." *Institute for International Economics, Working Paper 96-13*, October 23, 1996. URL: http://www.iie.com/publications/wp/wp.cfm?ResearchID=169

"North Korea Country Handbook." *United States Department of Defense*, May 1997. URL: http://www.dia.mil/Public/Foia/nkor.pdf

"North Korea Issues for the 109th Congress." *East Asia Education Project, The Friends Committee on National Legislation*, January 2005. URL: http://www.fcnl.org/pdfs/north_korea_security_in_109.pdf

"North Korea Missile Milestones." *The Risk Report*, vol. 6, no. 5 (September–October 2000). URL: http://www.wisconsinproject.org/countries/nkorea/missile-miles.htm

"North Korea—Denuclearization Action Plan: Initial Actions for the Implementation of the Joint Statement." *U.S. Department of State*, February 13, 2007. URL: http://www.state.gov/r/pa/prs/ps/2007/february/80479.htm

"North Korea Primer." *National Defense University*, November 3, 2005. URL: http://merln.ndu.edu/merln/mipal/reports/NorthKoreaPrimer03Nov05.doc

"North Korea Profile: Missile Overview." *Nuclear Threat Initiative*, 2003. URL: http://www.nti.org/e_research/profiles/NK/Missile/index_1667.html

"North Korea Profile: Missile Overview." *Nuclear Threat Initiative*, August 2006. URL: http://www.nti.org/e_research/profiles/NK/index_1667.html

"North Korea Profile: Nuclear Overview," *Nuclear Threat Initative*, September 2005. URL: http://www.nti.org/e_research/profiles/NK/Nuclear/

"North Korea Report: 2005." *Amnesty International*, 2005. URL: http://web.amnesty.org/report2005/prk-summary-eng

"North Korea's Nuclear-Capable Missiles." *The Risk Report,* vol. 2, no. 6 (November–December 1996). URL: http://www.wisconsinproject.org/countries/nkorea/nukemiss.html

"North Korea's Nuclear Challenge." *2002 Carnegie International Non-Proliferation Conference,* November 14, 2002. URL: http://www.ceip.org/files/projects/npp/resources/conference2002/northkorea.htm

Oberdorfer, Don. "The United States and South Korea: Can This Alliance Last?" *Nautilus Institute: Policy Forum Online 05-93A,* November 17, 2005. URL: http://www.nautilus.org/fora/security/0593Oberdorfer.html

Oh, Kongdan. "Misunderstandings About the Relocation of U.S. Bases in Korea." *Brookings Institution Paper,* June 21, 2003. URL: http://www.brookings.edu/views/op-ed/fellows/oh20030621.htm

Oh, Kongdan, and Ralph C. Hassig. "North Korea's Nuclear Politics." *Current History,* vol. 103 (September 2004). URL: http://www.brookings.edu/views/articles/fellows/oh20040901.pdf

———. *North Korea Through the Looking Glass* (Washington, DC: Brookings Institute Press, 2000).

O'Hanlon, Michael E. "A Master Plan to Deal With North Korea: Policy Brief Number 114." *Brookings Institution,* January 2003. URL: http://www.brookings.org/comm/policybriefs/pb114.htm

O'Hanlon, Michael, and Mike Mochizuki. "Bridging the Roh-Bush Divide on Korea." *Yale Global Online,* May 14, 2003. URL: http://yaleglobal.yale.edu/display.article?id=1615

———. *Crisis on the Korean Peninsula: How to Deal with a Nuclear North Korea* (Washington, DC: Brookings Institution Press, 2003).

Olsen, Edward A. "If the United States Had 'No' Policy Toward North Korea." *Strategic Insights,* vol. 4, no. 2 (October 2005), URL: http://www.ccc.nps.navy.mil/si/2005/Oct/olsenOct05.asp

———. *Korea: The Divided Nation* (Westport, CT: Praeger Security International, 2005).

———. "U.S.–North Korea: From Brinkmanship to Dialogue." *Strategic Insight, Center for Contemporary Conflict,* vol. 2, no. 1 (January 2003). URL: http://www.ccc.nps.navy.mil/rsepResources/si/apr03/eastAsia.asp

"Open Letter from Senators Clinton and Levin to Secretary Rice." *Website of the United States Senate,* April 28, 2005. URL: http://clinton.senate.gov/4.28.05.html

"Opening Remarks of Chairman Henry Hyde: Full Committee Hearing on the Korean Peninsula: Six Party Talks and the Nuclear Issue." *U.S. Congress, House,* 109th Session, March 10, 2005. URL: http://wwwc.house.gov/international_relations/109/hyde031005.htm

"Overcoming Humanitarian Dilemmas in the DPRK: Special Report 90." *United States Institute of Peace,* July 2002. URL: http://www.usip.org/pubs/specialreports/sr90.html

Park, Jae Kyu. President, Kyungnam University, Former Minister of Unification, Republic of Korea. Speech presented at the Woodrow Wilson Center for International Scholars, Washington DC, January 17, 2006. Videotape recording: www.wilsoncenter.org/index.cfm?fuseaction=events.event_summary&event_id=161541

Park, John S. "Inside Multilateralism: The Six-Party Talks." *Washington Quarterly*, vol. 28, no. 4 (Autumn 2005): 75–91. URL: http://www.twq.com/05autumn/docs/05autumn_park.pdf

Park, Syung-je. Board Member, Military Analyst Association of the Republic of Korea, Seoul, Republic Korea. Email interview by author, May 29, 2004.

————. Board Member, Military Analyst Association of the Republic of Korea, Seoul, Republic of Korea. Email interview by author, January 22, 2006.

"Participatory Government's National Security Policy Initiative: Peace, Prosperity, and National Security." *Republic of Korea National Security Council* (Seoul: Republic of Korea, 2004).

"Patterns of Terrorism." *Released by the Office of the Coordinator for Counterterrorism*, United States Department of State, 2003. URL: http://www.state.gov/s/ct/rls/pgtrpt/2003/31644.htm

Perl, Raphael F. "Drug Trafficking and North Korea: Issues for U.S. Policy." *CRS Report for Congress*, Congressional Research Service, Washington DC, December 5, 2003. URL: http://www.fas.org/sgp/crs/row/RL32167.pdf

Pinkston, Daniel A. "North Korea Conducts Nuclear Test." *Center for Nonproliferation Studies, Monterey Institute of International Studies,* October 10, 2006. URL: http://cns.miis.edu/pubs/week/pdf/061010_dprktest.pdf

————. "When Did the WMD Deals Between Pyongyang and Islamabad Begin?" *North Korea Special Collection, Monterey Institute of International Studies, Center for Nonproliferation Studies* (Monterey CA: Monterey Institute of International Studies, January 2003). URL: http://cns.miis.edu/pubs/week/021028.htm

Pollack, Jonathan. "The United States, North Korea, and the End of the Agreed Framework." *Naval College Review,* vol. 56, no. 3 (Summer 2003). URL: http://www.nwc.navy.mil/press/Review/2003/Summer/art1-su3.htm

"Post-Command Shift Joint HQ Planned." *Donga Ilbo*, August 18, 2006. URL: http://english.donga.com/srvservice.php3?bicode=050000&biid=2006081812778

Potter, William C. and Phillip C. Saunders, "Double Trouble: North Korean Talks are Imperative." *Center for Non-Proliferation Studies, Monterey Institute,* March 18, 2003. URL: http://cns.miis.edu/research/korea/potsaund.htm

Prahar, Peter A. "Prepared Statement: North Korea: Illicit Activity Funding the Regime." *Senate Sub-Committee on Financial Management Government Information, and International Security, Senate Homeland Security and Government Affairs Committee,* April 25, 2006. URL: http://hsgac.senate.gov/_files/042506Prahar.pdf

Price, Congressman David. Keynote speech presented at North Carolina State University, Centennial Campus Engineering Graduate Research Center. "Korean Peninsula: Time of Diplomacy and Development," April 24, 2003. URL: http://www.house.gov/price/issue_north_korea.htm

Radchenko, Sergey. "The Soviet Union and the North Korean Seizure of the USS *Pueblo*: Evidence from Russian Archives," *Cold War International History Project: Working Paper Number 47.* URL: http://www.wilson center.org/topics/pubs/CWIHP_WP_47.pdf

"Recognizing Iran as a Strategic Threat: An Intelligence Challenge for the United States." *Staff Report of the US House of Representatives Permanent Select Committee on Intelligence, Subcommittee on Intelligence Policy,* August 23, 2006. URL: http://intelligence.house.gov/Media/PDFS/IranReport082 206v2.pdf#search=%22Recognizing%20Iran%20as%20a%20 Strategic%20Threat%3A%20An%20Intelligence%20Challenge% 20for%20the%20United%20States%22

Reiss, Mitchell B., and Robert L. Gallucci. "Red Handed." *Foreign Affairs Online,* March/April 2005. URL: http://www.foreignaffairs.org/ 20050301faresponse84214/mitchell-b-reiss-robert-gallucci/red-handed.html

"Report No. 2000/09: Ballistic Missile Proliferation." *Perspectives, Canadian Security Intelligence Services,* March 21, 2001. URL: http://www.csis-scrs.gc.ca/en/publications/perspectives/200009.asp

"Report to the Speaker of the U.S. House of Representatives." *North Korea Advisory Group,* November 1999. URL: http://www.fas.org/nuke/guide/ dprk/nkag-report.htm

"ROK Participation in U.S. Peacekeeping Operations." *Ministry of National Defense, Republic of Korea,* 2003. URL: http://www.mnd.go.kr/

"ROK–US Alliance and USFK." *Republic of Korea, Ministry of National Defense,* June 2003. URL: http://www.mnd.go.kr/english/SCM/Documents/ ROK-US_Alliance_and_USFK.pdf

Roy, Denny. "China and the Korean Peninsula: Beijing's Pyongyang Problem and Seoul Hope." *Asia-Pacific Center for Security Studies Paper,* vol. 3, no. 1 (2004), URL: http://www.apcss.org/Publications/APSSS/Chinaandthe KoreanPeninsula.pdf

Rubin, Barry. "North Korea's Threat to the Middle East and the Middle East's Threat to Asia." *Middle East Review of International Affairs* (Book Studies). URL: http://meria.idc.ac.il/books/brkorea.html#Author

Rubin, Uzi. "The Global Range of Iran's Ballistic Missile Program." *Jerusalem Issue Brief, Institute for Contemporary Affairs,* vol. 5, no. 26 (June 20, 2006). URL: http://www.jcpa.org/brief/brief005-26.htm

Rutland, Peter. "Distant Neighbors." *CDI Russia Weekly,* vol. 2, no. 2 (January 21, 2003). URL: http://www.cdi.org/russia/241-9-pr.cfm

Samson, Victoria. "North Korea's Missile Flight Tests." *Center for Defense*

Information, November 20, 2003. URL: http://www.cdi.org/friendlyversion/printversion.cfm?documentID=1677

Schwartz, General Thomas A. "Statement of Commander in Chief, UNC/CFC and United States Forces Korea." *Before the Senate Armed Forces Committee*, March 7, 2000. URL: http://www.shaps.hawaii.edu/security/us/schwartz_2000.html.

Scobell, Andrew. *Kim Jong Il and North Korea: The Leader and the System,* Strategic Studies Institute Monograph (Carlisle, PA: U.S. Army War College, March 2006). URL: http://www.strategicstudiesinstitute.army.mil/pdffiles/PUB644.pdf

———. *North Korea's Strategic Intentions*, Strategic Studies Institute Monograph (Carlisle, PA: U.S. Army War College, July 2005). URL: http://www.nautilus.org/napsnet/sr/2005/0569Scobel.pdf

"Setting a Humanitarian and Human Rights Agenda for North Korea: Meeting Report." *Brookings Institution,* March 4, 2004. URL: http://www.brook.edu/fp/projects/idp/20040304idpnkorea.pdf

Shambaugh, David. "China and the Korean Peninsula: Playing for the Long Term." *Washington Quarterly* vol. 26, no. 2 (Spring 2003). URL: http://www.twq.com/03spring/docs/03spring_shambaugh.pdf

Shim, Jae Hoon. "'Protect Regime Now, Feed People Later." *Yale Global Online*, October 18, 2005. URL: http://yaleglobal.yale.edu/display.article?id=6385

Snyder, Scott. "Disciplining North Korea: The Bush Administration & U.S. Policy Toward North Korea." Paper presented at the *Korea Political Science Association*, "Inter-Korean Relations: Status and Prospects," July 25, 2002. URL: http://asiafoundation.or.kr/Asiafoundation/download/KPSA—Disciplining_Bush_pol.doc

———. "The Fire Last Time." A Book Review on *Going Critical: The First North Korean Nuclear Crisis*. Joel S. Wit, Daniel B. Poneman, and Robert L. Gallucci. Washington: Brookings Institution Press. *Foreign Affairs*, July/August 2004. URL: http://www.foreignaffairs.org/20040701fareviewessay83415/scott-snyder/the-fire-last-time.html

So, Chin Tae, Lt Gen. "Recasting the Viability of a Small Ally's Airpower: South Korea in Focus." *Air and Space Power Journal: Chronicles Online Journal,* October 1, 2002. URL: http://www.airpower.maxwell.af.mil/airchronicles/cc/tae.html

Sokolski, Henry "Hide and Seek With Kim Chong-il." *Nautilus Institute Policy Forum Online 05-80A*. September 29, 2005. URL: http://www.nautilus.org/fora/security/0580Sokolski.html

Song, Moon-hong. "After the Perry Report: The Korean Peninsula Game Enters the Second Round." *East Asian Review,* vol. 11, no. 4 (Winter 1999). URL: http://www.ieas.or.kr/vol11_4/songmoonhong.htm

"South Korea—Constitution." *International Constitutional Law Project*, November 2004. URL: http://www.oefre.unibe.ch/law/icl/ks00000_.html

"Special Report on the North Korean Nuclear Weapons Statement." *Center for Nonproliferation Studies, Monterey Institute of International Studies*. February 11, 2005. URL: http://cns.miis.edu/pubs/week/050211.htm

Squassoni, Sharon A. "Weapons of Mass Destruction: Trade Between North Korea and Pakistan." *Congressional Report for Congress, Congressional Research Service,* March 11, 2004. URL: http://www.fas.org/spp/starwars/crs/RL31900.pdf

Statement of Former North Korean High Ranking Government Official. "Drugs, Counterfeiting, and Weapons Proliferation: The North Korea Connection." Testimony Before the Senate Committee on Governmental Affairs, May 20, 2003. URL: http://hsgac.senate.gov/index.cfm?Fuseaction=Hearings.Testimony&HearingID=73&WitnessID=257

"Statement of Stephan Haggard and Marcus Noland for Hearings on the North Korean Human Rights Act of 2004: Issues and Implementation." *Subcommittee on Africa, Global Human Rights, and International Operations. United States House of Representatives*, 28 April 2005. URL: http://www.iie.com/publications/papers/noland0405.pdf

Steinberg, David I. (Ed). *Korean Attitudes Toward the United States: Changing Dynamics* (Armonk, NY: M.E. Sharpe, 2004).

Tate, Winifred. "Paramilitaries in Colombia." *Brown Journal of World Affairs*, vol. 8, no. 1 (Winter/Spring 2001). URL: http://www.watsoninstitute.org/bjwa/archive/8.1/Essays/Tate.pdf

"The 38th Security Consultative Meeting Joint Communique." *Defense Link*, October 20, 2006. URL: http://www.defenselink.mil/news/Oct2006/d20061020uskorea.pdf

"The Threat of Weapons of Mass Destruction." *Defence: Australia's National Security*, 2003. URL: http://www.defence.gov.au/ans2003/section5.htm

"Transcript: Update on the Six-Party Talks with Christopher R. Hill." *Brookings Institution Center for Northeast Asian Policy Studies*, February 22, 2007. URL: http://www.brook.edu/comm/events/20070228hill.pdf

Umebayashi, Hiromichi. "US Navy Set Missile Defense Operations Area in the Sea of Japan 190 Kilometers West of Okushiri: Japan as a Base for the Defense of the US Homeland." *Nautilus Special Report.* June 2, 2006. URL: http://www.nautilus.org/napsnet/sr/2006/0642Umebayashi.pdf

"The United States and South Korea; Reinvigorating the Partnership, Joint US–Korea Academic Studies vol. 14: 2004." *Proceedings of Symposium Conducted by the Stanford Asia Pacific Research Center, the Korea Economic Institute, and the Korea Institute for International Economic Policy*, 22 – 24, October 2003. URL: http://www.keia.com/2-Publications/2-3-Monograph/Monograph2004/Monograph2004.pdf

"U.S., Asia-Pacific Security Alliances." *U.S. State Department Fact Sheet*, 1998. URL: http://usinfo.state.gov/journals/itps/0198/ijpe/pj18fact.htm

Valencia, Mark J., and Jenny Miller Garmendia. "Yellow Sea Clash: North Korea Has a Point." *Northeast Asia Peace and Security Network Special*

Report, December 23, 1999. URL: http://www.nyu.edu/globalbeat/asia/Valencia122399.html

Vershbow, Alexander, United States Ambassador to the Republic of Korea. "The Changing US–ROK Alliance." Remarks to the Republic of Korea at the National Assembly Study Group on Parliamentary Democracy, Seoul, Republic of Korea, November 9, 2005. URL: http://seoul.usembassy.gov/nov_9_2005.html

Vick, Charles P. "The Closely Related Collaborative Iranian, North Korean, and Pakistani Strategic Space, Ballistic Missile and Nuclear Weapon Programs." *Global Security.Org,* May 23, 2006. URL: http://www.globalsecurity.org/wmd/world/iran/missile-development.htm

———. "Has the No-Dong B/Shahab-4 Finally Been Tested in Iran for North Korea?" *Global Security.Org,* May 2, 2006. URL: http://www.globalsecurity.org/wmd/library/report/2006/cpvick-no-dong-b_2006.htm

Von Hippel, David. "Estimated DPRK Military Energy Use: Analytical Approach and Draft Updated Results," paper presented at the "DPRK Energy Expert Study Group Meeting," Stanford University, California, June 26–27, 2006. URL: http://nautilus.org/DPRKEnergyMeeting/papers/DvH_DPRK_Military.ppt#270,1,EstimatedDPRK Military Energy Use: Analytical Approach and Draft Updated Results

Walpole, Robert D., National Intelligence Officer for Strategic and Nuclear Programs, "The Iranian Ballistic Missile and WMD Threat to the United States Through 2015." *Statement for the Record to the International Security, Proliferation and Federal Services Subcommittee of the Senate Government Affairs Committee,* September 21, 2000. URL: http://www.cia.gov/nic/testimony_WMDthreat.html

Ward, Adam, and James Hacket. "U.S. Troop Withdrawals From South Korea: Beginnings of the End for the Alliance?" *Strategic Comments: The International Institute of Strategic Studies,* vol. 10, no. 5 (June 2004). URL: www.iiss.org/stratcom

"White Paper: 1996." *Republic of Korea, Ministry of National Defense, Chapter Three,* 1996. URL: http://mnd.go.kr/mnd/mnden/sub_menu/w_book/1996/232.html

"White Paper: 1998." *Republic of Korea, Ministry of National Defense, Chapter Three,* 1998. http://www.mnd.go.kr/english/html/02/1998/133.html

"White Paper: 1999." *Republic of Korea, Ministry of National Defense, Chapter Three,* 1999. URL: http://www.mnd.go.kr/cms.jsp?p_id=01902000000000&CMSTrans=/jsps/w_book1.jsp&src=/english/html/02/1999/index.html

"White Paper: 2000." *Republic of Korea, Ministry of National Defense, Chapter Three,* 2000. URL: http://www.mnd.go.kr/cms.jsp?p_id=01902000000000&CMSTrans=/jsps/w_book1.jsp&src=/english/html/02/2000/index.html

"White Paper: 2004." *Republic of Korea, Ministry of National Defense*, 2004. URL: http://www.mnd.go.kr/etext2/main.jsp?dir=002&subdir=000& name=&popup=N&currentPage=1

Wickham, John A. Jr. *Korea on the Brink: From the "12/12 Incident" to the Kwangju Uprising, 1979–1980* (Washington, DC: NDU Press, 1999). URL: http://www.ndu.edu/inss/press/NDUPress_Books_Titles.htm

Wishnick, Elizabeth. "Nuclear Tension Between China, N Korea." *International Relations and Security Network*, August 11, 2006. URL: http://www.isn.ethz.ch/news/sw/details.cfm?id=16511

Woodrow, *Thomas*. "China Opens Pandora's Nuclear Box." *China Brief*, vol. 2, no. 24 (December 10, 2002). URL: http://www.jamestown.org/publications_details.php?volume_id=18&&issue_id=664

Wolf, Charles Jr., and Kamil Akramov. *North Korean Paradoxes: Circumstances, Costs, and Consequences of Korean Unification* (Santa Monica, CA: Rand Defense Research Institute, 2005). URL: http://www.rand.org/pubs/monographs/2005/RAND_MG333.pdf

Wolfsthal, Jon "No Good Choices: The Implications of a Nuclear North Korea." *Testimony to the U.S. House of Representatives International Relations Committee, Sub-Committees on Asia and the Pacific and on International Terrorism and Nonproliferation*, February 17, 2005. URL: http://wwwc.house.gov/international_relations/109/wol021705.htm

Wright, David C. "Assessment of the North Korean Missile Program." *Union of Concerned Scientists*, February 25, 2003. URL: http://www.ucsusa.org/global_security/missile_defense/assessment-of-the-north-korean-missile-program.html

Wright, David C., and Timur Kadyshev. "An Analysis of the No Dong Missile." *Science and Global Security*, vol. 4, 1994. URL: http://www.princeton.edu/~globsec/publications/pdf/4_2wright.pdf

| INDEX

| ABOUT THE AUTHOR

BRUCE E. BECHTOL, JR., is a former intelligence officer with the Defense Intelligence Agency and a retired Marine who has lived and worked in Korea and continues to visit there frequently. He received his Ph.D. from the Union Institute in Cincinnati, Ohio, and currently serves as an associate professor of international relations at the U.S. Marine Corps Command and Staff College and as an adjunct professor of diplomacy at Norwich University. Dr. Bechtol is also an adjunct professor at Excelsior College in Albany, New York, where he teaches graduate courses on global issues and rogue regimes, and served as a visiting adjunct professor at the Korea University Graduate School of International Studies in Seoul, Korea, during 2006–2007.

A contributing author to several books on North Korea, he has also written more than a dozen articles dealing with Korean security issues in peer-reviewed journals. Bechtol is the former editor of the *Defense Intelligence Journal* (2004–2005) and sits on the Editorial Advisory Board of the *East Asian Review* and the Board of Directors of the International Council on Korean Studies. He lives in Fredericksburg, Virginia.